Katie Hickman

was born into a diplomatic family in 1960 and has spent more than twenty-five years living abroad in Europe, the Far East and Latin America. She is the author of three previous books: *A Trip to the Light Fantastic – Travels with a Mexican Circus*, which was one of the *Independent*'s 1993 Books of the Year and was short-listed for the 1994 Thomas Cook Travel Book Award; *The Quetzal Summer*, a novel set in the Andes, for which she was short-listed for the 1993 *Sunday Times* Young British Writer of the Year Award; and *Dreams of the Peaceful Dragon – a Journey into Bhutan*. She is featured in the Oxford University Press guide to women travellers, *Wayward Women*.

KATIE HICKMAN

Daughters of Britannia

The Lives and Times of Diplomatic Wives

TED SMART

This edition produced for The Book People Ltd, Hall Wood Avenue,
Haydock, St Helens, WA11 9UL

Flamingo
An Imprint of HarperCollins*Publishers*
77–85 Fulham Palace Road,
Hammersmith, London W6 8JB

Flamingo is a trademark of HarperCollins Publishers Ltd

www.**fire**and**water**.com

Published by Flamingo 2000
9 8 7 6 5 4 3 2 1

First published in Great Britain by
HarperCollins*Publishers* 1999

Copyright © Katie Hickman 1999

The Author asserts the moral right to
be identified as the author of this work

Author photograph by Tom Owen Edmunds

ISBN 0 00 7624085

Set in New Baskerville

Printed and bound in Great Britain by
Omnia Books Limited, Glasgow

Contents

ACKNOWLEDGMENTS

Many people helped me most generously during the researching and writing of this book. I am very grateful to all the women (and a few brave men) who agreed to be interviewed, or who wrote to me about their experiences, and also to all the staff at the British Diplomatic Spouses Association (which since this book was written has changed its name to the Diplomatic Service Families Association) for their patience with my enquiries. My thanks, too, to all the women whose reminiscences, recipes, poems and multifarious experiences of diplomatic life over the last forty years are so vividly catalogued in the DSWA/BDSA archive. Of the many books, memoirs and diaries which I have drawn upon, I feel particularly indebted to two contemporary sources: Beryl Smedley's *Partners in Diplomacy*, and most especially Jane Robinson's excellent *Wayward Women*, without which I would truly have been at a loss to know how to embark on such a huge project. My greatest thank you, however, goes to my mother, Jennifer Hickman. Not only did she allow me freely to plunder her letters, but she also proved to be a most assiduous and thoughtful research assistant. Thank you so much, Muv.

I would also like to thank my editor, Michael Fishwick, for dreaming up this book and then twisting my arm until I agreed to do it; my wonderful agent, Gill Coleridge, for making it all happen, and for all her support and encouragement throughout the project; and Phyllis Richardson, at HarperCollins. Annabel Hendry (Black) and my father, John Hickman, both made invaluable comments on the manuscript; Dr Matthew Dryden gave me his expert advice on medical matters; James and Charlotte Heneage commented on the title and the cover; Peter Bursey at the Foreign and Commonwealth Office Library helped me with my picture research. Many people have most generously lent me photographs: my thanks to Nigel Nicolson, Veronica Atkinson, Lady Hibbert, Lady Trevelyan, Jennifer and Standley Duncan, Mary S. Lovell, Ghassem Khatib-Chahidi, Beryl Smedley, and Denis and Iona Wright. My grateful thanks, also, to The Society of Authors for awarding me a most generous grant with which to complete the writing of this book. A huge thank you, finally, to Tom Owen Edmunds, for having been as always such a loving, discerning and stalwart support.

Last of all my thoughts go to those whom I shall never be able to thank: those forgotten women whose brave and extraordinary lives form the bedrock of this book. It has been an enormous privilege to be the custodian of their stories. I can only hope that I have done them justice.

Katie Hickman
London, 1999

AUTHOR'S NOTE

Daughters of Britannia is about the lives and experiences of wives (and sisters and daughters) of British diplomats, a term which I have defined in the widest possible sense, and which for the purposes of this book includes members of the British Consular Service. The single exception to this is Mary Waddington, whose husband, although of British extraction, actually worked for the French Diplomatic Services. It does not include women who lived in countries formerly within the British empire (where diplomatic representation was, of course, unnecessary). Nor does it include women who are themselves diplomats, whose immense achievements are unfortunately beyond the scope of this book.

A list of the principal women in the book and the primary places where they served

Seventeenth Century	Date first went abroad
The Countess of Winchilsea (Constantinople)	1661
Ann Fanshawe (Portugal, Spain)	1662
The Countess of Carlisle (Moscow)	1663
Katharine Trumbull (Paris)	1685

Eighteenth Century	
Countess of Stair (Paris)	1715
Mary Wortley Montagu (Constantinople)	1716
Mrs Vigor (St Petersburg)	1730
Miss Tully (Tripoli)	1783
Emma Hamilton (Naples)	1786
Mary Elgin (Constantinople)	1799

Nineteenth Century	
Elizabeth Broughton (Algiers)	1806
Elizabeth McNeill (Persia)	1823
Harriet Granville (The Hague, Paris)	1824
Anne Disbrowe (St Petersburg)	1825
Mary Sheil (Persia)	1849
Isabel Burton (Brazil, Damascus)	1861
Mary Fraser (Peking & Japan)	1874
Victoria Sackville (Washington)	1881
Mary Waddington (Moscow)	1883
Catherine Macartney (Kashgar)	1898
Susan Townley (China, Washington)	1898

Twentieth Century

Ella Sykes (Kashgar)	1915
Vita Sackville-West (Persia)	1926
Marie-Noele Kelly (Brussels, Turkey)	1929
Norah Errock (Iraq)	1930
Iona Wright (Trebizond, Ethiopia, Persia)	1939
Evelyn Jackson (Uruguay)	1939
Pat Gore-Booth (Burma, Delhi)	1940
Diana Cooper (Paris)	1944
Diana Shipton (Kashgar)	1946
Masha Williams (Iraq)	1947
Peggy Trevelyan (Iraq, Moscow)	1948
Maureen Tweedy (Persia, Korea)	1950
Felicity Wakefield (Libya, the Lebanon)	1951
Ann Hibbert (Mongolia, Paris)	1952
Jennifer Hickman (New Zealand, Dublin, Chile)	1959
Jane Ewart-Biggs (Algeria, Paris, Dublin)	1961
Veronica Atkinson (Ecuador, Romania)	1963
Rosa Carless (Persia, Hungary)	1963
Angela Caccia (Bolivia)	1963
Sheila Whitney (China)	1966
Jennifer Duncan (Mozambique, Bolivia)	1970
Catherine Young (Syria)	1970
Annabel Hendry (Black) (Brussels)	1991
Chris Gardiner (Kyiv)	1994
Susie Tucker (Slovakia)	1995

LIST OF ILLUSTRATIONS

PROLOGUE

It was the late afternoon when His Excellency the Earl of Winchilsea, Ambassador Extraordinary from King Charles II to the Grand Seignior Mehmed IV, Sultan of Sultans and God's Shadow upon Earth, sailed into Constantinople.

To arrive in Constantinople by sea, even today, is to be presented with an extraordinary sight. In 1661 it was one of the wonders of the world. Built on seven hills, and surrounded on three sides by water, it was described by contemporary travellers as not only the biggest and richest, but also the most beautiful city on earth. The unequal heights of the seven hills, each one topped with the gilded dome and minarets of a mosque, made the city seem almost twice as large as it really was. On each hillside, raised one above the other in an apparent symmetry, were palaces, pavilions and mansions, each one set in its own gardens, surrounded by groves of cypress and pine. On the furthermost spit of land, and clearly visible from the sea, was the Seraglio,* the Sultan's palace, its turrets and domes reflected in the waters of the Bosphorus.

Few buildings in history have had the sinister beauty of this fabled pleasure dome. No contemporary Christian king, and only a few since, had aspired to anything that equalled it. Built around six great court-yards, and covering as much land as a small town, this city within a city was the focus of all life in Constantinople. The Seraglio was not only the symbol of all power in the great Ottoman empire but also, to the dazzled imagination of foreign travellers, the seat of all pleasures too. For it was here, too, that the Grand Seignior's harem was incarcer-ated – several hundred concubines, beautiful slave girls bought from

---

* The Topkapi Palace.

as far away as Venice, Georgia and Circassia and kept, out of sight of other eyes, for the Sultan's delight alone.

Here, every day, as many as 10,000 people were catered for – including the four corps of guards who protected the Seraglio, the black and white eunuchs, the palace slaves, its pages, treasurers, armourers, grooms, physicians, astrologers and imams, as well as the Sultan and his family. According to one estimate there were 1,000 cooks and scullions working in the palace kitchens which, in addition to staples such as meat and vegetables, produced jams, pickles, sweetmeats and sherbets in quantities 'beyond possibility of measure'.[1]

Opposite the Seraglio, and close enough to be easily visible from it, rose the graceful shores of Asia, a pleasing prospect of wilderness interspersed with villages and fruit trees. And on the narrow stretch of water in between them sailed the water traffic of the world.

It was three months since the ambassador's entourage had set sail, and the journey had not been an easy one. On New Year's Day, just after they had left Smyrna on the last leg of their voyage, a tempest had all but tossed them into oblivion. During the week of the storm their vessel had been cast upon rocks five times, leaving every man on board fearing for his life. It was an escape 'so miraculous and wonderfull, considering the violence of the storm, the carere and weight of our ship, as ought to make the 8 day of January for ever to be recorded by us to admiration, and anniversary thankfulness for God's providence and protection,' wrote one witness.[2]

Now, the ambassador's storm-battered, leaky little ship – its masts, yards and decks encrusted eerily with white salt from the continual spray of the sea, its flags and ensigns flying, its guns at the ready – sailed across the last stretch of the Sea of Marmara and into the Bosphorus at last. It must have seemed to those on board as if they had reached the very epicentre of the world.

In many ways, of course, they had. Whoever controlled Constantinople controlled not only the great gateway between Europe and Asia, but also one of the greatest water trade routes linking the northern and southern hemispheres. Looking north, the Black Sea gave access through the Volga to southern Russia, and through the Danube to the Balkans and eastern Europe. To the south, the Sea of Marmara led not only to the Aegean, but to the whole of the Mediterranean,

North Africa and beyond. In amongst the fishing boats and the caiques, the galleons and perhaps even one of the Sultan's magnificent gilded barges, sailed innumerable vessels from all four corners of the earth – merchant ships, slave galleys and vast timber rafts cut from the deep forests of southern Russia and floated down the Bosphorus for shipbuilding and fuel.

On the captain's orders the men lined the rigging, their muskets at the ready. As the ship drew close to the Sultan's palace, in a suffocating cloud of gunpowder, a salutation of sixty-one guns was fired. A little while later, when the ambassador finally disembarked, it was to a second deafening salute of fifty-one guns. His welcoming committee comprised not only his own servants, English merchants, and other travelling companions brought with them from Smyrna, but also many of the Grand Seignior's officers who had come to honour him. Their procession was so splendid that multitudes of people flocked from all parts of the city to watch them, and made 'the business of more wonder and expectation'. 'As we marched all the streets were crowded with people and the windows with spectators, as being unusual in this countrey to see a Christian Ambassadour attended with so many Turkish officers,' wrote the ambassador's secretary. He was so proud of their 'very grand equipage' – believing that 'none of his predecessours, nor yet the Emperour's Ambassadours, can boast of a more honourable nor a more noble reception' – that he recorded each element:

1. The Vaivod* of Gallata and his men
2. The Captain of the Janizaries with his Janizaries
3. The Chouse Bashaw with his Chouses†
4. The English Trumpeters
5. The English horsemen and Merchants
6. My Lord's Janizaries
7. The Druggerman‡
8. My Lord himself with Pages and Footmen by his side
9. My Lord's gentlemen
10. The officers and reformadoes of the ship.[3]

* Voyvoda, or Governor of Gallata.
† The chief guard and his guards.
‡ Dragomen, or interpreters.

From the brief account of the voyage which has come down to us, we know that the Sultan presented the embassy with ten sheep, a hundred loaves of bread, twenty sugar loaves and twenty wax candles. We also know that the ambassador distributed money among the people, and was visited by the messengers of other foreign ambassadors to the Porte. We know that he was given audiences with both the Grand Vizier, and with the Grand Seignior himself.

But we can only speculate about the Countess of Winchilsea's role in all this. The fact that we know she was there at all seems almost accidental. At the very tail end of the procession, in between 'my Lord's gentlemen' and 'the officers and reformadoes of the ship', the ambassador's secretary has inserted one simple phrase: 'My Ladies Coach'. With these three small words, my Lady Winchilsea slips into history.

INTRODUCTION

'English ambassadresses are usually on the dotty side, and leaving their embassies nearly drives them completely off their rockers.' These words, from Nancy Mitford's classic vignette of embassy life *Don't Tell Alfred*, were like a mantra of my youth. As children, my brothers and I used to chant them to my mother, in those days a British ambassadress herself, in her vaguer moments. Not because she was dotty (well, only occasionally) but because we knew, beyond doubt, that all other ambassadresses were.

From an early age, we were used to the tales of former ambassadresses – mad, bad and dangerous to know, they came to form part of our family culture. In New Zealand, my father's first posting as a young first secretary, there was the delightfully *distraite* Lady Cumming Bruce. She was far more interested in her painting than in her diplomatic social engagements, which often slipped her mind completely; according to legend, she could regularly be spotted crawling through the residence shrubberies, so as not to be spotted arriving late for her own parties. 'Dear Mummy and Daddy,' my mother wrote to my grandparents just a few months after her arrival in Wellington, 'Lady Cumming Bruce is very vague and difficult to pin down – says she'll do something and then doesn't. When Helen* went onto their boat to greet them on arrival she suggested to Lady CB that she should perhaps put her hat on before meeting the press. Lady CB opened her hat box inside which instead of a hat, was a child's chamber pot.'

During the twenty-eight years that my mother spent as a diplomat's wife, she wrote letters home. Today, at my parents' house in Wiltshire, in amongst the paper rubbings from the temples at Angkor Wat, the

* Helen Pickard, the wife of the deputy high commissioner.

Persian prayer mats and the bowls of shells from the beaches of Conne-mara – the legacy of a lifetime's wanderings – there is a carved wooden chest which contains several thousand of them. Once a week with almost religious regularity – sometimes more frequently – these letters were written at first to my grandparents and my aunt, but then later also to myself and my two brothers when we were sent home to board-ing school in England. During the last ten years of her travelling life it was not unusual for her to write half a dozen letters a week, recording all the vicissitudes of diplomatic life.

In these days of instant communications, of faxes and e-mails and mobile telephones, it is hard to describe the extraordinarily intense pleasure of what used, in old fashioned parlance, to be called 'a corre-spondence'. As a bitterly homesick ten-year-old at boarding school for the first time, I found in my mother's letters an almost totemic significance. The main stairs of my school house wound down through the middle of the building around a central well; in the hall below was a wooden chest on which the post was always laid out. For some reason only the housemistress and the matron were permitted to use these stairs (the rest of us were confined to the more workaday stone stairs at the back of the house), so the trick was to crane over the banisters and try to spot your letters. From two storeys up it was imposs-ible to read your name but, to a practised eye, the form of a certain handwriting, the shape of a certain envelope, its colour or its thickness, were all clues.

Occasionally my mother would use the official embassy writing paper – thick sheaves of a creamy sky-blue colour, lavishly embossed with the royal crest – but it wasn't really her style. For most of my school days she used the same big pads of plain white airmail paper, slightly crinkly to the touch, bordered in red and blue, which she bought in industrial quantities from an English stationer's. Often I would carry her letters around with me in my pocket, unopened, for a whole morning, until I could escape somewhere private in which to savour them. Their fatness, their pleasing weight, their peculiar texture against my finger-tips had an almost magical power to soothe. These letters carried news of my family, of course, but perhaps more importantly they described another world, and another way of life. They described another part of myself, in fact, which was as strange to my English friends as the land of the Jabberwock or the Yonghy-Bonghy-Bo.

I kept these letters, and many years later they were to be the inspiration for this book. Although I have quoted them here only occasionally, what they have given me is a strong sense not only of the value of the experiences they describe, but also of their fragility. One of my main aims in writing this book is to preserve them, and others like them, lest, like Lady Winchilsea's, their stories should drift into oblivion.

The lives of the women described in this book represent a lacuna in history. While the experiences of their menfolk were recorded and preserved for posterity even as far back as the sixteenth and seventeenth centuries,* what these women saw or felt or did is unknown. Because, with a few rare exceptions, they were not involved in affairs of state, they were quite simply not considered important enough. Because they were women, their experience had no value, and even their presence often went unrecorded. To quote the well-worn feminist joke, the history of diplomacy is very much a 'his-story'.

Of all the women whose experiences I have drawn upon in this book, Lady Winchilsea, who in 1661 made the long and perilous journey to Constantinople at her husband's side, is the earliest. I am in no doubt that there were others before her, for the custom of sending resident ambassadors abroad, initiated by the Italians during the Renaissance, had begun to spread through the rest of Europe by the beginning of the sixteenth century,† but any records for them are almost impossible to find.

Even when we do have a fleeting glimpse of them (as in the case of the Countess of Winchilsea) their stories are tantalizingly elusive.

---

* Manuscript copies of these documents, often written in the form of *relazione* ('A narrative of . . .'), were considered so valuable that they often commanded large sums, even in their own time.

† Previously, the role of an ambassador was usually to complete a short-term mission – to declare war or negotiate a treaty. England's first permanent ambassador, John Shirwood, became resident in Rome in 1479. In 1505 John Stile was sent to Spain by Henry VII, where he became the first resident ambassador to a secular court. By the mid-seventeenth century the idea of permanent missions abroad was no longer a novelty in England, but neither was it a universal practice. During the Restoration (1660–68) the crown sent diplomatic missions to thirty countries, but permanent embassies to only five (France, Spain, Portugal, the United Provinces and the Hanse towns of Hamburg, Bremen and Lübeck). Turkey and Russia were in a special category: ambassadors were sent there in the name of the monarch, but were in fact paid servants of the Turkey Company or British merchants settled in Moscow.

Did Lady Winchilsea, like one of her more famous successors, Lady Mary Wortley Montagu, ever visit a harem or one of the imperial city's glorious marble-domed *hammams*? Did she, like Mary Elgin nearly a century and a half later, go disguised in man's clothing to watch her husband present his credentials to the Grand Seignior? What of the everyday practicalities of her life? What were the conditions she had to endure aboard ship? Did she have children whom she was forced to leave behind? Perhaps, like her contemporary Ann Fanshawe, she fell pregnant and gave birth thousands of miles from home. If so, did her child survive?

Although we will never know what Lady Winchilsea thought and felt when she arrived in Constantinople in 1661, remarkably, many accounts of the lives and experiences of diplomatic women *have* survived. Until well into the first half of this century many of them wrote letters home; these letters are often the sole record we have of them. A handful are already well-known names – Mary Wortley Montagu, Vita Sackville-West, Isabel Burton. The vast majority are not. Who was Mrs Vigor, gossiping from St Petersburg in the 1730s about the scandals and intrigues of the imperial court? Or Miss Tully, incarcerated for over a year in the consulate in plague- and famine-torn Tripoli on the eve of the French Revolution? We know almost no personal details about them (not even their Christian names). Nor do we know who their correspondents were, only that their letters were precious enough to someone, as my mother's were to me, to have been safely kept. A great number of the sources I have used – collections of letters, private journals, or memoirs largely based on them – were never intended for public consumption at all: only a hundred or so copies were sometimes published through private subscription for family and friends. Why did they write these letters? No doubt they longed for news from home; but perhaps they also felt compelled to describe the circumstances of their lives abroad – so exhilarating, so strange, so inexplicable – to their family and friends. In Moscow in 1826 Anne Disbrowe enjoys the festivities which took place at the coronation of Tsar Nicholas I; in Peking, some fifty years later, at the heart of the Forbidden City itself, Mary Fraser takes tea with the legendary Chinese Dowager Empress Tzu Hsi; while at the turn of this century, during her seventeen long years in Chinese Turkistan, Catherine Macartney witnesses not one, but two full eclipses of the sun.

Others have more perilous tales to tell, of famines, plagues, tempests, earthquakes, wars, kidnappings, assassination attempts, and of the illnesses and deaths of their children. Even today – perhaps especially today – the world remains a hostile place for many diplomats. Their families, my own included, have often felt that the real substance of their lives is greatly, and at times almost wilfully, misunderstood. As one wife recently wrote in the *BDSA* (British Diplomatic Spouses Association) *Magazine*: 'All Britons KNOW that diplomatic life is one long whirl of gaiety (they have seen the films and read the books) . . .' Although this may be true for a few, most of the women represented here have very different stories to tell. 'I shall never forget the utter despair into which the sight of my new home plunged me,' wrote Jane Ewart-Biggs of her arrival as a young wife at her first posting in Algiers. From the outside their house – the central block of the old British hospital – seemed solid enough, but the interior was in a state of total disrepair, the paint flaking from the walls and doors hanging on single hinges. In the entrance hall a huge hole gaped through the ceiling 'through which pipes and wires hung like intestines'. By the time her husband Christopher came home she was in tears. He, by contrast, was buoyed up by the fascinating day he had spent learning all about his new job. 'It was then that I realised that the major problems arising from our nomadic life were going to affect me rather than him,' Jane wrote, 'and that the same circumstances creating political interest for him would make my life especially difficult.'[1]

Whatever the external circumstances, for the most part these are personal stories told from within. Their sphere is essentially domestic. Whether they are writing from Persia or St Petersburg, these women (mostly wives, but some daughters and sisters, too) describe the concerns of any ordinary Englishwoman: children, dogs, gardens, houses, servants, clothes, food. Politics, except on the occasions when they came into direct conflict with their lives, are only incidentally discussed. What they engage with instead is daily life. For the contemporary reader the women's subjectivity has a peculiar *veritas* which is frequently absent from their husbands' more distanced and perhaps more scholarly approach. What they do, brilliantly, is to describe what life was really *like*. It is this, more than anything else, which is their particular genius.

Who, today, would want to read Colonel Sheil's ponderous ethnographic dissertation on Persia in the mid-nineteenth century?* The memoir of his wife Mary, however, contained in the same volume, while politically almost entirely uninformative, has a freshness and drama which remains undimmed by time. Mary vividly describes her agonizing 1,000-mile journey with three small children and an invalid husband through the Caucasus Mountains from Tehran to Trebizond on the Black Sea (from whence they were able to sail to England). She recorded with simple stoicism how they waded up to their knees through the freezing snow, eating only dry crusts and sleeping in stables: 'I learned on this journey that neither children nor invalids know how much fatigue and privation they can endure until they are under compulsion.'[2]

In writing *Daughters of Britannia* I have drawn on the experiences of more than 100 diplomatic women. Their lives span nearly 350 years of history, and encompass almost every imaginable geographical and cultural variation, from the glittering social whirl enjoyed by Countess Granville in Paris after the Napoleonic Wars, to the privations suffered at the turn of this century by that redoubtable Scotswoman, Catherine Macartney, who in her seventeen years in Kashgar, in Chinese Turkistan, saw only three other European women.

Many of these women lived unique lives. Some saw sights which no other English person, man or woman, had ever seen. And yet, despite their vast differences – in character and taste as much as circumstances – a bond of shared experience unites them; a diplomatic 'culture' which was both official and intensely personal. Even though they are separated by nearly 200 years, when the anguished Countess of Elgin writes about her longing for news from home, it could be my own mother writing.

> Dearest Mother,
>
> Do not expect this to be an agreeable letter. I am too much disappointed in never hearing from home; the 17th July is the last from you, almost six months! ... I can't imagine why you took it into your heads that we were going home; for I am sure

---

* Colonel Sheil was the British minister in Tehran on the eve of the Crimean War.

I wrote constantly to tell you that we were at Constantinople, and why you would not believe me I know not. If you knew what I felt when the posts arrive and no letters for me, I am sure you would pity me. I shall write to nobody but you, for I feel I am too cross.[3]

In the Elgins' day the journey from England to Constantinople was not only long and arduous, it was also hazardous. Messengers were frequently attacked and robbed, and every single precious letter either destroyed or lost. Amazingly, even in the late twentieth century the non-arrival of the bag has been the cause of as much disappointment and pain. Here is my mother to my brother on 23 May 1978: 'Darling Matthew, Boo hoo! The bag has let us down, and there is gnashing of teeth here, and blood is boiling.' And to myself, on the same day: 'Darling Katie, The bloody bag has let us down yet again and we have no letters from any of you. We are so mad we could spit . . .'

What qualities were needed in a diplomat's wife? In Mary Elgin's day nobody would have thought it necessary to enumerate them. Of course, plenty was written on the qualities required in a man. In the sixteenth century, when the idea of sending a resident ambassador abroad was still fairly new, these were frequently listed in treaties and manuals. A man (in Sir Henry Wotton's famously ambiguous phrase) 'sent to lie abroad for the good of his country' was required to have an almost impossibly long list of attributes. He should be not only tall, handsome, well-born and blessed with 'a sweet voice' and 'a well-sounding name',[4] but also well read in literature, in civil and canon law and all branches of secular knowledge, in mathematics, music geometry and astronomy. He should be able to converse elegantly in the Latin tongue and be a good orator. He should also be of fine and upstanding morals: loyal, brave, temperate, prudent and honest.

An important ambassador's entourage could include secretaries and 'intelligencers', a chaplain, musicians, liverymen, a surgeon, trumpeters, gentlemen of the horse, 'gentlemen of quality who attended for their own pleasure', young nephews 'wanting that polish that comes from a foreign land', even dancing and fencing masters. But never a wife.

The ideal diplomatic wife was more difficult to describe: 'Just as the right sort can make all the difference to her husband's position,' wrote

Marie-Noele Kelly rather forbiddingly in her memoirs, 'so one who is inefficient, disagreeable, disloyal, or even merely stupid, can be a millstone around his neck.'[5] Although there have been some magnificent millstones – Lady Townley's infamous 'indiscretions' forced her husband to retire from the service – there is no doubt that all the staunchest qualities deemed necessary in men were required in their wives, too. Circumstances have often demanded of them unimaginable courage and reserves of fortitude.

This book is the story of how such women survived. It is the story of many lives lived valiantly far away from family and friends; and of the uniquely demanding diplomatic culture which sustained (and sometimes failed to sustain) these women as they struggled, often in very difficult conditions, to represent their country abroad. Although their role, in the eyes of 'his-story', lay very much behind the scenes, I believe that this is precisely why their testimony is so valuable: it was in coping with quite ordinary things, with the daily round of life, that their resilience and resourcefulness found its greatest expression.

My only regret is for the lives which, even after more than two years' searching, have continued to elude me. So it is only in my imagination that I can describe for you what it must have been like for Lady Winchilsea as she sailed into Constantinople, that city of marvels, by her husband's side that afternoon. Perhaps she, like the ambassador, was dressed in her court robes, still fusty and foul-smelling from their long confinement in a damp sea-trunk. Dolphins were still a common sight in the Bosphorus in those days, and I like to think of her watching them riding the bow-waves in front of the ship as it came into the harbour at last, the fabled city rising before them, its domes and minarets shining in the pink and gold light.

CHAPTER ONE

Getting There

Sometime at the beginning of April 1915 a lonely Kirghiz herdsman wandering with his flocks in the bleak mountain hinterland between Russian and Chinese Turkistan would have beheld a bizarre sight: a purposeful-looking Englishwoman in a solar topi, a parasol clasped firmly in one hand, striding towards the very top of the 12,000-foot Terek Dawan pass.

Ella Sykes, sister of the newly appointed British consul to Kashgar, was dressed in a travelling costume which she had invented herself to cope with the rigours of the journey. Over a riding habit made of the stoutest English tweed was a leather coat. On her legs she wore a pair of thick woollen puttees, while her hands were protected by fur-lined gloves. On her head she wore a pith helmet swathed in a gauze veil, and beneath it, protecting her eyes from the terrible glare of the sun in that thin mountain air, a pair of blue glass goggles. If the herdsman had been able to see beneath this strange mixture of arctic and tropical attire, he would have seen that her cheeks and lips were swollen, her skin so badly sunburnt that it was peeling from her face in large painful patches. But her eyes, behind those incongruous goggles, sparkled with a very English combination of humour and good sense. 'Such slight drawbacks', she would later record, 'matter little to the true traveller who has succumbed to the lure of the Open Road, and to the glamour of the Back of Beyond.'[1]

The glamour described by Ella Sykes is not of the kind usually associated with diplomatic life. This mysterious existence invariably brings to mind a vague impression of luxury – of diamonds and champagne, of vast palaces illuminated by crystal chandeliers, of ambassador's receptions of the Ferrero Rocher chocolates advertisement variety. While it is relatively easy to conjure with these fantastical images (for on the whole this is what they are) it is much more difficult to imagine the reality behind them. To contemplate Ella Sykes on her journey across the Terek Dawan pass* is to invite a number of questions. Who were these diplomatic women, and what were their lives *really* like? Where did they travel to, and under what circumstances? And, most important of all, how did they get there in the first place?

In 1915 an expedition to Kashgar, in Chinese Turkistan, was one of the most difficult journeys on earth. Following the outbreak of the First World War, the normal route for the first leg of the journey – across central Europe and down to the Caspian Sea – had become too dangerous, and so Ella and her brother Percy travelled to Petrograd (St Petersburg) on a vastly extended route via Norway, Sweden and Finland. From Petrograd they went south and east to Tashkent, the capital of Russian Turkistan, on a train which lumbered its way through a slowly burgeoning spring. At stations frothing with pink and white blossom, children offered them huge bunches of mauve iris, and the samovar ladies changed from their drab winter woollens into flowered cotton dresses and head-kerchiefs.

For all these picturesque scenes, even this early stage of the journey was not easy: the train had no restaurant car, and the beleaguered passengers found it almost impossible to find food. At each halt, of which luckily there were three or four a day, they would all leap off the train and rush to buy what they could at the buffets on the railway platforms, gulping down scalding bowls of cabbage soup or *borsch* in the few minutes that the train was stationary. The further east they travelled, the more meagre the food supplies became, until all they could procure was a kind of gritty Russian biscuit. Without the soup packets they had brought with them, Ella noted with some *sang-froid*, they would have half starved.

From Tashkent Percy and Ella took another train to Andijan, the end of the line, and from here they travelled on to Osh by victoria.† Here they found that Jafar Bai, the *chuprassi* (principal servant) from the Kashgar consulate, had come to meet them. Under his careful

---

* In recognition of her ground-breaking travels in Chinese Turkistan, Ella later became one of the first female Fellows of the Royal Geographical Society.
† A kind of small horse-drawn carriage.

ministrations they embarked on the final stage of their journey, the 260-mile trek across the mountains.

At first they met a surprising number of people en route: merchants with caravans laden with bales of cotton; Kashgaris with strings of camels on their way to seek work in Osh or Andijan during the summer months: 'Some walked barefoot, others in long leather riding boots or felt leggings, and all had leather caps edged with fur.' The long padded coats they wore were often scarlet, 'faded to delicious tints', and they played mandolins or native drums as they went. On one occasion they met a party of Chinese, an official and a rich merchant, each with his retinue, also bound for Kashgar.

> The ladies of the party travelled in four mat-covered palanquins, each drawn by two ponies, one leading and one behind [Ella wrote], and I pitied them having to descend these steep places in such swaying conveyances. They were attended by a crowd of servants in short black coats, tight trousers and black caps with hanging lappets lined with fur, the leaders being old men clad in brocades and wearing velvet shoes and quaint straw hats.

At night Ella and her brother stayed in rest-houses, which in Russia usually consisted of a couple of small rooms, with bedsteads, a table and some stools. Sometimes these rooms looked out onto a courtyard where their ponies were tied for the night, but often there was no shelter for either the animals or their drivers. Over the border in China these rooms became more rudimentary still, lit only by a hole in the roof. The walls were of crumbling mud, the ceilings unplastered, their beams the haunt of scorpions and tarantulas. Up in the mountains, of course, there were no lodgings of any kind. The Sykeses slept in *akhois*, the beehive-shaped felt tents of Kirghiz tribesmen, their interiors marvellously canopied and lined with embroidered cloths. In the remotest places of all they slept in their own tents.

According to Ella's account, these nights spent in the mountains were attended by a curious mixture of the rugged and the grandiose. Wherever they stopped, Jafar Bai would instantly make camp, setting up not only their camp-beds, but also tables to write and eat at, and comfortable chairs to sit on. While he heated the water for their folding baths, another servant prepared the food. After the gritty Russian biscuits and packet soups, a typical breakfast – steaming coffee and eggs, fresh bread and butter with jam – must have seemed like a banquet. The Russian jam, delicious as it was, had its drawbacks. In a state of ever-accelerating fermentation, the pots had a habit of exploding like bombs, causing havoc inside Jafar Bai's well-ordered tiffin basket.

The routine was one which the Sykeses were to adopt for all their travels in Turkistan: 'The rule was to rise at 5 a.m., if not earlier,' Ella wrote, describing a typical morning in camp,

> and I would hastily dress and then emerge from my tent to lay my pith-hat, putties, gloves and stick beside the breakfast table spread in the open. Diving back into my tent I would put the last touches to the packing of holdall and dressing-case, Jafar Bai and his colleague Humayun being busy meanwhile in tying up my bedstead and bedding in felts. While the tents were being struck we ate our breakfast in the sharp morning air, adjusted our putties, applied face-cream to keep our skins from cracking in the intense dryness of the atmosphere, and then would watch our ponies, yaks or camels as the case might be, being loaded up.[2]

Most days they would walk for an hour or so before they took to their mounts. Ella usually rode sidesaddle, but on these long journeys she found it less tiring to alternate with 'a native saddle', onto which she had strapped a cushion. Her astride habit, she noted, did for either mode. They would march for five hours before taking lunch and a long rest in the middle of the day, wherever possible by water, or at least in the shade of a tree. Then, when the worst of the midday heat was over, they would ride for another three or four hours into camp (the baggage animals usually travelling ahead of them) 'to revel in afternoon tea and warm baths'. This was Ella's favourite time of the day, not least because she could brush out her hair, which she had only hastily pinned up in the morning, and which by now was usually so thick with dust that she could barely get her comb through it.

At high altitude – sometimes they were as high as 14,000 feet – she suffered from the extremes of temperature. During the day, beneath a merciless sun, in spite of her pith hat and sun-umbrella, she often felt as if she was being slowly roasted alive, while the nights were sometimes so cold that she was forced to wear every single garment she had with her, with a fur coat on top. 'My feet were slipped into my big felt boots lined with lamb's wool,* and a woollen cap on my head completed the costume in which I sat at our dinner table.' Thus prepared, she felt perfectly ready, she wrote, 'to meet whatever might befall'.

In Ella Sykes's day a woman, diplomatic or not, was really not supposed to take with quite such aplomb to the challenges of 'the back of beyond'. It was not just her physical but her mental frailty, too, which was the impediment. If women themselves were in any doubt about this, then useful handbooks such as *Tropical Trials*, published in 1883, were on hand to tell them so.

> Many and varied are the difficulties which beset a woman when she first exchanges her European home and its surroundings for the vicissitudes of life in the tropics [warned its author, Major S. Leigh Hunt]. The sudden and complete upset of old-world life, and the disturbance of long existing association, produces, in many women, a state of mental chaos, that utterly incapacitates them for making due and proper preparations for the contemplated journey.[3]

Not only the preparations, but the departure itself, according to the major, were likely to reduce a woman to a state of near imbecility, coming as she did in moral fibre somewhere between 'the dusky African' and 'the heathen Chinee'. When embarking on a sea voyage, farewells with well-wishers of a woman's own sex were best done on shore, he advised, while 'a cool-headed male relation or friend' was the best person to accompany the swooning female on board.

In real life, of course, women were made of much sterner stuff, but nevertheless departures were often very painful. 'The parting with my people was unexpectedly terrible,' wrote Mary Fraser on the eve of her first diplomatic posting to China in 1874. 'Till the moment came I had not realised what it was to mean, this going away for five years

---

* These special 'double-lined native boots' were a present to her from the orientalist and explorer Sir Aurel Stein.

from everything that was my very own.' Revived by a glass of champagne, thoughtfully provided by her husband Hugh, she soon pulled herself together, however, and 'by the time the sun went down', she would remember, 'on a sea all crimson and gold, my thoughts were already flying forward to all the many strange and beautiful things I was so soon to see.'[4]

This poignant mixture of excitement and regret is probably superseded by only one other concern. Thirty years after Ella Sykes travelled to Chinese Turkistan, Diana Shipton was told by her husband Eric that he had been offered the post of consul-general in Kashgar. 'Mentally,' she wrote, 'I began immediately to pack and to plan.'[5]

The notion of travelling light has always been an alien one to diplomatic wives. 'We are like a company of strolling players,' wrote Harriet Granville, only half jokingly, en route to Brussels in 1824. Over the centuries many others must have felt exactly the same. When Lady Mary Wortley Montagu, whose husband Edward was appointed ambassador to Constantinople, arrived in Turkey in 1717, the Sultan lent their entourage thirty covered wagons and five coaches in which to carry their effects. Mary Waddington, who travelled to Russia in 1883, did so with a staff of thirty-four, including a valet and two maids, a master of ceremonies, two cooks, two *garçons de cuisine*, three coachmen and a detective. 'Four enormous footmen' completed the team, Mary recorded with gentle irony, 'and one ordinary sized one for everyday use'.[6] Even as recently as 1934, when Marie-Noele Kelly arrived by P & O in Cairo, she was accompanied by three European servants, three children, and fourteen tons of luggage.* The prize, however, must surely go to Lady Carlisle who, when her husband made his public entry into Moscow in 1663, accompanied him in her own carriage trimmed with crimson velvet, followed by no fewer than 200 sledges loaded with baggage.

When Elizabeth Blanckley's family travelled to Algiers, where her father was to take up his post as consul, they chanced upon Nelson and his fleet in the middle of the Mediterranean. 'Good God, it must be Mr Blanckley,'† Nelson is reputed to have exclaimed when he saw

---

* This was enough to furnish a very large villa. In those days only the houses of heads of mission were furnished by the government.

† Lord Nelson's father was a close friend of Mr Blanckley's.

their little boat, all decked out 'in gala appearance' with flags of different nations. 'How, my dear Sir, could you in such weather trust yourself in such a nutshell? . . . But I will not say one word more, until you tell me what I shall send Mrs Blanckley for her supper.'

> My father assured him that she was amply provided for [recalled Elizabeth Blanckley in her memoirs] and enumerated all the live stock we had on board, and among other things, a pair of English coach-horses which, to our no trifling inconvenience, he had embarked, and stowed on board. Nelson laughed heartily at the enumeration of all my father's retinue, exclaiming, 'A perfect Noah's ark, my dear sir! – A perfect Noah's ark.'[7]

Even the most determinedly rugged travellers, such as Isabel and Richard Burton, whose highly idiosyncratic approach to diplomatic life broke almost every other rule, travelled with prodigious quantities of luggage. On Isabel's first journey to Santos in Brazil, where Richard was appointed consul, she took fifty-nine trunks with her, and a pair of iron bedsteads. It is hard to imagine anyone further from Major Leigh Hunt's fanciful picture of the swooning and feather-brained female abroad than Isabel Burton. This was the woman who, when she learnt that she was to be Richard Burton's wife, sought out a celebrated fencer in London and demanded that he teach her. ' "What for?" he asked, bewildered by the sight of Isabel, her crinoline tucked up, lunging and riposting with savage concentration. "So that I can defend Richard when he is attacked," was the reply.'[8] Carrying out the order issued by her husband when he was finally dismissed from his posting in Damascus – the famous telegram bade her simply 'PAY, PACK AND FOLLOW' – was really a life's work in itself. Although Richard was little short of god-like in Isabel's eyes, when it came to the practicalities of their lives, she knew very well who was in control. 'Husbands,' she wrote, '. . . though they never see the *petit détail* going on . . . like to keep up the pleasant illusion that it is all done by magic.'[9]

One wonders who was responsible for overseeing the household of Sir William and Lady Trumbull when they travelled to Paris in 1685. The vast body of correspondence describing Sir William's embassy gives us almost no information about his wife other than that she had 'agreeable conversation' and once enjoyed 'a little pot of baked meat' sent to her by the wife of the Archbishop of York. We do know, however, the exact contents of her luggage. The Trumbull household consisted of forty people, including Lady Trumbull and her niece Deborah.

> Besides a coach, a chaise, and 20 horses, there were 2 trunks full of plate, 9 boxes full of copper and pewter vessels, 50 boxes with pictures, mirrors, beds, tapestries, linen, cloth for liveries, and kitchen utensils, 7 or 8 dozen chairs and arm chairs, 20 boxes of tea, coffee, chocolate, wine, ale and other provisions; 4 large and 3 small cabinets, 6 trunks and 6 boxes with Sir William and Lady Trumbull's apparel, and 40 boxes, trunks, bales, valises, portmanteaux, containing belongings of Sir William's suite.[10]

Handbooks for travellers, particularly in the late nineteenth century when the empire was at its height, were often aimed at readers who were going abroad, as diplomats were, to live for some time. They enumerated at length not only what to take for a two- or three-year sojourn, but also exactly how to take it. Major Leigh Hunt, perhaps because of his military background (Madras army), was very particular on the subject.

First there were the different types of trunk available. These include a 'State Cabin Trunk', made from wood with an iron bottom, for hot, dry climates; a 'Dress Basket', made of wicker, for damp climates; and a 'Ladies Wicker Overland Trunk', for overland travel (it was shallow, and could easily be stowed beneath the seat in a railway carriage). Then, of course, there was the ubiquitous travelling bath. One's china, he advised, 'should be packed, by a regular packer, in barrels'. Sewing machines were to go in a special wooden case; saddles in a special tin-lined case; paint brushes, he warned, should have their own properly closed boxes 'or the hairs will be nibbled by insects'. Even a lady's kid gloves, well-aired and then wrapped in several folds of white tissue paper, should be stored in special stoppered glass bottles.

Useful items of personal apparel include 'several full-sized silk gossamer veils to wear with your topee' and '*a most liberal* supply of tulle, net, lace, ruffles, frillings, white and coloured collars and cuffs, artificial flowers and ribbons'. Furthermore 'pretty little wool wraps to throw over the head, and an opera cloak, are requisites which should not be overlooked'. Among essential household items the major lists mosquito curtains, punkahs, umbrellas and goggles; when travelling by sea, a lounge chair; drawing materials, wool and silks for 'fancy work'; a water filter, lamps, a knife-cleaning machine; and no fewer than half a dozen pairs of lace curtains. Other recommended sundries include:

    a refrigerator
    a mincing machine
    a coffee mill
    a few squares of linoleum
    cement for mending china and glass
    Keatings insect powder
    one or two pretty washstand wall-protectors
    a comb and brush tray
    bats, net and balls for lawn tennis
    one or two table games
    a small chest of tools including a glue pot
    a small box of garden seeds
    a small garden syringe
    chess and backgammon
    a few packs of playing cards
    a Tiffin basket

Tropical Trials was, thankfully, by no means the only handbook of its kind to which a woman planning a life abroad could turn. Flora Annie Steel's celebrated book *The Complete Indian Housekeeper and Cook*, first printed in 1888, was so popular in its day that it ran to ten editions. Although it was dedicated 'To the English girls to whom fate may assign the task of being house-mothers in Our Eastern Empire', its sound good sense and truly prodigious range of recondite advice – from how to deal with snake bite ('if the snake is known to be deadly, amputate the finger or toe at the next joint . . .') to how to cure 'bumble foot' in chickens – made it just as useful to diplomatic women living outside the empire.

Unlike the major, Annie Steel had no time at all for fripperies.* 'As

* Although they were first published almost simultaneously, the difference in tone between these two handbooks is an interesting one. Annie Steel's recipe for hysteria in her fellow sisters is wonderfully brisk: whisky and water, 'and a little wholesome neglect'.

to clothing, a woman who wishes to live up to the climate must dress down to it,' was her sensible advice. Frills, furbelows, ribbons and laces were quite unnecessary, she believed. None the less, the clothing which even she considered essential would have taken up an enormous amount of trunk space. 'Never, even in the wilds, exist without one civilized evening and morning dress,' she urged, and listed:

6 warm nightgowns
6 nightgowns (silk or thin wool) for hot weather
2 winter morning dresses
2 winter afternoon dresses
2 winter tennis dresses
evening dresses
6 summer tea gowns*
4 summer tennis gowns
2 summer afternoon gowns
1 riding habit, with light jacket
1 Ulster†
1 Handsome wrap
1 umbrella
2 sunshades
1 evening wrap
1 Mackintosh
2 prs walking shoes
2 prs walking boots
2 prs tennis shoes
evening shoes
4 prs of house shoes
2 prs strong house shoes[11]

On the actual journey, however, circumstances were often rather more frugal than these preparations suggest. When Diana Shipton travelled to Kashgar it was so cold in the mountains that she and her husband put on every garment they possessed and did not take them

* A tea-gown was closely related to the modern dressing-gown, the difference being that a woman could perfectly respectably wear it in public.
† A stout waterproof cloak.

off again for three weeks. On one of her journeys in Brazil Isabel Burton once went for three months without changing her clothes at all. Sometimes, though, such spartan conditions were imposed more by accident than by design. When Angela Caccia, her husband David and their newborn son were posted to Bolivia in 1963 they made the journey by sea, taking with them an enormous supply of consumer goods, from tomato ketchup to soap powder. This luggage came with them as far as Barcelona, where it was lost, leaving them to face the six-week ocean voyage with little more than the clothes they were wearing. For the baby they did have clothes, but no food; 'David had 75 ties; I had 9 hats, and between us we had 240 stiff white paper envelopes.'

However, the journey itself was so entrancing that the Caccias soon forgot these inconveniences. Their route took them through the Panama Canal and then down the Pacific coast of South America to the Chilean port of Antofagasta, from where they took a train across the Atacama and up into the Andes. Angela was spellbound by the beauty of the desert, despite the fact that the air was so thin and dry that their lips cracked and their hands hissed if they rubbed them together as if they would ignite. The light was so intense, she recorded, that they wore dark glasses even inside their carriage with the curtains drawn.[12]

Very few diplomatic women were as experienced, or as naturally adept at travelling as Ella Sykes – or certainly not at first. The journey to a posting was often a woman's first taste of travelling abroad, and it left an indelible impression on her – although not always the same sense of wonderment experienced by Angela Caccia. Reading back over my mother's very first letters, written during the six-week sea voyage out to New Zealand in 1959, I find, to my surprise (for I have always known her as the most practised of travellers), a note of apprehension in her tone.

I suppose quite shortly we shall really be at sea [she writes from her cabin aboard the S.S. *Athenic*]. Atlantic rollers may begin, instead of the millpond the Channel has been up to now. We have been sailing in dense fog all day. It is a queer sensation to have thick mist swirling around with visibility about the length of the boat, the foghorn sounding every few minutes and bright sun shining down from above. We seem to be travelling at a snail's pace.

It is also a surprise to be reminded that even then such a voyage was still considered a special undertaking. My parents arrived at the London docks to find themselves inundated with well-wishers.

We were taken straight to our cabin and found a large box of flowers from Auntie Olive, also from Betty and Riki, and telegrams from Hilary and Tony, J's mother, Auntie Jo and Jack, Sylvia Gardener, and Richard Hickman. After the ship sailed at eight o'clock last night I found Mummy's wonderful boxes of Harrod's fudge and chocolates, and Hilary's [my mother's sister] stockings. Thank you so much both of you. It was all the nicer getting them then, after we had left the dock and were feeling a bit deflated. Thank you Mummy and Daddy also for the beautiful earrings, which J produced after dinner . . . I wonder if you realised how much I wanted something just like them?

There was no such send off for Isabel Burton when she took to the seas on her first posting in 1865. In her hotel room in Lisbon, where she stayed en route to Brazil, she was greeted by three-inch cock-roaches. Although she could not know it then, it was only a taste of what was to come. 'I suppose you think you look very pretty standing on that chair and howling at those innocent creatures,' was Richard's characteristically caustic response. Isabel reflected for a while, realized that he was right, and started bashing them instead with her shoe. In two hours, she recorded, she had a bag of ninety-seven.

For some women, the journey was the only enjoyable part of diplomatic life. The writer Vita Sackville-West loathed almost every aspect of it (the word 'hostess', she used to say, made her shiver), but her first impressions of Persia, recorded when she travelled there to join her husband, Harold Nicolson, in 1926, echoes the experience of many of these peripatetic wives. On crossing the border she wrote:

I discovered then that not one of the various intelligent people I had spoken with in England had been able to tell me anything about Persia at all, the truth being, I suppose, that different persons observe different things, and attribute to them a different degree of importance. Such a diversity of information I should not have resented; but here I was obliged to recognise that they had told me simply nothing. No one, for instance, had mentioned the beauty of the country, though they had dwelt at length, and with much exaggeration, on the discomforts of the way.

The land once roamed by the armies of Alexander and Darius had, to Vita's romantic imagination, a kind of historical glamour that its contemporary inhabitants never quite equalled. It was 'a savage, desolating country', but one that filled her with extraordinary elation. 'I had never seen anything that pleased me so well as these Persian uplands, with their enormous views, clear light, and rocky grandeur. This was, in detail, in actuality, the region labelled "Persia" on the maps.' With the warm body of her dog pressed against her, and the pungent smell of sheepskin in her nostrils, Vita sat beside her chauffeur in the front seat of the motor car with her eyes fixed in rapt attention on the unfolding horizon. 'This question of horizon,' she wrote musingly later, 'how important it is; how it alters the shape of the mind; how it expresses, essentially, one's ultimate sense of a country! That is what can never be told in words: the exact size, proportion, contour; the new standard to which the mind must adjust itself.'[13]

On that journey, she believed, Persia had in some way entered her very soul. 'Now I shall not tell you about Persia, and nothing of its space, colour and beauty, which you must take for granted –' she wrote to Virginia Woolf on her arrival in Tehran in March 1926, 'but please *do* take it for granted, because it has become part of me, – grafted on to me, leaving me permanently enriched.' But the exact quality of this enrichment even she found hard to put her finger on. 'But all this, as you say, gives no idea at all. How is it that one can *never* communicate? Only imaginary things can be communicated, like ideas, or the world of a novel; but not real experience . . . I should like to see you faced with the task of communicating Persia.'[14]

Such difficulties, however, were as nothing compared to the difficulties and hardships often involved in the actual travelling itself. When Mary Fraser set off from Venice to make the journey to Peking in 1874 she was unprepared for the rigours of her first diplomatic journey, even though, having lived in Italy and America, she was relatively well travelled for a young woman. At first all was well, even though she could not help noticing the strange smell on board their boat: 'the abominable, acrid, all-pervading smell of the opium cargo it was carrying'. By the time they reached Hong Kong, however, they had other worries: the worst typhoon in fifty years had all but destroyed the little island.

The P & O agent who came to meet their boat, 'ashy pale and still trembling in every limb', described how the storm had literally ripped apart the island in less than two hours. All shipping vessels had been wrecked, half the buildings ruined and not a single tree had been left standing in the Botanical Gardens. Worse than all this, though, was the fate of Hong Kong's coolies and their families who had been living in sampans in the harbour – an estimated 10,000 had been drowned. By the time the Frasers arrived the water in the harbour was awash with the floating bodies of men, women and children. As she disembarked, Mary accidentally stepped on one of them and thereafter, 'I could not be left alone for a moment without feeling faint and sick.' In the tropical heat the corpses were already beginning to putrefy. Pestilence was all around and the atmosphere, she recalled with horror, 'was that of a vast charnel house'.

The Frasers then travelled on to Shanghai without incident, and Mary recovered her composure enough to enjoy the rest of the journey, even the final stretch up the Pei-Ho river, although at first she surveyed the preparations with dismay. For the five-day river journey they had a fleet of five boats, each with five boatmen. Three of these carried their luggage; one was a kitchen and store room; while the fifth was fitted up snugly as a sleeping room and dining room. At night the boatmen pulled up the boards on the deck of their boat and, packed 'like sardines in a tin', they fitted the boards back tightly over themselves and slept peacefully. On the Frasers' boat there was a little deck at the front with two chairs and 'a tiny caboose sunk aft', where a mattress could be laid on the floor at night. By day it was replaced by a table. 'In the morning,' Mary recalled, 'poor Hugh used to hurry into his clothes, and go on shore for a walk, while I attempted to make my toilet, in all but darkness, with the help of one tin basin, muddy river water, and a hand glass.'

Although, unlike her husband, she was quite unused to these primitive travelling arrangements – 'the Frasers', she once commented, 'are all Spartans' – Mary was quick to learn a certain diplomatic stoicism. For most of the five days they spent on the Pei-Ho their servant, Chien-Tai, cooked 'with marvellous success' amidst her trousseau trunks in the kitchen boat and 'not a course that we would have had on shore was omitted'; but on one terrible occasion, amidst torrential rain, the boats became separated and they had nothing to eat for a whole day. The two of them passed the day gloomily in the blacked-out caboose, lighted only by two meagre candles.[15]

On her journey to Constantinople in 1716 Lady Mary Wortley Montagu, together with her husband and infant son, faced still greater hardships. On the mountain roads between Bohemia and Saxony she was so frightened by the sheer precipices that when she finally arrived in Dresden she could not compose herself to write at all. Their journey was all the more dangerous because they travelled at night, with only the moon to light their way.

In many places the road is so narrow that I could not discern an inch of space between the wheels and the precipice [she wrote to her sister Lady Mar]. Yet I was so good a wife not to wake Mr Wortley, who was fast asleep by my side, to make him share in my fears, since the danger was unavoidable, till I perceived, by the bright light of the moon, our postilions nodding on horseback while the horses were on a full gallop, and I thought it very convenient to call out to desire them to look where they were going.

As they travelled further south the danger of mountain precipices was replaced by another less dramatic but no less real peril: the weather. From Vienna Lady Mary wrote again to her sister on the eve of their journey through Hungary. It was January, and the entire country was so frozen by 'excessive cold and deep snows' that her courage almost failed her. 'The ladies of my acquaintance have so much goodness for me, they cry whenever they see me since I have determined to undertake this journey; and, indeed, I am not very easy when I reflect on what I am going to suffer.' Lady Mary's usually sanguine tone begins to waver a little at this point; but when no less a person than Prince Eugene of Savoy, the Austrian general, advises her against the journey she begins to sound genuinely frightened.

Almost everybody I see frights me with some new difficulty. Prince Eugene has been so good as to say all the things he could to persuade me to stay till the Danube is thawed, that I may have the convenience of going by water, assuring me that the houses in Hungary are such as are no defence against the weather, and that I shall be obliged to travel three or four days between Buda and Essek without finding any house at all, through desert plains covered with snow, where the cold is so violent many have been killed by it. I own these terrors have made a very deep impression on my mind, because I believe he tells me things truly as they are, and nobody can be better informed of them.

She ends her letter, 'Adieu, my dear sister. If I survive my journey, you shall hear from me again.' And then, in an uncharacteristically maternal aside: 'I can say with great truth, in the words of Moneses, I have long learnt to hold myself as nothing, but when I think of the fatigue my poor infant must suffer, I have all a mother's fondness in my eyes, and all her tender passions in my heart.'

As it turned out, Lady Mary's fears were not realized and the Wortley Montagus survived their journey. Although the snows were deep, they were favoured with unusually fine weather, and with their carriages fixed upon 'traineaus' ('by far the most agreeable manner of travelling post') they made swift progress. What they saw on the frozen Hungarian plains, however, shocked even their robust eighteenth-century sensibilities. Lady Mary recorded her impressions of the fields of Karlowitz, where Prince Eugene had won his last great victory over the Turks, in a letter to her friend, the poet Alexander Pope:

The marks of that glorious bloody day are yet recent, the field being strewed with the skulls and carcasses of unburied men, horses and camels. I could not look without horror on such numbers of mangled human bodies, and reflect on the injustice of war that makes murder not only necessary but meritorious. Nothing seems to me a plainer proof of the irrationality of mankind, whatever fine claims we pretend to reason, than the rage with which they contest for a small spot of ground, when such vast parts of fruitful earth lie quite uninhabited.[16]

But, as Lady Mary had found, the 'tender passions' provoked by the additional stress of travelling with small children were often difficult to bear. Catherine Macartney, yet another diplomatic wife to find herself posted to the wilds of Chinese Turkistan, describes the extraordinary precautions which she took to ensure the safety of her small son. Eric, her eldest child, was born in 1903 when the family was in Edinburgh on home leave, and was only five months old when they set off back to Kashgar. 'It seemed a pretty risky thing to take so small a traveller on a journey like the one before us,' Catherine wrote. Nonetheless, knowing what was ahead of them, she did all she could, almost from the day Eric was born, to prepare him for the journey. To harden him up she took him out in all weathers, and only ever gave him cold food (once they were in the Tien Shan Mountains she knew that it would be impossible to heat up bottles of milk). Eric apparently throve on it. Catherine described their travelling routine:

When we were in the mountains, his bottles for the day were prepared before starting the march, and carefully packed in a bag to be slung over a man's back. As they needed no heating, he could be fed when the time came for his meals, and just wherever we happened to be. And the poor little chap had his meals in some funny places – cowsheds, in the shelter of a large rock, or anywhere where we could get out of the wind.

At night he slept in a large perambulator which they had carried along especially for the purpose. According to Catherine, 'He stood the journey better than any of us.'

Five years later, in 1908, when the family went home on leave again, they were not so lucky. Eric was now five, his sister Sylvia two and a half. Flooding rivers had blocked the usual route through Osh, and instead the Macartneys decided to trek north over the Tien Shan, and then through the Russian province of Semiretchia, from whence they could reach the railway at Aris, just to the north of Tashkent. Catherine recorded it all in her diary. Despite her misgivings about travelling in the summer heats, she was overwhelmed by the beauty of the lakes and flower-filled meadows they passed through. The two children, who rode on pack ponies in front of two of the consulate servants, seemed to enjoy it too. It is not long, however, before a more anxious tone begins to colour her entries: '*Thursday, July 23rd*. We have beaten the record today and have done four stages, reaching Aulie-ata at about four o'clock this afternoon. Poor little Eric has been so ill all day with fever; but the travelling has not seemed to worry him much, for he has slept the most of the time in spite of the jolting. Our road has been across the grassy *steppes* and the dust was not so bad.'

The next day, to her relief, Eric was much better, and she was able to hope that it was just 'a passing feverish attack'. Two days later it was clear that it was something much worse.

Sunday, July 26th. Today's march has been done with the greatest difficulty, for the children have both been very unwell and can take no food whatever. They have not seemed themselves for some days, and today they have been downright ill. To make matters worse, I suddenly had an attack of fever come on, which decided us to stop at the end of our second stage at Beli-Voda. Eric and I had to go to bed, or rather to lie down on hard wooden sofas, and it was pitiable to see poor little Sylvia. She was so ill and miserable and yet wanted to run about the whole time, and seemed as though she could not rest. There was little peace for anyone, for we could only have the tiny inner room that was reserved for ladies, to ourselves. The whole afternoon travellers were arriving and having tea in the next room, talking and laughing and making a distracting noise. Happily we had the place to ourselves for the night. I am much better this evening, but the children seem to be getting steadily worse and we are becoming anxious about them.

The following day the two children were so ill that the Macartneys got up at dawn and made haste to the town of Chimkent, where they were told there was a doctor. The doctor advised them to stop travelling at once and, to Catherine's relief, found rooms for them in an inn near his house.

It is delightfully cool and restful here, after the hot dusty roads [she wrote in a snatched moment] and a few days' rest will, I hope, set us all up. The first thing we did was to give the children a warm bath, put them into clean clothes and get them to bed. They looked so utterly dirty and wretched when we arrived that I felt I must cry; and they were asleep as soon as they got between clean sheets ... a sleep of exhaustion. Both of them have lost weight in the last few days.

It was the last entry she was to make for many weeks.
On 23 August Catherine finally resumed her journal.

Our two or three days here have lengthened into nearly a month, and a time of awful anxiety it has been. The children, instead of recovering in a few days, developed dysentery, and to add to our troubles Nurse took it too. For three weeks it was a fight for Eric's life and several times we thought we would lose him. Sylvia, though bad enough, was not as desperately ill as Eric ... My husband and I did all the nursing and during that time we neither of us had a single night's rest, just snatching a few minutes sleep at odd times.

In spite of their rudimentary lodgings – two rooms so small that there was only space for the children's and the nurse's beds – they were comforted by the extraordinary kindness of the local people. The Russian doctor visited them sometimes as many as three or four times a day. And there were others, too, 'who, simply hearing that we were strangers and in trouble, were most helpful in sending us goat's milk, cake, fruit, and delicacies. It is when one is in such straits as we were that one discovers how many kind people there are in the world. But I never imagined that anyone could receive so much sympathy and practical help from perfect strangers as we did during that anxious month.'[17]

The Macartneys had been on the road for more than 800 miles before they finally arrived, exhausted, in Aris. From here they were able to pick up the Tashkent–Moscow train, and travelled onwards, first to Moscow, and then to Berlin via Warsaw. Although Eric suffered several relapses during that time, the family arrived safely in Edinburgh, three long and painful months after they had set out.

Like Mary Wortley Montagu with her traineaus, and Mary Fraser with her fleet of Chinese river boats, diplomatic women over the centuries have been obliged to take what transport they could find. Yet another Mary – Mary Waddington, who travelled to Russia to the Tsar's coronation in 1883 – had several luxuriously appointed private railway carriages at her disposal, but a diplomatic wife was just as likely to find herself transporting her family by camel, yak, horse, palanquin, coolie's chair, house-boat, cattle-truck, *tukt*,* sleigh or *tarantass*† as by more conventional methods.

Travelling to the most far-flung diplomatic posts has remained a logistical problem well into the present century. One diplomatic wife recalls her journey to Persia in 1930, with her husband and English nurse, her children Rachel, aged two, and Michael, aged nine months, and seventy pieces of luggage. The quickest route in those days was by train, through Russia, although it still took two weeks. There were no disposable nappies in those days, so the baby's washed napkins had to be hung out on rails in the corridor to dry, and when it came to crossing the Caspian Sea both her husband and the nurse were so sick she had no one to help her at all. 'I can still see my poor husband with Rachel on his lap, being sick, and she, infuriatingly cheerful, saying, "What's Daddy doing that for?"'

In 1964 Ann Hibbert's husband Reg was sent to Ulan Bator, the capital of Mongolia, to open the British embassy; she later flew out there on her own under very strange circumstances. It was at the height of the Cold War, and sometime in the middle of the night they came down to refuel on the Soviet–Mongolian border. Although Anne was allowed off the plane, the Russians went to some lengths to stop her from talking to the other passengers. 'I was told that I was not to go with the others,' she remembers. 'I was separated from them, and taken into a room by myself and the stewardess, very kindly, said, "I have to lock you in. Would you like the key on the inside or the outside?" I said, "On the inside, if you don't mind." So I was locked up, while the plane was refuelled.'

---

* A horse litter.
† A boat-shaped basket resting on long poles, drawn by three horses abreast.

Single women travelling on their own, even respectable married ones, have always been faced with special complications, as Sheila Whitney found when she went to China in 1966.

Ray said, 'You need a rest, come out on the boat,' which I did and it took me four and a half weeks – the slow boat to China. I didn't particularly enjoy it because I was a woman on my own, and in 1966 if you were a woman on your own, and one man asks you to dance more than twice you were a scarlet woman. I went and sat on the Captain's table and there was a young chap there, and he was engaged to somebody, so I said, 'Oh well, we're in the same boat. You're being faithful to your fiancée, and I'm being faithful to my husband, perhaps we can, you know . . .' I didn't invite him to dance or anything. But, no, they all had to be in bed by half past ten. On the journey before they'd all been in trouble, apparently, and so they all had to be in bed by half past ten at night. All the ship's officers. Anyway, that was that. I was sharing a cabin with a young eighteen-year-old girl, who was there with her parents, and I used to go out with her parents, because if I did anything else I was labelled. It was ghastly. I can't tell you how ghastly it was. But it was very funny, too. So I didn't have such a gay time as I thought I was going to have. You know, I was looking forward to it.

At the turn of the century a similar regard for propriety governed long sea voyages, although, if Lady Susan Townley is to be believed, the rules were slightly less strict then than they were in the 1960s.* On her journey to Peking from Rome in 1900 she noted the popularity of parlour games, especially musical chairs, during which a convenient lurch of the ship could always be blamed when a 'not unwilling Fräulein' fell into the lap of a smart officer. 'These fortunate incidents, resulted in several engagements before the end of the journey,' she noted wryly. 'No wonder the game was popular.'[18]

A woman's sex contributed to her difficulties on a voyage in many

---

* In the course of her long diplomatic career Lady Susan saw sex around every corner. Her brilliantly self-aggrandizing memoirs contain the heading, 'How I once diplomatically fainted to avoid trouble with a German swashbuckler'.

different ways. She was encumbered not only morally (especially if she was obliged to travel alone) by notions of 'respectability', but also physically, by the clothes she wore. Until the latter part of this century women's fashions were a serious handicap on anything but the shortest and most straightforward of journeys. Even an exceptional traveller such as Ella Sykes, who relished the harshness of the road, must privately have cursed the inconvenience of her cumbersome long skirts.

Recalling her long diplomatic career, which began just after the war in 1948, Maureen Tweedy claims that she knew, even as a child, that she had been born into a man's world. She was 'only a girl', and restricted, apart from her sex, by layers of underclothing. 'Children today cannot imagine how my generation were restricted. Woollen combinations, a liberty bodice on which drawers, goffered and beribboned, were buttoned, a flannel petticoat with feather-stitched hem, and finally a white cambric one, flounced and also beribboned.'[19]

For grown women, matters became even worse. The extensive clothing list suggested by the highly practical Flora Annie Steel was as nothing compared to the extraordinary number of garments which went underneath:

6 calico combinations
6 silk or wool combinations
6 calico or clackingette slip bodices
6 trimmed muslin bodices
12 pairs tan stockings
12 pairs Lisle thread stockings
6 strong white petticoats
6 trimmed petticoats
2 warm petticoats
4 flannel petticoats
36 pocket handkerchiefs
4 pairs of stays
4 fine calico trimmed combinations for evening[20]

Any woman following Flora Annie Steel's advice to the letter would therefore have made her journey with a total of seventy-four different items of underwear (not including the pocket handkerchiefs).

*   *   *

Mary Sheil would have been similarly restricted in 1849, when she made the three-and-a-half-month journey to Persia via Poland and Russian Turkistan. The introduction of the crinoline was still seven years off, but there were stays, combinations and yards of cumbersome petticoats to hamper her. A typical day-time outfit of the period, even for travelling, would have included long lace-trimmed drawers, a tightly laced bone corset supporting the bust with gussets, and a bodice or camisole over the top. In addition to these a woman would have worn a total of five different petticoats: two muslin petticoats, a starched white petticoat with three stiffly starched flounces, followed by a petticoat wadded to the knees and stiffened on the upper part with whalebone, followed by a plain flannel petticoat. Over these went her travelling dress.

Mary Sheil was a highly intelligent and educated woman. During the four years she spent in semi-seclusion in the British mission in Tehran she learnt to speak Persian fluently, and became something of an authority on many aspects of Persian history. However, like so many other women contemplating their first long-distance diplomatic journey, she must have been totally unprepared for the kind of hardships she encountered. But the sheer physical discomfort of the journey, although considerable, was eclipsed by her growing sense of the vast cultural chasms which she would somehow have to cross. Physically, she may have had the protection of her husband and his Cossack escort; emotionally, I suspect, she was entirely alone.

Colonel Sheil and his newly pregnant wife were luckier than most contemporary travellers for, as diplomats, they were provided with a messenger, an officer of the Feldt Yäger,* who rode ahead of them and secured, to the exclusion of other travellers, a fresh supply of horses. Nevertheless, the journey was not only uncomfortable, but occasionally extremely dangerous. Until a few years previously, Mary noted with some trepidation, no traveller had been allowed to proceed through the Russian hinterlands without an armed escort.

At one point they travelled in their carriage – 'an exceedingly light uncovered wagon, without springs, called a *pavoska*, drawn by three horses abreast' – for five days and five nights at a stretch. They stopped only for meals in flea-bitten inns along the way; sometimes, after a long and exhausting day on the road, they would find that there was abso-

---

* A government messenger, 'nearly as powerful at the post-houses as the Czar himself'.

lutely nothing for them to eat: 'not even bread, or the hitherto unfailing samawar [sic] . . . so we went dinnerless and supperless to bed.'

As they penetrated still further into the Russian outback the countryside became increasingly desperate. There was nothing to be seen but desolation and clouds of midges. 'It is marvellous,' Mary remarked sombrely, 'how little change has taken place in this country during fifty years.' In Circassia she noted down the price of slaves who, even in 1849, were still openly on sale. A young man of fifteen could be bought for between £30 and £70, while a young woman of twenty or twenty-five cost £50–£100. The highest prices of all, however, were fetched by young nubile girls of between fourteen and eighteen, who went for as much as £150 (just under £9000 today).

For the most part, the strangeness of these lands was something which Mary had to endure before she could reach her destination. Unlike her successor, Vita Sackville-West, she found little in the Persian landscape to excite her imagination. 'Sterile indeed was the prospect, and unhappily it proved to be an epitome of all the scenery in Persia, excepting on the coast of the Caspian,' she wrote.

If Mary's upbringing had ill-prepared her for the rigours of the journey, it had prepared her even less for the stark realities of life in Persia. At the border she veiled herself for the first time and, very much against their will, persuaded her two maids to follow her example.

At first the implications of this self-imposed purdah were lost amidst the excitement of their reception. The Persians welcomed them magnificently, as Mary recorded in her journal:

The Prince-Governor had most considerately sent a suite of tents for our accommodation; and on entering the principal one we found a beautiful and most ample collation of fruits and sweetmeats. His Royal Highness seemed resolved we should imagine ourselves still in Europe. The table (for there was one) was covered with a complete and very handsome European service in plate, glass and china, and to crown the whole, six bottles of champagne displayed their silvery heads, accompanied by a dozen other bottles of the wines of Spain and France.

More typical of her fate, however, was the 'harem' which had been prepared for her and her ladies – a small tent of gaily striped silk, with additional tents for her women servants, surrounded ominously by 'a high wall of canvas'.

Colonel Sheil's triumphal procession through Persia to Tehran is counterpointed in Mary's journal by her growing realization that, as a woman, she would play no part at all in his public life. In Tabríz, in northern Persia, where thousands of people turned out into the streets to welcome them, 'there was not a single woman, for in Persia a woman is nobody'. A tent was set up where the grandees of the town, who had come to meet them, alighted to smoke *kalleeans* and *chibouks*, to drink tea and coffee and to eat sweetmeats. Mary was obliged to remain in solitary seclusion while her husband received their visitors alone. Once the men had refreshed themselves, the entire procession was called to horse again, this time with a greater crowd than ever, including 'more beggars, more lootees or mountebanks with their bears and monkeys, more dervishes vociferating for *inam* or bakshish . . .'

Excluded from these courtesies, and relegated ingloriously to the very tail of the procession along with the servants and the baggage, poor Mary found the show, the dust and the fatigue overwhelming. To make matters worse, at every village a *korban*, or sacrifice, was made in which a live cow or sheep was decapitated, and the blood directed across their path.* Although this ceremony was carried out in their honour, Mary was repelled and disgusted by it. Every last vestige of romance which Persia – the land of *The Arabian Nights* and *Lalla Rookh* – might once have held for her was swept away. In the towns she saw only dead horses and dogs, and a general air of decay; in the countryside only desolation and 'a great increase of ennui'.

Mary Sheil completed her journey to Tehran in one of the strangest conveyances ever used by a diplomatic wife – a Persian litter known as a *takhterewan*, a kind of moving sofa 'covered with bright scarlet cloth and supported by two mules', while her two maids travelled in boxes, one on either side of a mule, 'where, compressed into the minutest dimensions, they balanced each other and' – no doubt echoing their mistress's private thoughts – 'sought consolation in mutual commiseration of their forlorn fate in this barbarian land.'[21]

---

* In order that all misfortunes and evils should be drawn onto the sacrificial animal rather than onto the travellers.

CHAPTER TWO

The Posting

To Mary Sheil, nervous and exhausted from nearly four months' travelling, the British residence in Tehran must have seemed like a haven from the horrors of the barbarous and teeming streets outside. 'I passed through a pretty English garden, and then entered an excellent, and even stately-looking English, or rather Italian dwelling of considerable size,' she wrote. But the house itself was not the only wonder in store for her. 'I was still more surprised when an extremely well-dressed Persian entered the room and said to me, in an accent savouring most intensely of the "Cowgate", "Wi' ye tak ony breakfast?" This was Ali Mohammed Beg, the mission housekeeper, who had acquired a fair knowledge of English from a Scotch woman-servant.'

Despite this auspicious beginning, it was not long before Mary came to realize that the house, beautiful as it was, was not so much a haven as a prison. As she had so forlornly discovered on her journey, in Persia a woman was no one. The journal which she wrote to alleviate the loneliness and almost total isolation of her four years in Persia records all too clearly the monotony of her life: 'To a man the existence is tiresome enough, but to a woman it is still more dreary.' As was so often the case in these diplomatic partnerships, her husband was occupied with his job, with sports, visits, and 'the gossip and scandal of the town, in which he must join whether he likes it or not'. The conditions under which a woman found herself obliged to live were very different: 'She cannot move abroad without being thickly veiled; she cannot amuse herself by shopping in the bazaars, owing to the attention she could attract unless attired in Persian garments.' But any European woman who managed to escape suffocation beneath the *roobend*,*

---

* A white linen veil fitting tightly round the head and hanging over the eyes with only a small open-worked hole to breathe through.

would surely have been half-crippled by the tiny shoes, barely covering half the foot, with a small heel three inches high in the middle of the sole.

Unlike so many of her successors – and predecessors – in postings in which the seclusion of women was practised, Mary was as much a victim of her own prejudices as the local customs. In her view the acquaintance of only a very few of the Tehran ladies was considered desirable at all; none of them were Persians. The Russian mission, she complained, was too far away for her to be able to cultivate the friend-ship of 'Princess D' and her 'aimiable daughter', while the remaining female society was limited to just one or two other ladies, the wives of foreign officers in the Shah's service. Tehran, she wrote rather plain-tively, was 'one of the most frightful places in the world' and her life there resembled that of a nun. Although on several occasions she did go to visit the Shah's mother in the palace harem, it does not seem to have occurred to her that such women might have been seen as equals rather than as exotic curiosities.

Later on, when Mary had learnt Persian and was in a better position to form an opinion, she conceded that the Persian women were both lively and intelligent. 'They are restless and intriguing, and may be said to manage their husband's and son's affairs. Persian men are made to yield to their wishes by force of incessant talking and teazing,' she noted, a frisson of disapproval in her voice. The Shah's mother in particular – 'very handsome, and did not look above 30 but must be 40' – was very clever: not only was she in complete charge of the harem itself; it was also said that she played a large part in the affairs of government.

The *Khanum* (the Lady), as she was known, received Mary kindly. She said 'a great many aimiable things to me and went through all the usual Persian compliments, hoping that my heart had not grown narrow and that my nose was fat.' Mary was entertained lavishly, and the *Khanum* asked her many questions about Queen Victoria: how she dressed and how many sons she had. She even made her describe the ceremonial of a Drawing Room, and a visit to the theatre. And yet despite these overtures, 'various circumstances render it undesirable to form an intimacy with the inmates of any Persian anderoon,' Mary wrote primly. 'If it were only on account of the language they are said to be in the habit of using in familiar intercourse among themselves, no European woman would find any enjoyment in their society.'

This memsahib-like prudery condemned Mary to a life of splendid isolation. At first she was amused by the way in which her escort seized any men who came too close to her and pushed their faces up against the wall until she had passed lest she should be 'profaned' by their glance. But once established at the mission Mary was allowed nowhere, not even for a drive, without an escort of fifteen or twenty armed horsemen. This was not so much for security, for Persia was a safe country, 'but that dignity so required'.

Since she could take no part in her husband's public life, almost her only pleasures were her pets, letters from home, which arrived just once a month, and her garden. At first she found the garden a melancholy place, full of lugubrious cypresses, in which 'the deserted, neglected little tombs of some of the children of former ministers occupied a prominent place', filling her with gloomy forebodings. But with the help of a Mr Burton, a first-rate English gardener who at that time was in the service of the Shah, she was soon astonishing everyone with the beauty of her celery and her cauliflowers, 'for these useful edibles occupied my mind more than flowers.'[1] To be thrown back on her own resources in this way, albeit in the humble cultivation of a vegetable patch, was to prove an invaluable training for the real hardships that she was later to face.

In the mid-nineteenth century there was nothing, and no one, to tell Mary Sheil what living in Persia was going to be like. While various forms of military and diplomatic intelligence existed for the use of Colonel Sheil and his colleagues, the female, domestic sphere was never considered important enough to merit attention. As a woman, and as a European, Mary was doubly isolated.

Present-day Foreign Office wives (and now of course Foreign Office husbands as well) may consult a well-developed system of post reports to tell them exactly what to expect when they arrive in a new country, from schools for their children to whether or not Marmite can be bought in Azerbaijan (it can't). But knowing the theory, of course, does not necessarily make the practice any easier.

Sometimes even the most basic physical conditions, such as the weather, can be the most daunting. Extremes of heat and cold (−45°C in the harshest Mongolian winters; +45°C in the hottest central Asian summers), of humidity or altitude, are only partly alleviated by modern central heating and air-conditioning. Although most diplomatic women are willing to adapt to a different geography, a different culture, even a different political system, they are often ill-equipped to meet the challenge. Learning the language, as Mary Sheil did in Persia, is vital, but sometimes even the most brilliant linguists find it unexpectedly tough. 'Why do grammars only teach one such phrases as "Simply through the courage of the champion's sword"',' lamented Vita Sackville-West, 'when what one wants to say is "Bring another lamp"?'[2] Jane Ewart-Biggs was able to learn quite fluent Flemish in Brussels, but even she was stumped when she had to introduce Baron Regnier de Wykerslooth de Rooyesteyn to the Comte de Crombrugghe de Picquendaele.

The very first impressions of a new posting are the most vivid. These fleeting insights can set the tone, all too brutally sometimes, for the next two or three years to come. Jane Ewart-Biggs arrived in Algeria with her two-month-old baby, Henrietta, in her arms, in 1961, at the height of the country's savage war of independence against the French. The first thing she saw on her journey from the airport was a man leaning out of a stationary car. It was only when she was past the car that she realized that the man's strange position, spreadeagled out of the window, could only have meant one thing: he was dead. 'I had never seen anyone dead before,' she commented faintly.[3]

Lady Mary Wortley Montagu was both refreshed and exhilarated by her first impressions: 'Hitherto all I see is so new to me it is like a fresh scene of an opera every day,' she wrote enthusiastically on first arriving in Turkey.[4] For others, such as Ella Sykes out in the wilds of Turkistan, part of the lure of the 'Back of Beyond' was simply the physical freedom from starchy drawing-room conventions.

There were other wives, however, for whom first impressions were not quite so liberating. When my mother finally arrived in Wellington, after six weeks on the high seas, she vividly expressed in her first letters home her own sense of dislocation at the strangeness of it all, tinged with a faint disappointment.

Dear Mummy and Daddy [she wrote a few days after her arrival in July], We arrived in Cooks Strait in lovely weather and docked at Wellington in bright sunshine and no wind. It was both exciting and sad. Firstly it was horrid having no family among the cheering crowds at the quayside, and secondly it was exciting to see this wonderful harbour. The Second Secretary and Chief Clerk were on the quayside, looking most English and conspicuous by the very fact that they didn't look excited and weren't waving to anyone . . . The town of Wellington has little to offer. It seems rather provincial, unfinished, and a cross between Montreal and some deep southern hick town. All the shopping streets have covered-in ways, with their signs flapping horizontally at you as you walk along, and it would never surprise me to see a posse come riding into town. One feels it should have saloon bars with swing doors.

When her husband was posted to Benghazi, in Libya, Felicity Wakefield was daunted not only by the conditions under which she was expected to live, but also by an acute sense of the life she was leaving behind.

I had just had two years living in our beautiful house in South Kensington. It was like a railway station because there were people in and out all the time, and we were having rather a good time living there. And the children were all there, and all one's friends were readily available. Life was very easy and very pleasant, and then suddenly one's taken out of that and put in a new place where you know nobody. And the physical things were very difficult. The lights were on sometimes, and often not on. The climate in some ways was idyllic, but then you got these terrible winds off the desert. The water in the tap tasted brackish. It was very salt. You *could* drink it, there wasn't anything else to drink at that stage. Eventually we got organised, and used to fetch water in an enormous tank down from the mountains, but everything tasted revolting because it was cooked with salty water – including the coffee for breakfast. The Libyans were unfriendly; if you invited them, they wouldn't come. In the end we learnt how they did things, and learned to love them. But my initial impressions were . . . I was horrified.

Many women, especially those with young families, found, like Felicity Wakefield, that their first impressions were dominated by purely practical considerations. In the harsher and more remote postings, shortages of light and water, and weird, if not downright dangerous electrical systems were commonplace. For Catherine Young, who arrived in Syria for the first time in 1983, it was the even more basic expedient of buying food for her family's breakfast the next day.

> I thought, oh my goodness, the children are going to school, I must go and get a few things. I went in to one of the shops and it looked like a grocer's shop and there I got some sugar. As for tea? No, no tea. Coffee? No; no coffee. Jam? No jam. Butter? The same. I had to go into four different shops to get enough for breakfast. And I came back and I was absolutely desperate. I thought, I'm going to spend my life doing this – how am I going to manage?

The first few glimpses of a new and unknown country could evoke powerful feelings. Loneliness and homesickness were commonplace, but these were often mingled with other, darker emotions. Angela Caccia struggled to come to terms with the effects of the physical landscape itself. Bolivia was a beautiful country, but its beauty had a disturbing quality to it. Nature, she observed, 'was prodigal here, contemptuous, aloof'. At midday the sun was so strong that even half an hour in it would burn the baby's cheeks to blisters, and yet at night they 'would huddle by the fire while frost fell outside'. Strangest of all, though, was the effect of altitude (La Paz is 11,000 feet above sea level) and the extraordinary mountain light. 'The air was so clear, the light so pure, it seemed almost to have sparks in it, like fluorescence in sea water. On some days the blueness of the sky had a dazzling intensity; on others it was white, as though the colour had gone into a range of radiance beyond human sight.' Despite this beauty, or perhaps because of it, during her first few weeks Angela felt miserable and isolated, surrounded by people 'whose languages and ways of thought we saw no hope of understanding'. And at first she was afraid, too: 'afraid . . . of these strange, different people, of the stories of violence, death, and brutality . . . I was afraid of the Indians, the men in the buses who smelt so strongly of dirty clothes, drink and excrement.'[5]

Her experience is echoed by that of Masha Williams, whose first impressions of Baghdad in 1947 were of a 'violent, cruel world'. Although she was fascinated by it strangeness and its mystery, she was a little frightened too. 'I was afraid of the Arabs,' she confessed. 'Socially we met them rarely, our time being taken up by the British, but it was a frightening world outside our British circle. In the streets – anonymous, faceless, shapeless women draped in black and the thin-lipped men who stared brazenly from under their head cloths at my bare arms and swollen figure.'[6]

It came as a shock to realize that these feelings were sometimes reciprocated. In Peking during the Cultural Revolution Sheila Whitney remembers the 'anti-imperialist' marches, specifically directed against foreigners, which took place every few months or so, during which the Red Guards would throw paint on cars in the British mission compound and smash their flower pots. 'We used to watch it, fascinated, really. I felt sorry for the Chinese, because they all had to do what the Red Guards told them.'

Other less drastic forms of culture shock could work both ways as well. When Mary Sheil visited the Shah's harem she was amused to find that not one of his ladies could be convinced that European women undressed at night before they went to sleep. 'Was it true,' she was asked, 'we put on a long white dress to pass the night in?' When Maureen Tweedy arrived in Seoul she, too, found the people friendly, but puzzled by Europeans and their ways. 'We had to learn many things in our new post; to say Western and not European in deference to the Americans; to say Asian and not Asiatic; to remember that when a servant giggled on being reprimanded it was a sign of embarrassment and not of impertinence.'[7] While blowing one's nose in public was frowned upon, spitting was perfectly acceptable, and to be thought old was a compliment. On her arrival Maureen was met by a group of journalists, and their questions brought home to her how unknown and far away Britain was to Koreans. Why do English girls wear dark clothes? Why does the sun not shine in Britain? What do English boys say to English girls? What is a deb (this was in the late 1950s)? Why do the English not have a national costume like the Scots? How well did she know the Queen and how often did she go and see her? Was it true that the English are such bad cooks they can only live on fish and chips?

* * *

The style in which a diplomatic wife first arrived in a new posting varied enormously according both to the country and to her husband's diplomatic status in it. When Maureen Tweedy's husband was posted to Kuwait in 1950 it was still only a little-known sea port on the edge of the desert. There was no airport and no one to welcome them, so they landed, unheralded, on a strip of beaten sand 'under the supercilious gaze of a couple of camels'.[8] Arriving in Tripoli in the late eighteenth century, Miss Tully found that great crowds of people had gathered at the docks for a good view of the strange new arrivals. The Bey's chief officers, 'splendidly arrayed in the fashion of the east' in flowing robes of satin, velvet and costly furs, had been sent to meet them. But the majority, she noted with revulsion, 'were miserable beings whose only covering was a piece of dark brown homespun cotton'.[9]

In the grander embassies arrivals were very different occasions. Although there was no public entrance or procession for the Elgins when they arrived in Constantinople in 1779 (as there had been for the Winchilseas in 1661), their reception was still designed to reflect the richness and magnificence of the Ottoman court. No fewer than ninety attendants were sent to the British embassy, each one carrying a round tray covered with beautiful flowers and quantities of exotic fruit; 'they placed the flowers and fruit on each side of our hall and made two rows from top to bottom,' wrote the Countess of Elgin to her mother. 'The Great Man [the Grand Vizier] then came into the room followed by eight trays with five pieces of fine Berlin china on each, filled with different sorts of preserves and painted handkerchiefs over each. Four trays for me and four for Elgin.'[10]

Similarly in 1664, when Ann Fanshawe and her husband, Richard, the new ambassador, first arrived in Spain, they were greeted with all the pomp and circumstance that the Spanish court could muster. Her view of Spain, perhaps not unnaturally, was profoundly influenced by her reception. The Fanshawes had sailed to Cadiz, where a barge, sumptuously covered with crimson damask and gold fringes, Persian carpets underfoot, was sent to meet them. As they disembarked from their own ship all the other vessels in the harbour saluted them with volleys of guns and cannons. At the dockside a great crowd of the town's 'quality' was waiting to honour them, and the streets were thronged with common folk eager to watch them go by. The King's representative, Don Juan de la Cueva, the Duke of Albuquerque and twice a Grandee of Spain, came to greet them personally. With a graceful flourish, Lady Fanshawe remembered with a little flutter, he deposited his plumed hat on the ground before her. 'This, with my family and life, I lay at your Excellency's feet,' he said.

From Cadiz they travelled in state all the way to Madrid. In addition to the Spanish courtiers and their entourages who now accompanied them, the Fanshawes had their own extensive suite, including gentlemen-of-the-horse, three pages, a chief butler, a chief cook, two undercooks, two grooms, two footmen, a governess for their children, a housekeeper, a waiting gentlewoman, a servant to the young gentlewoman, a chambermaid and a washmaid, three postilions, three coachmen and three grooms.

As befitted his status as ambassador, Richard travelled in the principal gilded state coach, which was lined with crimson velvet and fringed with silver and gold. Ann followed behind in a second, green-velvet-lined coach. Many gentlemen, perhaps including the gallant Duke of Albuquerque, rode in front and Ann's pages, dressed in matching green velvet liveries, rode behind her. Numerous coaches, litters, riding horses, and a string of covered wagons decorated with the Fanshawe coat of arms and carrying their trunks and clothes, brought up the rear. Along the way they were lavishly fêted, entertained with banquets, plays, comedies, music and *juegos de toros* (bullfights). In the King's palace in Seville, where they stayed briefly, Ann was presented with a pet lion. 'Yet I assure you,' she claimed, not wholly convincingly, in the memoir written for her only surviving son, '. . . that your father and myself both wished ourselves in a retired country life in England, as more agreeable to both our inclinations.'

And yet, while she remained in Spain, everything about the country seemed marvellous; better, in fact, to her dazzled eyes, than anything she had ever encountered in England.

Our house was very richly furnished, both my husband's quarter and mine, the worst bed and chamber of my apartment being furnished with damask, in which my chambermaid lay; and all the chambers through[out] the floor of them, covered with Persia carpets. The richness of the gilt and silver plates which we had in great abundance, as we had likewise all sorts of very fine household linen, was fit only for the entertainment of so great a prince as his majesty our master.*

In fact everything she saw or experienced in Spain, even the food, was fit only for kings.

There is not in the Christian world better wines than their mid-land wines are especially, besides sherry and canary. Their water tastes like milk; their corn white to a miracle; and their wheat makes the sweetest and best bread in the world. Bacon, beyond belief good; the Segovia veal much larger, whiter and fatter than ours. Mutton most excellent; capons much better than ours ... The cream called *nata* is much sweeter and thicker than ever I saw in England. Their eggs much exceed ours and so all sorts of salads and roots and fruits. That I most admired is melons, peaches, bergamot pears and grapes, oranges, lemons, citrous, figs, pomegranates ... And they have olives which are nowhere so good.[11]

As the travelling dust gradually settled, and the last fanfares died away, the blurred kaleidoscope of first impressions gradually gave way to a more measured appreciation of the conditions in store. The house which Ann Fanshawe was to preside over for the next two and a half years, the Casa de las Siete Chimeneas (the House of the Seven Chimneys), with its rich damask hangings, Persian carpets, gilt and silver plate, was one of the grander British residences abroad, but others found that they could be just as happy in more modest surroundings.

In the 1950s Maureen Tweedy was posted to Meshed, near the Persian border with Russia, a place of pilgrimage for Sharia Muslims and the burial place of Harun-al-Rashid, Caliph of Baghdad, a name exotically linked with *The Thousand and One Nights*. For Maureen the consulate there, still redolent of the last days of the Raj, had a romance all of its own, and 'the quietude of a purely English setting'. Despite its rudimentary Russian heating system and 'our old friend from Indian days, the thunderbox' as the only sanitation in their bathroom, she loved the house: it was a large, square, two-storeyed building with

* King Charles II.

green shutters and wide deep verandas all round it, standing in a beautiful garden shaded by great walnut trees. 'A sweep of lawn, flanked by herbaceous borders, led to the rose garden. Beyond were two tennis courts and beyond these again a formal lily pond, a swimming pool brooded over by an ancient mulberry tree, an enormous kitchen garden, and peach and apricot trees heavy with fruit.' Their servants, 'elderly Indian orderlies, grown old in the service of the British', stood stiffly to attention as the Tweedys drove through the gates. In addition to the five indoor servants, and five gardeners, their household included an aged Pakistani syce, or groom. Although the consul no longer kept horses, the syce still made sure that all the saddlery was in perfect condition, and was fond of reminiscing about the days when the Russian consul general never went anywhere without his Cossack guards, nor the British without an escort of Indian cavalry.[12]

Similarly, when Diana Shipton, Maureen's contemporary, arrived in Kashgar in 1946 she found the British consulate a rich repository of memories from other lives. There were photographs in the drawing room, 'a store full of horns and heads from many shooting trips', a game book, beautifully printed and bound, and another notebook in which to record sightings of birds and their migration. There was also a good collection of gramophone records, including everything from complete symphonies to old dance tunes. The greatest legacy was the library, which contained an eclectic collection of over 300 books, from improving tomes like *The Life of Mohammed, Arithmetic in the Mongol Language* and twelve volumes of the *Encyclopaedia of Religion and Ethics,* to the more wistful *Hunting Insects in the South Seas.*[13]

Other women found themselves considerably less well equipped. Catherine Macartney, the first woman to inhabit the Kashgar consulate, found no such luxury when she arrived there in 1898. The original building was little more than a 'native dwelling' built in traditional style around a courtyard. The walls were of sun-baked brick and mud, and there were no windows, only skylights covered not with glass (which had not yet reached that part of the world) but with oiled paper. 'Our furniture was very primitive,' Catherine wrote stoically, since most of it had been home-made by her husband, who had no very great experience of designing comfortable chairs. His first attempt 'was so high that I had almost to climb up to the seat, and must sit with my feet on the rail, or with them dangling. The back was quite straight and reached far above my head, and the seat was not more than about six inches wide. There was no possible chance of having a rest in it . . .'[14]

In 1947, when Masha Williams first arrived in Baghdad during the ferocious summer heat, she found that none of her heavy luggage had arrived, although her fur coat had been sent from the cleaners at Harrods. In the house itself there were no curtains, and no furniture (the office, which provided them with an allowance, expected them to buy these things for themselves) and, worst of all, no refrigerator or fans.

The culture, customs or politics of a particular country could also impose their own particular living restrictions. Sheila Whitney speaks for all the diplomatic wives who experienced communist regimes.

It was quite tough. We weren't allowed to move more than a twelve-mile radius from the centre of Peking. If you wanted to go any further you had to ask permission. And the Ming tombs were just about within that twelve-mile radius so you could go there. But when you did there was always a little man on a motor-bike with a boiler suit watching you. You weren't allowed to diversify off the main route to anywhere, so you didn't see any of the little villages, and suddenly you got two or three miles outside Peking and this little chap would appear on his bike. And he would follow you to the Ming tombs and, wherever you were, you would see him in the bushes.

Peggy Trevelyan's experience in the Soviet Union in the early 1960s was also typical. 'One had to presume our house was bugged. So if ever my husband wanted to tell me about anything – not that he told me much because he thought it was better that I didn't know – but if there was anything pertaining to individuals in the embassy that he thought I should know, we used to go for a walk in the botanical gardens.'

It was the dress restrictions that Norah Errock remembers from her lonely diplomatic childhood in Saudi Arabia in the early 1940s. When she and her mother went to visit the King's harems in Riyadh she was expected to wear Arab clothes. 'We had sort of bloomers first, then a long shift dress, then a sort of overdress with huge sleeves which you sort of pulled round and that acted as the veil if any male appeared – but in very beautiful colours. And if you went out you put on a black overdress – but then again the overdress was often beautifully embroidered.' On one occasion Norah's mother decided that it would be a good idea to show some films to the women.

> They had never seen films before. The only films we had of course were propaganda films. I was given instructions on how to run the projector. They were allowing some of the younger princes in, and there was one who kept saying, 'You should have your veil on when I'm in the room.' He was probably about eight or so, but he might well have been thirteen and by then, of course, women are supposed to veil in front of them. So I can remember trying to work the machine, and at the same time keep the veil over my face.
>
> The film they enjoyed most was when the previous person who had used the machine hadn't wound back the reel as you are supposed to do. It was of parachutists and there was this wonderful sequence of the parachute going up – to them of course it was probably just as extraordinary as parachutists coming down from the sky.

Just occasionally a climate, a landscape, a people and a way of life all combined so harmoniously that, even from the very first, a country seemed like nothing short of an earthly paradise. 'Whatever life brings or takes away ... whatever comes, Japan will always be my second home,' Mary Fraser was to write of her posting there in the 1890s. 'I do not think I have really been so far from Japan that I did not sometimes see the cherry blossoms drifting on the wind, did not sometimes hear the scream of the wild goose through the winter sky and hear the long roll of the surf thundering up on the Atami beaches.'

Mary Fraser was an American brought up largely in Italy. Her parents were wealthy, liberal, cosmopolitan and artistic. Her sculptor father, Thomas Crawford, rented the Villa Negroni in Rome, once the home of Pope Sixtus V. In 1851 Mary was born there. Its stone walls (the masonry was taken from the ancient baths of Diocletian), its vast warren of long galleries and 'dimly gorgeous rooms' were the perfect setting from which to absorb the splendours of Rome. As a young girl Mary met the Brownings, the American poets Lowell and Longfellow and, best of all, Edward Lear, who drew pictures for her youngest sister, Daisy, then still just a little child, and wrote poems for her, including 'Manyforkia Spoonfoolia', inspired by the strange meats and unmanageable cutlery of his hotel dining room, and most of the recipes for *Nonsense Cookery*.

How Mary came to marry the spartan Scot Hugh Fraser we shall never know. They met and became engaged in Venice. Although they seem to have been rather ill-matched, she always wrote of him affectionately. 'I always leave my real self in cold storage when I go to England,' she once confessed, 'and my dear Hugh had very little use at any time for the Mediterranean born side of my personality.'*

After her first posting to China Mary travelled to Vienna and South America. A photographic portrait of her shows a thin, thoughtful woman with a gentle face and pale blue eyes. Her hair is worn in the style of Queen Alexandra, piled up on the back of her head, a few curls swept carefully over her brow. It was this Mary, older and more wistful, who accompanied her husband, Hugh, when he was sent as minister to Tokyo in 1889.

From the beginning, Mary was bewitched by the beauty of Japan. With its gardens and its cherry blossom, Tokyo was one of the fairest cities she had ever seen: its streets and houses 'seemed to have grown up by accident – and are of no importance as compared with the flowers.' In her house, with its wisteria-sheltered verandas and its view,

---

* Mary tells the story of one of Hugh's earliest postings, before their marriage, in Guatemala. When his boss was sent on leave Hugh remained there as chargé d'affaires, with responsibilities in five republics in Central America. 'His headquarters were in the new town of Guatemala; his staff, a native clerk; and his only means of transport, a mule. He used to tell me how he would journey from capital to capital through the forest, in uniform, cocked hat and all, this latter for the benefit of any stray bandits that might have been drawn there for shelter. They would not touch a foreign representative in a cocked hat and gold lace, though they might have cut his throat in mufti. England was a word to conjure with in those days.' After a year and a half 'a dreadful doubt began to enter Hugh's mind. His mail grew scantier and scantier. His chief had not returned. Appeals for direction were unanswered and the FO turned a deaf ear to his suggestions of an exchange.' Eventually he decided to take the matter into his own hands. He packed his bags and left. When he reported, rather shamefacedly, to the office, 'authority was infinitely amused: "Good Lord, my dear boy!" it said. "We expected you home ages ago – we had no idea that you would last it out as long as that!"'

across a little moat, of the Emperor's new palace, she felt at the very centre of things. Her own upstairs balcony was 'so wide and cool that every breeze sweeps through it from end to end, and yet so sheltered that I can wander about and work or read in absolute privacy'. Japan seemed 'absolutely fresh'; 'All that one has read or heard fails to give any true impression of this vivid youngness,' Mary wrote. Although she still missed her own country, she felt immediately at home.

Outwardly Mary's life was still dominated by her diplomatic duties, particularly by the ceremonial of the imperial court; but she was becoming increasingly absorbed by the natural world around her. The plum blossom, 'eldest brother of the hundred flowers', came out when the snow was still on the ground, and she was entranced to find that a whole body of poetry and tradition had grown up around this early harbinger of spring. By the beginning of February the plum-gardens were in full bloom, and Mary visited them to admire what the Japanese called the 'silver world': 'a world with snow on the paths and snow on the branches, while snowy petals, with the faintest touch of glow-worm green at the heart, go whirling along on the last gust of wind from the bay'.

In the autumn, it was the maple trees. 'The autumn has come at last, and the maples are all on fire,' she wrote in November that year. 'Since one autumn, when I wandered through the New Jersey woods as a tiny child, I have never seen such a gorgeous explosion of colour, such a storm of scarlet and gold.' The Japanese sub-divided their maples again and again, and one Japanese gardener told her that he knew of no less than 380 distinct varieties.

Those which please me most are, I think, the kind which grow about ten or twelve feet high, with leaves in five or seven long points, exquisitely cut, and growing like strong fingers on a young hand. They always seem to be pointing to something, and one involuntarily looks round and about to see what it is. They are deep red in colour all the year round, and are constantly grouped with vivid greens, making splendid masses in the shrubberies.

But Mary's greatest rapture was saved for the cherry blossom. That first spring, the arrival of this fabled wonder coincided with a royal visit from the Duke and Duchess of Connaught. 'I hope you will not think me wanting in loyalty.' Mary wrote to her family, 'if I say that they have been almost more of an excitement to me than the royal visitors.' Mary had been ill, and the contemplation of the flowers in her garden, particularly the cherry blossom, meant more to her than if she had been up and busy: 'The crown of the year has come at last . . . an outburst of bewildering beauty such as no words can convey to those who have not seen it for themselves.'

On the streets of Tokyo every avenue was planted with cherry trees in long, close-set rows; every garden boasted its carefully nurtured groves. 'Over the river at Mukojima they dip to the water, and spread away inland like a rosy tidal wave; and the great park at Uyeno seems to have caught the sunset clouds of a hundred skies, and kept them captive along its wide forest ways.' The double cherry blossoms were the most magnificent of all, surpassing 'every other splendour of nature'. During the two weeks or so when the blossom was at its best, the Japanese flocked, day after day, to look at them. From her veranda Mary watched the tall grove of cherry trees in the garden, their branches waving softly against the sky, storing up 'the recollection of their loveliness until the next year should bring it round again'.

However, 'I would not want you to think that existence is one long series of cotillion figures out here,' she wrote in a more sombre mood; 'it can be very sad and very bitter.' At times there was an almost mystical quality to her response to the natural world – her 'cherry blossom metaphysics', as she liked to call it, which in her dark moments brought great solace. On her frequent travels around Japan the merest glimpse of Mount Fuji – or Fuji-san, the name reverently given to the perfectly cone-shaped, snow-capped volcano – was usually enough to lift her spirits and banish her lingering sense of disappointment with life. 'In Japan one cannot think of Fuji as a thing, a mere object in the landscape;' she mused, 'she becomes something personal, dominating, a factor in life. No day seems quite sad or aimless in which one has had a glimpse of her.'

This natural affinity with all things Japanese, which began with the natural world, opened Mary's mind to many other, more perplexing aspects of Japanese life. Throughout her time there she was almost startlingly open to what must have seemed a deeply alien culture. She was strangely aware of the bluntness of her own, western faculties when it came to describing the exquisite delicacy of Japanese sensibilities.

'English is a clumsy, square-toed vehicle of expression,' she wrote in exasperation, 'and stumbles along, crushing a thousand beauties of my Japanese thought-garden, which a more delicate language (or a more skilful writer!) might have preserved for you.'

Very soon Mary learned to love the Japanese people, as well as their country. Her natural peers were 'the little hot house ladies' of the imperial court, 'with their pretty shy ways and their broken confidences about the terror of getting into European clothes.'* The life of the court was very formal: the clothes, etiquette and food were all strictly regulated. The speech used by the imperial family differed from that of ordinary people. There were special terms for the royal-feminine and the royal-masculine, and courtiers had to take care when speaking to one of the princes to use certain words meant only for royal ears. 'Is this not a puzzling sum?' Mary exclaimed. Even when the Frasers attended the Emperor and Empress at Enryo Kwan, their palace by the sea, this formality persisted. A simple walk around the palace gardens was conducted with rigid protocol. Members of the court followed the sovereigns, in the strictest order of precedence, in all their uniforms and finery, 'like some huge dazzling snake, gliding in and out of all the narrow paths'.

Even the smallest details of imperial life, Mary observed, seemed to have a peculiarly Japanese grace. The chrysanthemum, symbol of the Japanese imperial house, appeared embossed in gold on royal invitations, on the panels of the court carriages, and even on the servants' liveries. Thursdays were reception days at court and Mary was fascinated by the refreshments offered to the diplomatic corps on these occasions, which included maple leaf shapes made entirely of sugar: 'Large and small, deep crimson, green and orange, with three leaves, or five or seven, they were piled on the delicate china in such an artistic fashion that I could not refrain from an exclamation of pleasure when they were offered to me,' she wrote.

Mary was intrigued by the ladies of the court, but she felt greater sympathy for the ordinary people of Japan, particularly her own servants. 'The very smart people here affect the most impassive countenance and a low voice in speaking,' she noted, while only the lower

---

* Western institutions, and western clothes and customs, were officially encouraged in Japan at this time.

classes could express their emotions and *joie de vivre*, although their habits did sometimes surprise her. She was supposed to enter her servants' courtyard only at appointed times, but she could not resist observing them from behind the blinds of one of the upper windows. Once, in the terrible heat of summer, when even she could bear no more than 'the thinnest of white garments' against her skin, she arrived in her kitchen to find, to her quiet amusement, her cook's grandmother 'without a shred of raiment on her old brown body'.

Big Cook San, as her principal chef was known, was a particular favourite. Ever since the influenza epidemic which had swept the country earlier that winter he had suffered from bad lungs, and so when Mary and Hugh went on a visit to Horiuchi, a fashionable seaside summer resort, they took him with them, hoping that the change would do him good.

Big Cook San descended to the platform, jingling like a gypsy tinker with all the saucepans that he had hung round himself at the last moment. An omelette pan and a bain-marie, miraculously tied together, hung over his shoulder; a potato-steamer from his waist; in one hand he carried a large blue tea-pot, and in the other a sheaf of gorgeous irises, carefully tied up in matting, for fear there should be no flowers at Horiuchi!

Mary's greatest affection, though, was reserved for Ogita, her samurai, guide and interpreter, her 'right hand in a thousand matters of life'. When he died, of influenza, she recorded his death with real grief. 'Do you wonder that I tell you so much about a mere servant?' she wrote. 'He has been so helpful and faithful, has carried out all my whims with such gentle patience, has piloted me through so many journeys, taught me so many quaint stories, that a part of my Japanese life has died with him.'

Ogita was a tall man of soldierly bearing, a master swordsman and a teacher of Japanese fencing. After his illness Mary was shocked to see death written on the face of this 'valiant, humble, upright soul'. Ogita lived in a little house in the British legation compound with his wife and five children, and when Mary visited him there and saw him lying on a couple of worn mats on the floor, she thought he looked pitifully long and thin, and much too large for the tiny room. Although he was often too weak to speak, until the very last his two hands always went up to his brow when she entered, and there was always 'a light of welcome' shining for her in his eyes. Once or twice he said to her: 'Okusama* is very kind; I would get well if I could; but I can never travel with her any more, and I am too tired to live.'

After his death, Mary went to visit Ogita one last time. Incense was burning in the house, and freshly gathered flowers had been placed near the coffin head.

> He lay very straight and stiff, with a smile of peace on his thin face. His hands were crossed on his breast, and his long blue robes were drawn in straight folds, all held in place with little packets of tea, which filled the room with a dry fragrance; the coffin was lined with these, and his head rested on a pillow of the same. Beside him on a stand lay his most precious possession, his sword; and before the weeping wife left me kneeling there, she touched my shoulder, and pointed to the sword, bowing her head in reverence, and whispering, 'Samurai, Okusama!'

Mary, a devout Catholic, had tried without success to convert Ogita to her faith. Although she was to remember this with regret after his death, she comforted herself with the thought that he had been 'a samurai and a gentleman to the last; and I do not believe that any true gentleman was ever shut out of heaven yet.'[15]

When Elizabeth Blanckley arrived in Algiers in 1806, where her father was posted as British consul, it was through her servants, too, that the spirit of the country was most vividly revealed. Not everyone in the Blanckley household was as favourably impressed by their first sight of the country as Elizabeth. Her Maltese nurse was so disconsolate 'at seeing herself surrounded by turbans' (from the moment they disembarked, she never ceased weeping and exclaiming, 'I must die, my heart is broke'; '*il mio cuore sta negro, il mio cuore sta negro*') that the family took pity on her and dispatched her back home. Instead they found a new nurse, Maria; her husband, known as Antonio the Stupid because he could never do anything right; and a butler who could

---

* Honorific by which Mary was addressed by her servants.

turn his hand to anything, but was particularly adept at making dolls' wigs. Most exciting of all for Elizabeth and her sister, who were then still quite young, there was Angela, a seventeen-year-old slave, who was presented to them by the Dey (the local ruler) along with her three-month-old baby.

As Christians the Blanckleys were not allowed to own slaves, who were usually hired out to them as domestic servants (Maria and Antonio the Stupid were both slaves of Maltese extraction). Angela and her baby, however, were gifts, which was just as well because 'the poor helpless unfortunate' appeared to be unable to do anything at all either for herself or for her baby, let alone in any capacity as a domestic. The Blanckleys, who were good-natured and rather intrigued by her interesting circumstances, took them into their household and cared for them all the same. The baby, who was known as Angelina, became a great favourite.

It was their janissary, however, who became their most important link with the country. Janissaries were not really servants at all, but aristocrats,* an elite corps of soldiers created under the Ottoman system of *devshirme* (a levy of at least one son from each non-Muslim family in the empire). The most talented of these boys either became janissaries, or went into the Turkish civil service; throughout the Ottoman empire at least one of their number was always assigned to the household of a foreign diplomat to act as bodyguard. As far as Elizabeth was concerned, though, Sidi Hassan had much more exciting duties to perform. He would hide behind their drawing-room curtains, for example, and pretend to be a lion in his den while she and her sister took the role of lambs or travellers whom he would proceed to gobble up. But, best of all, Sidi Hassan was a storyteller.

Elizabeth listened to these stories, these 'Algerian Nights' as she called them, with a delight that even in later years, when she had long left Algiers, never faded from her memory. These fascinating tales of genii and princesses were so long that some of them took the evenings of an entire week to conclude. One, which she never forgot, was the story of a girl whose eyelashes were so long that she always swept the floor of her chamber with them. Elizabeth and her sister would sit and listen to Sidi Hassan in his room at the back of their house; he

* The Dey was elected from their number.

would smoke his pipe, the smell of which clung so strongly to their skin and dresses that such visits were finally banned by their mother.

Elizabeth Blanckley spent six years of her childhood in Algiers, from 1806 to 1812. Like Mary Fraser in Japan nearly a century later, from the moment their boat landed (the Noah's ark so admired by Nelson) Elizabeth felt at home. They did not live in the town of Algiers itself, but in a country residence, a 'garden' just outside the city. The house was built on cliffs overlooking the sea. In the heat of summer it was delightfully cool, watered by fountains and shaded with vines which produced bunches of grapes at least three feet long.

Although the house was built in the Moorish manner, around an open courtyard, much of it was decorated in the English style. Elizabeth's favourite room was her bedroom, which was more dear to her even than the grand Parisian boudoir which became hers in later life. This room had a domed ceiling and was surrounded by four smaller *chiosks*, or domed recesses. The first was the door; the second was taken up with books and toys, while the third accommodated her bed, 'with its white muslin curtains, *drapé* by violet-coloured ribbons, and *couvre-pied* of scarlet and gold'. The fourth *chiosk* was a window, shaded by the branches of the vine, which overlooked the sea.

Away from the cliffs, the house was surrounded by groves of fruit trees – pomegranates, almonds, orange and lemon trees, as well as the bergamot, or sweet lemon – in which nightingales sang. The fig trees bore fruit of such perfection that it had hitherto been considered fit for the Dey alone, while the apricots were so abundant that two of their pigs died from a surfeit of them. (It was not only the pigs who became over-excited at the prospect of so much wonderful fruit: a local synonym for apricot was 'kill-Christians'.) Their vegetables grew in prodigious quantities, too. In her potager Elizabeth's mother grew cabbages, cauliflowers, broccoli, carrots, turnips, onions, leeks, peas, french beans, haricots blancs, artichokes, calabash, pumpkins, cucumbers, musk and watermelons, aubergines, tomatoes and several kinds of capsicums, okra, strawberries and potatoes.

The Blanckleys kept so many pets that their 'Garden' also became something of a Noah's ark. Their animals included a spaniel, a tortoise, a hare, a silver fox, a lamb, a tame gazelle and a goat called Phyllis. Mr Blanckley tried to keep wild cats, but they did not survive captivity. Nor did their pet lamb, which was eaten by jackals; nor their father's eagle, for whom an even worse fate was in store. One day, mistaking the bird for a guinea fowl, the cook killed it, plucked it, and hung it in their already well-filled Christmas larder. If Elizabeth and her sister had not missed it, no one was in any doubt that it would have been served up at table.

But even for Elizabeth there were intimations of something more disturbing beyond this vision of childhood utopia. For the convenience of Mr Blanckley in fulfilling his consular duties the family kept a second house in the town, and it was here that Elizabeth experienced the greatest thrill of all – greater even than Sidi Hassan's 'Algerian Nights'. As the sun began to set, exactly one hour before the muezzin began to call the faithful to prayer, she would make her way up onto the flat terrace at the very top of the house. Here, almost every evening, she would conduct a secret rendezvous with the secluded women of the neighbouring house.

> I doubt not that the *something* of mystery connected with the rendezvous, and its realization through one of the Gothic pigeon holes in the upper chamber of our terrace, from which our fond Mahommedan neighbours had by degrees completely annihilated all intervening glass, increased the interest of the interview, and caused a *battement de coeur*, a something inexpressibly delightful, beyond, or at any rate, certainly very different from what I have experienced in all other *liaisons* of simple *amitié*.

Although she was only a little girl of nine or ten at the time, these forbidden meetings had an extraordinary, almost sexual frisson, which derived only in part from their clandestine nature. 'I knew nothing of them,' she wrote of her Algerine friends, 'beyond the delight with which they ever sought and conversed with me, and the anxiety with which I ever ascended to the terrace and kiosk, and listened to their signals.'[16]

CHAPTER THREE

Partners

Compared to the innocent childhood idyll described by Elizabeth Blanckley, her mother's journal of life in Algiers makes altogether more sombre reading. Mrs Blanckley (we do not know her Christian name) was the devoted wife of Henry Stanyford Blanckley, whose family, of gentle rather than aristocratic birth, could trace its ancestry back to Sir Walter Ralegh. Before his appointment as British agent and consul-general at Algiers Henry Blanckley had been British consul in the Balearic Islands for nineteen years, an appointment he obtained after sixteen years' service in the army during which he fought in 'the American War' (the American War of Independence, 1775–83). It therefore seems likely that Mrs Blanckley was much younger than her husband, but very few facts about her survive. From the diaries she wrote, however (later published by her daughter alongside her own memoirs), we know a good deal not only about the everyday details of her life, but also about the role she played as the British consul's wife.

Many aspects of Mrs Blanckley's life in Algiers were delightful. The consular corps was a small, close-knit community, but large enough to provide an ample supply of balls, dinners, banquets and masques. It did not lack for elegance either: the wife of the French consul had connections at the imperial court in Paris, from whence she would bring back details of all the latest fashions. The Europeans in Algeria were always very well dressed, 'in accordance to the taste of the undisputed emporium of fashion', even more so than in London, where they 'sighed in vain for a copy of *Le Journal des Modes*'.

When not engaged in diplomatic entertainments, Mrs Blanckley spent a good deal of time visiting the Algerian women in their harems. Unlike Mary Sheil, whose Victorian sensibilities were shocked by the deliciously bawdy talk of the women's quarters, Mrs Blanckley, a woman of a more liberal age, was struck by the beauty and courtesy of the Algerines. One of the first calls she and her daughters paid was on their dragoman's (interpreter) new wife, whom they found sitting 'in lonely grandeur', laden with so many pearls and jewels that she could scarcely move beneath the weight of them. She wore so many rings in her ears, Mrs Blanckley recorded later in her journal, 'that her ears were quite bent down, hanging in the *elephant* style'. At the wedding of the daughter of the *Cadi*, or chief judge, a few months later she was even more amazed by the opulence of the Algerian women: 'My eyes were perfectly dazzled by the splendor of the jewels by which their *salamas* (caps) and persons were covered, whole bouquets of roses, jessamines, peacock feathers and butterflies were completely formed of diamonds,' she wrote. The bride herself was so bedecked with jewels that 'she was quite unable to bear the weight of her *salama* without the support of two of her attendants, who walked on either side of her and held her head.'

The greatest spectacle of all, however, came when she visited the Dey's wife herself. As the wife of the British consul, Mrs Blanckley was an important visitor, and the Dey's women took the greatest possible care over their preparations. They made iced sherbets of orange flower water, together with vast quantities of different foods – meat, poultry, pastries and sweetmeats – which she ate with beautiful rosewood spoons, their tips inlaid with amber and coral. Although she enjoyed this feast sitting cross-legged on the floor with the other women, Moorish fashion, every comfort had been thought of: the table on which the food was set was inlaid with silver and mother-of-pearl; her hands were washed with scented water poured from silver jugs; exquisitely embroidered napkins were brought for her to wipe her fingers on.

On her arrival at the palace harem, Mrs Blanckley had found that not only the women, but the whole room was heaped with jewels. There were jewels spread out over the tables and shelves; there were even jewels strewn across the floor – emeralds, sapphires and rubies which seemed to be growing up out of the cut-velvet carpets like so many fantastical flowers. Although Mrs Blanckley was perfectly sensible of the honour they were paying her – 'I am the first and only Consul's wife of any nation who has been so highly distinguished,' she recorded with pride – she found this extravagance rather overwhelming: 'My eyes were so dazzled with all the splendour I had beheld at the palace, that I felt quite glad when all these visits were concluded.'

There were other reasons why she might have been glad to conclude these visits. As the British consul's wife, Mrs Blanckley was not only able to enjoy the greatest refinements and courtesies that the Algerians had to offer. She was also exposed to an altogether more sinister side of life. The Blanckleys' position in Algeria was by no means as secure as it appeared. Although in theory they were protected by their diplomatic status, in practice they were entirely at the mercy of a series of petty despots, the Deys, who ruled Algiers under the nominal suzerainty of the Ottoman sultans.

Part of the Ottoman empire since the early sixteenth century, by the eighteenth Algiers had become a pirate state, preying mercilessly on shipping in the Mediterranean. Some aspects of Mrs Blanckley's account of their life in Algiers make gruesome reading. Daily life for the ordinary citizen was bloody, brutal and, all too often, short. Both smallpox and the plague were frequent epidemics, although it was a crime punishable by death to even refer to the plague, let alone take precautions against it, until the Dey chose to make the pestilence official.* Slaves and criminals were kept in the *bagnio*, or prison, from whence they were taken by day to work in the stone quarries. At night they were forced to wear chains so heavy that even a strong man could barely support the weight of them. The most vicious punishments were handed out with impunity for the most arbitrary of crimes. 'The poor Jew who was bastinadoed is not yet dead,' Mrs Blanckley wrote soberly, 'but has been obliged to submit to lose 3lbs of flesh from the part where the bastinadoes were inflicted.' His crime had been to disturb the Dey with the noise of his hammer.

Reminders of the tyrannical powers of the Dey were ever present, even within the diplomatic community. The Danish consul was thrown into the *bagnio* like a common slave when the expected tribute from Denmark did not arrive on time, and, to the horror of his distraught wife, forced to wear chains which weighed a crushing 60 pounds. When Mr Blanckley led a deputation of diplomats to plead for their

---

* All disease, but especially the plague, was considered to be the will of God. To take any preventative measures against it was therefore an impious, or even blasphemous act.

colleague, the Dey was so enraged that he 'bounced up from his seat and fell down again, his legs still retaining their tailor position, whilst he pulled his beard . . . and literally foamed'. The same fate later befell both the Dutch and the Spanish consuls, with the threat (happily never carried out) that the latter's wife and eight children would be taken to the market place and sold as slaves.

The Blanckleys themselves once came under a similar threat. 'I am much fatigued, having passed the last several nights in packing up our valuables and clothes, which I am obliged to do with great secrecy, lest our slaves might give information, and we know not from one hour to the next what may be our destiny,' Mrs Blanckley wrote anxiously. This time the Dey's wrath had been aroused by the fact that some vessels sailing under the Algerian flag had been seized by the British in nearby Malta. Although a British gunship, *La Volontaire*, was sent in to protect them from possible repercussions, Mrs Blanckley, perhaps remembering the Dey's previous rage, was still understandably agitated. 'The Minister of the Marina has been very unguarded and violent in his expression against the person of the Consul,' she wrote; 'and we have but too great reason to dread being put into chains.'

Although it was her father who held the position of consul, Elizabeth Blanckley was never in any doubt about her mother's crucial involvement in his work. While Mr Blanckley fulfilled the public role, behind the scenes Mrs Blanckley worked tirelessly to support him. To enable the family to meet all their expenses (a consul's salary at that time was nominal) Mrs Blanckley regulated her domestic affairs with the greatest possible economy. 'Rising early and retiring late', she oversaw not only the immediate household, but also the vegetable garden, orchards, dairy, and even the large tracts of land on which they kept their own herds and flocks. According to Elizabeth, 'From these resources our large family, and constant and numerous guests of all degrees, were in a great measure supported.'

It was against this background of domestic harmony that the Blanckleys' most important work was carried out. While they survived the worst excesses of the Dey's regime, some of their countrymen were not so fortunate. One of Mr Blanckley's main duties in this 'very nucleus of piracy' was to claim any British national taken into slavery by the Algerians. He was able to do this under the terms of a treaty agreed with the Turkish Sultan in 1761, known as the Ottoman

Capitulations, which also gave European consuls wide-reaching powers of jurisdiction over their countrymen in both civil and criminal cases, liberty of movement around the Dey's dominions, freedom from restrictions in commerce and religion, and (in theory at least) inviolability of domicile.

After these captured Britons had been identified and set free, it was to Mrs Blanckley that the care of these unfortunates most frequently fell. Sometimes they were English sailors, or a handful of travellers on board a foreign passenger ship which had fallen into the hands of Algerian pirates. Sometimes they were the crew of an English merchant vessel captured on the high seas with its cargo of cotton, opium or oil. If the captain of one of these ships (who was often accompanied by his wife and family) was not properly insured his capture would spell certain ruin. At least he would have been allowed to keep a change of clothing; the rest of the crew on board such vessels were routinely stripped of everything they possessed, right down to their underclothes. Mrs Blanckley grew adept at making up not only extra beds, but also new shirts with which to clothe her destitute countrymen.

On one occasion fifteen Englishmen were shipwrecked on the Barbary Coast, at a place called Gigery. The Blanckleys first received knowledge of their capture when a small piece of bluish-white paper was delivered to their house, much creased and soiled, on which a few scarcely legible lines had been scratched with charcoal and water. It told a distressing but all too familiar tale. The ship belonging to these English mariners, laden with a cargo of pigs of lead and barrels of gunpowder, had been on its way to one of the Mediterranean ports, when a storm had driven it onto the rocks. The 'inhospitable savages' who inhabited this remote piece of coast had overpowered the exhausted men and diverted them of everything, including all their clothes. Freezing with cold and half-starved, the fifteen men watched helplessly from the shore as, in their haste take possession of the ship's cargo, several of their captors tied pigs of lead to their waists, instantly sinking to their deaths as they attempted to swim back to shore. Another group later blew themselves up when they built a fire too close to one of the barrels of gunpowder. Perhaps anxious to be rid of these unlucky Christian devils, they were now demanding a large ransom.

It was only with difficulty that the outraged Mr Blanckley could be made 'to comprehend the truth of the Dey's reply, which was, that he had not the least command or influence with the men of Gigery . . . that they had ever continued a wild and completely savage people; and that had any Algerine subjects fallen into their hands, he, the Dey, would equally have been obliged to pay a ransom for their liberation.' The compassionate Blanckleys paid the ransom from their own pocket, and a few days later the thirteen mariners – 'two having sunk under their misery' – arrived in Algiers.

The men had scarcely a rag upon them, but Mrs Blanckley was well prepared and already had beds and clothing waiting for them. She tended their wounds and fed them, although her greatest anxiety over the following weeks was that 'they might be injured by taking too great a quantity of food, after their long state of almost starvation; and she used great caution in having nourishment distributed to them.' 'In this, and in every other instance,' Elizabeth wrote, 'did my excellent parents act a part worthy of the good Samaritan; their house, their purse, and even their wardrobe, being opened and freely bestowed according to the wants of their unfortunate fellow-creatures.'[1]

In no other profession has a wife been so intimately involved with her husband's work. While not everyone had the extraordinary task of sewing shirts for starving shipwreck survivors, it was a partnership which, in one form or another, had been taking shape from the very earliest days of diplomacy.

The Earl of Stair, ambassador to Paris in 1715, was noted for keeping 'the most splendid house in Paris next to that of the King, and having with him his Countess and her daughter, both ladies of the greatest honour and politeness'. Here the ambassador would entertain the principal lords and ladies of France 'with all possible elegance', but after about ten o'clock at night his custom was to 'pretend business, and leave the company to the care of his lady, withdraw to his Room, undress himself, and repair to the coffee-houses *incognito*; and, by a dexterous Method of Conversation, find out the secrets of the Day'.[2] In the 1730s Mrs Vigor, whose husband was consul-general in St Petersburg, liked to do her embroidery at the Countess of Biron's, where the Tsar was a constant visitor. This was in no way for her own amusement, she claimed, but for the advantage these contacts might bring her husband 'in the station he is in'.[3]

Marriage to a diplomat was a commitment not just to an individual but to an entire way of life. 'CONSIDER SMALL MEANS AND FOREIGN LIFE,' Lady Fane, herself the child of diplomats, telegraphed frantically to her own daughter when she announced her engagement to a young Foreign Service subaltern.[4] The vagaries of diplomatic life, its insecurities and discomforts as well as its privileges, meant that husbands often demanded far more of their wives than most women might legitimately expect.

The twenty-one-year-old Catherine Borland might have thought twice if she had had someone like Lady Fane to advise her when in 1898 she became engaged to George Macartney, the first and perhaps most famous British consul to Kashgar. Assuming that her fiancé was still safely *en poste*, Catherine was in her kitchen in Edinburgh, innocently baking a cake one Saturday morning, when the maid announced that George had arrived. Although they had been engaged for nearly two years, to her astonishment he calmly announced that they must be married within the week, 'for he had only got three months' leave from Kashgar, and already five weeks of it had gone'. Just one week later they set off on their 'great adventure'. 'To me it was a great adventure indeed,' Catherine later recalled, 'for I was the most timid, unenterprising girl in the world. I had hardly been beyond the limits of my own sheltered home, and big family of brothers and sisters, had never had any desire whatever to see the world, and certainly had no qualifications for a pioneer's life, beyond being able to make a cake.'

In the seventeen years that Catherine Macartney spent in Chinese Turkistan she had to master a far greater range of accomplishments. Fortunately, she seems to have been one of those women who was quite simply born to the pioneering life, and learnt to adapt both to a new husband and to a new life with extraordinary speed.

A journey of that sort is a pretty good test to one's temper [she wrote of her first arduous six-week journey to Kashgar] for one's nerves get strained, at times almost to breaking point. Everything seems to go wrong when one is utterly tired out, and sometimes very hungry. If two people can go through the test of such a journey without quarrelling seriously, they can get through under any circumstances. We just survived it, and it promised well for the long journey through life.[5]

There were others, however, who were not so lucky; others from whom, however devoted they may have been as wives, diplomatic life required sacrifices they found terribly hard to bear. 'You cannot imagine how sorry I am at giving up our snug country Darby and Joan life for all the plagues and tinsel of diplomacy,' wrote Anne Disbrowe in a letter from St Petersburg, where her husband was posted in the 1820s. The glitter of Alexander I's court was a far cry from the braying donkeys and dust storms of Kashgar, but for Anne it was just as hard: 'I once thought I was ambitious, but either I was mistaken in the conjecture or the quality is worn out, and perhaps having attained my wishes I want nothing more.'[6] Having been told that they would only be gone a month or so, she had left her two little girls behind in England. In the event it was three years before she finally returned to England and was able to see her daughters again.

Whether or not they wanted to, diplomatic wives almost always led a far more active role than that of a mere camp-follower and house-keeper to their husbands. But as the example of Mrs Blanckley shows, their role often extended into many areas beyond the conventional social ones. Although it was not until 1946 that women were able to enter the Foreign Office in their own right,* in the past, when diplomats were often obliged to work with very little formal backup, they frequently used their wives as unofficial secretaries, and occasionally even as their deputies when they were occupied elsewhere. Many women, such as Mary Fraser in Japan and Isabel Burton in Brazil and later in Damascus, frequently acted as a private assistant, copying reports and even getting to grips with complicated systems of codes and ciphers. When Elizabeth McNeill married her husband John, the British agent in Persia in 1823, she took over the management of all his expenses. She was so discreet 'that he could entirely trust her with all his diplomatic difficulties', and was soon involved in making copies of all her husband's letters. Their years in Persia were crucial ones as the country was an important buffer between an increasingly expansionist Russia and British India at that time. Although John McNeill

* After 1946 women were appointed diplomats on a permanent basis; during the war, however, there had been many successful temporary appointments. As far back as 1921 women had been able to enter the service as more junior clerical and executive officers.

was frequently away for months on end travelling the country, no one doubted that Mrs McNeill was more than capable of undertaking the more sedentary parts of his job. 'I am more than delighted with the promptitude and ability manifested by Mrs McNeill,' Colonel Macdonald, the envoy, wrote just a few years later in 1828; 'we have no need of an Agent at the capital so long as she is there.'[7]

Even earlier, in the eighteenth century, diplomatic wives showed themselves to be equally as capable. In 1789 Torrington, the British minister in Brussels, described his wife in a letter to the Secretary of State as 'the soul of my office'. When he came back to England he left her behind to supervise the work of his young (and of course male) chargé d'affaires. Although it was then unthinkable, for all her capabilities, that Mrs Torrington should herself have been appointed *chargé*, it was not unknown for women to be recommended for the less politically important post of consul. In 1752 Mr Titley, from Copenhagen, recommended the appointment, on the death of her husband, of 'a very notable woman', Mrs Elizabeth Fenwick, as consul in Denmark, so long as she should remain unmarried. In the event one of her sons was appointed instead, but some ten years later, in Tripoli, a Mrs White did indeed act as her husband's unofficial successor (and was paid by the Treasury) for two years until an official, male replacement was appointed.[8]

In particularly remote or dangerous postings, an even closer involvement was often necessary. Felicity Wakefield was posted to Egypt during the Suez Crisis in 1956, when President Nasser nationalized the previously neutral canal zone. Although no one in the embassy, not even the ambassador himself, knew of the Israeli and Anglo-French plans to invade Egypt at that point, there was no doubt that the situation was serious – 'We had a house out on the pyramids road and I remember convoys of Egyptian army vehicles going past.' Given tank recognition charts by the secret service, she was asked to identify and count the tanks going past her house – 'Which I did,' she recalls with satisfaction. 'I hid behind the curtain so that my servants didn't know what I was doing and I drew the tanks and I counted them. I suppose they could have accused me of spying – which is just what I was doing.'

Spying was one of the very few things that Ann Fanshawe did *not* do for her husband, but no doubt she would have, had it been necessary

– and relished it too. The marriage of Ann and Richard Fanshawe represented not only one of diplomacy's greatest partnerships, but one of its greatest love stories. They were married in 1644, during the Civil War. Richard was thirty-five, and the Secretary of the Council of War to the Prince of Wales (the future Charles II), then a boy of fourteen. Ann herself was just nineteen. A portrait of her in later life by Sir Peter Lely shows an exquisite oval face with a long nose and soft chin. Her small mouth is slightly pursed; her dark eyes, beneath the fashionable ringlets of the day, have a faintly resigned look about them. Thick ropes of pearls are strung at her wrists and looped around her neck and shoulders over magnificent lace cuffs and collar. By not so much as a flicker of a sloe-shaped eyelid is it possible to guess at the extraordinary swashbuckling life which lay behind the exterior of this placid, conventionally fashionable matron.

Ann was the eldest daughter of Sir John Harrison of Hertfordshire. Although she was brought up with 'all the advantages that time afforded', learning to sew, to speak French, to sing and dance and play the lute, she was, by her own admission, 'what we graver people call a hoyting girl'.* She learned her lessons well, 'yet was I wild to that degree, that the hours of my beloved recreation took up too much of my time.' Best of all she liked riding and running, 'and all active pastimes . . . But to be just to myself, I never did mischief to myself or other people, nor one immodest action or would in my life, but skipping and activity was my delight.'

From a boisterous, skipping girl Ann grew up into a deeply sensual, ambitious and capable woman. From the day of her marriage at Wolvercote church until Richard's death in 1666, she was passionately in love with her husband. 'I thought myself a Queen,' she wrote, 'and my husband so glorious a crown, that I more valued myself to be called by his name than born a princess; for I knew him very wise and very good, and his soul doted on me.'

It was only after the Restoration in 1660 that Dick Fanshawe became an officially credited diplomat, but for many years both during and after the Civil War, he acted as an envoy for the King in exile. He was very much a man of his times – highly educated, a great lover of both history and poetry, and something of a poet himself. As well as a writer

* A hoyden, or boisterous girl.

of his own verses he was a translator of Horace, and of Camoëns's *The Lusiads* from the Portuguese. In the memoir written for her son, also called Richard, so that he would know what manner of man his father had been, Ann describes him tenderly: 'He was of the highest size of men, strong, and of the best proportion, his complexion sanguine, his skin exceeding fair, his hair dark brown and very curling, but not very long, his eyes grey and penetrating, his nose high, his countenance gracious and wise, his motion good, his speech clear and distinct.' Both his 'masters', Charles I and Charles II, loved him greatly, 'both for his great parts and honesty, and for his conversation, in which they took great delight'. Even after his death, Ann never stopped loving him. Throughout their life together he was her 'North Star, that only had the power to fix me'.

Richard Fanshawe loved his wife as much as he was beloved by her. The first time they were parted after their marriage, when Richard went to Bristol on the King's business, he was 'extremely afflicted even to tears, though passion was against his nature'. From the very beginning he had complete trust in Ann, involving her unhesitatingly in many of his affairs. Not long after their marriage he entrusted her with his store of gold, saying to her, 'I know that thou that keeps my heart so well will keep my fortune, which from this time I will ever put into thy hands as God shall bless me with increase.'

His trust was well-placed. During the dangerous and uncertain years of the Civil War Ann undertook a number of missions on her husband's behalf. Alone, and almost continually pregnant (typically for those days, she bore Richard fourteen children), she travelled frequently on his business affairs: in November 1648 'my husband went to Paris on his master's business, and sent for me from London. I carried him three hundred pounds of his money.' In France she was received at the Palais Royal, and there her little daughter played with 'the lady Henrietta', younger sister to Charles II. This respite did not last long. Soon Richard 'thought it convenient to send me into England again, there to try what sums I could raise, both for his subsistence abroad, and mine at home'.

But these missions were only a small taste of what was to come. After the Battle of Worcester in 1651, which finally ended the cause of Charles II in England, Richard was taken prisoner and for ten weeks kept in solitary confinement at Whitehall. 'Cease weeping,' Richard told her when they met, 'no other thing upon earth can move me.' But Ann had good reason to weep. The conditions in prison were so bad that Richard contracted scurvy, and the effects nearly killed him. In order just to catch a glimpse of him, she would go 'when the clock struck four in the morning, with a dark lantern in my hand, all alone and on foot, from my lodging in Chancery Lane . . . to Whitehall . . . There I would go under his window and softly call him . . . Thus we talked together; and sometimes I was so wet with rain that it went in at my neck and out at my heels.'

Ann petitioned Cromwell in person to secure Richard's release, and in November that year he was finally let out on bail, although it was not until 1658, seven years later, that he was able to escape to France again. To her consternation, Ann was refused a pass to travel out to join him. At Whitehall she was told that her husband had gained his liberty through trickery; 'but for me and his children upon no conditions we should not stir'. Ann did not waste time arguing. She went to the pass office at Wallingford House, and obtained papers under her maiden name, Ann Harrison, for herself, 'a man, a maid, and her three children'. She then shamelessly proceeded to forge the pass, changing the capital 'H' to two 'f's,* the two 'r's to an 'n' and the 'i' to an 's', and the 's' to an 'h', the 'o' to an 'a', and the 'n' to a 'w', 'so completely that none could find the change'. She then hired a barge to take her family to Gravesend, and from thence a coach to Dover. Then, laughing merrily at the thought of their great escape, she and her family crossed the Channel, to Richard and freedom.

The Fanshawes' greatest adventure of all, however, had taken place in 1650, ten years earlier, when Richard was sent on a vital diplomatic mission to Spain: he carried letters from the future Charles II to the king of Spain, Philip IV, petitioning urgent funds to help the royalist cause. Ann, as always, was by his side.

The Fanshawes set out from Galway, which was then in the throes of the plague. Not wishing to enter the town itself, they were led 'all on the back side of town under the walls, over which people during the plague (which was not yet quite stopped) had flung out all their dung, dirt and rags, and we walked up to the middle of our legs in

---

* Until the eighteenth century Fanshawe was spelt ffanshawe or ffanshaw.

them'. By now covered in flea bites, they found the ship, a Dutch merchant vessel, which was to carry them as far as Málaga.

The boat was owned by 'a most tempestuous master, a Dutchman (which is enough to say), but truly, I think the greatest beast I ever saw of his kind'. All was well until they came to the Straits of Gibraltar, where they suddenly saw a well-manned Turkish galley in full sail coming towards them. The Dutchman's ship was so loaded with goods that his guns, all sixty of them, were useless. 'We believed we should all be carried away as slaves,' Ann wrote. But the 'beast captain' was not about to give up so easily. He called for brandy, of which he drank a good deal, called for his arms, called for his men, and cleared the decks of everyone else, 'resolving to fight rather than to lose his ship that was worth £30,000'.

'This was sad for us passengers,' Ann went on, 'but my husband bid us be sure to keep in the cabin, and no women appear, which would make the Turks think we were a man-of-war; but if they saw women they would take us for merchants and board us.' Leaving Ann down below, Richard took up his gun, his bandoliers and his sword, and went up to the top decks, where he stood waiting with the rest of the ship's company for the Turkish man-of-war to approach them. Ann, who despite being expressly forbidden to show herself, was merely waiting for her chance to join him, had not reckoned on the ploys of the 'beast captain'. When she tried the door, she found she had been locked in:

> I knocked and called to no purpose, until at length a cabin boy came and opened the door. I all in tears desired him to be so good as to give me his blue thrum-cap he wore, and his tarred coat, which he did, and I gave him half a crown; and putting them on, and flinging away my night's clothes, I crept up softly and stood upon the deck by my husband's side as free from sickness and fear as, I confess, from discretion; but it was the effect of that passion which I could never master.

The Turks were satisfied with a parley, and eventually turned and sailed away. 'But when your father saw it convenient to retreat, looking upon me he blessed himself, and snatched me up in his arms, saying "Good God, that love can make this change!", and though he seemingly chid me, he would laugh at it as often as he remembered that voyage.'

The most dangerous voyage of all, however, was undertaken very soon after this one on their return from Spain to France. In the Bay of Biscay their boat sailed into a storm which lasted for two days and two nights 'in a most violent manner'. The winds were so strong that they 'drew the vessel up from the water', and so destroyed the boat that by the end it had neither sail nor mast left. The crew consisted of six men and a boy: 'Whilst they had hopes of life they ran about swearing like devils, but when that failed them they ran into holes, and let the ship drive as it would,' Ann wrote. The final blow to their chances of reaching land came when even the ship's compass was lost, causing

such horrible lamentation as was as dismal to us as the storm past. Thus between hope and fear we past the night, they protesting to us that they knew not where they were. And truly we believed them; for with fear and drink I think they were bereft of sense. So soon as it was day, about six of the clock, the master cried out, 'The land! The land!' But we did not receive that news with the joy belonging to it, but sighing said, 'God's will be done'.

Eventually their ship ran aground and that night they all sat up

and made good cheer, for beds we had none, and we were so transported that we thought we had no need of any. But we had very good fires and Nantes white wine, and butter and milk, and walnuts and eggs, and some very bad cheese. And was this not enough, with the escape of shipwreck, to be thought better than a feast? I am sure until that hour I never knew such pleasure in eating, between which we a thousand times repeated what we had spoken when every word seemed our last.

Nothing was ever to equal the exquisite exhilaration of these two great adventures. After the Restoration the Fanshawes' diplomatic career reverted to a distinguished but far more conventional round of appointments. Richard was officially accredited ambassador, first to the court of Portugal in 1662, and then three years later to Spain. In between the births, and deaths, of her prodigious family, Ann slipped effortlessly into the role of the ambassador's lady, admiring Richard in all his finery as he presented his credentials, giving and receiving visits, and attending court functions; listing, with distinctly beady eye, all their silver, and plate, and fine brocades. But she would doubtless have given it all up, and endured a thousand more dangers, to be at Richard's side.

When he died in 1666, while still serving as Charles II's ambassador to Spain, Ann's heart was broken. 'O all powerful Lord God,' she wrote in a frenzy of grief, 'look down from heaven upon me the most distressed wretch upon earth. See me with my soul divided, my glory and my guide taken from me, and in him all my comfort in this life. See me staggering in my path. Have pity on me, O Lord, and speak peace to my disquieted soul now sinking under this great weight...'

Ann survived Richard by fourteen years, but the thought of him always made her eyes 'gush out with tears'. In her heart, as well as in life, they had always been as one. '*Glory to God* we never had but one mind throughout our lives,' she concludes her memoir, 'our souls were wrapped up in each other, our aims and designs one, our loves one, and our resentments one. We so studied one the other that we knew each other's mind by our looks; whatever was real happiness, God gave it to me in him.'[9]

Until well into the present century, the majority of diplomatic wives played a part which was very much an extension of the social role they would have fulfilled in England. Even Mrs Blanckley's good works, sewing shirts for shipwrecked sailors, had perhaps more to do with her own upbringing and devout religious convictions than with any more formally imposed ethos. In the first half of the present century, however, two important changes occurred within the Foreign Office which were to affect the roles of diplomatic wives quite as much as those of their husbands.

Towards the end of the nineteenth century the Diplomatic Service had been expanding, and the introduction of salaries in 1919 meant that it attracted those who lacked the minimum £400 per annum in private income which had formerly been essential. It now also merged with the previously separate Foreign Office. After the Eden reforms of 1943, however, the service was expanded still further, and recruitment became both more meritocratic and more middle class. Mirroring the increasingly structured and hierarchical nature of their husbands' jobs, the role of wives became subtly more codified.

This code was manifested not only in new diplomatic etiquette manuals, such as Marcus Cheke's* specially written book of instructions (tactfully compiled in 1946 for the benefit of those wives who may not have been brought up to know a fish knife from a finger bowl), but also in a kind of received 'in-house' culture perpetuated by the wives themselves.

At the beginning of this post-war period wives of the 'old school' deplored the lack of social sophistication amongst the new breed of middle-class wives coming up through the ranks, and were not shy of saying so. Marie-Noele Kelly, who was to become one of the great British ambassadresses, blamed the communist bloc for the disruption of the old social certainties of pre-war Europe – the sort of 'freemasonry' which had once characterized the whole diplomatic corps. 'This arose naturally,' she wrote, 'from members having the same background and training, from their use of a common language [French] and the universal code of courteous social formulae evolved by the French.'

Marie-Noele recalled how, as a young newly married wife in the 1930s, she was taken to one side by her own ambassadress, Lady Granville, and 'in smiling fashion' given some friendly words of advice. Although Lady Granville would no doubt have preferred her to have been English (Marie-Noele was of aristocratic, but Belgian stock), she recognized that she had been 'properly' brought up 'and that there were things which need not be stressed'. The same could not be said for many of the younger wives coming into the service in her own days as an ambassadress, a high proportion of whom had 'no conception that these mysteries even existed'.[10]

This was not just old-fashioned snobbery, although doubtless it played a part. For the more traditional diplomatic wives, of upper-class if not aristocratic upbringing themselves, this social know-how was an essential tool of the trade. Marcus Cheke's handbook, which by today's standards makes hilarious reading, was thoroughly approved of by the 'old school' because it showed the new recruits, both men and their wives, how to conduct 'those social relationships which it is [their]

---

* Marcus Cheke was then vice-marshal of the diplomatic corps.

duty to cultivate'.[11] It was the wives, however, who came in for Marie-Noele's most withering disapproval:

> They seemed to have little social sense and could not understand the idea of representation. Although, unlike an earlier generation, their husbands were given ample allowances for this very purpose, their ladies seemed to have exactly the same outlook as if the husbands were working in offices in London and their homes were in suburbia. If they spent their allowances, it was on the cosy job of entertaining each other, or members of the colony; if and when they were forced into wider society, they tended to huddle together in the corner until they could slip away.

The word 'duty', so unfashionable today, was all too familiar to diplomatic women of my mother's generation. By the beginning of the 1960s the code of behaviour which had been gradually gathering force over the previous twenty years was finally given a formal mouth-piece with the foundation of the Foreign Service Wives' Association.* One of the association's first newsletters reprinted a speech given by Lady Kirkpatrick, wife of the Permanent Under-Secretary of State Sir Ivone Kirkpatrick, in November 1960. The talk, entitled in a suitably no-nonsense way 'Serving Abroad', gave formal expression, perhaps for the first time, to the role of the 'new wife':

> Our lives have to be dedicated. The work of the Foreign Service does not begin and end between office hours, its family life is often disrupted and it has to observe a degree of self-discipline and sacrifice unknown in most other callings ... I have chosen the title *Serving Abroad* because *service* is the key note: and if we realise that the Service is more important than we are, we shall do our work abroad properly.

The submersion of women not only into the individual sphere of their husbands' lives abroad, but into the wider embrace of the service itself, was complete.

---

* Reflecting modern trends, this association is now the BDSA (the British Diplomatic Spouses Association). Masha Williams was one of its founder members in 1959.

The time and energy freely given by wives like Mrs Blanckley in Algiers had become a duty which was expected, even demanded, of all diplomatic women. According to Lady Kirkpatrick, the duty of the Foreign Office wife was, principally,

> to make a comfortable centre where you can return hospitality and enable your husband to invite and talk to the people of the country in an informal way. To do this properly means work, and 90% of the work involved revolves on you. It would be fairer if all or most of the entertainment allowance were paid direct into your account. But we live in an unjust world, and there would be a collapse if everyone went on strike until they got justice.

In this rarefied world receptions and cocktail parties were 'a cross which had to be borne',[12] especially since it was also the wife's duty 'to look after the bore whom everyone else was wisely shunning'.

Intelligent diplomats, particularly the more senior ones, have always recognized the importance of their wives' contribution to their careers. According to Lord Tyrell, ambassador to Paris in the 1930s, 'A woman with the right personal gifts who marries a diplomat or a consular officer and is conscientious about the performance of her duties is, as you know, invaluable to the public service and one can think of many Ambassadors and Ministers in the past, who have owed a great part of their personal success and of the success of their best work to their wives.'[13] But as the service expanded, the partnership between a diplomat and his wife became, in one sense, more formally recognized. Questionnaires filled out by heads of mission assessing the productivity of their officers now began to include commentaries on the 'performance' and suitability of their wives (a practice only very recently discontinued). In another sense, however, these same changes brought with them new restrictions. The informality of previous years had given women a freedom and a scope which were now largely denied them.

In 1960, at the time of Lady Kirkpatrick's speech, anything more intellectually taxing than entertaining or charity work was definitely not on the agenda. Unquestioning loyalty was expected of wives, but only within certain strictly defined limits. Politics were proscribed. 'You are not required to discuss politics at all, and indeed must be careful to confine yourself to intelligent listening, since anything you say will be taken as the opinion of your husband and therefore of the Ambassador and the British Government,' was Lady Kirkpatrick's stalwart advice. 'It is better to be thought stupid and amiable (above all amiable),' she concluded, 'than dangerous. Madame de Staël would not have been an asset as a diplomatist's wife.'* On the still more delicate question of contact with members of the press, her advice was: 'I can only suggest that you sweetly reply that you don't know as your husband never discusses anything with you.'

Inevitably, some wives found the prospect of marrying into this strict new world a daunting one.

> I must say, I was very frightened [recalls Rosa Carless, Brazilian-born wife of the diplomat Hugh Carless]. I was working in a museum in São Paulo, and I had a lot of friends of all different types. I mixed with a lot of artists. I led a rather bohemian life, but in a decent way, not a crazy way. The thought of being in an Embassy, it was almost like a boarding school. I received a letter before I went to Tehran saying that the ambassadress liked the women to wear stockings and gloves – even in the heat.

'I was used to doing a job,' complained Masha Williams, who before her marriage in 1946 had worked as a high-level interpreter with Reuters, 'not being an appendage.'[14]

But for many others, who were perhaps responding to the increasing opportunities for women elsewhere, the diplomatic partnership which they forged with their husbands was indeed a job. 'An ambassadress's job is arranging dinners, not writing books,' a particularly curmudgeonly reviewer commented on the publication of Marie-Noele Kelly's book on Portugal, *This Delicious Land*. Characteristically, she was delighted that he (for it must have been a he) had at least admitted that arranging dinners *was* a job. It was quite unrealistic to suppose that 'a distinguished and civilized entertainment' could simply be improvised 'out of the void', she wrote approvingly.[15]

---

* Madame de Staël, of course, *was* a diplomat's wife. Hers was a marriage of convenience, to Eric-Magnus de Staël, the Swedish ambassador to Paris, although the question of whether or not she was an asset to him in his work is too complex to be covered in this footnote.

Although they were unpaid, and by today's standards lamentably unrecognized, the work carried out by many of these women at their husbands' sides was the source of enormous satisfaction to them. 'Paul and I had a vast desk,' recalls Pat Gore-Booth, whose husband was an ambassador to Burma and India in the fifties and early sixties, 'and he would sit on one side, and I sat on the other, and we spent a lot of time together working. It was the partnership angle which was the biggest blessing of all. And those who are fortunate enough to go through life in that state I think are very lucky.' Her feelings are echoed by her contemporary Peggy Trevelyan: 'The partnership was one of the pleasures of it really – that you were in it together, making it work.'

Even if a woman had her own profession or career, there was a clear, and almost entirely unquestioned understanding that her husband's job took precedence. As recently as 1976 Mary Henderson, who was a highly paid journalist before her marriage to Nicholas Henderson, British ambassador to Bonn, Paris and Washington, gave a talk at a 'Going Abroad' course organized by the Foreign Office. 'I now manage to write about one article every three years,' she said. 'I do not regret it. It is more rewarding to be working with and for one's husband. You can discuss things together, laugh about things together and enjoy or hate things together. And then I believe that being the wife of a member of the Diplomatic Service is a job in itself and is a career. In some posts it is a full-time and exacting career.'[16]

Increasingly, the most successful diplomatic partnerships were ones in which the 'duty' demanded of the wife was leavened not only by a love of the job, but also by a healthy sense of her own value. In the sixties and seventies Jane Ewart-Biggs and her husband Christopher were considered good diplomatic partners because each possessed qualities which complemented those of the other. 'My contribution was to create the well-organised, relaxed background which gave Christopher the confidence to project his original intellect and individualistic humour so appreciated by the French,' she wrote. While Christopher welcomed their guests, it was Jane who then took over the formal introductions 'because I was better at it'.

For a woman of energy and ambition even something as apparently mundane as a dinner party could be elevated into an art form. For Jane, the most enjoyable part of the evening was the post-mortem:

Sometimes from my vantage point between the two leading guests I might have gleaned some political tit-bit for Christopher. Sometimes Christopher might even have set me the task of extracting certain information, basing his hopes on Belgian politicians or civil servants being less guarded when talking to their hostess than to their host. If successful, I laid these trophies before him like a dog with a bone.

Jane Ewart-Biggs had other, more finely honed diplomatic instincts, too. When her husband was in the running for the job of minister in Paris,* the ambassador at the time, Christopher Soames, sent for him to see if they would 'take' together:

I had never met Christopher Soames, but I instinctively knew that my Christopher, with his shyness and misleading old-fashioned look, might not immediately impress the kind of person I understood Soames to be. On the other hand, I knew that my more outgoing style might impress him ... So I made complicated arrangements for the children to be looked after, bought a new dress ... and took the plane with him, the result being that Christopher's journal *should* have read: 'He took *us*.'[17]

* Number two in the embassy and a very senior post.

CHAPTER FOUR

Private Life

'I get up at six, so ungenteel am I grown,' wrote Mrs Vigor, wife of the minister resident in St Petersburg in 1730, 'have done looking about, and giving orders in the family, to come to breakfast by eight. When that is over I spend an hour with my instructor in French; then retire to my room, and either work, or read, 'till twelve, when I dress for dinner at one; after dinner we chat a little; then I work, or read again, 'till six, when we either go out to take the air in the coach, or walk, 'till eight, at which hour we always sup, and go to bed at ten.'[1]

After the initial shock of arriving and absorbing, as best she could, the conditions of her new posting, a diplomatic wife had to get her house in order. As Mrs Vigor hints, the graceful order of her day in early eighteenth-century St Petersburg marked a good deal of ungenteel hard work. By 'the family', she would not have meant her relations (the minister, Claudius Rondeau, was her newly acquired second husband and she had, as yet, no children) but her household.

The description is a telling one. In our own servantless age, it is hard to imagine how much diplomatic women depended on their domestic households. When Mary Sheil arrived in Tehran, her first important encounter was with Ali Mohammed Beg, the weirdly Scots-accented mission housekeeper. There can be few diplomatic women, from any era, who do not have similar memories. In the days before modern embassy infrastructures came into being – with their post reports and their liaison officers – a diplomatic wife's servants were sometimes her only coherent link with the strange new world which lay beyond the embassy walls. It was the servants who knew where the shops and bazaars were, how to access reserves of food which might be in short supply, how best to keep the house cool or warm; who knew, in short, how things worked.

The number of servants assigned to a diplomatic household varied enormously. In 1799, at the embassy in Constantinople, Mary Elgin was overwhelmed to find herself with a household of sixty to feed every day. In post-war Rotterdam, on the other hand, Maureen Tweedy's domestic help was provided by 'a dear old daily' who only came in the mornings and answered to the unsuitable name of Mrs Mink. In her encyclopaedic *The Complete Indian Housekeeper and Cook* of 1888, Flora Steel opined that three indoor and one outdoor servant and a groom were the very minimum required by two people. If punkahs were used in hot weather (as they were up country in India from 15 March until 1 November, and in many other hot countries), then for both day and night work a further three men were required.

Flora Steel devoted a large section of her manual to essential tips on how a housewife living abroad should deal with her servants. The oriental servant, she observed, 'is a child in everything except age, and should be treated as a child; that is to say kindly, but with the greatest firmness'. Western notions of cleanliness and hygiene were particularly difficult to enforce. The efficient housewife in foreign climes had to be especially vigilant with her 'native' cook, whose dirty habits, such as stirring the eggs into the rice pudding with his finger, would be deeply engrained. There were many wives, Mrs Steel noted reprovingly, who never went into their kitchens at all lest their appetite for breakfast be spoiled by seeing a servant 'using his toes as an efficient toast rack . . . or the soup strained through a greasy turban'.[2]

This was exactly the experience of Catherine Macartney when she first entered her new home, Chini-Bagh, in Kashgar. Feeling rather nervous at the ordeal of being introduced to her staff for the first time, she entered the kitchen, a dark and smoky room lit only by a skylight overhead. Her new Indian cook was sitting on the mud floor with a basin of eggs in front of him, 'breaking each into his dirty brown hand, letting the whites slide through his fingers into one basin and putting the yolks into another'.[3] Although he produced some very good cooking over the years, Catherine always wished that she had never actually seen him at work – a sentiment heartily shared by Susan Townley who, during her first few weeks in China, once innocently walked into her kitchens to supervise the preparations for a dinner party only to find her cook boiling up a rat in the soup.

For particularly recalcitrant servants Mrs Steel recommended a good dose of castor oil: their inability either to learn or remember her instructions must, she believed, have a physical cause. While few wives of later generations would have dared to use this particular ruse, there must have been many who secretly longed to.

The task of training foreign servants in what must have seemed inexplicable English ways could be an enervating one. Shortly after her arrival in Persia in 1849 Mary Sheil organized a dinner for thirty-six guests, at which all the attendants, down to the last footman, were Persians. 'When it is considered that ... everything is conducted as like Europe as possible,' she wrote wearily afterwards, 'it may be imagined what time and labour were expected in drilling the Diggories of the Mission'[4] Similarly, my mother once wrote to me in exasperation from Chile: 'My Darling Katie, the more I think about it the more I think how clever I am to have thought up the name of Gertrude Towers for this house.* Our Juan is straight Manuel, though he says *"muy bien"* instead of *"que?"* – usually when things ain't at *all* "muy bien". And I am frequently to be heard raising a shrill voice to anyone who crosses my path on a bad day.' Even Marie-Noele Kelly was occasionally plagued with less than perfect staff. 'Excellency!' her chef in Moscow, a lonely Dutchman, once accosted her early one autumn morning, 'a woman, or a bottle – I must have one or the other.'[5]

All around the world, even in the most far-flung diplomatic outposts, there were standards to be kept up. Ella Sykes was horrified at the state of her new household when she arrived in Kashgar to take over from Catherine Macartney in 1915, little guessing at the vast improvements her predecessor had struggled to make. Despite receiving the 'princely sum' of £5 a month, her cook Achmed, she discovered, could produce only two or three soups, and roughly the same number of meat dishes; 'his bread, moreover, was uneatable, and not a single pudding or cake found a place in his repertory.' The other servants were dirty, and used their sleeves as dusters. Worst of all, though, was the difficulty in finding anyone to boil and starch her brother Percy's shirt fronts and collars.

Beneath her gentle exterior, however, Ella had not only nerves of steel but great reserves of energy, qualities which were especially useful,

---

* The street was named after a woman called Gertrudis Echenique.

she noted, 'when dealing with the slackness of the oriental'. Even so, at first she found it a constant struggle to maintain even the most modest standards of cleanliness and order. Her butler Sattur, 'a gnome-like little man, perfectly honest, but with the mind of a boy of twelve', had an irritating habit of stretching across them when serving either food or drink at the table, and 'a constitutional inability to put the lid on a biscuit tin or close a door'. It was a proud moment for both Ella and Sattur when, 'after many a reprimand, he knocked at my bedroom door instead of bursting in without notice'.

Other changes to the daily routine were less easy to implement. Any attempts to persuade Sattur to use a damp cloth on the end of his broom when dusting, instead of merely whisking the dust from one spot to another, reduced the poor man to such a state of nerves that eventually Ella had to give up. On the personal hygiene front, too, she had to be content with insisting firmly on clean garments, and (shades of Flora Steel) 'well-washed hands and faces'.

The boiling and starching of Percy's shirts, and of her own numerous petticoats, however, were standards which were not to be given up so lightly. Eventually Ella discovered a man who was prepared to take on the job. Puzzled by the strange noises coming from the ironing room one day, she looked in to discover him laying out one of her dresses on his board and, taking a large gulp of water from a jug at his side, ejecting 'a fine spray of water from his mouth upon it'.[6]

Coping with 'servant problems' remains one of the more arcane tasks faced by diplomatic wives. Even in the most perfectly drilled households, strange hierarchies and rivalries abound. In Santos Isabel Burton was forced to have no fewer than five sittings for each meal in her household. The first, for Richard, herself and her guests, was followed by one for her Irish maid, who had been elevated from plain Mary to 'Dona Maria', and her brother. Then her German servants dined, because they would not sit down with her black servants, who in turn would not sit down with the slaves, 'who were obliged to stand or sit in corners where they gave them the leavings'.[7] In Ecuador, over a hundred years later, my mother remembers an identical punctiliousness amongst her own staff: 'The hierarchy in our Embassy kitchen forbade Jorge the gardener from sitting down with the indoor staff. Every day he would eat his lunch on a solitary stool sitting by the sink.' Not even the grandest households were immune. An implacable hatred raged between Marie-Noele Kelly's Dutch chef and her dauntingly misogynistic butler, John Smith. This manifested itself in a tug-of-war with the rope to the kitchen-lift, where their dinners would often sit suspended, cooling rapidly, in mid-shaft: 'Each hoped the complaint for meals cold or late would be laid at the other's door.'[8]

Dealing with staff in Muslim countries often carried an additional penalty clause. Many male servants considered it demeaning to take orders from a woman, and so wives found that they had to fight to maintain any kind of authority in their own households. During her first posting in Iraq after the war Masha Williams found that extreme tact, worthy of the most delicate diplomatic negotiations, had to be employed when dealing with her Arab servants, Hassan and Mahomet. She was advised never to give orders, but always to request the jobs she wanted done. They worked well, she found, 'but when and how they wished, not as I asked'. Wisely, she accepted the status quo. Another keen new wife in the same embassy, who came armed with an enticing collection of international recipes which she tried to teach to her cook, ended up with an ulcer. Worse still was Catherine Macartney's predicament when she employed a Chinese servant who refused point blank not only to take orders from her, but even to serve her at table, on the grounds that she did her own cooking and could not, therefore, be a real lady. (Her children's governess, on the other hand, who sat inside and read books all day, was completely acceptable.)

Few of the critics back home in England who carped about extravagant diplomatic lifestyles were aware that a common problem was not so much acquiring large numbers of staff as getting rid of unwanted or superfluous ones. In many Iron Curtain and other communist countries domestic staff who worked in embassy households were also government spies. Most diplomatic families, accepting this to be the case, took it in their stride, some even kindly providing especially interesting talk at the dinner table on the evening before they were known to have to make their reports. In Hungary in the early 1960s Rosa Carless's chauffeur confessed to her that he was obliged to report even the smallest details of her life, such as what kind of soap she used, so that it could be put in her dossier 'just to have a complete picture'. Others, like Sheila Whitney in Peking, found that they were paying a rather heavier price.

'We discovered at our first party that the cook wasn't really a cook at all but a spy in the household,' she recalls. His role was to report not on the Whitneys but on the other servants, which would not have mattered so much if he had showed at least some culinary skill. 'The first dinner party that I gave was an absolute disaster. It was supposed to be a stew and the meat was ghastly. I don't know what it was but it wasn't cooked properly. You know, stews have to be cooked for hours and hours, and it was obviously cooked too quickly.'

Shortly afterwards Sheila's husband Ray found a notebook in his quarters which made it clear that, as they had suspected, their 'cook' was a young army corporal. The entire household, including the other servants, heaved a sigh of relief on his day off, but they were unable to replace him. The Whitneys had been assigned a total of five servants, including a gardener, even though their 'garden' consisted of only a few plants in little pots: 'But we couldn't sack anybody. We might have said, "Well, we don't really need the gardener, so-and-so could do it." But no, no, you couldn't do that because the unions wouldn't allow you. And if you had done, you wouldn't get a replacement because all the servants would disappear. So it was impossible.'

The formidable Flora Steel and her doses of castor oil notwithstanding, by the standards of many other countries the British were generally kind and generous employers, and were profoundly shocked by the conditions they observed elsewhere. Travelling through Russia – a country where, until the abolition of serfdom in 1861, fortunes were measured not by money, but by the numbers of peasants owned – Mary Sheil was appalled by the universal disregard shown by the upper classes towards their servants. On long journeys they were never provided with rooms, but expected to sleep on bare benches or even on the floor, across the doorway of their master's room. 'They seemed to me to look on and to treat them as inferior animals,' she observed.[9]

By contrast, British diplomatic women often regarded their servants with the greatest respect and even affection. Rosemary Watts, wife of the military attaché in Pakistan in the early 1980s, lovingly kept the old shopping lists written by her cook, which she found in an old kitchen drawer:

carats	graeps	tomto
garrets	graps	tòkmto
anion	orags	magos
onyon	orgets	maggos
enion		
eneun	garaforat	plumps
onuin		plumes
oinion	apal	blubs
	appall	
cabig		peair
kabaj	tarnaps	
kabij		potots
cabje	bononas	patota
cebaag	banaa	
	bana	lama
passely	bein	laman
pasle	biness	
koliflor	suagr	malien
colefloor		
	spanch	pippers
	sapench	poppers[10]
chkakn	spina	

In the past, in the loneliest and most segregated postings, servants provided not only practical but also emotional support. Mary Fraser's beloved Japanese samurai, Ogita, and Elizabeth Blanckley's janissary, Sidi Hassan, offered not only protection but companionship, too. When she was living in Brazil, one of the most solitary periods in her life, Isabel Burton engaged a number of slaves as servants, building them a chapel (they were Catholics) and paying them as well as their masters, like freemen. She remained very attached to one in particular – Chico, a recently emancipated slave – even after she caught him roasting her favourite cat over the fire. 'Black as coal and brimming with intelligence', he remained her 'right hand' until the day she left Brazil.

Together, Isabel and Chico were resourceful to a fault. Conditions were always difficult in Santos, but never more so than during the Paraguayan War, when provisions were so scarce that for several months the town was in a state of virtual famine. Undaunted, Isabel and Chico would sally forth, large panniers on their arms, to forage in the jungle. About ten miles out of town one day they came across some large flocks of geese and other poultry, which Isabel, with a completely brazen disregard for the truth, described as being 'chiefly kept for ornament'. The two of them returned triumphantly, their horses laden with stolen fowl. 'So as I passed through the town the squawking was immense,' Isabel explained with characteristic bravado, 'and most of the Grundy,* respectable English tried to avoid me, which made me take an especial pleasure in riding up to them and inquiring after their wives and families, and entering into a conversation, which I, perhaps, should otherwise not have done.'[11]

In Bolivia, where her husband Stanley was posted as ambassador in the early eighties, Jennifer Duncan's right hand was her cook:

There was hyper-inflation in the country at the time, and as a result there were often strikes and the roads would be blockaded. It was often very difficult to get food. I'm not talking about fancy things. Even to get sugar, flour, basics like that, meant queuing for a long time. Meat was almost impossible to get hold of. When I went shopping I often used to take my cook with me because it was important to be able to identify what little was on sale. I learnt from her that you had to ask to see the head of the animal. If it was a sheep, that was all right, but people who didn't know the ropes would often be sold dog instead.

In communist countries obtaining food was a particularly complex task. Veronica Atkinson, who was posted to Romania during the bitter last days of the Ceauşescu regime, believes that without her staff to help her she would have found the system totally impenetrable. Although as diplomats they had access to more supplies than ordinary Romanians – an embassy shop provided them with basics such as olive oil, cereals, butter and milk – when it came to buying fresh meat or vegetables,

* Mrs Grundy was a character in a play of 1798 by Tom Morton, *Speed the Plough*. She came to epitomize a strait-laced neighbour.

the situation was very difficult indeed. Although there was no war, wartime conditions prevailed: 'If you imagine a store, the window – empty. No jars of anything. No fresh food,' she remembers. Using packets of cigarettes – Kent, for preference – her cook would barter for their supplies with her Communist Party contacts. 'Obtaining food was easy for the cook because she knew that so-and-so could get it from Bulgaria, or from the Black Sea, or from Turkey. She knew, she had a network.'

Sheila Whitney's cook had no trouble buying fresh fruit and vegetables in Peking, but could find only one variety at a time. 'There was usually a glut of things like vegetables. They didn't rotate crops at all. So for a whole month and a half you all had beans. And even when you went out to parties you were served beans, because there was nothing else on the market. Or cabbage. Or carrots. So you know, if it was March it was carrots.'

The process by which Marie-Noele Kelly's servants obtained food for her was more complex still. Nothing was ever delivered to the house and so one servant queued for hours every morning to buy milk – and often came back with none. In winter no fresh vegetables were available except cabbage. There were a number of *gastronoms*, or food emporiums, for foreigners and high officials, where excellent Russian food – cheese, cream, fish and sometimes fruit – were available, but at a price. In the winter a single orange cost eight shillings. Marie-Noele's chef did the shopping personally, but spoke no Russian; he therefore had to be provided not only with a car, but with his own interpreter too. Meat came from another market; local, seasonal produce, such as mushrooms or wild strawberries, from a third. 'He told me more than once,' she wrote, 'that Russian women had kissed his hand for allowing them to pick up the potatoes that fell out of his weekly sack.'[12]

Iona Wright, posted to Trebizond, on the Black Sea coast of Turkey during the war, confesses to 'going native' in culinary matters. Even their basic supplies, which came in by ship across the Black Sea, were erratic, and were often consumed by the passengers en route:

At the moment we have, in the Consulate, no sugar at all [she wrote in her journal in 1941]. There has been none available in town for a month, and yesterday the small stock that we had ran out. For our tea it does not matter as we do not take it, but for coffee and cooking in general it is very difficult, also for cocoa and other hot drinks now that the weather is colder. The sweet shops are practically empty, as everyone is buying anything sweet that they can find, and I am just going to buy some chocolate that is left, in order to make a drink out of it with some milk.[13]

Feelings of loneliness and what Mary Fraser once described as 'the famishing homesickness for Europe and one's own people' could be alleviated to some degree by familiar food. Many diplomatic women went to enormous lengths to obtain at least some of the things which reminded them of home. During my childhood by far the most exciting room in the various houses we lived in was the huge walk-in cupboard, always known as 'Aladdin', which contained my mother's supplies. Painstakingly ordered from a firm called Braham Masters, they included such English delicacies as three years' supply of Christmas puddings, Marmite, Worcestershire sauce, Bath Olivers, Ribena, jars of mincemeat (for making mince pies), Coleman's mustard and Cooper's Oxford marmalade. Over the years my mother developed a close relationship with her contact in the company, who would go out of his way to procure special luxuries, such as her favourite lapsang souchong tea, which were not on the Braham Masters list. 'He used to write me lovely letters, telling me where he was going on holiday, and that sort of thing,' she recalls. 'I was terribly sad when he retired. It was never quite the same again.'

Through the ages there have been very few diplomatic wives who have not had such arrangements. In 1806 there were no *épiciers* in Algiers, so Mrs Blanckley relied on a similar supply of stores, obtained wholesale from Gibraltar, Marseilles and England. Mary Fraser, on her first posting in China, describes vividly the enormous tribe of trades-men who supplied the legation compound, from the purveyors of jewels and precious stones to the camel caravans which brought their fuel in winter. But none of this, however picturesque, ever exceeded the excitement which accompanied their twice-yearly deliveries, in dozens of sturdy wooden cases, from the Army & Navy Stores.

The process of selecting groceries and provisions from the Army & Navy's vast catalogues (new price lists were issued four times a year, and paid for by subscription) was an occupation which in itself took several days – if not whole weeks – to complete, and the huge range made our Aladdin's supplies of Marmite and mincemeat look pitifully meagre by comparison. In Mary Fraser's day nearly fifty different types of biscuit, from the whimsically named Dew Drops to Dessert Rusks, could be ordered alongside tins of caviare, asparagus, lobster and potted meats (twenty-one varieties), endless sauces, pickles, marmalades and fancy fruits (crystallized or *glacés*, sixteen varieties). Soaps, pomades, colognes and tooth powders (from the spartan 'Calvert's Carbolic' to 'Atkinson's Circassian Rose Opiate for the Teeth') were listed next to a huge selection of 'Perfumes for the Handkerchief' (thirty-two varieties, ranging from 'Fantaisie Parisienne' to the manly 'Guards Bouquet'). Other sundries included everything from bunion plasters, bottles of smelling salts and enemas, to green baize aprons for your butler, worm powder and poultry food.

The ubiquitous travelling bath was handsomely represented. Seven varieties came in twenty different sizes and finishes, and included an immense contraption known as the 'Cabinet Portable Turkish Bath', which came in pine, ash, mahogany and exotic black walnut. One year the drugs and perfumery section also carried this intriguing note: 'Arrangements have been made with a manufacturer for the supply of Artificial Limbs and Eyes at a Discount, if ordered through the Society, of 20 per cent from ordinary prices.' I have often wondered how much call there was for them.

In more recent times diplomatic wives have had to resort to even more drastic means to do their shopping. Catherine Young, posted to Syria in 1983, discovered that while few foodstuffs were available in Damascus, over the border in Lebanon it was a different matter. She and some of the other embassy wives organized regular shopping expeditions there: 'Sometimes we made it a day out, sometimes I used to go with a friend. About once a month. In Lebanon – in war-torn Lebanon, because it was then at the worst of the civil war – you could get everything. You could go and you could pay in anything, too. I used to write Midland Bank cheques. And if I had gone with my French cheque book they would have been happy. I even think they would have taken sea shells.' But even these shopping expeditions had their drawbacks. Crossing the border was no easy matter – at times they had to negotiate as many as seven checkpoints. 'You know, seven armed-to-the-teeth chaps with Kalashnikovs stopping you. On your way to a shopping expedition.'

In the toughest postings it paid to be as self-sufficient as possible. In the early sixties food supplies in Russia were still so uncertain that Peggy Trevelyan, the British ambassadress there from 1962 to 1965, took no less than £500-worth of frozen food with her, mostly meat. 'If you suddenly found you had twenty people coming to lunch you might find that you could only get two chickens in the market,' she explains. At other times the entire basement of the embassy (a vast sugar baron's mansion overlooking the Kremlin which, then as now, contained both the ambassador's residence and the chancery) was stuffed with food supplies, mostly British goods in tins or sacks, which were distributed monthly to all embassy staff. Few visitors can have guessed that throughout the winter months the attic of this stupendous building became a chicken-coop, which meant that they enjoyed the luxury of fresh eggs; the yolks, due to the lack of natural light, were almost entirely white.

Diana Shipton found the Kashgar consulate well set up with its own cow, for milk and butter, hens for eggs, and a substantial vegetable garden. Two donkeys were kept for bringing water up to the house from the river. Everything else, except for flour, rice and meat, which were procured from the local bazaar – was ordered up from India at least three months in advance.

In many countries not only food, but everyday household items and services were very hard to come by. In St Petersburg in 1825 Anne Disbrowe lamented the prohibitive cost of having her laundry done; while over a hundred years later her successors in Moscow were forced to send their clothes and shoes back to the UK for dry-cleaning and repairs. In Trebizond during the war, Iona Wright found that shampoo, and even soap, were impossible to get hold of, as were cosmetics of any kind. She was lucky in that she managed to get an acquaintance, the old French consul, to buy her some face powder in Istanbul. 'He is about sixty, quite a dandy with a small pointed beard, buttoned boots and high stiff collars,' she wrote in her journal. 'He is quite an encyclopaedia and can talk about all sorts of unusual things. He seems to know all about face-powder, although he is a bachelor, so I asked him to choose some for me when he went on holiday to Istanbul, and a careful selection of very subtle shades was the result.'[14]

Other women had to go even further afield, writing home to beg family and friends in England to send them the things they needed;

in the most remote outposts this could take many months. Clothes were a problem for Mary Elgin when she went to Constantinople in 1799. Her letters home to her mother are filled with shopping requests, including 'some gauze stockings for me to wear under my silk, and some flannel socks'. She was disappointed, too, in not finding the muslin dresses which she had expected to be able to buy there, noting that she had been obliged to send all the way to India for them instead. 'The people here admire coloured muslins amazingly, you can have no notion how much applause *your* blue muslin has met with. I advise you to bring plenty of coloured muslins with you, they will be more thought of than white,' she wrote before her parents' proposed visit to Turkey, adding parsimoniously, 'and then when we go they will sell wonderfully.'[15]

Elizabeth McNeill, who in 1823 accompanied her husband to Persia, experienced similar difficulties. Back home in Edinburgh her sister kept a little account book in which to record the sums she received and those she paid out for Elizabeth's numerous commissions, which were sometimes quite substantial: 'John wishes me to get a murone [sic] velvet gown, trimmed with Vandyke lace, for paying royal visits in,' Elizabeth wrote soon after her arrival. 'I would like it with longish sleeves, and half up to the neck. If you can get broad Vandyke lace to stand up around the skirt, I think it would be admired here. Let it be rich-looking.' In the same letter she also requested a bobinette dress with long sleeves and 'a yard or so of bobinette lace for handkerchiefs'. Also, 'a neat drest cap – something in the Queen Mary style, of materials that would wash or last. A common morning cap. Two pairs of stays with steel busks. 2 prs white satin slippers. 2 prs black satin slippers. 2 prs black kid ditto. 2 prs neat walking ties. 2 prs of ties of Denmark satin. A tortoiseshell comb with a high head, the largest you can find . . . a few pairs of habit gloves, drest and common.' And, 'a wreath of moss-roses, with buds for my hair, and one or two artificial flowers'.

She also asked for a good supply of toys to give as presents to children in the royal harems – 'snuff-boxes with figures that start up in them, serpents, a small Noah's Ark, and a nest of boxes'. Other treats sent out by her sister, again mainly intended as presents, included: 'some Loch Fyne herring' and 'a little box of oatmeal in which a few bottles of Highland whisky might be packed . . . also in a tin case a few cakes of Rankine's shortbread and a pound or two of Mrs Waddell's gingernuts'. The condition in which these foodstuffs arrived is not on record, but Elizabeth's packing instructions were very specific: 'P.S.,' she wrote, 'fill up any spare corner with darning cotton and white floss silk.'[16]

For Catherine and George Macartney such difficulties were compounded by the fact that no parcel bound for Kashgar could exceed seven pounds in weight. (When George ordered a pair of thick winter boots he received them in two parcels – one boot in each.) Packages from India took two months; those from England, three. After placing an order they might wait four or five months for their goods to arrive. Like Diana Shipton forty years later, they found that deliveries sometimes arrived in a terribly battered condition after their journey over the mountains. Tins were dented, and George's cigars (eighteen different varieties were available at the Army & Navy) were once so crushed that he was forced to smoke the powder in his pipe instead.

Kashgar's extreme remoteness made almost every aspect of the Macartneys' daily life there unusually challenging. Despite its apparent insignificance, this tiny, fly-blown oasis settlement on the western fringes of the Taklamakan Desert was for more than fifty years one of Britain's most crucial outposts in the 'Great Game', that long and shadowy campaign for supremacy in Asia against Tsarist Russia. George had arrived there as a very young man in 1890, and was to spend the next twenty-eight years – his entire career, in fact – first as the British agent, and then, in 1908, as British consul.* His official job was to represent the interests of the handful of British Indians, mostly small-time traders, living in Kashgar. Unofficially, he ran a vital listening post, reporting on Russian movements just across the border, most especially the machinations of the Russian consul in Kashgar, Nikolai Petrovsky.

Life in Kashgar was always tough and often very lonely. For the first eight years George had only one European friend there, a Dutch priest called Father Hendricks, with whom he conversed in their only

---

* The British government would have appointed him consul sooner but, under pressure from the Russians, the Chinese government refused permission for this until 1908. Two years later George Macartney became consul-general. He was knighted in 1913.

common language – Latin. With the arrival of his young bride, Catherine, in 1898, George's life improved immeasurably. Not only did she provide companionship and, later, three children; she also set about converting his spartan house, Chini-Bagh (at that time not only windowless, but practically furnitureless too), into a proper home.

Although Catherine approached her new life with unusual resourcefulness, at first even the most simple task, such as shopping in the bazaar, was a test of her courage. On her first expedition there, curious onlookers surrounded her by the hundreds, touching her coat and dress and peering into her face, fascinated by their first glimpse of a female *Feranghi* (a Frank, or foreigner). Literally unable to move through the crowd, she was forced to take refuge in one of the shops, and it was many months before she dared venture there again. One day she overheard two men discussing her: 'One said I could not be a woman, because I wore a belt; the other replied that I might be a man, because I did not show my trousers and had no hair; but they both agreed that I looked like a woman, as I had no beard. Evidently I was a great puzzle to them.'

Catherine lived the life of a true pioneer. She grew vegetables, milked cows, churned butter, made most of her own and her children's clothes, and even supervised the butchering of her own animals, a task she dreaded, but undertook because it was the only way to get edible cuts of meat. Although she rarely complained, any small luxuries, on the rare occasions when she could get them, assumed an almost agonizing importance. Once, her mother wrote to her describing the beautiful new winter hat she was sending out from Edinburgh: it was made from a rich brown velour, trimmed with ostrich feathers, and was quite the height of fashion. After months of anticipation, the eagerly awaited parcel arrived. But instead of the expected sturdy wooden box she received a strange package like a long hard sausage with her hat rolled up as tightly as possible inside, ostrich feathers and all. Clearly the original box had come undone, and a helpful Indian postmaster had repacked it for her. Bravely, Catherine wore the ruined hat (she had no other that winter) but disappointments of this kind were very hard to bear.

On another occasion a half-crazed thief broke into their house, and although he did not steal much he managed to wreak havoc on their stores, turning everything upside down and filling Catherine's fur coat with soap and sugar. Later the man was caught and brought to the house by the authorities. 'When he saw me, he smiled and salaamed, and then took a bundle out of his coat which he presented to me. It was an almost new coat to a winter costume I had hardly worn, all cut up into ribbons,' Catherine recalled bitterly. 'I nearly wept before them all, for the winter was coming on, and I could not replace it.'[17]

As with the crucial domestic arrangements of staff and daily supplies, so the private pleasures and routines of diplomatic women varied enormously. Jane Ewart-Biggs's highly sophisticated whirl of a busy Parisienne bears little relation to Iona Wright's lonely existence in the highly segregated and conservative backwater of wartime Trebizond. At weekends Iona and her husband Denis would go to bathe along the coast, sometimes taking picnics of cucumber, tomatoes and hard-boiled eggs (two each). There was very little else for her to do. She would have liked to play tennis, but in those days women did not play at the club there. When she went to the cinema, a rat ran over the balustrade of their box. 'The Turks here are friendly, but they live so differently from us that we do not get beyond a certain point with them,' she wrote in her journal. 'I would like to have some European women to go out with, and have a chat over coffee somewhere. I don't know what would happen if two women went into one of the coffee shops. Nothing of course, but I couldn't get any woman here to do it.' Three times a week she met some of the other non-Turkish people at tea parties, but found it 'rather ridiculous having nothing to do all day long, and then having to dress up and parade out as if at last you were going to relax . . . when there is still nothing to do or talk about.'[18] Rosa Carless, posted to Angola in the 1960s, knew this conversational *ennui* as *cri-cri*, after its usual subject matter, *criados* (children) and *criadas* (maids).

Despite the ever-popular image of embassy women as ladies of leisure, hordes of servants at the ready to carry out their every wish, the strict order and discipline of Mrs Vigor's St Petersburg day was in fact far more typical of their private lives, whatever their circumstances. In a letter to Alexander Pope, Lady Mary Wortley Montagu described her week's routine at her summer retreat, known as Belgrade Village, near Constantinople in 1717.

I endeavour to persuade myself that I live in a more agreeable variety than you do, and that Monday setting of partridges, Tuesday reading English, Wednesday studying the Turkish language (in which, by the way, I am already very learned), Thursday classical authors, Friday spent in writing, Saturday at my needle and Sunday admitting of visits and hearing music, is a better way of disposing the weeks than Monday at the Drawing Room,* Tuesday Lady Mohun's, Wednesday the opera, Thursday the play, Friday Mrs Chetwynd's, etc; a perpetual round of hearing the same scandal and seeing the same follies acted over and over, which here affect me no more than they do other dead people.[19]

Although she would not perhaps have made such claims to erudition, Diana Shipton was equally vigorous when it came to organizing her day at the Kashgar consulate. 'We did not allow ourselves to flick through a novel, or sit listening to dance records to pass the time,' she recorded.[20] Instead, she would take an hour's walk every morning; in spring and summer she and Eric played tennis three times a week, and set themselves strict times for reading and writing, for fear of frittering their time away. Even their reading material was vetted: no romances or thrillers, but serious tomes like *War and Peace* and Boswell's *Life of Samuel Johnson*.

Living so far away from home, often divorced from all the usual occupations and benchmarks, diplomatic wives found that private daily routines such as these could keep at bay the demons of loneliness, homesickness, and even boredom. Iona Wright made the best of it:

I do housework in the mornings, but in a very general sense, picking and arranging flowers, sewing, framing pictures, making small bits of furniture etc. In the afternoons we usually go for a walk, either into the country or round the old ruins of Trebizond, where you can, bit by bit, see the old form of the town as a fortress . . . Then there may be a tea-party somewhere, or perhaps we call on a Turkish family after office hours and have coffee and a sweet liqueur with them.[21]

* i.e. at St James's Palace.

A daily routine was also considered vital to one's health, especially in hot climates. Major Leigh Hunt had much to say on the evils of indolence when living in the tropics. Regular exercise, he admonished his lady readers, was essential not only for health, but for bodily comfort and cheerfulness, too. The wise female should make sure never to miss her morning and evening walk or ride:

> In the early morning the tropical world is seen at its best, and the temporary discomfort of rising at dawn, and hastily dressing, often by candlelight, is amply repaid by the delicious enjoyment of the fresh morning air, and the bright healthy colours, and keen appetite for *chota hazree* [early breakfast] that is produced by the brisk exercise. The good results of such an effort do not end here, for you will experience a delicious lightness and buoyancy that will carry you through the day, enabling you to make light of the heat that utterly prostrates your indolent neighbour.[22]

Amongst the most adventurous women, partly due to the extreme remoteness of their posting, were Diana Shipton (whose husband Eric was better known as the mountaineer than as the British consul) and her predecessor in the Kashgar consulate, Ella Sykes. During her time in Chinese Turkistan, Ella undertook some remarkable journeys, becoming the first Englishwoman ever to negotiate the Katta Dawan Pass in the Pamirs. As Younghusband had pointed out, the foothills of the Pamir Mountains are level with the higher summits of the Alps; at their base camp Ella's party was already at a height of 13,000 to 14,000 feet. 'I was actually on that Roof of the World,' she wrote ecstatically after the climb, 'which in my wildest day dreams I had never imagined that I should visit.'[23]

During that time Ella also became the second western woman ever to visit Khotan, the extraordinarily remote sub-desert region 300 miles east of Kashgar known as the 'Kingdom of Jade'. She was amazed by the shyness and docility of the people there, many of whom had never seen westerners before. The women would vanish 'like rabbits into their mud hovels' when they saw their party approaching. A group of peasants who had posed, without a murmur of protest, to have their photographs taken, told one of Ella's servants afterwards that they had thought they were going to be shot.

Although few diplomatic women were such intrepid travellers, many have been, in their own ways, inspired and loving explorers of the countries they were posted to. In the 1780s Miss Tully described the exquisite pleasure of visiting a private pleasure garden in the Libyan desert, 'a wilderness of sweets' even during the worst heats of summer.

One of Marie-Noele Kelly's greatest pleasures was riding near the Egyptian pyramids at dawn and at dusk. Later, the family kept a permanent tent out by the Cheops pyramid, where her children rode a camel called Princess, and she could enjoy breathing in 'the thin, dry, envigorating air of the desert'. The tent was a beautiful structure complete with bedrooms and a feast chamber, and was the perfect place to escape the noise and pomp of embassy life back in Cairo.

Even Mary Sheil, incarcerated in her house for most of her time in Persia, found to her relief that she could make excursions to the various ruins and mosques around Tehran, including the ancient city of Rei, destroyed 600 years previously by Genghis Khan. 'There is not much choice of action,' she wrote, 'but, such as it is, it is free and uncontrolled.' As a woman, Anne Disbrowe was prevented from joining in the bear, elk and wolf hunts which took up much of her husband's time in St Petersburg. Instead, as well as writing prodigious numbers of letters (perhaps the most popular private occupation of all), she collected seeds to send home: cucumber seeds, Siberian seeds and the seeds of 'transparent apples'.*

Ann Hibbert, too, started collecting plants as a way of occupying herself during her lonely posting to Ulan Bator in the early 1960s. 'Somebody had told me that the flowers in Mongolia were simply extraordinary, and so I wrote to Kew Gardens and, of course, because it was communist they hadn't been able to get out there for a long time. They were delighted, and they sent me things for pressing flowers, and so we used to drive out and gather them.' Mongolia is a vast country – about the size of Mexico – and in those days had only a million inhabitants, and Ann used to drive for thirty or forty kilometres across the steppes, or the wide mountain valleys, without seeing a single soul. 'I'm not a botanist, but I used to press these things, write down where

---

* Soft yellow-skinned apples with translucent flesh. They bruised very easily, which is why they never retained their popularity. Occasionally they can still be found in old cottage gardens.

I found them and all that sort of thing, and the Queen's Messenger used to come out once a fortnight and take them back with him.'

Some of the more familiar aspects of private life back home, such as Sunday worship, were often difficult, or even impossible to keep up abroad. There were often no churches or even a priest to officiate at services (although many of the bigger embassies employed their own chaplains). In Persia both Mary Sheil, who was Catholic, and Elizabeth McNeill, an Episcopalian, felt the lack keenly. For Elizabeth, who endured not only twelve years of isolation there (from 1823 to 1834), but also the deaths of all but one of her young children, the absence of a priest was hard to bear. Although one of their staff read the Sunday service when they were at the embassy, like a true Scot she missed the comfort of a sermon.

Although many women enjoyed the novelty of adapting to their new and exotic surroundings, for others family celebrations, particularly Christmas, were never quite the same. Mary Sheil did her best to keep Christmas as much as possible 'in the English fashion'. Instead of holly she bravely decorated the house with ivy and the few flowers which she had left in her garden, but this was never entirely successful. Diana Shipton, too, felt that all attempts to stage an English Christmas at the consulate in Kashgar were doomed to failure. 'It was not only because the bazaar could offer nothing in the way of presents and decorations,' she explained, 'nor because holly and "Christmas Trees" did not grow, but because the festival meant nothing to the people there and our traditions were unknown to them.'[24]

In such distant and often lonely postings, it was important to maintain both spiritual and emotional ties with home. With their family, friends – and perhaps even their children – thousands of miles away, diplomatic women often turned to their pets. These living, breathing reminders of home were often especially cherished household companions and friends. When Mary Sheil made her epic journey to Persia, as well as her four servants she took her precious dog Crab, a Scotch terrier 'of great sagacity and most exemplary fidelity'. In her memoir she apologizes for referring so often to her dogs, 'but they were so much of companions to me in Persia, I cannot avoid referring to them'.

Mary Fraser, too, was greatly attached to her dogs, including a dachshund, Tippoo Tip, known affectionately as the Brown Ambassador, and a beautiful Gordon setter who came to them off a pirate sealer, 'whose captain, when sent to prison [for murder], made the most careful arrangements for his dog's welfare'. Tippoo Tip was notorious for stealing her servants' clogs and burying them in the garden, and had a particular fondness for sitting on the laps of ladies wearing white satin gowns, believing (cat-like) that they set him off to his best advantage. When Mary acquired another dachshund from England, the Emperor himself came to hear of this wonderful new creature. 'I felt cold for a minute,' she wrote, 'fearing that politeness would require me to place Toney Bones as his Majesty's disposal. But – I did not!'[25]

In Damascus the Burtons, too, had a large menagerie of animals (one of Richard's pet names for Isabel was 'Zoo'), including numerous dogs and a donkey. At one point they also had a pet panther who used to play hide and seek with Isabel in the garden. When he died – poisoned by the frightened local villagers – she held him in her arms like a child, and both she and Richard were inconsolable.

Happily, though, many of these pets, like their owners, survived the vicissitudes of diplomatic life to return to a long and happy retirement in England. A typical tale is told by one contemporary diplomatic spouse, Alex Sutherland, who simply could not bear to part with his dog, Nero, salvaged from a German family in the Ivory Coast. Despite Nero's considerable age he was brought back to England, put through Britain's still stringent quarantine, and installed in the Sutherlands' London flat. 'He was a guard dog, but we let him into the house,' Alex explains, 'and he's been with us ever since. He speaks four languages, and disobeys orders in all of them.'

CHAPTER FIVE

Embassy Life

Setting up home almost anywhere abroad could lead to feelings of isolation and loneliness, but it was only in the very smallest and remotest missions that women were truly alone. As Sir Marcus Cheke pointed out, in many embassies 'the whole Embassy staff forms a sort of family, of which His Majesty's Ambassador is *pater familias.*'[1] British missions abroad, especially the bigger ones, functioned as ready-made communities which represented 'a way of thought, a manner of life', as Marie-Noele Kelly put it, 'that "forever would be England".'[2]

These 'Little Englands' have taken many forms. Large missions, like those widely found today, were relatively rare in the past. In the late 1860s, for example, only five embassies and nineteen legations existed overseas. Junior secretaries and aides – who until 1919 were unsalaried and often related to the incumbent ambassador – were usually accommodated at the embassy itself, there often being no distinction between the ambassador's residence and his office, keeping the same table and living more or less *en famille* with the ambassador and his wife. When Ann Fanshawe accompanied her husband Richard to Spain in 1664 she travelled with a household of nearly sixty people, which included not only her servants but the embassy secretaries, too. The chief secretary is listed as a Mr Lyonel Fanshawe, almost certainly a kinsman of Richard's. 'We settled now our family in order, and tables,' she wrote on first arriving at the embassy in Madrid, La Casa de las Siete Chimeneas. 'Our own consisted of two courses of eight dishes each, and the Steward's of four,' she added with a touch of pride. 'I dine in my morning gown with the *attachés*,' wrote Harriet Granville, from The Hague in 1824, 'who are very merry, obliging, intelligent people.'[3] It was not only inclination, but also the prestige of the ambassador, as the personal representative of his sovereign, which made these little worlds as comfortable and self-contained as possible. His status, and that of his wife, were reinforced by an extended entourage which included not only domestic staff such as valets, chefs and coachmen, but professionals such as physicians, priests, dancing and fencing masters and, in the case of Mary Waddington, who travelled to the new Tsar's coronation in Russia in 1883, even a detective.

In the twentieth century, as missions became larger following the expansion of the Diplomatic Service, they began to resemble not so much a family as an entire community. When Vita Sackville-West went to Tehran in 1926 she found that the other members of staff – the counsellor, the consul, the military attaché and numerous secretaries among them – lived in houses built amongst the plane trees of the legation gardens. Apart from the muddy car which arrived once a fortnight bringing their letters, life there was entirely self-contained. Every morning an old white horse did the rounds, delivering two barrels of drinking water to each house; a sanitary cart came to take away the night soil.

Although Vita was not naturally inclined towards this kind of communal living, she learnt at least to be sanguine about it.

'Compound life means that at 8 am the Consul's son aged ten starts an imitation of a motor horn,' she wrote to Virginia Woolf,

that at 9 am somebody comes and says have I been letting all the water out of the tank; that at 10 am the Military Attaché's wife strolls across and says how are your delphiniums doing; at 11 am Lady Loraine appears and says wasn't it monstrous the way the Russian ambassador's wife cut the Polish Chargé d'Affaires' wife last night at the Palace; that at 12 noon a gun goes off and the muezzins of Teheran set up a wail for prayer; then at 1 pm it is time for luncheon, and Vita hasn't done any work.[4]

Even in our own times, living within a compound is a feature of embassy life (and is sometimes obligatory, for either security or financial reasons) in many countries.* Although the obvious constrictions

---

* There are embassy compounds in Abu Dhabi, Addis Ababa, Bangkok, Dubai, Istanbul, Jedda, Karachi, Kathmandu, New Delhi, Singapore, Tehran and Ulan Bator. Some compound accommodation is available in Accra, Bahrain, Banjul, Cairo, Freetown, Islamabad, Kingston, Kinshasa, Luanda, Muscat, Seoul and Tokyo.

and lack of privacy are offset by the advantages of communal facilities such as a swimming pool, a club, or a shop, it is a way of life which inevitably suits some people better than others. For many women, this strong sense of community remains amongst their happiest memories of diplomatic life. Iona Wright, whose husband Denis was ambassador in Ethiopia in 1960, remembers the long lazy days in the embassy compound in Addis Ababa in her private memoir, *Black Sea Bride*:

> . . . the cool early morning with the mist below the house, over the 'Ladies Mile' . . . Abdullah rushing in with breakfast and spilling the tea into the tea-cosy . . . Denis walking off down the drive to the office after listening to the nine o'clock news . . . and Gabre Mariam, the groom, bringing 'Whisky' to the door, for me to go riding with Betty and Ann. Trotting through the tukuls and out onto the plain, deciding who would gallop and who would go slowly . . . discussing our horses and their ways, and gossiping a bit. Coffee with Ann, or Betty, or with Pamela Parker on the way home, or straight back in order to go shopping.
>
> Drinks in the garden on the swing seat before lunch, with the Peels from the Consul's house next door wandering over to join us, or going over to them where they sat under a big tree and Warbishet their house-boy scurried in and out, with bare feet, carrying tonic water and beer . . . Michele Peel coming back from school in the landrover . . .

And so on through the hot afternoon until evening. Later, if they had a dinner party, their staff would often stay behind to chat for a few minutes after the other guests had left before walking down the hill to their own homes. At night hyenas prowled in the servants' 'village' behind their house, and 'one could see the moon over the giant eucalyptus on the hill.'[5]

In the past it was not unusual for entire embassies to move up into the hills, or down to the sea, in search of cooler weather during the summer months. The summer temperatures in Baghdad could reach 120°F, so Peggy Trevelyan used to take her family up north to the mountains of Kurdistan. As a child growing up in China in the late 1930s Alethea Knatchbull-Hugessen remembers the embassy summer residence on the coast: 'There was a bungalow with, I think, four bedrooms, a dining room and a sitting room, and that was about all. It was an embassy compound, so there were other families there, too. The whole embassy used to migrate there. Telegrams used to come there, and so on. Right by the sea, it was a lovely place.'

'We have encamped at the Mission village of Goolahek, seven miles from town, near the foot of Elboorz,'* wrote Mary Sheil on 29 May 1850. From their camp she looked out over the mountains, the villages and mulberry trees interspersed with a sea of white tents, for the Russian mission was also nearby, as was the Shah himself, at his summer palace at Niaveran. The Sheils' household had numerous sleeping tents, a nursery tent, and Mary had a private sitting-room tent, all enclosed within a high wall of canvas which formed an *anderoon*, or harem.

The logistics for an exodus of this kind, even to the relative informality of the Sheils' tented camp, were complex. It was not a question of packing up a few suitcases, but of moving an entire household, furniture and all. Had Mary Sheil lived fifty years later she might perhaps have taken the advice of Flora Steel, who gave instructions on the minutest details, right down to the number of camels necessary to carry the luggage. For a lady, her three or four children, and an English nurse, the following were required:

1st camel load:	2 large trunks and 2 smaller ones with clothing.
2nd camel load:	One large trunk containing children's clothing. Plate chest. 3 bags. One bonnet box.
3rd camel load:	3 boxes of books. One box containing folding chairs. Light tin box with clothing.
4th camel load:	4 cases for stores. 4 cane chairs. Saddle stand. Mackintosh sheets.
5th camel load:	One chest of drawers. 2 iron cots. A tea table. Pans for washing up.
6th camel load:	Second chest of drawers. Screen. Lamps. Lanterns. Hanging wardrobes.
7th camel load:	2 boxes of house linen. 2 casks with ornaments. Ice pails. Door mats.

* The Elburz Mountains.

8th camel load:	3 casks of crockery. One cask of ornaments. A filter. Purdah bamboos. Tennis poles.
9th camel load:	Hot case. Milk safe. Baby's tub and stand. Sewing machine. Fender and Irons. Water cans and pitchers.
10th camel load:	3 boxes saddlery. Kitchen utensils. Carpets.
11th camel load:	2 boxes drawing room sundries. Servants coats. Iron bath. Cheval glass. Plate basket.

A piano required a cart to itself and should be swung to avoid jolting. In addition, breakables such as lamps and glasses were best carried on mules; 'camels are not patient,' she noted, 'except in poetry.'[6]

But even at Goolahek, at 3,800 feet, Mary still found the heat almost unbearable. 'I am disappointed beyond measure,' she wrote; 'the dust and heat being intolerable, in spite of a stream of water which I had caused to flow through my tent.' There were days when it was impossible to go out until the sun had actually set; 'and even then the ground is reeking with heat,' she wrote despairingly. 'At that hour we mount our horses, and take a slow languid ride about the hills and villages . . . walking is out of the question. Decidedly, Persia is not a country to select as a residence of choice.'[7]

Nothing could have been more different than the experience of Gertrude Bell, the future orientalist and explorer, who as a young girl went to stay with her uncle, Sir Frank Lascelles, one of Colonel Sheil's successors in Tehran. By this time the mission camp, in which most of the legation staff would spend the hottest months of July and August, had been moved much higher into the mountains. 'From our camp in the Lar – greeting!' Gertrude wrote in a letter on Tuesday 9 August 1882. At 8,000 feet the Lar Valley was a very different place to the broiling, dust-choked Goolahek. The legation tents were pitched by a river facing rocky cliffs. Beyond, the narrow valley opened out into a flat grassy plain where nomads had set their black tents, their herds of camels, goats and horses grazing nearby. Gertrude was entranced: 'And such air!' she wrote. 'Cool, cool winds till about eleven in the morning, cold enough to make a cloak necessary, then hot, hot sun . . . at about four in the afternoon clouds blow up and the wind rises a little again; then the water is ready for fishing and we sally forth with rods and with much delight.'[8]

Seventy-five years later the British embassy summer camp at Lar was still in existence, and some of the original tents still in use. These were elaborate constructions, Iona Wright observed during one of her summer visits in the 1960s, 'with heavy bamboo poles, decorated cotton walls with tasseled pockets, small windows with "panes" of knotted blue string, and washing compartments at the back.' The names of the tent-makers in Delhi and Cawnpore were still stamped on the back. 'They are taken up on mule-back at the end of June, and remain, with a servant to guard them and to look after their various occupants, until the end of August, when the nights become too cold for comfort.'[9]

As well as the mountain camp, the legation kept its summer residence at Goolahek, or Gulhak. In place of Mary Sheil's tented harem, there was now an old-style Persian house. 'At the moment we have hardly any furniture,' Iona wrote on her first posting to Persia in 1954, 'as new things are due from England, instead of bringing it all up from Teheran as they used to do . . . Our cat is getting used to it now. We brought him by car, following the Embassy lorry with our suitcases, china, glass, candlesticks, etc. And he howled all the way, with his ears back.'

The house, designed by an Indian architect, had wide balconies and verandas all the way round. 'We lived mostly outside on the balconies really,' she remembers. 'They had these enormous rush blinds – I think in India they made them out of a kind of straw – huge blinds which you pull down when the sun comes out and they throw water on them which makes the air cool. So we always had these blinds down during most of the day, and then we just pulled them up in the evenings.' From the balconies the view was of enormous plane trees and a blue-tiled swimming pool. There were oleanders on the veranda steps, lavender and zinnias in the gardens below. 'There was a blue dome, like a mosque, beyond, but it was really the small temple that was built in the British War Cemetery. We could see this blue turquoise dome at the end of the garden. It was a very pretty view.' At night, in the garden, nightingales sang.

The embassy compound at Gulhak was even bigger than the one in Tehran. Summer life, although informal, followed a regular pattern. 'We used to get up about 8 or 8.30. Then my husband went to the office early because he always came back early – he didn't work in the afternoons. I used to either go out to something – a coffee party or the shops down in the town – or people came up to me. And there were four tennis courts, so we used to play tennis about once a day, usually in the evening.' There was riding every day, too (although the stables did not compare to those in Ethiopia, where an army of syce kept as many as fifteen horses in the embassy stables): 'There were stables there for only about four horses, I think. But I had one there and I used to ride about twice a week with the other wives.'

Pleasure and companionship, while pleasant enough in themselves, were by no means the only reasons behind the relative isolation of compound life. There were times when it was an actual physical necessity. For Mary Fraser, the vast compound which housed the British legation in Peking served as a refuge from a hostile outside world.

Although she later became fascinated by China, and especially by Peking, 'the enormous, ancient, wicked city, all "sand and ruin and gold",' during her first two or three months Mary barely ventured outside the compound walls, except to pay courtesy calls at the other legations. She was acutely aware that the streets outside, for all their squalor and poverty, were 'full of enemies'. After the First Opium War (1839–42), fought to prevent the Chinese Emperor from curbing the illegal but highly lucrative trade in Indian-grown opium, the British had used their victory over the moribund Manchu dynasty to gain extremely advantageous trading rights within Chinese territory. Under the Treaty of Nanking, the treaty ports of Canton, Fuzhou, Amoy, Ningbo and Shanghai were opened to British trade and residence, and the island of Hong Kong ceded to the British. Even before this, the naturally xenophobic Chinese had held out for nearly half a century against giving full diplomatic representation to European countries, but this further concession was eventually forced on them after the Second Opium War (1856–60), which ended with the occupation of Peking. As foreigners, diplomats were detested figures, and none more so than the British.

But the palpable hostility of the Chinese, fuelled by these recent events, was not the only reason for Mary's seclusion. Surrounded by an immense and impregnable wall, the legation was 'a little world in itself'. Once the residence of one of the imperial princes, the British legation lay within sight of the yellow roofs of the Forbidden City itself, from where, Mary wrote, 'grim tales of cruelty floated over the walls to us'. The principal building in the compound was the residence of the envoy and his wife, its wooden beams painted in the Chinese style in the richest peacock greens and blues and golds, its pillars 'of that vivid Asiatic scarlet that neither sun nor rain can pale'. The Big House, as it was known, stretched over several courtyards down the entire length of the compound. Leading from it on one side were the houses of the mounted constables who formed the envoy's escort; on the other were a number of student quarters and the chancery buildings. At the centre of the compound was a large open space occupied by the various bungalows of the other legation staff. At the east end was a substantial arsenal containing a reassuring collection of arms and ammunition,* while the western periphery was given over to the large legation stables, since every member kept at least two or three ponies for private use.

All year round the legation courtyards were filled with flowers and shrubs in porcelain pots. When the winter came their gardeners would replenish them with beautiful blooms mysteriously grown in a series of underground pits. Mary remembered the head gardener, a wizened old man with an extra thumb on each hand, and his pride when he once brought her a bunch of roses from his 'secret catacombs' on Christmas morning.

Another constant source of amusement in the legation was the daily visits of the various dealers in furs, embroideries and other curiosities.

The regulation hour was the one after the twelve o'clock breakfast (we never talked about 'Tiffin' in the North) [Mary wrote] when everybody was likely to be in a good temper and there was leisure for the everlasting bargaining which is as dear as money to the Chinese soul. Coming out of the dining-room we would find our merchants established on the verandah, all their wares artistically spread out for inspection, and rarely did they leave without something large or small having been added to one's collection. Of course, everybody collected; half the time there was nothing else to do; and the only quarrels that occurred in the peaceful com-

---

* Although the worst revolt against foreigners, the Boxer Rebellion, did not occur until 1900, there were numerous minor uprisings and massacres in the provinces during this period, including at least one witnessed by Hugh Fraser.

munity broke out when some too ardent acquirer infringed the law and began bidding for what another was already bargaining for.

Early December was an important turning point in the legation year, for now winter set in. Ice closed the Gulf of Pechili, which would remain frozen until the following spring. There were no more steamers, and although the legation continued to receive precious deliveries of mail (brought overland from Shanghai), for nearly half the year it was almost entirely cut off from the outside world.

Along with the rest of the beleaguered diplomatic community in Peking, the Frasers would set out with vigour to occupy the long winter months between December and April. 'Tiny as the society was,' Mary wrote, 'it kept the ball rolling quite cheerily for four or five months. Everybody dined everybody else quite solemnly till the stores began to run short, for every atom of grocery and all the necessities of a civilised table had to come from Shanghai or – and most people preferred this method – from Europe.' With so little else to occupy their time, there was fierce rivalry between the wives as each tried to surpass the rest with the refinements of their table. Towards Easter, however, when their precious supplies began to run short, Mary noted a change in tone: 'one glanced anxiously at the fast emptying shelves wondering whether one dared give a dinner-party without asparagus, green peas, truffles, *foie gras* or fondants.'

However low their stocks of *foie gras*, the members of the British legation seemed to thrive on this curious cocktail of conditions. Their isolation only served to enhance their sense of solidarity. Like many a 'foreign' wife espoused to a British diplomat, at first the American-born and Italian-raised Mary confessed to feeling far more at ease in the more cosmopolitan company of French or Russian women than in that of her husband's countrywomen. Although the Frasers were, of course, frequently entertained within the wider diplomatic community, Mary soon found that it was considered just as important to socialize within her own legation:

> The funny thing about all this entertaining, was that each family in our Compound, including the bachelor Second Secretaries, felt obliged to invite all the rest just so many times in the season.

Our bungalows were scattered about the place, none more than a stone's throw distant from another, but with the true English instinct for privacy, each was its owners' castle, and we sent each other cards of invitation as gravely as if we had been living in Mayfair.[10]

However odd she found it, Mary had to admit that this very English combination of respect for privacy and formal fraternizing paid off. She found it very laudable that, in all her time in Peking, she could not remember a single quarrel amongst the women.

It is a well-known paradox of diplomatic life that embassies in the smaller, more beleaguered, and sometimes even hostile postings are often the happiest. (Conversely, it is in the biggest embassies, in the more familiar cultures – Paris and Washington would be two examples – that feelings of alienation and loneliness amongst women are often the greatest.) For many women this *esprit de corps* is one of the most precious, if unlooked for, elements of a diplomatic career. Almost exactly 100 years after Mary Fraser's posting to Peking, Sheila Whitney experienced similar feelings of camaraderie amongst the British embassy wives. 'We helped each other out, and we did as much together as we could, because of course there was nothing else to do,' she remembers.

In the best British tradition their activities included not only staging pantomimes and Edwardian evenings, but also sweeping up the plant pots in the embassy compound which, every few months, were smashed by the Red Guards. Often, when their servants were ordered to go on strike, they would go shopping together, too.

We had to get up at six o'clock in the morning and a little bus was provided, and we all went in convoy to the market together. You saw great big slabs of meat – they weren't cut into joints or chops, or anything like that – just great big slabs of meat. Of course, very few of us could speak Chinese, and you'd just have to point and say 'about this much'. And they'd wrap it up, not in a bit of newspaper exactly, but in a bit of coarse sort of sugar paper, and then dump it in our baskets. It could have been anything – donkey!

A shared sense of humour often helped to alleviate some of the tenser situations.

There was one time when the Queen's birthday came in June and all the servants were told that they couldn't help, and so they all disappeared and were all on strike for the whole day. So we had no servants to help with the canapés. So all the wives were asked to go to the residence and help make them. And so we made all the canapés and what have you, but when we looked out of the window we suddenly saw that we had been surrounded by all these millions of Chinese. We could see them all shouting and shaking their fists at us, and Denise Hopson [wife of the chargé d'affaires], who is French, said, 'Oo, I must go and put my knickers on, you never know what might happen!' And we all laughed ... we all thought that was very funny.

The reality, of course, was very far from funny:

They were shouting at us, 'Down with British imperialism, down with British imperialism!' Our chaps were allowed to come into the residence for the party, but only one guest out of the hundreds that we invited was able to get in, and he only managed it because he climbed over the wall from the Indian embassy next door. So we all went into the garden and drank bottles and bottles of champagne, because we only had one guest, and we all got rather tipsy.

As a very young wife in the British embassy in Tokyo in 1941, Pat Gore-Booth was interned by the Japanese. All the British from outside the embassy compound were brought in, and so the two happy newly-weds, who had had the whole house to themselves, quickly found themselves in a mixed household of eight.

Each household was given a ration of dry stores, and there was a marvellous woman, the mother of one of the Japanese language students, who was given the job of organising the food. The Japanese sent in fresh supplies every day: a certain amount of meat, fish and vegetables, and so that was all divided up, and we managed as best we could.

We stayed inside the compound, although the ambassador was given the opportunity to go up to the hills and he did go. But we all said, 'No way, we will sit here and take it.' And we had a high old time. Ninety people: can you imagine it?* Everything was highly organized, real British phlegm coming to the top! We learnt everything from jiu-jitsu and flower arranging to Spanish. And there was a marvellous chap called Himatsinhji, our Indian military attaché, who was the brother of Ranjitsinhji, the famous cricketer, who was a very great sportsman, and he made us all learn how to play squash and keep exercised. And my husband wrote two light operettas (we had one of the two pianos in the compound; the other was in the residence). Altogether we had a very extraordinary time.

On Pat's twenty-first birthday, Paul Gore-Booth was to recall in his memoirs, they celebrated with a nightclub party at their house, which was illuminated briefly with the sign PAZZI's.[11]

The notion of an embassy as a refuge from a hostile world was not only held during times of war or revolution. Traditionally, the mission was free from both the laws and jurisdiction of the host country, and the advantages of extraterritoriality were not confined to its members. Mary Sheil soon found that the Tehran mission, like a religious shrine, was considered a legitimate place of asylum. It was not uncommon for Persians of all classes to take refuge in her house. These were often deserving cases, such as slaves escaping from cruel masters, but even if they were common criminals it was considered bad form to throw them out.

In Algiers Mrs Blanckley regularly gave refuge not only to ship-wrecked or ransomed Britons but also to Jews of any nationality, who during times of political unrest were subject to such frequent pogroms that the Blanckleys' house was 'almost filled with them'. During times of unrest embassies are still frequently sought out by political refugees. In Mozambique in 1975, during the white right-wing backlash after

---

* Thirty people had been living there before.

101

Portugal's decision to hand over power to FRELIMO,* Jennifer Duncan found her house, the British consulate-general, besieged by people seeking asylum. However, none of these influxes could rival the great *bast* (sanctuary) of July–August 1906, again in Tehran, when during the constitutional struggles an estimated 16,000 Tehranis took refuge in the British compound. Life in the city was so paralysed by this mass defection that the Shah was forced to grant the people a constitution and a National Assembly.

Its very real function as a haven or escape from the outside world is one reason, perhaps, that the notion of an embassy as a 'family' has proved so persistent. 'Going abroad is not like going to another planet; abroad is very much like home,' Lady Henderson, a former ambassadress to both Paris and Washington, was to write encouragingly as late as 1976. 'An Embassy is a family, in some ways rather an old-fashioned family. But you will find that if and when you need help, as in a family you will always find someone who will help you.'[12]

In more peaceful times the embassy continued to be something of a hermetic world, but an increased formality replaced the jolly camaraderie described by Sheila Whitney and Pat Gore-Booth. 'Helping at a Residence party really means doing what you would do if your parents gave a party,' Mary Henderson was to exhort, not a little ingenuously; but it is extremely unlikely that any of the 'junior wives' ever saw it in quite this way. Nor were they really encouraged to. In almost all embassies, right up until the present day, a rigid etiquette was observed which centred largely on the 'extraordinary and plenipotentiary' person of the ambassador, the paterfamilias himself, and his wife. Although this was largely, as Marcus Cheke explains, 'to exalt his Ambassador and Ambassadress in the eyes of their foreign colleagues', within the embassy itself it was an equally effective means of maintaining the status quo.

Marcus Cheke's 1949 handbook was expressly directed at the more junior – and increasingly middle-class – diplomatic officers and their wives who, at the outset of their careers, would have had little or no knowledge of these arcane diplomatic practices. Its tone was kindly, but stern. 'An invitation to the British Embassy† must be regarded as

* Frente de Libertação de Moçambique – the Mozambique Liberation Front.
† In this context, the ambassador's residence.

a Command . . . as Mr and Mrs Bull must realize, they are not being invited primarily because the Ambassador and Lady Sealingwax* like their company or their conversation; they are being invited to assist the Ambassador and Lady Sealingwax in the performance of their social functions.' With this rather dampening thought, Mr and Mrs Bull were further instructed that illness, absence or private mourning were the only legitimate reasons for ever refusing an embassy invitation. Furthermore, they were always to arrive at the residence five minutes† before the hour at which the function officially began, because 'this will enable Lady Sealingwax to welcome them before her attention is concentrated on more important guests'.

Unimportant and uninspiring, Mr and Mrs Bull were to be left under no illusions that they had been invited to Lady Sealingwax's party to enjoy themselves, either. They were not to spend all evening 'glued to each other's sides', or even talking to other members of the embassy staff, yet it was also incumbent upon them 'to avoid standing in gloomy and solitary silence' (although since one of their chief duties was 'to be affable to bores' this must, at times, have been rather a tall order). Instead, they were to consider themselves on duty at all times. Their job was to take the arriving guests off Lady Sealingwax's hands, and to introduce guests to each other, while being careful to do so only amongst those of a corresponding rank. Mrs Bull, in particular, 'should not . . . unless specifically asked to do so, introduce to each other persons of exalted rank'. She should keep an eye out for her ambassadress at all times to see if she needed any assistance.

Even before the current system, which clearly distinguishes the Foreign Office grades which carry representational status and obligations (usually from third secretary upwards) from those that do not (secretarial, clerical and junior administrative staff), diplomatic wives usually had a clear understanding of what their social life was really about: it was simply part of a wider mandate – that of representing one's country abroad

To a young wife, newly entering the embassy world, it must have

---

* These names were, of course, fictitious, as was the country 'Mauretania', which Cheke used as his example country – not to be confused with the West African Republic of Mauritania.
† This was a precise time, which applied to lunches and dinners. For a larger reception it was usual for the staff to arrive ten minutes before.

seemed as if even the most apparently straightforward actions were potential breaches of etiquette. At lunch or dinner parties she had to take great care not to walk out of the door in front of other people: 'The Ambassadress will be leading the way with the most important lady present, and Mrs Bull must go behind all the other ladies.' Even if she was dropping with fatigue, poor Mrs Bull could not go home until the very last guest had left. This last was most important for, as Marcus Cheke pointed out severely, 'it is a grave discourtesy to foreigners to leave a luncheon or dinner party before them. To a foreign Ambassadress, or the wife of an eminent Mauretanian official, it is practically an insult.'

Embassy etiquette, as the baffled Mrs John Bull would soon discover, extended beyond these purely social occasions. If either of the Bulls were offered a lift by the ambassador in his car, they had to make sure they sat on the left-hand seat, with their 'Chief' – who should always be allowed to enter the car first – on their right. When they were dropped at their destination the correct procedure was to wait respectfully on the pavement for the car to move off before turning away. They should never, of their own accord, light a cigarette when in the ambassador's company; should always stand up when he entered the room; and in public only ever refer to him respectfully as 'my Ambassador', 'His Excellency', or, at an informal pinch, 'Sir Henry'.[13]

In 1883 Mary Waddington claimed that she would miss the 'family life' of the Moscow embassy, although nothing could have been less cosy than the rigid formality she and her husband encountered on their return home each evening. 'Our *rentrée* to the Embassy is most amusing,' she wrote, 'the whole mission precedes us, and when we arrive we find them ranged in a semi-circle at the foot of the staircase, waiting to receive us. Richard* says he never understood the gulf that separates an Ambassador Extraordinary from ordinary mortals until he accompanied his brother to Moscow.'[14]

Until the very latter part of this century, formality in almost every situation was the order of the day, not only towards the ambassador and his wife, but with almost everyone of higher rank. In 1947, when Masha Williams first arrived in Baghdad, she was taken by one of her husband's colleagues to the Alwiya, the main club for diplomats and

---

* Mary's brother-in-law.

western expatriates. With a strict regard to protocol he would not introduce Masha to any of the other wives there because she had not yet paid her courtesy calls on the 'embassy ladies'.

Marcus Cheke would have given him top marks. When faced with two alternatives, 'one easy but appearing somewhat overfamiliar, the other respectful but appearing somewhat pompous or old-fashioned', Cheke strenuously advised plumping for the latter. 'If his wife is hesitating whether to appear at the beach picnic of the Counsellor's wife (who has been most friendly to her) with or without stockings,' ran what was to become one of his most famous adages, 'let her (if she is unable to telephone and ask) wear stockings.'

Things have come a long way since the days of Marcus Cheke. Pat Gore-Booth was amazed at the lack of formality when she visited her daughter-in-law Mary, who also became a British ambassadress, at the embassy compound in Saudi Arabia. 'There was much more cosiness, in a way,' she found, 'but staffs are so enormous now that you can't get in among them so easily.' But even in our own less formal times a surprising amount of the traditional embassy etiquette remains in place. 'I don't know what it is about the Foreign Office and tradition,' says one puzzled present-day 'Mrs John Bull'. 'I never got used to calling the ambassador "Ambassador". He was a perfectly normal person – all the ambassadors are really very nice people – and I just wanted to refer to this person by his name. I never really got used to that. I mean, you sort of get into the habit, but it still strikes me as odd. It's still very hierarchical, I suppose, the Foreign Office.'

Although some women found it hard to bend to the traditions and hierarchies of embassy life, conformity brought its own rewards. Not least of these was the feeling that they had membership to an exclusive club. Both old-fashioned social snobbery and, in the colonial past especially, racism have of course played their part in generating embassy exclusiveness; but so too has a perfectly legitimate desire to belong.

Despite the privileged access to many aspects of the host country, the sense of being perpetually 'foreign' or 'alien' could be both wearying and demoralizing. 'One of the things you get in the Foreign Office is this curious position of being an outsider and an insider at the same time,' says one young, liberal-minded wife, recently returned from her first posting abroad. The most successful, and happiest diplomatic wives have been those who instinctively understood and made the most of this ambivalence. As a member of an embassy, she points out, 'you're an insider in a small group of other British people which, if you need it, gives you that sense of belonging, and a place to go back to when you can't face being an outsider any longer.'

But membership of the embassy 'club' is not automatic. Those who, for whatever reasons, feel excluded can find it a bitter experience. 'Our family do not belong to the "jolly good show, dump your kid at boarding school brigade",' says one deeply disenchanted diplomatic daughter. 'My mother does not, and indeed, has not for the last fifteen years, followed my father around the world acting out the role of the do gooder wife who makes the tea and cakes while being an active member of the bridge club.' Women who dared to break with convention ran the risk of never being truly accepted into embassy circles; their families were particularly vulnerable:

It didn't matter where we went: Africa, Asia. People in the service would always look down on us and patronize us for going against tradition. My brother and I did not converse in the public school tones one expected of diplomatic children ... We didn't go to boarding school, we didn't have that common reclusive manner or that in-built feeling that we were superior to children who did not belong in diplomatic circles.

By no means all embassies functioned as one big happy family. Mary Fraser's experience in Peking was unusual: very few British missions have remained entirely immune from snobbery and petty jealousies. In-fighting between the different branches of an embassy – the chancery, consulate and commercial sections – was only too easily duplicated amongst the wives. The predicament of junior wives was noted by Masha Williams in Baghdad: 'They're miserable. They're lonely. They drink too much,' remarked Masha's friend Simone, herself the wife of one of the embassy clerks. 'They want to have a good time but they don't know where to turn, and they blame their husbands. There'll be a few divorces very soon.' Masha could well believe it: 'Alone all day, unable to speak to the locals, and their husbands' salaries not sufficient to join any club. I wished I could help but "No

busy-bodying," Alan insisted. "We've enough on our hands."'
Although Masha invited them to join her sewing circle, she was not
surprised when they did not turn up as 'they would not have been
welcomed by the other women'.[15]

No matter what internal rivalries or snobberies might beset a mission,
as far as the outside world was concerned it presented a united front.
Through arctic winds, desert storms and tropical rains, in hundreds
of embassies all around the world, these little gardens of Englishness
continue to be cultivated. Certain key events in the embassy calendar
have persisted at British missions for hundreds of years: the children's
Christmas party, the St Andrew's Day dinner, the Queen's (or King's)
Birthday Party. 'Oh! how familiar,' my mother wrote to me when she
first read Mary Fraser's description of the children's Christmas party
in Tokyo in 1889; 'I could have written this myself.'

The Queen (or King's) birthday remains the most important
national celebration of the year. Recently the QBP, as it is known, has
usually taken the form of a large cocktail party or reception, but at
the consulate in Algiers Elizabeth Blanckley gave a great dinner and
ball for eighty-four guests to mark the birthday of George III, making
up fifty spare beds at her house for the occasion. More unusually, to
celebrate Queen Victoria's birthday Mary Sheil gave a banquet for all
the beggars in Tehran. 'Nothing could exceed the confusion and
contention and clamour for admittance,' she wrote afterwards. The
Persians estimated that 7,000 men and women had attended; the English, more conservatively, 3,500. Whatever the figure, the uproar was
so great that the legation was like 'a town taken by assault'. In Ecuador
in 1978 even my mother's dog, a fat Cairn terrier called Joshua, was
roped in to do his bit:

Mariana [the cook] did all the food which was jolly good and
appreciated by everyone including especially Josh who had a whale
of a time hoovering up all the bits and pieces [she wrote in a letter
to my brother Andrew]. At one point a whole tray of cocktail
goodies fell to the floor – and Josh was right there. He would have
scoffed the lot if Pat Houlburg, my doggy friend, who knows about
Josh's weight problem, hadn't been there to restrain him! He had
a red carnation tied to his collar and looked very smart.

At Christmas especially these rituals mirror the familiar ones of home in every possible way. Plum puddings are boiled, turkeys are basted, crackers are pulled; mince pies and mulled wine are produced for carol concerts around the residence Christmas tree. At other times of the year, too, an essential Britishness is maintained: in Kabul in 1966 Betty de la Mare set up a Scottish dancing group; in 1969 the wives in Islamabad organized cricket matches, swimming galas and a marionette play of *Treasure Island* for their children during the long, hot school holidays; Peggy Trevelyan remembers how, in Moscow during the 1950s, the embassy tennis court was flooded in winter and used for skating parties; my mother, stationed in Chile in the 1980s, organized croquet matches in her garden; while in 1951, at the British consulate in Meshed, Maureen Tweedy kept up the tradition of Sunday evening tennis parties. 'The standard of play was not high,' she confessed, 'but the tea we gave was without rival, thanks to our wonderful Goanese cook Victor. All his considerable skill was put into a great variety of sandwiches, scones and cakes. Set out on the green lawn under the peach and apricot trees, it was a thoroughly English tea except for the brightly burnished samovars.'[16]

Even in the most remote posts, visible emblems of Britishness abound: Union Jacks, lions and unicorns, the posters in chancery lobbies all round the world of Big Ben, Beefeaters and Buckingham Palace Guards in their red coats and bearskins. Portraits and photographs of the royal family look down from embassy walls: Peggy Trevelyan remembers with the greatest affection an old portrait of George V which still hung at the residence in Moscow in the early 1960s. 'The Russians always used to come in and say, why do you have a picture of our Czar? The similarity was quite extraordinary. And that was a great subject of conversation always, especially at rather tricky dinner parties.'

To the disenchanted, an embassy may seem like an exclusive and snobbish club, keeping all outsiders at arm's length, but a large part of its *raison d'être* has always been to disseminate as widely as possible the idea of Britain and British culture. Although it must have been largely irrelevant to the beleaguered wives who survived the punishing Mongolian winters on powdered eggs and mutton fat in Ulan Bator, for certain protocol purposes British missions abroad were – and still are – considered to be part of the Court of St James. 'We, believe it or not,' my mother wrote home from Madrid in August 1968, 'have gone into court mourning. Isn't it dreadfully sad about Princess Marina? It was all so sudden. We are officially supposed to refuse invitations all this week. Our flag flies at half mast and J goes round in a black tie.'

My two brothers and I learnt to 'fly the flag' from an early age. We would stand still when the National Anthem was played, read lessons at the embassy carol service, and when my father was appointed consul-general in Bilbao we felt proud to fly the Union Jack on our car. When we moved to Singapore in the late 1960s, the ground-breaking BBC documentary on the royal family was much shown, as it was in practically every British embassy, high commission and consulate. We watched with bated breath, along with the rest of the world, as Prince Philip barbequed the royal sausages. Twenty years later videos of the royal wedding exerted a similar fascination.

Not all screenings of British life have met with such success. Diana Shipton and her husband Eric once requested some suitable films on British cultural life from the Indian government. The great day arrived and a large crowd of Turkis gathered expectantly at the Kashgar consulate's outdoor volley ball court – accompanied, to Diana's horror, by an equally large carnival crowd of traders hawking bread, sweets and fruit – only to find themselves obliged to sit through a long documentary on the coconut and its by-products. Afterwards, as the puzzled audience filed out, one man was heard commenting on the extraordinary things they could do with melons in India.

Charity work, too, was endemic to embassy life. Reading through the back copies of the BDSA magazines,* I see that fêtes, coffee mornings and bring-and-buy sales, bridge afternoons and bazaars, raffles and Remembrance Day services, charity events of every conceivable hue, have been held beneath the British flag from Toronto to Tehran. 'The days of the charity bazaar are over,' Catherine Young, a former chairman of the BDSA, is anxious to assert. 'People would much rather

* The first one was issued in July 1960 as the *Foreign Service Wives Association Newsletter*. In 1965 the association was merged with the Commonwealth Relations Office Wives Society to form the Diplomatic Service Wives Association (DSWA). In 1991 the DSWA changed its name again to the British Diplomatic Spouses Association (BDSA). In 1998 it changed its name a fourth time to the Diplomatic Service Families Association (DSFA).

give money instead of getting the wives to knit revolting little things that nobody wants any more.' But even in the 1990s, in amongst the advertisements for courses on personal safety and stress management, and articles with arcane titles – 'Cake and Shrapnel for Tea' was one offering from a wife in Beirut – the impression, overwhelmingly, is of Middle England on the move.

Whatever their family commitments or other personal interests, wives were expected to participate. When my mother first arrived in Chile, protocol required that as the new British ambassadress she should call on the wife of the head of state, who at that time was the military dictator General Pinochet. The conversation, like the visit itself, was formal, and could be relied on to follow a certain well-worn pattern.

I came to the conclusion that they never want any real answers [she wrote a touch wearily in one of her letters home]. 'What was I going to do with my time here?' I stupidly answered by talking about travelling about the country, their wild flowers, birds, etc. to see a look of horror on their faces. What they wanted to know was what charitable form my Lady Muck line was to be. Was it *defectos* [the handicapped], delinquents, oldies or orphans? I had obviously been away from the game too long and forgotten what my purpose in life was.

In Chile at that time the list of charities espoused by the British embassy was typical. It included the British Legion, the Salvation Army, an old people's home and one 'house' of an orphanage for teenage girls. With the exception of the orphanage all these had strong British links, but the embassy wives would often raise money for local causes on other occasions as well – after national disasters, for example, such as the 1985 earthquake, which reached seven on the Richter scale and devastated large parts of Santiago. As the ambassadress, my mother was responsible for liaising with the other embassies, with varying degrees of success.

There is some splendid quarrelling going on between some of the ambassadresses who are now all vying with each other in the earthquake victims fundraising stakes [she wrote in secret amusement to my grandmother in April that year]. The Europeans are organising a joint concert in one of the old – and damaged – churches. I went to their final committee meeting this morning. Holland isn't talking to Norway, Spain's gone off to Madrid right when there's work to do. Germany won't do anything, and Switzerland's fed up with being a mediator!

On the whole, charity work which took place within the confines of the mission itself was easier to control. Indeed, once a dedicated team of British embassy wives had put one of their projects in motion, it would move with the inexorability of an Exocet missile, impervious to all obstacles in its way. Not even a revolution could put off the embassy fête organized by Maureen Tweedy in Seoul. 'As revolutions go it could, I suppose, have been a great deal worse,' she wrote of the April 1960 uprising which put an end to the regime of President Syngman Rhee. All the same, 500 Korean students were killed, the police lost control, and the Tweedys caught sight of the constable from their own guardroom escaping out of a window dressed in civilian clothes. In the middle of this, understandably concerned about the fate of her fête, Maureen decided, 'as in the blitz', that it would be 'business as usual'.

A week later, 'the band of the Korean Navy blaring away gaily on the verandah of Number One House', the public were let into the embassy compound to sample the delights of Ye Olde Bottle Stalle, the tombola, bingo, a judo display, fortune tellers and, of course, a White Elephant stall. All this was set up within sight of the Duk Soo Palace, temporarily occupied by thousands of steel-helmeted troops who peered over the wall 'lost in wonder at the antics of the foreigners and enjoying every minute of it'.[17]

CHAPTER SIX

Ambassadresses

Literature has not been kind to ambassadresses. One of Britain's most famous, Lady Diana Cooper, is lampooned in Nancy Mitford's *Don't Tell Alfred* as Lady Leone – the beautiful ambassadress to Paris who is so driven off her rocker at the prospect of leaving her embassy that she turns back at the Gare du Nord, still clutching her farewell bouquets, and holes up in the embassy entresol. Unbeknown to the new ambassadress, Fanny Wincham, it soon becomes the fashion to visit her there. Society ladies, bearing gifts of gramophone records and baskets of food, stream through the courtyard to her hideout, where she lies 'like a beautiful stag dying in the forest', firmly refusing to budge.

When she is not being carried off screaming from her embassy, the ambassadress appears as the other most favoured stereotype, that of a Dragon Empress terrorizing 'her' embassy wives into producing 1,000 meatballs for the forthcoming QBP (Queen's birthday party). In William Boyd's *A Good Man in Africa*, the high commissioner's wife, Chloe Fanshawe, forces Morgan Leafy to dress up as Santa for the children's Christmas party. Mrs Fanshawe 'had a chest like an opera singer, a single wedge of heavily trussed and boned undergarmentry from which the rest of her body tapered gradually . . .' Her hair is held immovably by 'fearsomely strong lacquer'; her only other cosmetic tool being scarlet lipstick, 'which only served to emphasise the thinness of her lips'.

When it comes to real ambassadresses, of course, fact is pleasingly stranger than fiction. The delightfully dotty Lady Cumming Bruce, who kept a child's chamber pot in her hat box, was only one of many such ambassadresses. My mother remembers her with affection. 'She was very relaxed. The only thing we junior wives had to do was occasionally remind her to change her shoes. She once came downstairs for a big reception still wearing her bedroom slippers.'

Conscious of their role at the very pinnacle of the embassy hierarchy, not all heads of mission's wives were so laid back. In Singapore, the High Commissioner's wife was 'a terrible bully'. 'She used to refer to us as "her wives",' my mother recalls. 'Her great passion in life was *ikebana* [Japanese flower arranging] at which she was a great expert. None of us had the slightest interest in it, but we had to turn up to the classes she gave anyway, otherwise it was bad form. It was rather like being back at school. We'd sit in the back row being naughty.'

Stories of this nature are as old as the profession itself. In the Paris embassy in the 1930s Lady Clerk was, unlike her rather formal husband, Sir George,* of a bohemian turn of mind. Instead of the hot house orchids or carnations that were usual at grand diplomatic functions, she would strew the dinner tables with ivy, creating a sort of bistro effect. Once she forced an astonished crowd of Parisian aristocrats to play musical chairs. Jacques Février, one of Europe's most eminent pianists, was instructed to play, and to stop when she hit him.

The Paris embassy seems to have been a particularly rich source of dotty British ambassadresses. In addition to Lady Clerk there was Lady Bertie, who had an unsuitable fondness for poker, and Lady Tyrell, who spent most of her time up a tree in the embassy gardens, where she was engaged in writing a history of the world beginning with the year 2000 BC. When she was wanted her husband would send a footman to fetch her by whistling below. The French, who were impressed by the excellence of her brain, thought rather less of her powers as a hostess. She is said to have spent a whole evening talking to Lord Birkenhead, then Secretary of State for India, under the impression that he was the Turkish ambassador.

Even if they cannot put a name to her, most diplomatic wives will recognize the type. People knew about them, and talked about them, not because ambassadresses were particularly predisposed to be dotty

---

* His private life was apparently not quite so formal, as he was said to have had a fondness for nightclubs. It is alleged that Queen Mary once said to the King: 'They tell me that Sir George Clerk goes to nightclubs.' To which the monarch replied, 'Nonsense, my dear. It cannot be true. It's just as if you and I went to nightclubs.' Quoted in Cynthia Gladwyn, *The Paris Embassy*.

(although some might dispute this), but because they were prominent people of whom a very particular role was expected; their 'eccentricities' were often vastly magnified by the public lives they led. Masha Williams's husband had a little book in which he lovingly recorded the sayings of their ambassadress to Iraq, Lady Mack. ('Such charming people,' she is alleged to have said of her successors in Vienna, 'we never saw them at all.')

The transition from plain embassy wife to ambassador's wife, all diplomatic women are agreed, is enormous. The role of an ambassadress is unique. While all diplomatic wives have to cope with the problems of leaving friends and family – sometimes young children and ageing parents – and setting up home on the other side of the world, for an ambassador's wife there is the added strain and isolation of her status, and a greatly increased social life. 'You are the person who is seen to be "Mrs Britain",' explained Virginia Crowe, whose husband was ambassador in Vienna, 'so you are always on show.'

As the new British ambassadress in Chile just after the Falklands War in 1982, my mother found her public persona something of a mixed blessing. She wrote to me shortly after her arrival in June that year:

> Being English is a great positive advantage here, and being the British Ambassador even better. Our progress in a wheeled chair at the German clinic where I was taken after my rather ignominious accident [a dislocated toe] was royal ... 'It is a pleasure to do something for you after what you have done for us' says the doctor! And this is the sentiment and feeling one gets generally here. The hairdresser couldn't wait to establish my identity before a crowd surrounded me congratulating me on England's stand, etc. etc. I could have done without this as she wasn't making too much of a success with my hair as it was and after that it was even worse.

If the ambassadress herself was always on show (even at the hairdresser's), so was her house. Some of Britain's residences abroad are famous buildings – the Lutyens-designed house in Washington, and the palace on the Faubourg Saint-Honoré in Paris, bought by the

Duke of Wellington from Napoleon's sister, Pauline Borghese, after Waterloo, are two examples – but not all ambassadresses are compensated by living in such beautiful and expensive embassies. Elisabeth Young, whose husband was sent to open a new mission in Azerbaijan in the early 1980s, found herself living in a suite of three rooms in what was formerly an Intourist hotel, shared between the French, Pakistani and Iranian ambassadors. 'It's amazing,' she remembers cheerfully, 'what you can do with a microwave oven and a Baby Belling under the hall table.'

Whatever the conditions, embassy residences are not just places where ambassadors live; they are public buildings, often quite large ones, which must function smoothly at all times – not unlike discreet but extremely busy hotels. Visiting businessmen, MPs and ministers are not unknown to treat them as such. My mother was once enraged by one of her house guests, an MP, who informed her that breakfast the next day would be a working one, and that her presence was not required. There are tales, too, of people leaving their shoes outside the door to be cleaned, as if they were staying at the Hilton or the Hyatt. The unpaid manageress of this hotel – as well as its housekeeper, florist, book-keeper and, occasionally, cook – is the ambassadress. 'The Americans have a classic expression for it,' Virginia Crowe explains; 'a "twofer". As a couple we come as two for the price of one.'

In the past ambassadors and their wives lived in extraordinary style. In Constantinople the young Mary Elgin noted that when travelling through the city she had a suite of eight janissaries, four footmen and a dragoman who marched in state before her. Nearly a hundred years earlier her predecessor, the more world-weary Lady Mary Wortley Montagu, often found the formality of her position wearying. Not only the English, she complained, but quantities of Greeks, French and Italians 'make their court to me from morning till night'. The young French ambassadress of the time became a great friend of hers, but even a simple friendship was not without its difficulties:

her conversation would be a great relief to me if I could persuade her to live without those forms and ceremonies that make life formal and tiresome. But she is so delighted with her guards, her twenty-four footmen, gentlemen ushers etc., that she would rather die than make me a visit without them, not to reckon a coachful of attending damsels y'cleped maids of honour. What vexes me is that as long as she will visit with this troublesome equipage I am obliged to do the same.

As a twentieth-century ambassadress, my mother also became used to travelling with an entourage. In 1983, when she and my father spent two days visiting the Lauca National Park in the remotest corner of northern Chile, they were accompanied by a television reporter and 'two very nice camera men, recording our every sneeze'. The pomp and circumstance surrounding their visit, however, were in keeping with an altogether different set of expectations. On their arrival, tired and dusty, in the village of Putre, they were immediately summoned to an official welcome by the governor of the district, an army colonel. In front of the assembled village, speeches were made and commemorative plaques were presented. 'Then the school children danced for us,' my mother wrote home to my grandmother afterwards, 'and finally a group of a dozen immensely old, gnarled Indian grannies and granddads, all with flower-decked hats, came on the scene to sing and dance a local fertility dance. They sang a reedy, cracked, high-pitched chant about potatoes etc., and to cap it all John and I were "invited" to join in.'

At whatever end of the spectrum an ambassadress might find herself, hers was a position of enormous privilege. There were times when she seemed to experience life in an altogether different stratosphere to that of ordinary mortals. At the coronation of Tsar Alexander III Mary Waddington was quite serious when she wondered if 'the sight of all this splendour will destroy my mental equilibrium'. 'I think that I shall never again see anything like the dinner of the Emperor and Empress on the day of the coronation,' she wrote from Moscow. 'It looked exactly like some old medieval picture as they sat there in their robes and crowns in that old dark-vaulted room of the old palace . . . all the modern life and luxury grafted upon that old half-Eastern, half-barbaric world.'[1]

Meetings with royalty, both abroad and at home, are moments which are particularly precious to some. Present-day heads of mission and their wives are given an audience with the queen at the beginning and end of each posting. One of Pat Gore-Booth's most treasured memories is of dining *à quatre* with the Queen and Prince Philip on the

Queen's state visit to India in 1961. For Ann Hibbert, a former ambassadress to Paris, it was dancing with the Prince of Wales. But Beryl Smedley, wife of the high commissioner to Ghana, actually *became* a queen herself. Visiting a rural area of the country in 1966, the Smedleys were amazed by a request to 'enstool' Beryl as an honorary queen mother.

These honours and privileges, however, are earned at a price. Even in a medium-sized embassy the job of ambassadress can be an all-consuming one, requiring enormous reserves of energy and good will. 'I do sometimes get the feeling of being like the Ambassadress in *Don't Tell Alfred*,' my mother wrote to my grandmother, describing what was, for her, a fairly average day:

> On Easter Monday I had over 60 Anglo-Chilean women here playing bridge. The only problem is that the contract bridge players can't bear to wait until 6 o'clock for their tea and the duplicate lot don't finish before. So, a good deal of organisation has to go on. In the middle of all this, John and Andrew [my youngest brother] arrived back from Juan Fernandez, clasping in their hands a sack containing 24 lobsters, needing instant freezing, and also at the same time the two backpackers arrived – charming polite Etonians, but nevertheless not exactly in tone with the bridge ladies . . .

For an ambassadress engaged in running one of the bigger embassies, however, this 'Day in the Life of . . .' probably seems like a holiday. In Paris in 1992 Lady Fergusson officially entertained 238 house-guests, gave tea or coffee to 593 people, lunch or dinner to 3,492 people, and invited a further 3,447 to either drinks or a reception (this number was down by 1,000 on the previous year since, following the Queen's state visit that summer, they did not hold the usual Queen's Birthday Party).[*2] In the same year, Maria Fairweather's first at the Villa Volkonsky, the British residence in Rome, she oversaw a total of 380 house-guests and entertained a further 5,000. Between September and

* I am grateful to Ruth Dudley Edwards for the figures on the Paris embassy, which are quoted in her book *True Brits*. Maria Fairweather supplied the figures for Rome.

Christmas that autumn the Fairweathers spent only two nights on their own. 'By the end,' Maria admits, 'I was almost crying with fatigue.'

It was a feeling which many ambassadresses, 'those poor drudges of society', as Countess Granville once called them, will recognize. Their schedules could be punishing. After only six weeks in Russia Mary Waddington complained that she should never do as a permanent ambassadress, since just six weeks of diplomatic functions had left her both physically and mentally exhausted. For the coronation, she learnt, the entire diplomatic corps was expected to stand throughout the ceremony, a total of three and a half hours. 'I believe the Russian Court never sits down except at meals,' she wrote despairingly.

'You have no idea how tiring last night was,' wrote an exhausted Harriet Granville in a similar vein to her sister in 1825. 'A ball at the other end of Paris, entirely full of English Catholic bulls, at Lady Constable's . . . Before it I went to two *soirées*. We dine with Mme de Raguse to meet Leopold,* and there is another ball at Mrs Mitchell's . . . I pine for Lent exactly in proportion as the *élégantes*† dread it,' she added with feeling a few days later. 'The height of my earthly aspirations is to be allowed to abstain from pleasure.'[3]

Clever, witty, and a letter-writer of extraordinary brilliance, Harriet Cavendish was born in 1785, the second of the fifth duke of Devonshire's three children. Her mother was the celebrated Georgiana, Duchess of Devonshire. According to her first cousin, Charles Greville, 'Lady Granville had a great deal of genial humour, strong feelings, enthusiasm, delicacy, refinement, good taste, naiveté which just misses being affectation, and a bonhomie which extends to all around her.'[4] It appears to be a blueprint for the perfect ambassadress. In fact, few women have taken to their role with greater reluctance.

Although she was born into the very heart of the English aristocracy, Harriet's upbringing in the eccentric, amoral world of Devonshire House was a curiously inappropriate training ground for the brittle sophistication and formality which she would later encounter in Paris

---

* Leopold of Coburg, married to Princess Charlotte, and later first king of the Belgians.
† The principal society hostesses.

society. The habitués of her childhood world lived a life governed almost entirely by their own rules. The ladies often did not rise until two in the afternoon and did not separate until dawn. They spoke to each other in their own language, a kind of baby talk, corresponding with endless little notes: 'Dearest one, how does 'oo do? ... As 'oo do, so does poor little I . . .'[5] When Harriet was married in 1809, it was to a man who for many years had been the lover of her aunt, Lady Bessborough. Despite his gambling and his bad handwriting (Canning, the Foreign Secretary, once had to send a special messenger to Paris to find out if he had written Madras or Madrid in one of his ambassadorial dispatches), Charles Granville, it was once said, 'could make a barren desert smile'.[6] Harriet, who was conspicuously plain, adored him, adopting his two illegitimate children without a murmur.

By 1824, when Granville was first posted abroad, Harriet was thirty-nine, the devoted mother of five children. With her family and friends around her, her life was as comfortable and settled as she could wish. As for many a diplomat's wife both before and after her, leaving these certainties was unexpectedly terrible. 'We are just setting out, my beloved sister,' she wrote to her eldest sibling, Lady Morpeth. 'I do not know how my nerves could have stood parting with you.'

Although Canning had always intended Granville for the Paris embassy, where he was to become one of the first British ambassadors to the newly restored Bourbon court after Napoleon's final defeat at Waterloo in 1815, he decided to send him to The Hague first. Having settled in quite comfortably to the less exacting life of ambassadress in Holland, Harriet was filled with consternation at the news of their move to Paris only a few months later. In a letter to her brother, the Duke of Devonshire, in June 1824, she confessed to 'a selfish fear of any change of a place and a life I like so much, a dread of all the worries and duties of Paris, late hours, *grande parure*, visits, presentation, all my favourite aversions'. In short, the life of an ambassadress. For all her blue blood, Harriet was simply not cut out for the diplomatic life, let alone for the special rigours of the Paris embassy. She was, by her own admission, 'quite insensible' of the *éclat* of being ambassadress there. It was quite simply too glittering, too worldly, too superficial. She could not take it seriously enough.

Four months later Harriet was still trying valiantly to talk herself into some enthusiasm for it. There were compensations. She was delighted by the plans of the embassy, which had by now reached her ('It seems an incomparable one'); by the boxes Granville had secured for her at the French Opera, the Italian Opera and the Théâtre Français; by the fact that there would be English doctors there. But still she could not convince herself. 'I patted myself on the back and said: "It is a very fine thing to be an ambassadress,"' she told Lady Morpeth, her principal confidante, in October that same year. 'All this without the slightest effect, and I plunged back into "what if the calomel* should operate too much" with redoubled intenseness. This is foolish, unaccountable, and I combat it, but so it is.' The move itself was a trauma too: after their life of indolence and enjoyment 'it is like the waking of a doormouse, which I have always thought must be uncommonly distressing'.

The Hague, with its relaxed, almost provincial ways, had suited her far better. After three days of 'grand representation' when she first arrived, with 'all Holland pouring in', life soon resumed an air of normality and she could sink into the comfortably domestic routine which she enjoyed best. She drove to the sea and went for walks on the beach with her children. In the evenings they had sing-songs round the drawing-room fire. To her relief there was no custom of morning visits at The Hague, a subject on which she became, by her own admission, 'Quixotic'. 'There is no saying what is gained by lopping them off,' she wrote. 'Time in bushels, repose ditto, coming quite fresh and alive into the gaiety of the evening.' Of the two hundred visits she paid on her arrival, she was admitted only seven times. 'We may have whole hours to ourselves without offending anyone,' she wrote, almost incredulously. In Paris, she knew, there would be no such reprieve.

For a start, Paris was full of the French. In a letter, prudently marked 'Private and Confidential', written to Lady Morpeth shortly after her arrival in December, she complained that

> French people are – what shall I say? – what I don't like, as most comprehensive. They now show themselves to me at their best ... but there is a fonds of ill-breeding, insolence, conceit, and pretension *qui se fait jouer* all through their countenances, manners and attentions. They are one and all factitious, and were

* Mercurous chloride, used as a purgative.

I young, *désoeuvrée*, and seeking intimacy or enjoyment amongst them, *je me perdrais*. Luckily, *je n'en ferai rien*, for they run off me like rain upon oilskin, and the only grievance is to give up a portion of every day to a society in which I feel in every taste, feeling, and idea so wholly *étrangère*.

The 'exquisite set', dominated by *les élégantes*, into which she was admitted, came in for her particular opprobrium. 'There is not so much mind,' she wrote scathingly, 'as would fill a pea shell.'

Nevertheless, Harriet was a loyal wife, and she made up her mind to do her best. First on the agenda was to look the part. Her appearance had always been homely, and she knew it. ('My face, as Mr Hill once said, "Lord help it".') Trying hard not to think of her predecessor, the exceedingly rich Lady Stuart, who was said to have spent £1,000 a year on her wardrobe alone (well over £45,000 by today's reckoning), she did her best to smarten herself up.

In Brussels she bought new corsets, new silk dresses, and had her hair '*crêpé* into the solidity of a wig', all of which for a time gave her a new sense of confidence. But the *élégantes*, for all their pea-shell brains, were not so easily appeased. 'But, O Lady Morpeth, it is the woman made by Herbault, Victorine, and Alexandre,* the woman who looks to see if you have six curls or five on the side of your head, the woman who talks, dictates, condescends and sneers at me – quos ego. It is odd that their effect upon me is to crush me with the sense of my inferiority,' she wrote only half-jokingly, 'whilst I am absolutely gasping with the sense of my superiority. What a thing to write, but it is only to you.'

The social round was as relentless as she had feared. In the evenings they went to at least two *soirées*,† and dined out 'literally every day'. Things would not have been so bad if she had been able to see a point to it all. 'My days are all so alike that I can hardly hope at present to vary much in my accounts,' she wrote. Even the *soirées*, which began and ended early, were all very much the same – about fifty of the 'select' conversing *en cercle*. The custom which particularly weighed on her spirits, though, was the time-consuming but utterly pointless 'receiving and returning visits and curtsies'.

---

* Fashionable Parisian hairdressers of the time.
† Precursor to the modern cocktail party.

This tidal wave of duty submerged her own private life almost completely. 'Never come to me in the winter, dearest,' she wrote in frustration to Lady Morpeth. 'I would not buy even you, at the price of annoyance and fatigue to you, perpetual regret and privation to myself ... I seize an idle moment, as a cat does a mouse.'

Gradually, Harriet began to acclimatize to her new life. Her hard work began to pay off. By going at her work as an ambassadress 'like a dray horse' she was rewarded by meeting 'civil and conciliated faces at every turn'. Although she still found some of the younger duchesses insolent and artificial – she had a private theory that they would decide one day exactly what they were going to say the next – she began almost to like some of the older ones. She took great trouble over her house and her dinners and, to her secret delight, began to be something of a success.

In January 1826 she wrote describing the preparations for a great ball which she was to give at the embassy.

My house ... looks more brilliant and enormous than I can describe. I have asked 1,150, and as the Russians* and several great mournings in private families have brought me a number of excuses I have no fear of a crowd. We open the *rez de chaussée* – the *serre*, with a carpet doubled of scarlet cloth, eighteen lustres with lamps and six divans, the same temperature as the rooms, with all the doors and windows taken off in the ball- and drawing-rooms. Three *salons au premier*, five whist-tables in the *salon vert*, *écarté*, newspapers and books of prints in the state *couleur de paille* bedroom.

The opening of her *serre*, or conservatory, in particular, was a great success (a true Englishwoman, Harriet was secretly delighted at the thought of the *élégantes* being upstaged by her camellias and her orange blossom). 'I hear people go about the balls saying: "*Ah, mon Dieu, il n'y a pas de serre ici,*"' she reported with satisfaction.

Although Harriet still found the pace of life relentless, after six months in Paris the tone of her letters became one of amused resignation. 'We are now in the very kernel of the fêtes,' she wrote to her

* Tsar Alexander I had died the previous year.

brother in June 1825, 'and I notch them off as a prisoner does the days of his captivity.' Most importantly, she was finally beginning to get the measure of the French. 'Society is not the sort of puzzling maze it was to me at my first arrival,' she was able to write in December, when she had been in Paris a year. 'I like some people better, and know how to keep off those I do not.' The key to it all, she found, was really very simple. 'Their object is to be amused and received. They are like children, clever, lively, troublesome children, without tact, without *suite*, noisy and rude – if you spoil them. If kept in order, gay and animated, easily pleased and rarely offended.'

Harriet was clear-sighted enough to know that she could never be like the *élégantes*: 'the truth is, they have an aplomb, a language, a dress *de couvenance*, which it is as impossible for me to reach as it would be for one of them to think five minutes like a deep-thinking, deep-feeling Englishwoman.' It was far more enjoyable to outwit them. 'I seldom, now that I know their dear little habits and outings, find anybody at home,' she recorded with cool cunning in the autumn of 1825, of the new season's enervating round of calls. With similar aplomb, on a day when she found that her dinner and dance was to clash with that of the Esterhazys, she declined to put it off. Instead, she carefully sent word to all the *élégantes* that she would not expect them, and not to put themselves out. As she had predicted, they at once made Paul Esterhazy give up his dinner, and rushed to her house as early as possible. 'It was a bold stroke,' she wrote afterwards, 'for the fact is I should have lost all my best dancers and prettiest women had I failed, but I trusted to my knowledge of them and was not disappointed.'[7]

Although they were written nearly 200 years ago, Countess Granville's letters seem strikingly modern. Here was a woman – intelligent, educated and of an independent disposition – with an urgent need to retain a sense of herself, and to create her own space, amidst the all-consuming but artificial trappings of her role. The qualities required to cope with the job in our own times, listed for me by three ambassadresses of the 1990s – Virginia Crowe, Veronica Goodenough, and Catherine Young – proved to be almost identical to those shown by Harriet Granville. 'A good relationship with your husband,' said Veronica; 'adaptability,' added Virginia, 'and cheerfulness.' 'En-*dur-*

ance,' they laughed, warming to their subject. 'A strong stomach and good legs,' joked Catherine Young – and by that she did not mean limbs that look good in Chanel, but legs that would not become varicosed from all the standing about at endless National Days.[8]

If the tone of an embassy chancery emanates largely from the character of its current ambassador, the morale and even, it has been suggested, the mental health of the embassy women, has always been heavily influenced by that of his wife. Lady Henderson recalls how the embassy doctor in Paris once asked to see her about two of 'her wives': 'She asked me very seriously: "What is this entertaining you force your wives to do?" I found this question rather difficult,' Lady Henderson recalls, 'since I was not conscious of forcing anyone to do anything, least of all entertain.'[9] The doctor then explained that she had the two women under sedation because they were so worried about their social duties within the embassy. (It turned out that the two women also had personal problems.) But for better or for worse, an ambassadress's personality affects every other wife in the embassy.

Many have been greatly loved. Mrs Wade, the wife of the head of mission in Peking in the 1870s, was 'everything that the wife of an official in the East should be', according to Mary Fraser, 'thoroughly and fundamentally British, cheery, kind, intelligent, a woman who never made a mistake'. 'Warm, witty, with a fantastic sense of humour' was the accolade given by Catherine Young to her former ambassadress in Paris, Sarah Fergusson. Lack of formality, especially in the stricter days of Marcus Cheke, was always a popular trait. In the 1960s Iona Wright earned the affection of the embassy wives in Tehran because she did not make them dress up for her. 'I got letters from the clergyman's wife later,' she recalls, 'who said, "You were popular because you didn't make people wear their hats and gloves." I don't know, perhaps I should have. I did tell them if they did something extraordinary (one woman once wore a red suit to a funeral), but I never sent out a note or anything.'

Although many women were infuriated at being referred to by an ambassadress as 'her wives', the term could imply a degree of protectiveness, as well as possessiveness, which others found comforting. Marie-Noele Kelly remembered laughing 'perhaps a little loudly' in her ambassadress's hearing when a Belgian friend criticized the councellor's wife, Mary Knatchbull-Hugessen, for the impersonal style of her entertaining. 'Lady Granville* gave me an icy look and paid a suave compliment to Mary, thus gathering one of her flock to her bosom,' Marie-Noele recalled, leaving her feeling 'very hot and uncomfortable for a moment'.[10]

In the past it was considered perfectly normal for an ambassadress to steer her junior wives through some of the choppier diplomatic waters. Mary Fraser was to remember all her life the terror of being 'put through the mill' by her new ambassadress when Hugh was posted as secretary of the embassy in Vienna in 1880, a stark contrast to the cosy camaraderie of the legation in Peking:

My beautiful grey-haired Chiefess† laid her hand firmly on my arm and sailed away with me, through room after room, each fuller than the last, as it looked to me, of gorgeously bedecked dowagers with historical names, who gazed at me sadly over breastplates of diamonds, murmured a few polite words as I made my curtsey, and then faded out of my consciousness, as I was hurried off to the next group. When it was over – it took all the evening – my monitress gave a big sigh, as well she might, and informed me that I must leave cards with every one of those women within twenty-four hours, and be sure to remember their names and faces when I met them again.[11]

Marie-Noele Kelly, too, was the recipient not only of the occasional icy stare, but also of a good deal of wisdom from the 'kind but formidable' Lady Granville. 'As your husband gets more senior, be "all things to all men"', was one of her golden rules, 'and don't take sides ever.' This absolute impartiality was necessary, but isolating. It was difficult, if not impossible, to make friends among the other wives. 'I remember Lady Harrowby's‡ advice,' wrote Harriet Granville when she first arrived in The Hague, 'and do not let myself go to any likes and dislikes, but, like the sun, rather a dim one by the way, I shine on all alike.' Like many other women in her position, she found this part of her role very difficult to pull off. To cultivate that 'degree of repelling

---

* Another Lady Granville, born Nina Baring, the niece of Lord Cromer, for whom she entertained in Cairo in the 1880s.
† From the nineteenth-century French term, *chef de mission*.
‡ Her sister-in-law.

civility of manner, to have no preferences and create none . . . all this will rub my back up the wrong way'.[12]

To be on the receiving end of this 'repelling civility of manner' was not always easy, either. Many ambassadresses appeared more than just a little distant. Pat Gore-Booth was 'absolutely terrified' of her first ambassadress, Lady Craigie. 'She was quite a phenomenon,' she remembers. 'She was an American to begin with, so one never quite knew whether she was going to play the role of an American or of a British ambassadorial wife. That didn't matter so much, but she was of the old school, and I came in when I was just nineteen. I was a cypher. I used to go with her to call on the other ambassadresses, and pass the cookies.'

For the ambassadress herself, finding exactly the right note to strike could be an extremely delicate operation. While she could not be seen to be too relaxed, too great an emphasis on formality was equally unpopular. Traditional etiquette within the embassy, of the kind insisted upon by Marcus Cheke, only served to emphasize the gulf which already existed between an ambassadress and the other embassy wives. (Masha Williams remembers how she was obliged to take formal leave of her ambassadress in Baghdad before she went off to have her first baby.) People had a vague, but idealized image of them, which ordinary flesh and blood could in no way live up to, which is perhaps why so many of the stereotypes of ambassadresses have been negative ones. All too often they were judged not for what they were, but for what they were not. 'An excellent woman . . .' wrote Harriet Granville, apparently in some surprise, of the ambassador's wife in Brussels in 1824, 'with none of the representation or insolence of an Ambassadress.'

The grandeur of the lifestyle, and the prestige of the role, particularly in the bigger and more formal postings, often seemed daunting. Those who were unsure of themselves could end up placing too much emphasis on relatively unimportant details. At the beginning of her diplomatic career, Paraguayan-born Veronica Atkinson remembers being reprimanded by one particularly protocol-minded ambassadress who found fault with her for not introducing guests to her in the correct way. 'She said to me, "You should not introduce like that," and of course this was said in the middle of a big party. And then I was sort of tearful and I said to Michael, "What have I done wrong?" And he said, "How did you introduce?" And then I learnt. To the superior person, the person who is higher up the ladder, you say, "Can I introduce Mrs Smith to you?" instead of saying, "Can I introduce you to Mrs Smith?"'

After visiting Masha (by then Lady) Williams, the ambassadress in Madrid in 1966, my mother, in those days one of the more junior wives, found herself in a rebellious frame of mind. 'I paid my duty call on Lady Williams last week,' she grumbled in one of her letters home to my grandparents, 'sat in state for half an hour in a most sumptuous palace of a Residence, with a butler and a footman bringing us round coffee . . . I thought of all that unused garden – except for the Queen's Birthday Party – and my children with no-where to play. I wonder if we ever reach anything like such an exalted position whether my memory will stretch back and act with some understanding towards the problems of junior staff.'

The ambassadress in Peggy Trevelyan's first posting in Baghdad 'was a very, very difficult lady. She was not very good at her job, and resented the fact that anybody below her, junior to her, was doing it.' Tales of *folie de grandeur* abound. Iona Wright's ambassadress in Persia had been a friend of hers back in England.

But when she came out she said to me, you mustn't call me Constance, you must always call me Lady Stevens in front of other people. Well, I'd known her for years, since she'd married. She was rather fun in England, but she did get very grand out there. She was always telling people off all the time . . . she was the sort of person who always used to say 'you must arrive before the ambassador at every party' and so we'd go chasing round to get there in good time before they did. She worried about that sort of thing all the time. She once asked us to dinner, but I said, 'I'm afraid we can't come because we've invited this man on a motor bicycle who's going out from England to India.' We thought he was a rather interesting person, we'd met him at the Tehran Club and asked him to dinner. And she said, 'But this is your *ambassadress* talking.' She was like that, really. And after that she wouldn't talk to me. I met her later at a cocktail party and she completely ignored me. She was trying to be frightfully grand. I think it must have been insecurity really. She was really much nicer before she became an ambassadress.

Iona's successor found the Dutch-born Lady Stevens equally difficult to get along with.

> She took to drink, she really did. She was an amusing person, only about thirty-five, from a very good family in England. She loved parties, and things like that, but she really drank far too much after she was treated so badly by this woman. She was always being told to run round and get in the right side of the Rolls, and things like that. She really couldn't take her. Her nickname for her was Belsen, and several people started calling her that after we left.[13]

Others simply had too many other demands on their time to worry about such details:

> I didn't have the sense, seeing her pallor, the strained look on her face, to realise that she needed help as much as I had done on my arrival [Masha wrote of her ambassadress in Baghdad]. New post, new people, a different culture, different situation, incredible climate. She was like a new girl at school. Past experience would be of little help to her here and she would never admit to not being able to carry out the duties she supposed other ambassadresses had managed successfully. I didn't realise that literally she did not have time for us.[13]

Some were simply not cut out to be ambassadresses at all, a 'job' which, after all, they had married into rather than taken up from choice. As Philip Ziegler mused in his biography of Lady Diana Cooper, 'to be, or not to be, a good ambassadress depended largely on what one believes an ambassadress is supposed to do and be.' With her great personal *élan* and her legendary beauty – 'an orchid amongst cowslips, a black tulip in a garden of cucumbers, nightshade in the day nursery,' Raymond Asquith described her as a girl – Diana Cooper had many qualities. They were not the conventional ones of an ambassadress. 'Some expect her to be a benevolent mother hen, clucking lovingly over the migraines of the secretaries and the table manners of the Head of Chancery. This certainly Diana failed to be.'[14]

'Although she is capable of great heroism and devotion,' wrote one of her friends, Bridget McEwen, in a letter to her husband, 'she is not capable of enduring boredom: and to endure boredom with the good manners that don't show it is half the duty of an ambassadress.' She, for one, did not hold out much hope at all for the success of her posting. 'Diana will be no good at all,' she concluded brutally. 'She will be rude to the bores, and she will wear trousers because they are comfortable, and offend everyone. Only if there is an earthquake or a revolution will she show her true mettle,' she added. 'But who knows, there may be both.'[15]

On their first Christmas in Paris, in 1944, the Coopers held three parties: one was given for their French friends – 'très digne', wrote Diana afterwards; a second for the whole embassy staff and their friends – 'a nightmare'; and a third for 400 little embassy children – 'a bad smell'.[16]

Back in London, the Foreign Office's suspicions were deep. 'I fear the worst from her, that idle useless woman who scarcely speaks French,' wrote one senior official. Diana's most intimate circle of friends, *la bande*, were either too bohemian, or too grand, for traditional diplomatic tastes: 'riff raff', collaborators and fifth-columnists, spluttered the Foreign Office.[17] But no one could dispute the fact that she brought glamour 'in buckets' to Pauline Borghese's dusty and neglected palace on the Faubourg Saint-Honoré, which had been used as a furniture repository during the war.

The style which Diana Cooper brought to the Paris embassy was all her own. Her philosophy – 'Oh, just give them plenty of booze and hope it will go' – was unorthodox, but it worked. 'People went there to enjoy themselves but with the pleasing reflection that they might be outraged as well,' wrote Philip Ziegler. The historian Anthony Beevor (husband of Artemis Cooper, Lady Diana's granddaughter) describes her genius in creating not only a centre for Parisian artistic life, but a place where all sorts of people who would normally have refused to see one another for political reasons could meet on neutral ground.

She had a genius for throwing people together absolutely recklessly – and getting away with it. There was one famous occasion when she invited the Marchioness of Bath and Daisy Fellowes, two of the most *mondaine* women imaginable, to a lunch for

Tito's ambassador and Marcel Cachin, the doyen of the French Communist Party. Daisy Fellowes, revered among the French as one of the best dressed women in the world, sat opposite Madame Cachin, who although she was extremely cultured, looked like an old concierge. Against all the odds it was a tremendous success.

Despite the grandness of the surroundings, Lady Diana's *salon vert* had 'all the intimacy and excitement of a midnight feast'.

Happily for the other embassy wives (but sadly for literature) the days of the Dragon Empress are over. Whatever her personal relationship with the other spouses, the modern ambassadress is neither able, nor willing, to crack the whip in quite the same way as before. Whereas in the past it was considered perfectly acceptable for her to call upon 'her wives' for support or practical help, today this is no longer the case. Increasing numbers of diplomatic wives now have careers of their own, and do not have either the time or the inclination to involve themselves with embassy matters too closely.

Despite the many changes which have taken place over the last twenty years within the embassy hierarchy, the role of an ambassadress, perversely, has remained remarkably constant. The problems and stresses of a posting abroad have always centred on her; now, with the changes in the circumstances surrounding her job, she has become an increasingly solitary figure. 'The things which used to be shared between the head of mission spouse and all the others are now *all* on the head of mission spouse's shoulders,' explains Catherine Young. Once the linchpins of an entire embassy network, today's ambassadresses are more likely to be on their own. In spirit they resemble far more closely the social 'dray horses' of Countess Granville's generation than they do the ferocious and heavily trussed Chloe Fanshawes of more recent diplomatic mythology.

With this fact in mind, the BDSA now runs a two-day course for prospective heads of mission wives. The 'old school', it must be said, tends to be somewhat dismissive of this recent innovation – 'never, never, *never* leave your bedroom in the morning without make-up and earrings' used to be one of its adages – but the course's main function is simply to pool people's experience. It concentrates not so much on how to get in and out of a Rolls-Royce, or whether or not to kiss the President, but on a much more mundane subject – catering. 'After all have *you* ever been into a kitchen which feeds 150 people at a sitting?' points out Virginia Crowe, a former course organizer. 'On the way up, most of us have done it ourselves in our own kitchens, but we've never had to oversee that scale of entertaining, and it can come as a bit of a shock.'

Some ambassadresses are simply overwhelmed by the sheer volume of the work which is still expected of them (much of it, they privately confess, 'deadly dull'). Georgina Armour, wife of the consul-general to Dubai, admits to leaving the course feeling like 'a lamb to the slaughter', and her sense of foreboding was amply fulfilled when she arrived at her new posting in 1997.

'Oh, hello – you're on the BCAF committee' was the first reaction of the lady to whom I had been introduced. 'What committee?' I asked, stunned; I hadn't even heard of this one. It was the third time in 24 hours I had been treated so by expectant expatriates, and each time about a different committee. It had been a stressful day already and I'd arrived feeling thoroughly battered. Suddenly my hand began to shake uncontrollably, the cup clattered on its saucer and I burst into tears. The women looked totally surprised, then sympathetic, then disappointed.[18]

Part of the problem, she feels, is that for all the assurances of the Foreign Office in London that wives are not obliged to fulfil any expectations, 'living with the consequent resentment from the people you've disappointed (and many of them are not easy to avoid if you are often in the same room at a party) requires not just a thick skin but the hide of rhinoceros.' Tradition, particularly amongst expatriate communities abroad, cannot be turned off at will; 'you have to let it drip for a bit.'

While Georgina did receive a good deal of support from the other consulate-general wives, not all women in her position are so lucky. As Peggy Trevelyan puts it: 'Quite a number of people, perhaps a bit younger than me, who have become ambassadors' wives have had quite a difficult time. I wouldn't say that the younger wives were bolshy, but when I was doing it I knew that I could rely on somebody to come and help me with whatever it was that was going on. But now you don't.'

CHAPTER SEVEN

Public Life

'Diamonds are my weak point,' wrote Countess Granville anxiously to her sister on the eve of her presentation at the French court in 1824, 'and I have been obliged to borrow some from Mme De Gontaut, as they tell me a quantity must be worn, and those who have not enough must and do borrow.'

Before the turn of this century, when all the principal British embassies were still based in Europe, the high point of an ambassadress's public life was her presentation at court. The ceremony, which formally marked her entrance into society at the very beginning of her residence abroad, often proved to be something of an ordeal. Harriet Granville, normally the most socially sanguine of women, endured many weeks of anxiety: 'My presentation is thought of such consequence,' she wrote to Lady Morpeth. 'How I dress, how I behave, how I curtsey, so commented upon, so discussed, that I feel as if I was going to be hung.'

Even at Harriet's previous posting in The Hague, where the court was famously relaxed, the ceremony was extremely formal.

This morning I went all over diamonds and black satin to Court [she wrote in March 1824]. A little grand-chambellan leads me from the door to an ante-room where four *dames d'honneur* receive me, till the folding doors open and I walk in alone to the Queen, standing in the middle of a very large and handsome *salle d'audience*: she is a shy, quiet, well-behaved woman, in miserable health and thinner than Mme de Lieven.* We talk of our Royal Family,

---

* Princess Lieven, the wife of the Russian ambassador to the Court of St James, was a well-known figure in London society.

of the loss of our horses,* of the size of my house, and of the weather. A little back door opens and the King drops in. Five minutes more small Royal talk, and then I back out with a train five yards long, squiddle a little with the grand-maître, and that is all that belongs to my duties vis-à-vis the court.

Unlike the Dutch, the French were renowned for their love of diplomatic ceremonial. Harriet knew that her presentation in Paris would be a very different matter. The *traitement*, as the ancient presentation ceremony was known, had only recently been revived at the court of the newly restored Bourbon king, Louis XVIII. Lady Elizabeth Stuart, the British ambassadress to Paris immediately before Harriet Granville (and the first since the fall of Napoleon)† had been so frozen with terror during her *traitement* that she had barely been able to speak throughout the ceremony. It was not an encouraging precedent. Harriet was impatient with herself for giving too much thought to these trifles, but it was hardly surprising that she felt nervous.

As usual she wrote to her sister, Lady Morpeth, with all the details:

I found myself this morning feeling annoyed at my Court dress being too short on the sides, and very much pleased when Frederique dressed me *en cheveux*‡ to-day, as a rehearsal, to think it looked very well, and to hear Granville's compliments about it. Is this the woman who would not have cared if she had been seen in an old tattered garment with a masquerade red silk petticoat under it? ... Do not think *en cheveux* is my own idea. It is *de rigueur* for a presentation, and even old Madame§ receives me with her old grey careworn head bristled up by Frederique.

Her coiffure, her court dress and the prodigious quantities of diamonds which she was expected to wear were only a small part of the

---

* All their horses had died in transit.
† The first ambassador after the Napoleonic Wars was the Duke of Wellington, but his wife, Catherine Packenham, with whom he was not on good terms, stayed at home in England.
‡ i.e. without a hat.
§ The Duchesse d'Angoulême, a daughter of Louis XVI and Marie Antoinette, was always known at the French court as 'Madame'.

elaborate diplomatic etiquette which governed the presentation of foreign ambassadresses at the French court. If the ceremony in which Lord Granville presented his credentials, which took place only a few days before, was more formidable, it was only because his speech was slightly longer. 'I am to make a little phrase to the Dauphine about the honour, and her virtues, and my gratitude, twelve ladies standing behind her,' Harriet recorded with trepidation. The presentation, at five o'clock in the afternoon, was to be followed by a great dinner given in her honour, to which she was desired to invite a number of companions – 'Lord Granville cannot go if I do not name him.'

Her selection of twelve English ladies of the highest rank turned out to be a considerable difficulty in itself. For fear of offending more ladies than she honoured, she decided to ask only peeresses, but even then her problems were not solved.

Lady Abercorn did not feel very equal to it, and had never been presented, which precludes it. Lady Newburgh, to whom I proposed it, wrote me unbounded thanks for the very great honour intended her, but not being able to keep up a conversation in French, was obliged to decline it. Lady Caroline was charmed with this 'dear woman', oh! what a dear woman.' Lady Northland had never been presented, Lady Belfast ditto. Lady Granard too ill.

Her company, when it was finally settled on, consisted of only seven ladies: Lady Thomond, Lady Waterford, Lady Aylesbury, Lady Worcester, Lady Aldborough, Lady Glenlyon and Lady Strathallan, a daughter of the Duke of Atholl.

'My dearest Sis,' she wrote with relief after her ordeal was over, 'I think you will not worry to hear before the usual time that my labours are over and that my presentation *traitement* went off very smoothly.' Although she claimed that she never could describe ceremonies she confided, 'I hope you will be glad to hear that I never can think anything formidable again.' On the day, Harriet was so nervous that she forgot her 'compliment' altogether; 'but I am assured I did not disgrace myself, and the delight of having it over is beyond expression.' The dinner, she added, had been magnificent.[1]

Few other courts could rival the richness and splendour of Paris, and French protocol on the knotty questions of precedence, and diplomatic audiences and visits, had been extremely influential, and widely emulated, since the days of Louis XIV. The ceremony of an ambassadress's presentation, for example, had followed the same basic pattern in all the courts of Europe for well over a hundred years. Here is Ann Fanshawe describing her presentation to the Queen of Portugal in 1662:

> The Queen sat in a black velvet chair with arms, upon a black velvet carpet, with a state of the same. She had caused a low chair without arms to be set some distance from her, about two yards on her left hand, on which side stood all the noblemen, on her right all the ladies of the court. After making my reverences, due to her Majesty according to custom, and said those respects which became me to her Majesty, she sat down and then I presented my daughters to her . . . and then she made her discourse of England, and questions of the Queen's health* and liking of our country, with some little hints of her own and her family's condition, which having continued better than half an hour, I took my leave.[2]

Lady Mary Wortley Montagu described a similar ceremony in Vienna in 1716 when she was presented to the Empress† for the first time. 'I had a private audience, according to ceremony, of half an hour, and then all the other ladies were permitted to come make their court,' she wrote to her sister, Lady Mar.[3] 'I was delighted with my presentation,' commented Anne Disbrowe, the young wife of the Minister Plenipotentiary to St Petersburg, just a year after Harriet Granville's *traitement* in Paris. 'The Emperor [Alexander] kissed my hand, and I pretended to salute his cheek, à la Russe. The Empress [Elizabeth] would not allow me to kiss her hand, but embraced me, and they were both so gracious and so affable, that I was quite sorry to be sent away.'[4]

Although neither Lady Mary nor Anne Disbrowe was required to

---

* The Queen of Portugal's daughter, Catherine of Bragança, had married King Charles II earlier that same year.

† Elisabeth Christine, daughter of the Duke of Brunswick-Wolfenbuttel, who married Charles VI in 1708.

make a speech, both shared Harriet Granville's alarm on the subject of their court dress. Lady Mary found that she had to delay her first audience at the Viennese court for nearly a week while she sent for exactly the right gown, 'without which there is no waiting on the Empress'. When the dress finally arrived she found it a 'very inconvenient' article into which she had to be forcibly squeezed. Over the top of it a gorget was worn – a kind of ornamental collar covering the neck and shoulders. While the gorget showed 'the neck and shape to great advantage', the same could not be said for some of the other fashions at court, most of which, she wrote, were 'more monstrous and contrary to common sense and reason than 'tis possible for you to imagine . . . Their whalebone petticoats out-do ours by several yards' circumference,' she went on, with only a modicum of exaggeration, 'and cover several acres of ground.'

This was as nothing, though, compared to the monstrous hairpieces with which the ladies of the Viennese court adorned their heads: 'They build certain fabrics of gauze on their heads, about a yard high, consisting of three or four storeys, fortified with numberless yards of heavy ribbons.' The foundation for these stupefyingly large hairpieces was a huge roll of cloth, known as a *bourle*, shaped like an outsized milkmaid's pannier, over which they arranged both their own, and a great quantity of false hair. 'Their hair is prodigiously powdered to conceal the mixture,' Lady Mary went on, 'and set out with three or four rows of bodkins [hairpins] . . . made of diamonds, pearls, red, green and yellow stones.' The finished edifice was so heavy and cumbersome that it required 'as much art and experience to carry the load upright as to dance upon May day with the garland'.

In St Petersburg a hundred years later Anne Disbrowe did not have to cope with such exaggerated fashions, but the required court dress, which included a long train at the back, was never an easy thing to manage. 'My gown was made here,' she wrote home to her mother, 'very simple of tulle over white satin, with a long train, which I managed wonderfully well, and had not one tumble.' Like Harriet Granville, her relief when her presentation was successfully over, while tinged with regret, was almost palpable. 'They were all quite kind to me, and I wish my presentation was still to come, though I was dreadfully frightened at the thought of it before it took place.'

*　　*　　*

The presentation of ambassadresses was the only piece of formal ceremonial which exclusively involved women.* Most diplomatic protocol was centred on the ambassador, who for ritual purposes was the embodiment of the monarch he represented. It was an enormously complex code, largely determined by the slow accumulation of precedents, which had evolved steadily since the late fifteenth century. Since its principal purpose was to reflect the power of an ambassador's sovereign, even the smallest details, such as the exact placement of an ambassador's signature on a document, or whether or not he gave his hand to another envoy on his own house, came to acquire enormous symbolic importance.

By the seventeenth century an ambassador was required to take part in a number of elaborately stylized ceremonies. Although the courts of each country imposed their own traditions and variations upon them, as with the *traitement* of ambassadresses they followed a similar basic framework. A mission usually began with the ambassador's magnificent public entry into the capital, closely followed by his first formal audience with the king, when he would usually present his credentials (his letters of introduction). During the first few weeks of his mission he would also exchange visits with other ambassadors and envoys accredited to the court – a procedure governed by a complex set of rules – and on leaving he would be granted a formal farewell audience, known as an audience *de congé*.

Although an ambassador's wife was never formally involved in these ceremonies, she was a frequent witness. Occasionally, as a courtesy, she would be invited to take part. When the Countess of Carlisle and her husband, who was King Charles II's ambassador to Russia, went to Moscow in 1663, she accompanied him at his public entry into the imperial city. High-ranking courtiers, known as the *pristasse*, whose duty it was to welcome ambassadors, flanked them on sledges laden with bear skins. The ambassador's own sledge, drawn by two white horses, was decorated with blue velvet and silver lace, and his pages were especially dressed for the occasion (at a cost of £30 each) in liveries richly embroidered with silver and plumes. The Countess followed behind in her own carriage, richly trimmed with crimson velvet,

* To this day ambassadresses and other heads of mission's wives are still received by the wife of the head of state of the country to which they are accredited.

while her son, Viscount Morpeth, rode in a glass coach; trumpeters and drummers, gorgeously dressed and mounted on horseback, preceded them, while their two hundred sledges loaded with baggage brought up the rear. At the entrance to the city, musicians and *boyars* came to greet the Carlisles' entourage, and conducted them to their residence.

As potent symbols of the might and glory of their country, these public entries aimed to dazzle the local populace. One of the most glittering entrances of all, and certainly one of the most famous, was made by the Earl of Stair in Paris in 1719. The Earl had been the Minister Plenipotentiary to France since 1715, but it was only when he was raised to the rank of ambassador four years later that he was entitled to make a public entrance. Since his Countess lived with him in Paris 'in a princely fashion' and entertained lavishly on her husband's behalf, it is almost certain that she too would have taken part.

The Earl, who was known for his flamboyance, made sure it was worth waiting for. The state coaches were preceded by thirty-six footmen, twelve gentlemen on horseback and twelve pages, all wearing the Stairs' own livery: orange cloth trimmed with velvet lace in blue, white and crimson. Their silver lace shoulder knots were embroidered with silver thread, and decorated with blue and white feathers. On their legs they wore cherry-coloured stockings with silver clocks,* and even their gloves were richly embroidered with silver, four inches deep. Their hats were decorated with cockades and blue and white feathers. The ambassador's own entourage was five coaches strong, and these were followed by the coaches of several English lords and gentlemen. His six horses, led by six liveried grooms, were richly caparisoned in gold and silver, while all the others had their manes adorned with knots and ribbons mixed with thick tufts of gold and silver. The Earl's own coach was the most magnificent of all – a glass coach lined with Persian crimson velvet, with a groundwork of gold, and curtains made from Genoa crimson damask.

By the end of the eighteenth century such public entrances were becoming less common, and by the beginning of the nineteenth they had almost died away. When another diplomatic countess, the twenty-

---

* The triangular insertion at the heel of the stocking, which was often used to decorative effect.

two-year-old Countess of Elgin, arrived in Constantinople in November 1799 her entry was a very low-key affair compared to the huge procession of janissaries, bashaws and gentlemen-at-arms which had accompanied her predecessor, Lady Winchilsea, in 1661. 'On my going out of the boat, I found a fine gilt chair with six men to carry it, waiting for my arrival,' she wrote, adding simply: 'I was very happy to find it for the streets are sad walking.'[5]

Other aspects of diplomatic protocol presented far more of a threat than the perils of a muddy street. The exact order of precedence taken by ambassadors and other envoys and their wives at a foreign court was subject to violent dispute. Pope Julius II had drawn up the first formal list of precedence in 1504, and the arguments had raged ever since. The pope's list fixed the order as follows: the German emperor was first, followed by the king of the Romans,* the king of France and then the king of Spain, with England ranking seventh in this list, after Aragon and Portugal. Philip II's succession to the Spanish crown in 1556 (which he inherited after the abdication of his father, Charles V,) but not to the imperial title (which went to Charles V's brother, Ferdinand) led France and Spain into almost continual battles over the coveted second place. The bitter feud remained unresolved by a new list drawn up in 1564, which used the antiquity of the royal title as its criterion. After the pope and the Holy Roman emperor came France (AD 481), Spain (AD 718) and England (AD 827).

Almost no one seems to have agreed with either list, which added considerable spice to diplomatic life. One of the most famous disputes over precedence was at the public entrance of the Swedish ambassador to London in 1661, when neither the Spanish nor the French ambassadors would give way to the other in the procession. The result was a pitched battle between their respective entourages in which the French, to the great joy of the Londoners watching, were soundly trounced. 'And indeed we do naturally all love the Spanish, and hate the French,' wrote Samuel Pepys, who had been to watch the fun, in his diary.

---

* A title often held by the Emperor's son, in order to secure the succession (which was in theory an elective one). Maximilian I, who was the German emperor at the time this order was drawn up, had been elected king of the Romans in 1486. He became emperor in 1493 on the death of his father Frederick III.

The truth is, the Spaniards were not only observed to fight most desperately, but also they did outwit them; first, in lining their own harnesses with chains of iron that they could not be cut, then in setting their coach in the most advantageous place, and to appoint men to guard every one of their horses, and other for to guard the coach and other the coachmen ... There were several men slain of the French, and one or two of the Spaniards, and one Englishman by a bullet. So, having been very much daubed with dirt, I got a coach, and home; where I vexed my wife in telling of her this story.*

Although few had such serious consequences, disputes over precedence were so common that almost all diplomatic wives had their own tales to tell on the subject. According to Mrs Vigor, at a Russian court wedding in the 1730s all the foreign envoys had to be put in a room together to watch the procession. In the church itself another special enclosure was provided, 'to which they were to go as soon as the procession passed, because the ceremonial could not be settled for them to be in the procession, as no-one would submit to have the lowest place'.[6]

Diplomatic wives were no less touchy than their husbands. Lady Mary Wortley Montagu was particularly caustic on the subject when she briefly visited Ratisbon, the seat of the German imperial diet, on her way to Constantinople. 'You know that all the nobility of the place are envoys from different states,' she wrote to her friend, Anne Thistlethwayte. 'Here are a great number of them, and they might pass their time agreeably enough, if they were less delicate on the point of ceremony. But instead of joining in the design of making the town as pleasant to one another as they can, and improving their little societies, they amuse themselves no other way than with perpetual quarrels.' Precedence, and the granting of the title of 'Excellency' were the two chief bones of contention. All claimed the title for themselves, and would not allow anyone else to use it. When Lady Mary suggested that, for the sake of a peaceful life, *all* should have the title, 'such a dishonourable peace' was met with indignation. 'And I began

---

* The King of France was so outraged by the affair that he is said to have threatened to declare war on Spain if he was not righted in the matter, and forbade any of his ambassadors to yield to Spain at any of the courts of Europe in the future.

to think myself ill-natured to offer to take from them, in a town where there are so few diversions, so entertaining an amusement.'[7]

By the beginning of the nineteenth century the problems of protocol which so plagued the seventeenth and eighteenth centuries were no longer subject to such hot dispute. At the Congress of Vienna in 1815, after the fall of Napoleon, it was finally agreed upon by all the European powers that diplomatic precedence should follow a simple alphabetical expedient.* But even though the honour of a country was no longer seen to be at stake, the problems of diplomatic protocol never went away entirely. There were always plenty of other pitfalls to keep diplomats and their wives busy.

Countries outside Europe were not immune to such problems. In Persia, 'for want of more important subjects of contention,' wrote Mary Sheil, more in exasperation than in truth, 'trifles assume a magnitude unintelligible in Europe.' Indeed, the Russians had gone so far as to draw up a treaty on the subject of how their envoys should be received there, 'defining all the honours, the sweetmeats, the sugar, the visits from the Prime Minister downwards, which they are entitled to exact', while the Turkish ambassador, Salmee Effendi, had fought two arduous battles, 'one about a pair of shoes, the other concerning a chair'.[8] In Algiers, too, 'a most strict regard to etiquette was on all occasions observed among the different Consuls in their intercourse with each other,' according to Elizabeth Blanckley. 'My mother was the first lady handed out, I sat above all the other demoiselles, and Sidi Hassan headed the Janissaries at the lower end of the long numerously-flanked table.'†[9]

By the late nineteenth century it was considered a serious breach of protocol for either a diplomat or his wife to embark on formal public engagements before being presented at court. When they arrived in

---

* Today precedence is worked out by the length of time an ambassador has served at any posting. In Catholic countries, however, the papal nuncio – the pope's ambassador – always takes precedence over everyone else regardless of how long he has served.
† Elizabeth also tells a story of her father's predecessor, the irascible Mr Falconer, who went to extraordinary lengths to avoid giving precedence to the French consul: climbing the stairs at the palace on their way to offer congratulations at some local celebration, 'Mr Falconer suddenly caught his antagonist round the waist, threw him over the bannisters, then composedly walked forward and paid his respects to the Dey, amidst the shouts of laughter and applause of all present.'

Munich in 1882, Lady Anne Macdonell and her husband were forced to keep a low profile while they waited to see 'mad' King Ludwig of Bavaria. Weeks and weeks went by, but still the King delayed her husband's presentation (he never received ladies). 'During all these delays I could not accept an invitation for fear of meeting either a Prince or Princess whilst my husband had not been received by the King,' she remembered. In the meantime Anne had to content herself with snippets of court scandal about the King, who was becoming increasingly unstable. Having built himself a 'Versailles', he then proceeded to imitate every detail of the court of Louis XIV – even the servants wore brocade coats, knee-breeches and powdered wigs. Every day a banquet was laid for thirty people. 'He would arrive bowing low to imaginary guests, and the attendants would all wear black satin masks as he hated human faces.'[10] Although she never met the King, who was six foot three, with 'somewhat defective teeth', Anne once waited for two hours in deep snow at the back entrance of the palace to see him leave in a covered sleigh, wrapped in sables.

Although the custom of an ambassador's public entrance gradually declined, other ceremonies, such as the presentation of credentials, never did (it is still carried out today). When she arrived in Constantinople Lady Elgin was granted an extraordinary privilege which quite compensated for the lack of pomp at her arrival. As a woman in Turkey, however distinguished, she was not allowed to attend her husband's audience with the Sultan, so on that freezing winter's morning it was not his wife but a mysterious new attaché called 'Lord Bruce'* who formed part of the ambassador's company.

Mary rose at four o'clock that morning to make herself ready. Her maid, Masterman, helped her into her riding habit and her great coat, 'my little round beaver hat with a cockade, and black stock', and the two women were ready to leave the house by five. It was still pitch dark outside. Mary was escorted to her chair by her janissaries, who waited with flaming torches to light her way to the waterside. From Pera, where Europeans – including foreign ambassadors and their suites – usually resided, she crossed the Golden Horn to the sultan's† palace, where a carriage had been sent for her.

---

* Bruce was the Elgins' family name.
† Selim III, who was assassinated in 1808.

Just as morning began to dawn, we arrived at the gates of the
Seraglio which were not opened, so I remained in the carriage,
and saw all the guards and people assemble [Mary wrote]. It was
really the most amusing sight you can imagine. When the gates
were opened, we went into the court where I remained until the
Ambassador arrived, as I preferred seeing the fun to being shut
up in a room.

The procession continued to the divan, where the Grand Vizier sat
in state, 'the Grand Seigneur peeping through a lattice at us'. At ten
o'clock, after what seemed to Mary like an interminable wait, a dinner
was served. 'E and the Grand Vizier dined together; I, and some other
men, dined with a Great Man who knew who *Lord Bruce* was, and was
amazingly polite. We dined on a large, round massy silver table.'
After the dinner was eaten, and the ritual gifts – magnificent sable
pelisses for the Elgins – received (a ceremony which ended in a shame-
ful riot as the 'mob' of onlookers came to blows over the last few
kaftans), a select party followed Elgin to the Sultan's throne room,
through the Gate of Felicity into the Third Court, the Sultan's own
private residential quarters and the very heart of the Topkapi Palace:

We each had two men in superb gold embroidered dresses, who
put a hand on each shoulder, and in this form we entered the
room where the GS was setting on his throne. It was a very small
room and dark, but of all the magnificent places in the world I
suppose it is the first. His throne was like a good honest English
bed, the counterpane on which the Monster sat was embroidered
all over with immense large pearls. By him was an inkstand of one
mass of large Diamonds, on his other side lay his sabre studded all
over with *thumping* brilliants.

The Sultan's robe was of yellow satin trimmed with black sable, and
in his turban he wore his famous aigrette. In a window just beyond
him were a further two turbans, each covered with diamonds.

You can conceive nothing in the Arabian Nights equal to that
room . . . As soon as we were in the room E had to make his speech
which was answered by some Great Man. The Grand Seigneur had

to prompt him three times, the poor Creature's voice almost failed him, but you cannot think how good humoured the GS looked, he knew his speech by heart. Only think of my having managed to get Masterman into that room. We did not get home til half past 12 o'clock.[11]

Even in those countries which lay outside the courtly traditions of Europe, diplomatic women were received by the wives of their rulers and leading statesmen with similar ceremony. As the wife of the British consul to Lagos in 1861, Mrs Henry Foote was given a royal reception by the King of Lagos's 100 wives, all of whom were dressed in identical blue cotton cloth. And in Constantinople in 1718 Lady Mary Wortley Montagu was invited to dine with the wife of the Grand Vizier; an entertainment which, she claimed grandly, 'was never before given to any Christian'.* The visit took place in the harem, or women's quarters, of the Grand Vizier's house. In honour of the occasion Lady Mary took care to wear her finest clothes – the court habit of Vienna, 'which is much more magnificent than ours'.

As a mark of respect Mary Elgin, too, wore her court dress when she was first received by the Valide Sultan – the Sultan's mother and most powerful woman in the Ottoman empire. Her whole apparel, especially the trimming of beads and spangles on her dress, and her long gloves, which the Valide made her take off, were closely examined and admired. Although many accounts of the imperial harem had been written since it was first moved into the Topkapi Palace by Suleiman the Magnificent in the mid sixteenth century (the old harem, situated in a different building, had burnt down), Mary Elgin's is one of the very earliest first-hand accounts by a European of this most mysterious and fabled place.†

As before, Mary took a boat across the Golden Horn to the palace.

Upon my arrival at the Seraglio, I was received by a number of Blacks, and as soon as the Great door was closed, I was met by a

---

* This was actually not the case, although she was certainly one of the very first Englishwomen to describe it at first hand.

† Mary Wortley Montagu never actually visited the Sultan's harem. Her visit to the 'Sultana', formerly the principal concubine of the deposed Mustafa II, took place at the house of her second husband, the Minister for Foreign Affairs, Ebubekir Effendi.

vast number of women most magnificently dressed [she wrote in a letter to her mother on 4 October 1800]. Two led me by the arms, whilst one Great Lady walked before me with perfumes smoking in a beautiful gold thing; in this State, I was led upstairs; upon the top stood Hanum (the Pasha's sister) screaming with joy at seeing me. She led me into a room where I arranged my dress, the women holding a glass for me; Masterman told me it was worth looking at the back of the glass; it was completely covered with large pearls and diamonds!

In this anteroom Mary was given coffee and sweetmeats, and when she had finished the Valide herself sent for her. As ceremony required, Mary made her three bows. After the speeches – first Mary's and then the Valide's – had been read out and translated, the Valide made Mary come and sit down on a little sofa placed opposite her.

You can have no idea how excessively polite the Valida was. She said she received me publickly that all the world might know it, for that both she and her son were under such obligations to the English, that they could not sufficiently express their thanks; that they hoped Elgin was to remain here, for that his superior sense, prudence, and abilities, added to his friendship for them, had been of the greatest utility to her Son.

The exceptionally close alliance which existed at this time between the British and the Ottoman empire had been brought about by Napoleon's designs on Ottoman lands, particularly in Egypt. The Battle of the Nile, Nelson's great victory over the French in 1798, would still have been fresh in their minds. This, combined with other military aid and advice given by the British to the Ottoman forces, was the reason for the marked favour with which Mary was received.

'She was very stately,' she wrote of the Valide simply, 'only the Great Ladies were allowed to stand about the room, and all the attendants stood below the step.' She was not wearing many diamonds, but those she had were 'thumpers'.

She had about eight excessively large table diamonds on her head, I never saw any near as large, and on her little finger, she wore the finest and largest brilliant by far, that I ever saw, much larger I think (excuse a traveller!) than the 12,000 pounder we saw at Bridge & Rundles! On a cushion by her lay a watch covered with diamonds, and an inkstand, and a large portfolio studded all over with rubies and diamonds, also a smallish round thing covered with precious stones, which I fancy was a looking glass.[12]

It was a display which was designed to impress. And it did. Lady Mary Wortley Montagu was equally staggered by the sheer opulence displayed by the imperial women on these formal occasions. Despite being both an older and an altogether more cynical traveller than the impressionable Mary Elgin, on a visit to the 'Sultana' Hafise (the principal concubine of the deposed Mustafa II), in 1718, she was hypnotized by the enormous quantity of jewels on view. Unlike Mary Elgin's Valide, the concubine wore a dress almost entirely encrusted with diamonds: 'Round her neck she wore three gold chains which reached to her knees, one of large pearl at the bottom of which hung a fine coloured emerald as big as a turkey egg, another consisting of two hundred emeralds close joined together, of the most lively green, perfectly matched, every one as large as a half crown piece and as thick as three crown pieces, and another of emeralds perfectly round.' But it was her earrings which eclipsed all the rest.

They were two diamonds shaped exactly like pears, as large as a big hazelnut. Round her talpack [head-dress] she had four strings of pearls, the whitest and most perfect in the world, at least enough to make four necklaces every one as large as the Duchess of Marlboroughs, and of the same size, fastened with two roses consisting of a large ruby for the middle stone and round them twenty drops of clean diamonds to each. Besides this, her head-dress was covered with bodkins of emeralds and diamonds. She wore large diamond bracelets and had five rings on her fingers, all single diamonds, except Mr Pitt's, the largest I ever saw in my life.[13]

The whole, she estimated, was worth more than £100,000, by today's reckoning more than £10 million.

On formal occasions such as these, their diplomatic status gave women access to places and people which were forbidden – in Arabic, literally, *harem* – both to their husbands and to ordinary female travellers. In Peking both Mary Fraser and Susan Townley were given audiences by the formidable Empress Dowager Tzu Hsi, who received them in the 'Holy of Holies', at the very heart of the Forbidden City. In 1901, just a year after the Boxer Rebellion, Susan Townley described her journey there along with a number of other ladies of the diplomatic corps.

Borne rapidly along in her official sedan chair, she was at first only dimly aware of her surroundings: numberless vast courtyards flashed past her, each one connecting into the next through Chinese gateways decorated with dragons. At a certain point these chairs were forbidden to pass any further, and so the ladies were transferred into a fleet of palace chairs, upholstered in scarlet satin and slung upon two poles. On the shoulders of their imperial bearers they were carried through yet more courtyards, right into the Great Hall of Audience itself. There, waiting to receive them at the foot of the steps, was 'a gorgeous company of mandarins, court ladies and attendants'.

After the blazing sunlight outside the interior of the audience chamber was cool and dim. At the very centre stood a huge vase in which a vast block of ice had been placed to cool the air. Although the Emperor was present at their audience – the man whose very name was so sacred that it could neither be spoken nor written down in the common form – even he took second place to the Empress Dowager herself. Sitting exactly opposite the door by which they entered, the Empress received them behind a high table covered with yellow silk bearing a glass case containing 'a carved coral sceptre of exquisite workmanship'. It was only when she pushed aside the case in order to shake hands with the ladies who were presented to her that Susan Townley was really able to study 'this remarkable woman of whom I have heard and read so much'.

The Empress Dowager

sat upon a kind of Turkish divan covered with figured Chinese silk of a beautiful yolk of egg colour; being low of stature, her feet (which are of natural size, she being a Manchu) barely touched the ground, and only her head and shoulders were visible over the table placed in front of her. She wore a Chinese coat

Victoria Sackville in Washington, c. 1882. Despite the 'terrible stain' of her illegitimacy, the eighteen-year-old Victoria became a celebrated success as her father's hostess in Washington, receiving no less than fourteen proposals of marriage. She inherited her famously beautiful hair from her mother, the Spanish flamenco dancer Pepita.

Swashbuckling Ann Fanshawe. Her marriage to Richard Fanshawe, Charles II's ambassador to Spain and Portugal, was one of diplomacy's greatest love affairs.

Emma Hamilton as Circe, 1782, by George Romney. A legendary beauty, Emma had many years of social climbing before being accepted as a diplomat's consort.

Lady Harriet Cavendish (later Countess Granville), by Thomas Barber, 1809. An early model for the perfect ambassadress, she secretly enjoyed outwitting the Parisian élégantes.

Mary, Countess of Elgin, by Henry Bone. In 1800, disguised in male clothing, she had the unprecedented experience of attending her husband's presentation to the sultan at the Ottoman court.

Lady in a 'tonjon' or ladies' carriage, R. Ackerman, 1828.

Isabel Burton (standing, far left) in Rio de Janeiro, 1866. 'The Rio Club' was a small coterie of Europeans, mostly diplomats, who dined and picnicked together, and with whom Isabel was much in demand on her occasional trips to Rio. Santos, some two hundred miles up the coast, where Isabel's husband Richard was posted as Consul, was an altogether lonelier place, and Isabel was often forced to ride barefoot to dinners, guiding her pony over streams, while she carried her dress, stockings and shoes in a parcel.

Unloading supplies at the British Legation in Peking, 1900. In remoter postings the arrival of essential stores from Europe was one of the highlights of the year. Companies such as the Army & Navy Stores in London could supply almost anything, from travelling baths and poultry food, to potted lobster and asparagus tips.

Children's Christmas parties, such as this one celebrated in China c. 1890, remain one of the most familiar events in the embassy calendar.

The Chinese Empress H'zu Tsi (1835–1908) with princess Der Ling and her sister Roon Ling in a garden on Peony Hill, Peking. Their diplomatic status gave many women privileged access to people, and places, that were otherwise forbidden to foreign travellers.

The British Legation, Tehran, c. 1900.

European ladies at the British Legation Races at Gulhak, Persia, 1908. The Legation's summer residence was stationed in the hills at Gulhak, just outside Tehran. Women and their families always came here for several months each year to escape the burning heat of the plains.

Riding was an essential part of everyday embassy life for Iona Wright (centre) during her time in Ethiopia. In the 1950s there were still as many as fifteen horses kept in the embassy stables with a string of syce ('grooms') to look after them.

The British embassy's permanent summer camp in the Lar Valley (Persia) was used when the heat even in Gulhak became unbearable. In 1882, a young Gertrude Bell described it in her letters home. Nearly a hundred years later, in the 1960s, Iona Wright was to use the same camp, right down to its elaborately made tents. She recalls how the names of the original tent-makers in Delhi and Cawnpore were still stamped on the back.

The coronation of the Shah in Tehran, 26 October, 1967. According to protocol, the wives of senior diplomats were regarded as part of the court to which their husbands were accredited. Here, the diplomatic corps take their place to the right of the Shah's throne as the Prime Minister reads his address. Iona Wright, then the British ambassadress in Tehran, is seated in the front row, sixth from the left.

A supper given by Emperor Napoleon III for Queen Victoria at the Chateau de Compiegne, 1855. For all its glamour, diplomatic social life in the larger embassies required enormous reserves of stamina, and was not to everyone's taste. 'It is frivolous, eternally frivolous,' lamented Harriet Granville. 'At my age the head is not turned by incessant dissipation; but the time is filled, the result much the same.'

Guests at a diplomatic party, Warsaw, c. 1920.

The Queen's Birthday Party, the largest annual event in the embassy calendar, is celebrated at the Paris Embassy, 14 June 1979. The residence on the Faubourg-St Honore – once the home of Napoleon's sister, Pauline Borghese – was bought for Britain by the Duke of Wellington after the Napoleonic Wars.

Charity fashion show at the residence in aid of the Hertford British Hospital in Paris, June 1980.

Norah Errock (right) and her mother, Lady Stonehewer-Bird, photographed in 1946 with HRH Emir Abdullah of Transjordan. 'He had a strong sense of humour,' Norah Errock recalls, 'and wanted to be photographed with two unveiled women.'

Iona Wright curtseys to the Ethiopian Emperor Haile Selassie. The occasion was the National Liberation Day Reception at the Old Palace in Addis Ababa, 5 May 1960.

Beryl Smedley being 'enstooled' as honorary Queen Mother, in Abesim, 1966. Her husband, Harold, was British High Commissioner to Ghana at that time.

Peggy Trevelyan and her husband receive Brigadier Abdul Karim Kassem (far left), head of the left-wing military regime which overthrew the Iraqi monarchy in 1958, at the Queen's Birthday Party in Baghdad, 1959.

Repair work starts at the British Embassy Residence in Bucharest after the ravages of the 'Christmas Revolution' which overthrew the dictator Ceausescu in 1989. Hiding in the basement, Veronica Atkinson and her family said what they thought were their last prayers as troops aimed gunfire and mortar bombs at their house. To this day, her pictures are marked with bullet holes.

Wreckage of the car in which the British Ambassador to Eire, Christopher Ewart-Biggs, was assassinated by the IRA on 21 June 1976. The car hit a landmine which was concealed under the road just a few hundred yards from the Residence. Jane Ewart-Biggs was to hear the news on her own car radio.

Left: Escorted by soldiers, Jennifer Duncan arrives by boat to visit a British missionary hospital in northern Mozambique just before the outbreak of the Revolution in 1974.

Right: As British ambassadress in Bolivia, Jennifer Duncan joins in the celebrations to mark the building of a British-funded school on the Andean altiplano, 1982.

Jennifer Hickman writing letters home, aided by the author's cat, Minnie. The yearning for contact with home is the emotional experience which unites every woman in this book. In the past, letters could take many months, sometimes as much as a year, to reach their destination.

The author, aged five, arriving in Madrid in 1966, where her father was posted as First Secretary.

loose and hanging from the shoulders, of a diaphanous pale blue silk material covered with the most exquisite Chinese embroidery of vine leaves and grapes. Round her neck was a pale blue satin ribbon about an inch and half wide, studded with large lustrous pearls, pierced, and sewn to the ribbon. Her head was dressed according to the Manchu fashion, the hair being parted in front and brushed smoothly over the ears, to be afterwards caught up at the back and draped high and wide over a kind of paper-cutter of dark green jade set, like an Alsatian bow, crosswise of the summit of the head. The ends of this papercutter were decorated with great bunches of artificial flowers, butterflies and hanging crimson silk tassels. Her complexion is that of a North Italian, and being a widow her cheeks are unpainted and unpowdered according to Chinese custom in such cases. Her piercing dark eyes when not engaged looking at the ladies roved curiously about amongst her surroundings.

Her hands, Susan noticed, were beautifully shaped, but disfigured by the Chinese custom of growing the nails to an inordinate length. 'The nails of the two smaller fingers of the right hand were protected by gold shields which fitted to the finger like a lady's thimble and gradually tapered to a length of three or four inches.'

After the formal presentation was over ('Where has she learnt the ease and dignity with which she receives her European guests?' was Lady Susan's exclamation of surprise) the Empress Dowager conducted the ladies through her private apartments to the banqueting hall. Men were prohibited from entering this part of the Forbidden City, and the Empress led her guests away from the throne room in a yellow silk chair borne by twelve of her eunuchs, a thirteenth eunuch holding a yellow silk umbrella over her head. The European ladies followed behind her, each one supported under the elbows by two girl-attendants.

Susan found herself walking through countless rooms, the contents of each explained to them by the Empress Dowager through an interpreter. The banqueting hall itself was decorated in elaborate Chinese style, its columns gorgeously painted with dragon motifs, but in the middle of it a long European table had been placed and rows of ordinary dining chairs. 'They were evidently procured for our special comfort, but they looked strangely tawdry and out of place in their present surroundings. An ordinary cloth was spread upon the table, but in order to preserve its whiteness immaculate it was covered with shiny American oil-cloth, the ground of which was black, besprigged with coloured flowers.' Although the banquet was a very splendid one, they were given cheap knives, forks and spoons 'of an inferior metal' to eat with and strangely gaudy napkins 'hailing evidently from Manchester' of coarse mauve cotton patterned with large white flowers. 'The liquor consisted of tepid beer poured into a wine glass,' Lady Susan wrote in astonishment, 'or champagne in liqueur glasses!'[14]

Whether in Peking or Paris, life at court was not always everything it was made out to be. Despite the privileged access, despite the glamour of all the external trappings, the jewels, the diamonds, the court dresses – the *grande parure*, as Harriet Granville described it – there were other elements to the public face of diplomatic life which were not enviable at all. A woman posted to one of the larger European capitals found that she had effectively become a member of the court to which her husband was accredited.

This enormous social privilege carried with it an obligation to conform to certain rules and modes of behaviour, and above all, of course, to adhere to the rigid court etiquette of the day. 'Upon 4th January I waited on the Queen, Prince and Empress,* to give them the *buenas pascuas*, as the custom of this court is,' Ann Fanshawe recalled of her first New Year in Madrid.[15] And in The Hague Harriet Granville was obliged to interrupt one of her innumerable letters when she heard canons firing, in order to hurry off and write her name down at the palace, where the Princess of Orange had just given birth.

Other courts, however, made considerably more onerous demands. Mary Fraser and her husband were posted to one of the grandest and most formal courts of all – Vienna. The Empress Elizabeth,† who famously disliked society, deputized most of her duties to her *grande*

---

* Queen Ana Maria, the wife of King Philip IV of Spain. Her daughter the Infanta Margarita Teresa (whose portrait was painted by Velázquez in his masterpiece, *Las Meniñas*) married the Habsburg Emperor Leopold I in 1666. Although she was only fourteen at the time, she took precedence over every other lady at court, including the Queen.
† Wife of Emperor Franz Joseph.

maîtresse, Countess Goess, upon whom the ladies of the diplomatic corps 'were expected to call often and regularly'.

Thursday was the 'Place Day', when the Countess was officially 'at home' to receive calls.

> I was rather overcome by the solemnity of it [Mary wrote the first time she attended one of these receptions]. The hostess sat on a sofa just large enough for two from which a ring of chairs extended and met opposite her in a perfect circle.* She only rose from her seat for Ambassadresses; the rest of us went up and made a 'plongeon' about one third as deep as the curtsey reserved for Royalty. The Grande Maîtresse then extended her hand to be shaken, and, if the lady on the sofa were of lower rank than the new arrival, the seat was instantly vacated, and the latter dropped into it . . . No tea was served, and the conversation had to be general and utterly impersonal, three interesting subjects, the Imperial Family, politics, and gossip, being tabooed. One never did overtime on those visits!

Although these Thursday calls were made by the women alone, court balls and receptions at the Hofburg Palace were, of course, attended by diplomats as well as their wives. Dress, for both men and women, was extremely formal. 'How an Englishman hates a uniform!' Mary wrote, describing how their husbands fumed and cursed at having to don their gold lace and cocked hats. Although the monstrously large hairpieces which had so amazed Mary Wortley Montagu had long been out of fashion, the dress for the women in the 1880s was no less of a trial. This was especially the case when functions, such as the reception held on New Year's Day for the diplomatic corps and 'society', took place in the morning.† Full court dress, which they gamely struggled into at nine o'clock on a wintry January morning, comprised 'a low gown, court train and feathers'.‡

---

* The custom described here is referred to by many diplomatic women who attended court functions, and was often described as conversing *en cercle*.
† It was the rule at the Austrian court that only those with sixteen quarterings – those who could claim unbroken noble descent for four generations – could attend.
‡ As late as 1926 court dress in England consisted of 'a train not more than two yards long and a veil surmounted by three feathers'. A bouquet and fan were optional extras. (From Lady Troubridge, *The Book of Etiquette*.)

At court balls the dress for those in the diplomatic corps was no less formal (although trains were not worn and every move was dictated by protocol). The carriage of an ambassador and his wife, which always carried a green-plumed *chasseur*, or footman, on the box, was allowed to gallop at full speed across the squares of the city. Everyone else was required to travel at a walking pace. All, regardless of rank, had to be in their places by eight o'clock precisely.

Before the ball started, the ambassadors and their suites would make their way to the great mirror salon, where they would line up in strict order of precedence. The Emperor and Empress would then enter through a pair of double doors, accompanied by the chief members of their household, pause a moment, and then separate, 'he taking one side of the circle and she the other, passing each other at the bottom of the room and meeting again at their original place at the top, having said a few words to each individual there'.* After the members of the diplomatic corps had been formally received, they lined up in pairs and were led in procession, the Emperor and Empress at their head, into the *Weisse Saal* or White Ballroom, towards the great raised dais at the far end of the room on which the imperial family would preside over the evening's entertainment.

It was a moment of extraordinary splendour. As the doors opened the crowds of assembled guests parted to receive them, the women ablaze with silks and diamonds, the men in their outlandish Austrian uniform – with their panther-skin cloaks, skin-tight breeches, their scarlet and gold or pale blue and silver tunics – which seemed to Mary to have come straight out of *The Arabian Nights*, and were impossible to imagine as having anything to do with a real battlefield. The room itself, lit by thousands of candles, was one of the most beautiful that she had ever seen, 'spacious and perfect in its proportions, and forming with its soft old white-and-gold walls a charming background for all the glitter and colour that filled it on such occasions.'

This glitter and colour were regulated with true Austrian precision:

---

* At the receptions still given once a year at Buckingham Palace for the diplomatic corps in London, my mother was able to observe the Queen and Prince Philip, and other members of the royal family, receiving foreign diplomats in an identical ceremony.

Everyone else was in place already, the Viennese great ladies all in a group on the right of the dais, the girls, looking like a flock of pretty butterflies, half-way down on the same side, the crowds of men in national costumes and military uniforms filling up all the rest of the floor space except that reserved for the Diplomatists to the left of the dais, where we had to 'stay put' till supper-time.

Such evenings were exhausting for most of the women concerned. Harriet Granville complained of the relentless pace and discomfort of her public duties: *'Fondez-vous comme beurre?'* the Duchesse de Berri once called out to her as she danced a quadrille in a tiny space squeezed out of a crowd of thousands at a great ball at the Hôtel de Ville. The sheer scale of some of these functions meant that even getting away from them was a problem. According to Harriet, she and Granville would frequently be stuck for as long as two hours in the jam of carriages at the end of an evening. The more junior wives often found their lives even more demanding. No refreshments were served, and in Vienna, however grand one's position at the upper end of the ballroom, there were only ever two 'small and inhospitable' marble seats for the use of only the most distinguished dowagers and ambassadresses. 'Everyone else had to stand all night,' Mary Fraser recounted ruefully; when she looked close to fainting, Princess Reuss and Comtesse Robilant took pity on her and 'used to spread out their finery and make room for me to sit down behind and between them . . . screening the awful breach of decorum by putting up their fans, and no one can say how grateful I was for those few inches of resting place after standing on my high heels till they felt like spear-points.'[16] (Twenty years later, in Berlin, Lady Susan Townley breached a similar 'etiquette of the sofa' at one of the Kaiser's balls.)

There are times, even today, when public life as a diplomat's wife seems to require almost impossible levels of stamina. As British ambassadress in Ecuador, my mother wrote with relief to my brothers in May 1980:

Well, the King and Queen of Spain have come and gone, and I think the visit was a great success. We were used as the same old rent-a-crowd and rushed from place to place trying to get there ahead of them. All of which was pretty difficult in view of the fact that they had outriders etc and we didn't . . . Our first occasion was the military parade. The Ecuadorian Army march really quite well providing you don't mind their ridiculous goose-stepping. To add to that they wear helmets like the Prussians and the Kaiser used to wear with a pointed steel tip on the top. These wobble madly while they're goose-stepping and one sat there wondering which one was going to come off . . . We got up and down like yo-yo's as national anthems were played repeatedly, and the Egyptian ambassadress next to me nearly passed out with all the standing.

Angela Caccia found that she needed even greater resilience when she attended a solemn ceremony for the reinauguration of one of Bolivia's many presidents in the 1960s. As usual, the entire diplomatic corps was required at the cathedral for the inauguration mass, the high point of which included a ceremony known as the Washing of the Feet.

The choirboys across the aisle, instructed by their hoarse *masestro*, one by one whipped up their long white surplices and removed their black boots and grey woollen socks. The smell of their feet billowed across us, hot and foetid like a breath from the jungle. The President's wife coughed into a lace handkerchief, and a symphony of coughing, sniffing and blowing broke out among the surrounding ladies. The French Ambassadress looked about to faint.

The President had either great self-control or no olfactory nerves. He moved slowly with a large gilt bowl of water up the row of grubby children, washing and drying each pair of feet.

We shuffled out, gasping and spluttering still, through the rows of soldiers and the trumpet blasts, into the square.

In the European capitals, though, it was the requirements of court life that were nearly always the most brutal. Mary Waddington, who complained frequently of the exhausting weight of her court dress and diadem, once found a pair of lady's shoes discarded behind a sofa after one of the palace balls in Moscow, and heartily sympathized with the unknown rebel who preferred to go home barefoot rather than endure further agony. At the funeral of the much-loved Tsar Alexander I, who died of typhus fever in 1825, Anne Disbrowe recorded how the entire diplomatic corps had to remain standing in their places in the cathedral from nine o'clock in the morning until the proceedings finished at four o'clock that afternoon. Despite the cold, the women were not allowed to wear wrappings of any kind, and nearly froze into the bargain. (It was little consolation to know that the monarchs themselves frequently suffered most acutely on these occasions. Mary Waddington recorded how Queen Victoria was made ill by the continual curtseying and bowing at her own Drawing Rooms at Buckingham Palace: 'the constant movement of the people bending down and rising has the same effect upon her as the waters of the sea.')[17]

Younger and altogether less battle-weary than either Mary Fraser or Harriet Granville (whose exact contemporary she was), Anne Disbrowe wrote marvellously gossipy letters home from St Petersburg in the late 1820s; they illustrate perfectly the intimate connection between a court and its diplomatic corps. 'Nothing can exceed the handsome manner in which the *corps diplomatique* is treated,' she confided to her mother with pride, 'in no country are they so *fêté.*'

Indeed, at the numerous fêtes given by the Tsar at the Peterhof Palace just outside St Petersburg itself, Anne and her husband received truly royal hospitality. One of the first fêtes they attended lasted for three whole days, and carriages, house, board and servants were all provided for them by the Tsar. Their every comfort was looked after by Count Salahoub, one of the court's masters of ceremonies, who was deputed to take charge of all the diplomats. 'We sat down about fifty to dinner, at three, a most splendid repast,' Anne wrote, after which, at seven, the Tsar's carriages came to take them to the ball.

An estimated 130,000 people attended the Peterhof that day; and a total of 4,000 carriages, each driven by four horses (as was the requirement for those admitted to the court). No fewer than 4,000 of the Tsar's own horses were employed for the occasion. Not everyone was so fortunate as the Disbrowes. Such enormous numbers flocked to these entertainments that it was impossible for everyone to find lodgings, and it was not unusual to see guests – ladies as well as gentlemen – dressing in their carriages. 'It was a most extraordinary sight to see the bivouacs, carriages of all sorts and descriptions converted into dressing and sleeping rooms. In one you might see a fair lady adorning herself, in another a party at dinner.'

But it was not only the grandees who had access to the Tsar's fêtes; any of his subjects who cared to attend were free to do so, as Anne, with no small degree of wonder, went on to describe.

Here a group of white-haired scared-looking Fins [sic], there some neat German colonists, Tartars, Calmouks, Jews, horses, carts, men, women and children covered the ground, and formed altogether the strangest assemblage it is possible to conceive. People of every class were admitted to the palace, and it was a striking spectacle to see courtly dames in gold and jewels, Emperor, Grand Dukes and Duchesses, Princes and Counts, whirling through crowds of rustics, men with long beards, women with russet gowns, who gazed in respectful astonishment, and though in close contact with those grandees, showed no symptoms of rudeness, and were as quiet and unpresuming as if they had been bred to palaces and balls.

Diplomats may have had a privileged *entrée* at the St Petersburg court but, like that of Vienna, it was none the less extremely strictly controlled. Although Anne was able to take advantage of her diplomatic status to sit in the circle formed around the Empress mother, who played at piquet with some of her courtiers, protocol dictated that none of the diplomatic corps was able to move except at the command of the *maître de cérémonies*, who conducted them in an orderly way around the palace, not unlike a sheepdog with his flock. It was not always a felicitous arrangement. At one fête Anne saw almost nothing of the proceedings at all: 'at least three hours squeezed in a crowded corridor only procured me a glimpse of the Imperial headdresses.'

Anne adapted quickly to her exotic new life in St Petersburg. The Disbrowes took a large and comfortable house in the Quai des Anglais with beautiful views over the Neva. In the winter she was able to watch the great river freezing over, a curious spectacle in which the water appeared to boil before the ice covered it, 'and vapour or smoke was so thick that the opposite bridge was entirely hid'. To while away the long winter months there were horse-races and skating, *montagnes-russes* and numerous other entertainments on the ice. She walked along 'Newsky Perspective', watching the Russian ladies promenade 'in very gay attire, some in white satin pelisses with sable, others in ditto cloaks, pink, blue, and all the finest colours'.

Anne's wardrobe was always of the greatest importance to her. 'Yesterday I had the felicity of unpacking my Parisian boxes,' she wrote home in excitement, shortly after her arrival in 1825. 'The things are charming, but nothing extraordinary, flounces and full trimmings, no tucks, gigots* and blouses.' At court many of the great ladies, including the Empress, liked to wear Russian dress, and at a costumed ball given by Prince Yowrousoff Anne followed suit. It was 'a pretty little compliment we strangers pay to the natives in adopting their costume: light blue and gold for a serafin or gown, and *ponceau* embroidered in gold and pearls for a cap, not exactly like my old blue one in shape, but very nearly. I am still without a veil, and am now going to hunt for one.' Perhaps the strangest fashion statement of all, however, was one in which she was not allowed to indulge: '*Sposo* will not let me have a verdigris gown,' she wrote disconsolately, 'and they are so lovely I am longing for one ... it is rather odiferous and occasions much sneezing but it is a splendid colour notwithstanding these trifles.'†

The death of Tsar Alexander I in December that same year brought all these musings to an end. Anne was horrified: 'I hear ... that we positively must wear black flannel ... alack a day! I sigh over my velvet pelisse, worn three times, and five gowns never worn at all.' In fact, it was even worse than she had anticipated. As *de facto* members of the court, all diplomats and their wives were expected to take part in the official mourning which followed the Tsar's death. 'The mourning will last a year,' Anne wrote home sorrowfully. 'The first part will be dreadfully dismal. The order is not yet announced, and so I do not know exactly what it is to be except that gowns are to be common black flannel, quite frightful.' In the politically turbulent months that followed, despite witnessing the aftermath of the Decembrist Revolt‡

---

* Leg-of-mutton sleeves.
† Verdigris was a particularly brilliant shade of green. The green copper acetate which was used in the dyeing process clearly had an extremely disagreeable smell.
‡ The anti-tsarist revolt which took place after the death of Alexander I. It was organized by military officers who were disillusioned with their country's reactionary government.

– 'pools of blood on the snow, and spattered up against the houses' – the horrors of black flannel remained uppermost in Anne's mind. 'We all look so dismal in our black cloth gowns, high with falling colours* hemmed in *white*, according to our rank,' weepers† of the same width, black caps, and last night we rehearsed the Points or Schneps, a pointed black band across the forehead hiding almost all the hair: it should be quite hid, but modern coquetry steals out a curl or two.'[18]

Harriet Granville could not agree. 'The poor Duke's death brings me great reprieves,' she wrote with scarcely contained glee after the Duke of York's death in 1827. 'I have already been saved from Pozzo's great drum, a concert at the Palais Royal . . . We have not been told the length of mourning, but as we are to put our household into mourning it cannot be short, and while it continues dancing is out of the question, and when it is over,' she concluded triumphantly, 'Lent will be begun.'‡[19]

Every detail of public life was strictly regulated for diplomatic wives, from the number of diamonds they wore to their presentation, to the depth of their *plongeon* and the length of the court mourning observed. They had to work hard to fulfil the duties expected of them at court and some, like Harriet Granville, complained bitterly of the essential uselessness of it all. 'It is frivolous, eternally frivolous, and at fifty I shall at best be no wiser and better than I am now,' she wrote, adding drily, 'At my age the head is not turned by incessant dissipation; but the time is filled, the result much the same.' Most wives, however, lacking her essential social austerity, were content to see the public face of diplomatic life for what it was.

As silent but privileged witnesses in society, these women found much to enjoy. 'In spite of fatigue, I found constant amusement in watching the ways of this new world,' wrote Mary Fraser of her time at the Viennese court. The vivid descriptions that are their legacy portray a world of luxury and courtly pleasure now gone forever. In 1826 Anne Disbrowe did the honours at the great ball given by the

* Non-transparent veil hanging from the back of the head down to the shoulder.
† A widow's black veil.
‡ Lent marked the end of the social season.

Duke of Devonshire, the Ambassador Extraordinary sent to the Tsar's coronation. The entire marble-white ballroom was decorated with pink roses; an immense circle of wax lights supported on a wreath of roses dangled from the ceiling on such fine wires that the whole seemed held in place by magic. (The candles were lit by a man suspended from the ceiling by a rope.)

Nearly a hundred years earlier Mrs Vigor described the Tsarina Anna Ivanovna's birthday celebrations at 'the new hall that is just finished' in St Petersburg.* It was winter, and the hall was even bigger than St George's Hall in Windsor, but the room was kept warm by ornamental heated stoves. Orange trees and myrtles in full bloom were arranged into two rows, or walks, on either side of the hall, leaving a good space for dancing in the middle. Mrs Vigor was especially glad of these walks, she said, because they made it possible for the company to sit down and rest, unobserved by the sovereigns. Amongst the ladies of the court 'stiffened bodied gowns of white gauze with silver flowers' were the fashion, with quilted petticoats of different colours. The monstrous headpieces of a few decades earlier were no longer worn; instead 'on their heads was only their own hair, cut short, and curls in large natural curls and chaplets of flowers'.

> The beauty, fragrance and warmth of this new formed grove, when you saw nothing but ice and snow through the windows looked like an enchantment, and inspired my mind with pleasing reveries [she wrote in a letter to her English confidante]. In the rooms adjoining were coffee, tea and other refreshments for the company, and when we returned into the hall, the music and dancing in one part, and the walks and trees filled with beaux and belles, in all their birthday finery, instead of the shepherds and nymphs of Arcadia, made me fancy myself in Fairy-land, and Shakespeare's Midsummer Night's Dream was in my head all the evening.

Occasionally, a more active role was required: at the marriage of the Princess Anna Leopoldovna, a niece of the Tsarina, to the Prince

---

* The exact location of this great room is difficult to identify. Anna Ivanovna built many palaces in St Petersburg, none of which has survived.

of Brunswick, protocol required that Mrs Vigor, as the wife of a foreign minister whose master (George III) was related to the Prince, should be present on the wedding night. Her duty was to undress the Princess and help her into her night-clothes. It was an intimate – but not altogether welcome – glimpse into the life of the court. 'And thus ended the grand wedding, from which I am not yet rested,' she wrote on her return home, after she had been escorted by the grand marshal and was 'half dead with fatigue' at three in the morning. 'And what is worse, all this rout has been made to tie two people together, who, I believe, heartily hate one another.'[20]

Others, like Anne Disbrowe and Mary Waddington, and Vita Sack-ville-West, who attended the Shah's coronation in 1926, were suitably aware of the historical moment. Following the coronation of Nicholas I Anne could hardly wait to disrobe from her finery ('my silver gown, you know, and a silver embroidered train over lilac satin, English plumes on my head') and sit down to describe the extraordinary sight from which she had just returned.

> At half past seven this morning the *Corps Diplomatique* assembled in the ancient Palace of the Tsars,* in a low hall whose walls were covered with gilding and saints at full lengths [she wrote on 2 September 1826]. The procession began to enter the Cathedral of the Assumption about half-past eight, the Empress-Mother opened it, and took her seat upon a small throne entirely covered with turquoises . . . The Emperor was attended by his two brothers, the Grand Dukes Constantine and Michael, and the Emperor and Empress were seated on great chairs yclept thrones, under a canopy, the great officers of State arranged on either side of them, the Grand Dukes close to the thrones, the *Corps Diplomatique* stood on the left on raised benches.

'Now what can be more absurd than a coronation?' wrote Vita Sack-ille-West, but even she put aside her cynicism when the moment came. 'There is that in us which revels in ceremonial, and makes us crane to see the enthronement as though we assisted indeed at some moment

* The Kremlin.

of august transfiguration.' Like Cinderella, the Shah travelled in a glass coach drawn by six horses.

Escorted by his generals and his ministers bearing jewels and regalia, the aigrette in his cap blazing with the diamond known as the Mountain of Light, wearing a blue cloak heavy with pearls, the Shah advanced towards the Peacock Throne. The European women curtseyed to the ground; the men inclined themselves low on his passage ... Only the silence seemed strange; one expected a blare of trumpets, a crashing of chords, and nothing came; ... With his own hands he removed the cap from his head, with his own hands he raised and assumed the crown ... Then from outside came a salvo of guns, making the windows rattle, proclaiming to the crowds in the streets that Reza Khan was King of Kings and Centre of the Universe.[21]

CHAPTER EIGHT

Social Life

While Richard Burton, the British consul to Santos in 1865, was off exploring the interior of Brazil, sometimes for months at a time, his wife Isabel fought the crippling loneliness of her situation by sending to Rio for music – 'any of those gay little Andalusian songs, bull-fights, contrabandista or gypsy things,' she wrote bravely, '. . . I am spoony for anything Spanish and have got a guitar and castanets.'

Social life at the British consulate in Santos, then little more than a mangrove swamp, was a very different affair to the pomp and splendour of Vienna, St Petersburg or Paris. Dividing her time between Santos, on the coast, and São Paulo, in the interior, Isabel found that her life was extremely simple, 'very like farmhouse life, with cordiality and sociability with other farmhouses'.

Occasionally all the English living in the area would assemble in honour of some arriving or departing railway swell. There were no carriages with green plumed *chasseurs* to convey Isabel about, and she would often ride barefoot to these dinners, guiding her pony over streams while she carried her dress, stockings and shoes in a parcel. On their arrival, the hosts would show the ladies into a room where they would put on their stockings and shoes, and add the finishing touches to their toilette. 'However, we were not *décolleté*,' she wrote (and how very far away her old English life must have seemed to her at these times), 'nor did we wear flowers or diamonds on that lonely coast.'

Ever resourceful, Isabel made the best of it, with or without Richard (usually without). She made friends with Mr Aubertin, the head of the railway, a useful person with 'a very tidy cellar' to whom she would send down bossy notes: 'Dear Mr Aubertin, bring up the drink – I have got the food. Dinner seven o'clock.' Fortunately, perhaps, for Mr

Aubertin, Isabel had other neighbours to engage her energies and attention. There was a local tribe of Indians, the Botacudos, who wore their underlip distended by a piece of wood, and always marched in single file. When they passed the Burtons' house, they had the curious habit of throwing their arms out towards it 'as if the whole file were pulled by a string'. Another neighbour was a woman known to Isabel as the Marchesa de Santos, who had been mistress to the father of the Emperor of Brazil. The Marchesa was 'a great bit of interest' to Isabel. She had beautiful black eyes 'full of sympathy and intelligence and knowledge' and had led 'a very brilliant and stormy life'. Finally banished by the Empress to Santos, she lived only a few doors away from the Burtons. 'I used to see a great deal of her,' Isabel wrote. 'She was quite *grande dame*, most sympathetic, most entertaining, full of stories of Rio and the Court, and the Imperial people, and the doings of that time.' The Marchesa had been obliged to adopt 'up country habits', however, and took to receiving Isabel *en intime* in her kitchen, where she would sit on the floor gossiping and smoking her pipe.[1]

As these fragments from Isabel Burton's memoirs show, diplomatic social life was not always centred on royalty and grand public events. Much of it was on a much smaller scale – and for good reason. Up until the First World War the numbers of British diplomats appointed to the exalted rank of ambassador were always kept to a minimum, and so there were relatively few embassies. In the eighteenth century the more powerful nations would have declined even to receive an ambassador from a country which they did not consider to be their equal, let alone send one of their own. In the 100 years between 1689 and 1789, for example, only sixty-nine British ambassadors were appointed.* It was a tradition which persisted well into the present century; as recently as 1910 there were still only eight.

It was more usual, from the seventeenth to the nineteenth century, to find missions headed by diplomats of lesser rank – depending on the powers invested in them, these were known as agents, residents, envoys, and then later as ministers or ministers plenipotentiary – who carried out less complicated and important work than ambassadors.

---

* This did not include Turkey, which was a special case. During this period its ambassadors were appointees of the Levant Company.

In the nineteenth and early twentieth century these missions were more commonly known as legations, the head of which carried the rank of minister.

Most numerous of all, but with considerably less *éclat* than either embassies or legations, were consulates, which, in the eighteenth century, were usually created following the signing of a commercial treaty with a foreign power. Whereas embassies and legations were appointed to capital cities, the centres of political and social power, consulates were chiefly sited in centres of trade – in the eighteenth century they were commonly found in the Mediterranean ports of Europe, the Levant and the Barbary Coast. Although consular privileges were considerably less extensive than diplomatic ones – they did not (and still don't) include diplomatic immunity, for example – it was generally recognized that special protection was due to consuls under the law of nations, and 'a certain respect shown'.[2] The chief difference, however, was a social one.

This was not to say that the less politically important British missions and consulates did not have a social role to play. Far from it. The custom of paying and receiving calls – until the Second World War an essential element of all European social life – was no less important in diplomatic missions further afield. However, the etiquette governing such calls varied enormously. At the turn of the century Susan Townley learnt the conventionally polite Chinese enquiry: 'How is your Excellency's favoured wife?' To which, unvaryingly, would come the equally conventional reply: 'Thank you, Madam. The foolish one of the family is well.'[3]

At the same Peking legation, Mary Fraser once received a visit from the ladies of a high Manchu dignitary. In Europe and America a morning call would usually last between fifteen and thirty minutes. In China it was a rather more lengthy operation. These exquisite figures as gorgeously attired as butterflies were marvellous to look at (having spent five hours or more on their *toilette*) but Mary found it 'something of an ordeal to have the wife of a great dignitary arrive at eleven or twelve o'clock and stay till sunset'. During their stay – 'call' being perhaps too ephemeral a word – they would 'flit around from room to room fingering everything, trying on one's clothes, turning out wardrobes and asking the name of every article, and strange to say, carrying off all the toilet soap in sight'.[4] Susan Townley, hosting a similar visit from some of the imperial princesses, found them as 'playful as kittens', at teatime surreptitiously filling their big sleeves with English cakes.

All three of the diplomatic wives who wrote of their experiences in Kashgar found the social customs of Chinese Turkistan a puzzle. When Catherine Macartney arrived in 1898, people began calling on her at once to see what sort of a wife her husband George had found. One of her first visitors was the wife of one of the Indian munshis or secretaries, who sat and talked and ate sweets for so long that poor Catherine grew almost desperate. 'Then she began to yawn,' Catherine recalled, 'but still she stayed, and I racked my brains to think of a way to get rid of her. The strain of entertaining someone I could not understand or speak to for nearly two hours was making me feel hysterical.' At last their gong went for dinner and Catherine stood up, whereupon the munshi's wife also jumped up, looking nearly as relieved as Catherine herself, and hurried off. Later George explained to her that, as hostess, it was she who should have given the poor woman the sign to leave.

On another occasion, when George's Chinese munshi brought his wife to call on Catherine, her piano had just arrived from Edinburgh (it had been specially packed for the long mountain journey in zinc-lined cases). The pair were evidently so fascinated by the instrument that George asked Catherine to sing something, which she did, 'feeling very pleased with the impression I was evidently making'. They sat and listened, never taking their eyes off her, as though enraptured; 'but to my utter astonishment,' Catherine later wrote, 'when I had finished, they just collapsed in peals of laughter.' Although, she admitted, 'it was rather a shock to my vanity,' she quickly realized that the only way to save the situation was to laugh too, 'and we all roared with laughter together.'[5]

The grand public events attended by diplomatic wives in the larger postings had many parallels in the smaller and more obscure ones. Quieter and less ceremonious, these occasions were in their own ways equally memorable to the women who witnessed them. Very often they carried the added mystique of being forbidden to male eyes.

Both Masha Williams and Diana Shipton vividly remembered the purdah parties they attended. Masha's took place at the residence in

Baghdad, where under their gowns and veils, which they took off at the door, all the women appeared in smart dresses, 'much too tight'. In Kashgar, Diana Shipton gave the party herself, on Boxing Day, as part of her Christmas celebrations. She had no idea of the exact numbers of women hidden away in 'the rabbit warren' of the consulate, and so she simply laid out as many cakes as she could find, and banned her servants from the drawing room for the afternoon.

The slow trickle of women soon turned to a flood.

> There was no stiff silence and restraint. The room bulged with women; those who had no chair sat on the floor; everyone talked at once and screamed across to friends opposite; helpers picked their way about with trays of cakes and tea, falling over crawling babies or bumping into each other, so that tea poured onto the carpet and cakes were trampled underfoot. The babies were being fed by their mothers or were howling, others chewed any available cake, ashtray and cigarette, or made a quiet pool to add to the general fun.

Despite the chaos, she always enjoyed these parties far more than 'the stiff, embarrassed parties of men'.[6]

Miss Tully's letters, written between 1783 and 1793, have left a detailed record of social life on the Barbary Coast. The Netherlands, Sweden, Denmark, Spain, the Italian states and France all kept consuls in Tripoli and Miss Tully paints a familiar picture in which, amongst the Europeans, 'the custom is to have a general party, or (as the Italians term it) a *conversazione*, alternately at each of the Consuls' houses, where all the rest of the families meet.' Of far greater interest, however, are the uniquely detailed descriptions she was able to give of the entertainments that she regularly attended at the Bashaw's castle.*

During their unusually long residence – Richard Tully was consul in Tripoli from 1772 until 1793 – the ladies of his family had attained a unique position there: his daughters spoke the language fluently,

---

* The bashaw was Ali Koromanli. The Koromanlis were an Arab dynasty who ruled the Regency of Tripoli under the nominal suzerainty of the Ottoman Sublime Porte (see also p. 208).

and were known by the affectionate sobriquet '*Bint el bled*' (children of the country). Although many other diplomats visited harems at one time or another, few experienced the close intimacy these English women enjoyed with women such as Lilla Amnani, the Greek-born wife of the Tripolian ambassador to England, and, most strikingly, Lilla Halluma, the Bashaw's own wife.

Despite her privileged position, on her first visit to the royal harem Miss Tully could not prevent a frisson of fear from passing through her as she made the long journey to the forbidden quarters at the very heart of the Bashaw's castle. It was a forbidding place, and became all the more so during the frequent periods of political unrest which characterized Ali Koromanli's reign.

We passed through some subterraneous passages almost entirely without light . . . when we arrived at the entrance of the last of these gloomy passages, a door nearly all of iron, securely fastened, prevented our advancing further till our names were reported. After some time, we heard the eunuch advance, push back the iron bolt, and, with great difficulty, remove two immense heavy bars, with which this pass has lately been guarded. . . . [Miss Tully recorded, her style owing not a little to the gothic novels so popular at the time]. As soon as this gate was opened, a lantern, carried by one of the eunuchs, gave just enough light to discover a part of their formidable figures, and the glare of their arms; but when they held it up to take a better survey of those to whom they had just given entrance, it shone fully in their faces, which, black as jet, were rendered more striking by the fierceness of their eyes and the whiteness of their teeth, and thrilled us with horror.

The gloom and the darkness of their sinister subterranean journey into the harem was an extraordinary contrast to the light and splendour within. Like Mary Fraser's Manchu ladies, the women always took the most elaborate pains over their appearance, and would spend many hours dressing themselves 'in gala'. They would plait and perfume their hair, using scented waters and large quantities of Arabian perfumes – as much as eight ounces of powdered cloves at a time. During the course of the day they would repeatedly change their dress, each time for a still richer habit.

On one occasion, when Miss Tully attended a feast after the birth of one of the Princess's children, she found herself in company with several hundred other women. The gallery overlooking a central court-yard had been richly decked with Indian matting, Turkish carpets and silk cushions, while the feast itself – consisting of thirty to forty dishes of meat and poultry – was laid out on long, low tables raised only a few inches off the ground. After the meat courses came 'a dessert of Arabian fruits, confectionaries, and sweetmeats'. They drank sherbets, and the juice of raisins, pomegranates and oranges. 'These sherbets were copiously supplied in high glass ewers placed in great numbers on the ground,' Miss Tully wrote, 'reminding one much of the ancient scriptural paintings.'

On other simpler occasions, such as the 'visits of etiquette' paid to the principal ladies at the castle, they were received as formally as in any drawing room in London or Paris. Slaves were on hand to wash their hands with perfumed waters, and they were offered a choice of sherbets and coffee to drink. Miss Tully recalled how the coffee, sweet-ened and heavily spiced with cloves, cinnamon and saffron, was served in tiny cups on golden trays 'so large that they are carried round to the company by two black eunuchs'. (On one occasion they were received on western-style chairs, a great novelty in an Arab household at the time.)

During such visits they were also allowed to witness much rarer domestic scenes. When in the presence of Christians, Muslim women would express regret at their lack of liberty, but they were never unemployed, as Miss Tully explained:

The Moorish ladies are in general occupied in overlooking a numerous set of slaves, who make their sweetmeats and cakes, clean and grind their wheat, spin, and in short, are set about whatever seems necessary to be done. The ladies inspect by turns the dressing of the victuals, and during the time spent in this way, two sets of slaves are in attendance; one set perform the culinary operation, while another station themselves round their mistress, removing instantly from her sight any thing that may annoy her, and using fans without intermission, to keep off flies or insects, while she leans on one or other of the slaves, walking about to direct and overlook what is doing.[7]

Such engagements could be lengthy ordeals, especially in the east. Both Isabel Burton in Damascus and Mary Elgin in Constantinople found that it was considered perfectly normal to spend several days at a stretch visiting female friends in the harem, while in Persia Mary Sheil once attended a mystery play which lasted ten days. The play was a Shiah representation of the slaughter in the desert of 'Imam Hoossein' and his family (commonly performed in the month of Moharren), and the audience displayed such real grief at the enacted events that at first Mary, with her tendency to Victorian starchiness, was shocked. From behind the purdah screen, where she sat with the other women, she described how several thousand people gave vent to their grief 'in the style of schoolboys and girls'. But, to her confusion, the 'contagion', once it had started, spread to all. 'I too felt myself forced, would I or not, to join my tears to those of the Persian women around me,' she confessed, 'which appeared to give considerable satisfaction to them.'[8]

Once, having spent two and a half hours sitting on a hard narrow bench at the Turki Cultural Association in Kashgar, Diana Shipton turned to the wife of the Russian consul-general to ask, in a whisper, how much longer the entertainment would last. 'Six years,' came the confident reply.*

For her predecessor, Catherine Macartney, Chinese banquets demanded a strong stomach. One day, shortly after her arrival, a formal invitation arrived from the Ti-tai, the provincial commander-in-chief in Kashgar, and his wife. The invitation – a thin piece of red paper about two feet long – was to a first-class banquet, an indication that the great delicacies of swallow's nest soup and suckling pig would both be served. Translated, the invitation read: 'Respectfully, and with goblet in hand, I await the light of your countenance on the sixth day of the first moon at midday.'

At the appointed time Catherine and George set off, but on arriving at the Ti-tai's *yamen*, or residence, they were at once spirited off to different parts of the house, and did not see each other again until the feast was over. Unable to speak a word of the language, Catherine was left to fend for herself. In the women's quarters everyone was very friendly to her. As the principal guest she was led to the *kang*, or raised bed, at the end of the room, and made to sit at her hostess's left hand.

* Happily, this was not actually the case.

The other women crowded round to see how she was dressed: 'They opened my fur coat to see what I wore beneath it, stroked the feather in my hat, and seemed highly amused at my serviceable winter clothing.' Her feet, in particular, in their thick black shoes and black stockings, caused much excitement and hilarity. 'The little ladies put out their tiny embroidered satin shoes to compare with them, and went into peals of laughter at mine, till I tucked them away under me, hoping they would forget all about the ugly black things.'

When the food came it was a welcome relief. Or so it seemed at first. The banquet began with 'ancient eggs', which were 'not as bad as I expected they would be, and when one tried to imagine that they were what they very much resembled, gorgonzola cheese, and not bad eggs, they were quite possible to eat.' The eggs were followed by about forty different courses – including 'meat, vegetables, poultry, dried fish of many kinds, sea slugs, ducks, shark's fins, seaweed, lotus seeds, and roots, fungi of various sorts, sweet dishes and the very special delicacies, sucking-pig, which seemed to be simply the crackling served sweet, and swallow's nest soup'.

The swallow's nest soup, which Catherine had heard so much about, was a great disappointment to her. 'It is made from the gelatinous lining of the nest of a special breed of swallow that lives in south China and builds in most inaccessible places on the cliffs . . . the idea is not a very nice one, I know, but it seems that the birds themselves make this gelatinous stuff with their saliva to line their little nests.' Exotic as it sounded, Catherine reported that it tasted like nothing so much as onion- and garlic-flavoured vermicelli: 'I could not find anything very delicious about it whatever.'

But when it came to the sea slugs, Catherine's Scots phlegm, which had carried her valiantly through the ordeal, deserted her completely. If only they had been minced up, or simply disguised in some way, she lamented, it would not have been so bad; 'but they were served boiled whole, and when I saw these huge black slugs, covered with lumps, wobbling about in front of me, I wondered how I should live through the ordeal of swallowing one.' But there was no avoiding it. Her servant, Jafar Bai, had thoughtfully provided her not only with knives and forks but with salt and English mustard, all of which had appeared at her place on the table. Now, covering one of the slugs liberally with mustard, she shut her eyes and bravely swallowed one whole. But 'The ladies were so pleased with me that they insisted on me eating another,' she recalled piteously, 'and three or four times I had to go through the awful ordeal.' It was many days before she forgot the sight and the taste of slug, and they made her horribly ill.[9]

Pat Gore-Booth's husband, Paul, once wrote that diplomats 'must be able to contrive anything, bear anything, eat or drink anything and appear to like it'. The same could be said of their wives. Miss Tully was obliged to eat omelettes made from ostrich eggs and a fried cake of uncertain origin which looked like a toasted crumpet and was 'too disagreeable to be partaken of by Europeans'. She also tasted a delicacy, once sent as a gift by the Greek Patriarch of Alexandria, called *beccafigos* – tiny birds about half the size of larks, that feasted on figs and were then pickled whole in jars 'fit to eat without further dressing'. In Korea Maureen Tweedy was introduced to the joys of abalone, which had 'all the enticing texture of a piece of Wellington boot', and in Japan Mary Fraser battled with pickled horseradish, 'so pungent and horrible, that it might be employed as a danger signal at home'.

The American-style menu, produced for Mary's delectation at their hotel in Atami (where she was taking the hot waters for her rheumatism), was probably not much of an improvement:

Carrots Soup
Fish fineherbs
Beef Tea Pudding
Dournat
Boiled Sponge
Praised oeufs devil Sauce
Eclairs ala Onjam
Fish Squeak
Dam Pudding[10]

Foreign food was not always the object of suspicion. It could be delicious, and luxurious too. Diana Shipton recalled with pleasure the twenty-six exquisite different varieties of melon available in Kashgar, while in La Paz Angela Caccia experimented with almost infinite varieties of Bolivian potato, the buying of which her cook considered to be an art form in itself. She also drank *tisanes* made from coca leaves (the basic ingredient for cocaine, and commonly used to ward off altitude sickness). Susan Townley was amazed to be sent an entire sturgeon as a gift by the Empress Dowager in Peking, while Margaret Bullard recalled a feast given in Jordan in 1972 at which the main dish was a camel stuffed with a sheep, stuffed with a goat, stuffed with a turkey, stuffed with a chicken, which was itself stuffed with rice and hard-boiled eggs.[11]

Miss Tully wrote lyrically of the beauty of the fruit which grew in the gardens of Tripoli, of the 'sweet orange of Barbary, water melons, pomegranates, Indian and Turkey figs, apricots, musk melons and peaches. Several sorts of fine plums and some very high flavoured sweet grapes.' Best of all, however, was the exquisite heart of the date tree, a delicacy only ever eaten at the most important feasts and weddings, at the birth of a son, or the return of an ambassador to his family. The heart, which weighed between ten and twenty pounds, was eaten only when the tree was 'at the height of its perfection'. 'When brought to table its taste is delicious,' she recorded carefully for her English correspondent,

and its appearance singular and beautiful. In colour it is composed of every shade, from the deepest orange and bright green ... to the purest white; these shades are delicately inlaid in veins and knots in the manner of the most curious hook. Its flavour is that of the bannan and pine; except the white part, which resembles more a green almond in consistence, but combines a variety of exquisite flavours that cannot be described.[12]

This preoccupation with food was hardly surprising. Producing meals – not just for family consumption, but for the numerous official parties, dinners and lunches – was an all-consuming task for most diplomatic wives. However, the scale of such entertaining varied enormously. Isabel Burton's diamondless dinners on the lonely coast of Brazil, where the fare was likely to be plain *fejao* (beans) or *milho* (maize), can hardly compare with the ball and banquet for 900 people given by Marie-Noele Kelly in Istanbul one starry night in 1948. While Isabel's guests met in the simple white-washed convent which she had converted into a consulate, Marie-Noele's assembled at the embassy's summer residence in Pera, a 'great imperial pile copied from the Barberini Palace in the Rome of Victoria's days'.

This palace overlooked the Bosphorus, and possessed a ballroom so vast that even the 900 guests hardly filled it. Marie-Noele's Italian chef Antonio had called in all his friends, the chefs from other embassies, to help him, and when she visited the kitchens 'the scene was a setting from Hieronimous Bosch, so tense was the atmosphere, so gargantuan the preparations'. Later that evening her 900 guests consumed 500 chickens, 'and piles of Turkish *dolmans* and *bureks* two feet high were arranged in architectural splendour at regular intervals with French *pièces montées* on groaning tables'.[13]

Even in the grandest diplomatic households with numerous domestic staff, an embassy wife's own role in the culinary process was all-important. In previous postings, Mary Henderson had personally cooked for as many as 200 people, which was of invaluable help to her when she had to discuss large parties with her chef at the Paris embassy in the 1970s. In her *Vegetable Book* the cookery writer Jane Grigson quotes a recipe for stoved potatoes from the collection of Lady Clark of Tillypronee. Lady Clark collected recipes all her life – not only from her native Scotland, but from the numerous chefs she employed in Paris, Brussels and Turin. After her death, in 1901, the collection which she had amassed (which included no less than five versions of Bagshot clear soup* in thirteen different variations) were eventually edited and published by a family friend.

Almost all embassy women collected recipes at one time or another. Rosa Carless developed a passion for Persian cooking during her posting to Iran, while my mother's own recipe collection includes everything from how to make a real Spanish omelette to Ecuadorian *pollo boracho* (drunken chicken), and the delicious *locro de papas* (potato soup).† A popular stand-by in our household was *The International*

---

* A consommé made with shins of beef, veal and lean ham, flavoured with celery, leeks, carrots; flavoured with a bunch of herbs, garlic, peppercorns and cinnamon. It was simmered for six to eight hours.

† Mariana's *locro de papas*: 'Fry 3–4 finely chopped leeks, some garlic and a chopped tomato in fat to which *achiote* (turmeric) has been added to make a good orange colour.

'Add 2–3 lbs coarsely chopped peeled potatoes, and fry gently til they begin to look transparent. Add salt, pepper. Add a litre of milk (or milk and water) and boil for about ½ an hour til potatoes are beginning to break up.

'Mash slightly to thicken soup and crumble in a good handful of ordinary soft white cheese. Stir til cheese has melted. Serve with coarsely chopped avocado (perhaps tossed in lemon juice) and fresh parsley.'

Recipe Book, compiled by the Diplomatic Service Wives Association in the 1970s from just such individual and, at times, highly idiosyncratic sources. Alongside the usual cocktail dips and avocado mousses so beloved of that era one could find more exotic offerings: groundnut stew from Sierra Leone, Seth's fish balls from Ghana, macrobiotic salad from Japan (from Rosa Carless) and Zanzibar fish mould.

Even in the most remote postings there were culinary standards to be maintained. In Kashgar Ella Sykes not only battled to keep her brother Percy's shirt fronts boiled and starched, but used all her ingenuity to produce the kind of dinners which she believed appropriate to grace the consular table. Here is one of her menus:

Hors d' oeuvre

Caviar on toast   Salmon mayonnaise   Fried sausages

Tomato Soup

Meat Courses

Chicken aspic   Steaks à la Tournados   Indian Curry
Vegetables

Sweets

Trifle   Jam Tarts   Ices

Savoury
Cheese Straws

Dessert

The sheer effort involved in producing a six-course dinner in Kashgar in 1915 must have been stupendous. Not only did Ella have to drum the recipes into her cook – since he could neither read nor write the only way to teach him was to demonstrate each dish herself, repeatedly, until he could remember the right quantities and be trusted to make it on his own – but she had to find all the ingredients. All the beef and fish were diseased (her salmon, like so much else, would have come from the inevitable Army & Navy tins), and only the toughest of mutton and chickens could ever be procured. Although they grew their own vegetables and had their own eggs and milk, there were innumerable other shortages. The war in Europe had put a stop to their supplies of imported white flour, and Ella was forced to use 'native' flour, 'with its large admixture of grit and dust'. Instead of butter she used suet in the form of *dumba*, the fat from the tail of the central Asian sheep. It was a valiant effort, and under the circumstances her dinners were at least as brilliant a gastronomic achievement as any number of French *pièces montées* (although just how much they were appreciated by her guests is not on record).[14]

For many women the constant headache of producing meals was compounded by the desire to fly the flag by serving specifically *British* food. 'I have found that foreigners like our traditional dishes, which are a change for them,' wrote Mary Henderson in an article on 'Entertaining Abroad', 'so I have often served roast beef and Yorkshire pudding to Foreign Ministers. I rather want to serve treacle tart in Paris, but Nicko is a little uncertain about this!'*[15]

Nicko was not the only one. The economic effects of two world wars, and the culinary ones of rationing, meant that until the recent renaissance of British cookery not all foreigners were as keen as they might be to sample the delights of British cuisine. (The Paris embassy, where the Hendersons served from 1975 to 1979, was a little different, since it had no less than four French chefs.) But with some ingenuity much was achieved, such as this May Day buffet luncheon:

Fish Soup

Salmagundy†   Galatine of Hare   Pork Pie

Green Salad   West Country Mackerel   Spicy Beetroot

Baked Potatoes

Mrs Cochran's Sauce   Home made rolls

Trifle   English Walnut Cake   Lemon Curd Pancakes

Old English Herb Cheese and Oatcakes[16]

Some attempts were more successful than others. In Chile my mother remembers her joy at getting hold of some almost unobtainable

---

* Lady Henderson later went on to publish a book of her chef's recipes, *The Paris Embassy Cook Book*, Weidenfeld & Nicolson, London, 1980.

† Salmagundy is a recipe taken from the English eighteenth-century cookery writer Hannah Glasse; it is a plate of hors d'oeuvres, including ham, celery, hard-boiled eggs, mussels and olives.

smoked salmon for an important dinner party of visiting VIPs, and her silent consternation as she watched it dished up, boiled to a pulp, to the guests round her table.

After the lengthy and often laborious process of buying, preparing and cooking the food, it still had to be served. Ella Sykes was particularly despairing on the subject:

> When we were seated at table my anxieties were by no means over, for, in spite of my coaching, the waiters were fond of getting into one another's way, and occasionally there were unseemly wrangles between Sattur, who considered that he was the head, and masterful Jafar Bai, who would sometimes wrench the bottle of wine from him as he was endeavouring to fill up the glasses of our guests.[17]

In Ulan Bator organizing formal meals was never less than a 'challenge and a nightmare', even in the 1970s, according to Ann Hartland-Swann. Milk had to be mixed from powder; cream emulsified from butter and milk; all bread and bread rolls had to be home made, and the meagre supplies, which came from Denmark on erratic Soviet trains, would suddenly and inexplicably disappear from the shops. Ann gradually realized that the easy life she had envisioned, 'cushioned by servants', was simply not to be. 'No Mongolian maid can ever honestly be called "trained",' she wrote with resignation. 'One *could*, perhaps, describe as "training" the continuous process of supervision, gentle bullying (they are a diffident and quiet nation) and correction ("No, the host is served *last*, *not* first, and from the *left*, please, and the chocolate sauce was meant for the pudding *not* the fish"), but I doubt it . . .'

Ann described how at first, marooned at her own dinner table, she used to wait in terror to see what had become of her laboriously prepared dishes (cooks were unknown in Mongolia). 'To talk about the weather in three languages, trying to ignore plates and glasses which had been empty for fifteen minutes while ominous crashes (or, worse, a deadly silence) emanated from the kitchen, was not conducive to the assured poise of the ideal hostess.' The only solution – possible because of the extraordinary degree of comradeship which existed there – was to call upon one's diplomatic sisters. On the evening of a dinner party one of the other embassy wives would volunteer to mastermind operations from the kitchen, 'heating up dishes, serving out, thrusting wine and rolls into the maid's hands, cajoling and managing'.[18]

There were some disasters, however, which no amount of managing could circumvent. Bridget Keenan, stationed in Africa, described a dinner party at which her butler, Ceesay, simply disappeared.

> The plates needed clearing away, but Ceesay was not to be seen. 'Ceesay' my husband whispered louder and louder, getting a bit desperate. Suddenly Ceesay was back at his side. 'Ceesay, where have you been?' asked my husband in an undertone. 'Sorry Boss,' said Ceesay loudly and totally unabashed, 'I was just taking a piss.' The guests looked appalled. 'Well, I hope you washed your hands,' said my husband, deciding there was nothing left to do but make a joke out of it. 'Oh NO Boss!' said Ceesay, indignant that anyone would think he had wasted his time.[19]

In the past most diplomatic social life was not significantly different from that enjoyed by almost all the British upper classes – with its formal presentation parties and Drawing Rooms at Buckingham Palace, its concept of the Season, and its elaborate visiting rituals. With only a few changes, diplomatic women simply did what seemed quite natural to them. This is not to say that there was not a very real degree of skill, even artistry, involved.

'The idea that anybody can acquire popularity or respect in a foreign capital without taking real trouble and treating these social duties as an artistic craft, such as acting or politics, is . . . unreal,' wrote Marie-Noele Kelly with feeling. She had been brought up rather formally in the Belgian aristocracy, but she was realistic enough to realize that most truly great hostesses are made, not born. She was fascinated by the technique behind what she called 'the chequer board' of a diplomatic gathering, and the way in which a really accomplished hostess could make or mar a party by her social skills. 'What I really admired was the manner which, natural and smooth as it looked, was, I sensed, acquired.'[20]

Victoria Sackville, one of British diplomacy's most flamboyant personalities, must be one of the few exceptions which prove this rule.

Although she was only eighteen when, in 1881, she was sent to Washington as her father's hostess, it was said of her that during the seven years she presided at the British legation she never once made a mistake. And yet, according to her daughter Vita Sackville-West, she was a woman in whom artifice played no part whatsoever:

> Many people have told me what a clever woman my mother was, and what good taste she had; it was a sort of label tied onto her; but it was utterly wrong. She was anything but clever, and her taste was anything but good. Like a child, she neither analysed nor controlled her moods; they simply blew across her, and she was first one thing, then the other, without exactly realising which side was uppermost. She never thought, she merely lived.[21]

The circumstances surrounding Victoria's entry into diplomatic life are some of the most extraordinary in its history. The second of the seven natural children of Lionel, second Lord Sackville, and Pepita, the Spanish gypsy dancer who was his mistress for nineteen years, Victoria was brought up in almost total seclusion. After the death of her mother when she was just eleven years old, Victoria was sent to a convent in Paris, where she remained for the next seven years. The stigma of her illegitimacy was such that, on the rare occasions when she was at her guardian's apartment in Paris, she was expected to leave the room if visitors arrived.

Her father, a British diplomat, was almost always abroad and saw his children infrequently. Victoria was trained as a governess, and might well have become one, had not her father been appointed British minister to Washington. In the 1880s the British legation there, while not on a par with the major European postings, was of growing political importance,* but American ladies did not attend entertainments in households where there was no hostess to receive them. Lionel was still unmarried. It was imperative to find someone to play the part for him.

Lady Derby, one of Victoria's aunts, had observed her niece closely when she came to England on a brief visit, and decided to take a gamble. Until only a few years previously her husband, the earl of

---

* The legation became a fully fledged embassy some ten years later in 1893.

Derby, had been Foreign Secretary* and Lady Derby now used all her political influence with both Lord Granville, the current Foreign Secretary,† and the Queen, to persuade them that Victoria should go to Washington. It was a bold move. The 'terrible stain and stumbling block'[22] of illegitimacy meant that her niece had never been presented at court, the *sine qua non* of entry into European society. Amazingly, the Queen agreed, but with one proviso: Washington society must agree to accept her first.

Back in Washington a committee was formed comprising all the most important political hostesses of the day. These included the wife of the President, Mrs Garfield, the wives of the Secretary of State and the Under-Secretary of State, and the wife of one of the leading Republican senators, Don Cameron of Pennsylvania. 'The question put to these ladies was whether society could accept as the hostess of the most important diplomatic mission in Washington an 18 year-old, illegitimate daughter. The answer was favourable.'[23]

When Victoria Sackville stepped off the boat in America on 22 December 1881, she had no knowledge at all of the world she was about to enter. Innocent, barely educated, her English still far from perfect, she had nothing but her youth and her charm to recommend her. Alluring rather than conventionally beautiful, she had a flawless skin, a tiny waist, and had inherited her mother's astonishing dark hair, which when let down fell to below her knees.

> West, the new Minister, and his daughter, who was just come over, came in [wrote Mrs Adams, one of Washington's most influential society hostesses] ... and I thought her charming; she is the daughter of a Spanish ballet dancer, now dead, and has been educated at a convent in France, is quite pretty, rather elegant, and speaks with a most charming foreign accent. It's a curious position for a girl of eighteen, to be put at the head of a big establishment like the British Legation. She is delighted with her first week here.[24]

---

* The second Earl of Derby was Disraeli's Foreign Secretary between 1874 and 1878. Under Gladstone he became a Liberal, and was appointed Colonial Secretary in 1882.
† George Leveson-Gower, second Earl Granville, was Countess Granville's son (Foreign Secretary 1880–85).

And Washington was delighted with her. Just ten days after her arrival, dressed in 'a heavy, dark green satin walking dress, with a simple bonnet to match', Victoria made her debut at the President's New Year's Day reception. She was an immediate sensation. All the reporters present succumbed instantly to her charm, and 'rushed for their notebooks to cram them with superlatives', declared her biographer, Susan Mary Alsop. 'No other women in the DC was to receive such coverage.'

As Victoria herself often expressed it, '*Quel roman est ma vie!*' After the dullness and seclusion of the convent, her new life was to involve her in a truly punishing social schedule. In addition to running a large household (Lord Sackville had brought over a dozen French and English servants, and three carriages), she had to attend not only state occasions, but dinners, dances and ladies' lunches. These last were the most elaborate affairs, at which as many as twelve different courses were offered, taking up to two and a half hours to serve. A lunch given by a Mrs Blaine offered the following menu: oysters on the shell, mock turtle soup, broiled chicken and fried potatoes, sweetbreads and peas, asparagus, Roman punch, partridge and salad, ices, charlottes, jellies, sweetmeats, fruits, coffee and tea.

Like many other diplomatic wives both before and after her, Victoria found the custom of 'calling' by far the most burdensome of her social duties. During the winter season, which lasted from New Year's Day until Lent, she paid up to 300 calls, which that year would have worked out at more than five calls a day, not including Sundays. (Anne Disbrowe would have sympathized: 'Mr Disbrowe and I actually paid 9 and 20 calls on Easter Monday,' she wrote. 'Are you not overcome at the very idea?')

The stamina needed for this kind of social life was enormous. In 1881 an extremely rigid system was still in place. On their afternoons 'at home' most ladies received visits between three and five o'clock. Monday was the day allocated for the wives of justices of the Supreme Court, and the wives of army generals and navy admirals. Tuesday was the day allocated for prominent families, especially senators' wives, living in the West End. Wednesday was the day for cabinet wives and the wife of the Speaker of the House. Thursday was the day reserved for diplomatic calls, while Friday and Saturday were 'a mixed bag' of all the rest, 'sometimes announced by the newspaper and sometimes by invitation'.

The etiquette surrounding calling and card-leaving was extremely complicated. In the 1880s it was not considered correct to leave cards when a hostess was found at home; when a married woman called upon another married woman but found her out, she always left three cards: one of her own (for the wife), and two of her husband's (one for both the husband and the wife). If the hostess was either unmarried or widowed, only one of her husband's cards would be left. A bachelor, or a married man calling without his wife on a married couple would leave two of his cards. However, a lady never left her card for a man, and a married man never left his wife's card.

Although in England both card-leaving and calling had more or less died out by the end of the Second World War, in some diplomatic circles, until as late as the mid 1970s, it was still customary to leave cards at the hostess's house after a concert, a ball, a lunch or an evening party (it took the place of a letter of thanks); after an introduction had taken place (if one wished to further the acquaintance); or on a special occasion to convey a specific message. In such cases the cards would be initialled, usually in pencil, at the bottom right-hand corner. The 'language' of card-leaving was always in French:

p.p.	*pour présenter*	to introduce (often used by a head of mission when enclosing the card of a member of his staff)
p.r.	*pour remercier*	to thank
p.f.f.n.	*pour féliciter fête nationale*	to congratulate you on your National Day
p.f.n.a.	*pour féliciter nouvel an*	to congratulate you on the New Year
p.c.	*pour condoléances*	to send condolences
p.p.c.	*pour prendre congé*	to take leave (usually sent when leaving the posting)

In Victoria Sackville's day it would have been considered incorrect to send a servant to leave one's cards, but more recently cards could quite legitimately be sent by messenger, or even by post. Turning down the top left-hand corner of one's card indicated that it had been delivered personally.* On receiving a visiting card it was customary to return the call within twenty-four hours.

In some posts, even as recently as the mid 1960s, all diplomats would send calling cards to each member of staff of every accredited diplomatic mission in the capital. By the 1970s the sheer numbers involved had caused the practice to fall into disuse, although in 1979, when my grandfather died, I can remember cards being left at our house, the British residence in Quito, Ecuador, by some of my mother's friends. They were marked 'p.c.' and the top left-hand corner had been duly turned down.

In the 1940s it was the duty of Marcus Cheke's Mrs Bull to pay numerous calls, but the numbers now involved make this impossible. However, in many countries heads of mission and their wives still pay a formal call on their opposite numbers at the beginning of a posting, and return such calls. In practice, even this custom is rapidly dwindling.

Victoria Sackville emerged from her lonely convent schooldays to become a brilliant and innovative hostess, guided, it appears, almost entirely by instinct. She was the first person to break with diplomatic tradition in having gate-crashers thrown out of her house, and is credited with having introduced the *bal masqué* to Washington. By 1890 she had received fourteen proposals of marriage. But not everyone found such social skills easy to acquire.

'Entertaining,' according to Mary Henderson in 1976, sounding rather more severe than she perhaps intended, 'means making people enjoy themselves.'[25] But, by now, younger generations of women were beginning to question the expectations of wives of the 'old school'. The formal and ritual nature of diplomatic life, with its ready emphasis on protocol and etiquette, seemed old fashioned, even anachronistic, and increasingly out of kilter with 'ordinary life'.

Back in England there was increasing criticism of the perceived extravagance, funded by the taxpayer, of diplomatic entertaining. 'It is the picture of an inbred group of people, cushioned from the hardships which beset the rest of humanity, regularly drinking duty free liquor in each other's homes, that critics of diplomatic entertaining sometimes conjure up,' wrote Stanley Tomlinson, whose 1974 *Hand-*

* According to some experts on etiquette, it should be the *right*-hand corner.

book on Diplomatic Life Abroad was a successor to Marcus Cheke's *Guidance*.[26] And there were many wives, disillusioned by the long hours, the cost to their family lives, and the sheer effort of it all, who would have heartily agreed.

Ann Hartland-Swann painted a gruesome picture of the diplomatic social scene in Mongolia in the 1970s. 'At all functions here, senior wives are treated like puppets, rigidly segregated, condemned to spend long hours discussing their children, the weather and their imaginary illnesses (though there is nothing imaginary about their overweight and boredom). Ambassadorial dinners never include Mongolians or other staff and are painfully formal and very long (five or six inedible courses are the general rule).' Nonetheless, even those wives who privately shared this dissenting voice continued to play their part in the elaborate social scheme of diplomatic life. 'I had at last acquired the technique of chatting brightly, saying "Ghastly weather, isn't it?" and "Good time for the roses" over and over again to different guests,' wrote Masha Williams.[27] 'Pointless as it may sometimes seem,' Ann Hartland-Swann agreed stoically, 'appearances must be kept up and the "Corpse" must be entertained.'

The social role, however it was viewed, was still a defining one. Although individuals may have voiced discontent – some aspects of a diplomatic social life were indeed both tedious and time-consuming – overall it was still agreed that it contributed to something much more lasting and subtle. Diplomacy has always depended on the quality of its human relationships, and the social life which helped to foster them was a serious business. Marcus Cheke believed that social intercourse amongst diplomats, and the elaborate good manners involved, was an essential means of maintaining harmony amongst the nations of Europe, and quoted Winston Churchill to this effect: 'Many quarrels that might have led to war have been adjusted by the old diplomacy of Europe, and have, in Lord Melbourne's phrase, "blown over".' Even in the modern world, where diplomats have much less direct power, and where the chief function of a diplomatic mission is as likely to be commercial as political, diplomacy plays an important role. A profound understanding of a foreign nation and its people cannot be achieved overnight. 'Contacts between governments or businessmen are not just about two people meeting,' explains Maria Fairweather, British ambassadress in Rome in the mid 1990s. 'You need to know the mental climate of a country, too. No one, however clever they are, can arrive in a country they don't know, and talk to people they don't know, and get anything like the depth of information they really need. And that's where we come in.'

Perhaps one of the reasons why diplomatic entertaining has often been so largely criticized is that its results are hard to quantify. However, in situations where social life is very greatly reduced, the negative effects can be seen very clearly. In countries like those formerly in the communist bloc, where diplomats were deliberately segregated, both they and their wives experienced real feelings of impotence and isolation. This lack of contact, not just with high officials but with ordinary people too, was perceived to be a serious impediment to their job.

Sheila Whitney remembers the strange vacuum in which the diplomatic corps was forced to exist when she first arrived in Peking. 'Ray was a Chinese specialist, and I paint a bit, so I thought I'd be able to take up Chinese painting. And perhaps learn the language,' she recalls, 'but by the time we got there the schools were all closed.' The xenophobia of the Cultural Revolution soon put paid to such ideas:

We had no contact with the Chinese whatsoever. They weren't allowed to even say hello to us in the street or anything. Our neighbours weren't allowed to be neighbourly. I remember Ray came home one lunchtime to find the teacher (I only saw him once) who was supposed to be teaching me how to speak Chinese, and he was giving a great tirade against the ghastly imperialists, but of course I couldn't understand a word of it. There he was solemnly telling me how horrible the English and Americans were, and then left. And that was all I saw of my Chinese teacher.

It was not until twenty-two years later, long after Ray had retired, that they were able to speak to one of their neighbours. On a visit to China they went to see their old house:

a dear old man came along, wheeling his bicycle, with a straw hat on . . . he came along and stopped about two or three yards from us and said, in Chinese, to Ray, 'You're the man who lived next door to us all those years ago.' It's amazing that we met him. He took us into his house, which was the next door house to us, a tiny little place. His wife had had a stroke, but he insisted that she got up because it was discourteous to stay in bed when your guests arrived. He told us all about his four sons, one of whom was a taxi driver. And he said how much he had regretted not being able to get to know us, because they are very courteous, the Chinese, usually.

It was a similar story in Soviet Russia. According to Peggy Trevelyan, the ambassadress in Moscow in the early 1960s, 'It was quite difficult because we didn't really meet Russians.' Although they used every possible excuse to invite them to the house, very few ever came.

They were scared. It all changed so much afterwards that it's difficult to realise how restricted we were. Rostropovich, the cellist, gave a concert for heads of mission, and afterwards he came up to my husband, who was a pianist, and said, 'I'd love to come and play in the embassy with you'. We had two pianos in the big white drawing room. So Humphrey was very flattered and delighted and said, 'Yes, do, by all means.' He said, 'How about next Thursday?' So Humphrey said, 'That's fine – four thirty.' And so half past four came and Humphrey said to me, 'Don't be surprised if he doesn't turn up.' Half past four. Half past five. Half past six. And he didn't come.

A few days later we had the Queen's birthday party, and Rostropovich was standing in a corner amongst all the other concert people, surrounded by them, and so my husband went up to him and said, 'Salva, we were very disappointed you didn't come the other day.' And he shrugged his shoulders and said, 'I'm terribly sorry, something happened and I couldn't make it.' Two months later we got a message from London, from his agent there, saying Salva [Mstislav] Rostropovich had asked me to tell you that he asked permission to come that day and was refused. So he wasn't even allowed to come and make music. And that was disappointing, of course. But it was very difficult to get any kind of friendship because they couldn't come unless they came as engineers or whatever it was.

National sensitivities affect all forms of diplomatic dealing, and it is largely because of this that certain forms of behaviour, and a certain etiquette, have always been given great emphasis. Marcus Cheke quoted approvingly from Wladimir d'Ormesson's *Enfances Diplomatiques*,* sketches of diplomatic life before the First World War: *'Qu'on ne sourie pas quand je dis que la première vertu des diplomates, c'est d'être des gens bien élevés.'* Even Stanley Tomlinson, the tone of whose 1974 *Handbook on Diplomatic Life Abroad* was significantly more soothing on social matters than Cheke's, had to admit that in diplomatic circles 'the rules of courtesy can be a shade more formal and elaborate than might otherwise be the case'.

It comes as something of a surprise to learn that in many other countries the British are actually considered to be one of the least formal of nations. Marie-Noele Kelly expressed astonishment at the general informality in England, where a hostess would say vaguely, 'Oh, let's sit down anywhere.' 'People of most other countries would not like such lack of ceremony among themselves and they would never tolerate it at all from people who were themselves "foreigners", particularly if they were official representatives.' In all things social, she claimed, not only Europeans, but Asians and Latin Americans tend to be 'much more punctilious and formal than their opposite numbers in Anglo-Saxon countries'.

Whether they were born into diplomatic circles or not, almost all modern diplomatic wives have had to adjust to the formality of social intercourse. As a young and inexperienced diplomatic wife, my mother was put through her paces before dining with the governor of New Zealand and his wife.

I don't think I ever told you about our dinner party at Government House [she wrote in a letter home to my grandmother], which in spite of all our qualms beforehand was quite fun. When we arrived we were taken into an ante-room by the lady-in-waiting and shown the seating arrangement at dinner, when to curtsey and how deep a curtsey to make. A bob is not good enough and something between this and a deep curtsey is expected ... The Cobhams were announced about ten minutes later by one of the

* First published in *La Revue de Paris*, 1 May 1932.

English aides, and lined up, we were all introduced to their Ex's in turn and drinks were then produced. There were about 18 of us at dinner, and it was a relief to find that we knew nearly all the guests present. We had an excellent dinner, and after the port and coffee which were given at table, the women all file out behind Lady C. She first curtseys to Lord C who takes up a position near the door, and then we all do the same in turn. This is a horrid moment as all the men are still standing at the table watching us do our bit, to the sound of creaking knee-joints.

In strange contrast to this formality were the after-dinner games proposed by Lord Cobham. My mother was initially horrified at this idea: 'We had to draw a picture of a subject written down on a piece of paper by the person sitting on your right. I had Lady C sitting next to me and she gave me "Lord C giving an impromptu sermon to a lonely Pacific island."'

Dress codes, too, were often far more formal abroad than at home. In New Zealand in the 1960s stockings, hats and gloves were *de rigueur* not only for big parties and receptions (and, of course, for any occasion at all at the high commissioner's residence), but also for quite ordinary coffee mornings and tea parties. 'And of course it was a terribly windy place – Windy Wellington, it used to be called – so your hat was always blowing off. It was absolutely ghastly,' my mother remembers. Then there were the gloves. 'There were always four or six little buttons at the wrist. So when you sat down to have your tea you would undo the buttons to loosen the glove. And then, instead of taking the glove off, you simply rolled the glove part back over your wrists, and drank your cup of tea, or whatever it was, that way.'

Despite the many changes that have taken place within the Foreign Office, nearly two generations later it is surprising how many similar social hurdles remain to perplex the modern wife. Annabel Black, whose husband was posted to Brussels in the early 1990s, is surely not the only person who has been sent Marcus Cheke as a joke, but has found parts of it genuinely helpful when trying to unravel the mysteries of *placement*, precedence and arcane visiting rituals. Even for the most naturally courteous, the formalities can still be daunting. Here is one young working wife, recently returned from a posting in Paris.

One of the things which is always done is that you are always served from the right. I don't know if you have ever tried to scoop out a piece of an ice-cream *bombe* with your right hand when you are extremely left-handed, and you've never met anybody of the people around you, and it's all incredibly posh, and everybody's watching you because conversation has gone silent . . . It's a bit of a worry really.

On another occasion I got the wives of two ministers muddled up at some official function. One of them had been looking for her husband, and I told the other one that her husband had arrived, and she came back to me and said, 'Je ne SUIS PAS Madame whoever-it-was.' I did feel quite embarrassed about that. It *is* quite formal. And I suppose the etiquette is important, although I didn't have much idea about that when I first got here. I was a bit worried about it before I went.

Few embassies remain as formal as the one in Paris. Today, when it would be neither possible nor desirable to try to impose the rules of European diplomatic etiquette in countries where they are understandably less well known, the conditions governing social life are as variable as they ever have been. British embassies, particularly in more remote countries, have almost always followed the wise expedient of adopting local customs as much as possible. Arranging formal *placement* at dinner parties, for example, when it was impossible to know who would appear, and at what time, was beyond even the most accomplished hostess.

Grizel Warner remembers how, on one occasion, 'an ambassador from a neighbouring African state, who was known always to dine out alone, arrived with not one but two of his wives in tow.' His hostess, a well-trained but exasperated diplomatic wife, tried vainly to find out which one took precedence, but 'as we went into the dining room, the two ladies walked hand in hand, and on reaching the table, refused to be separated. Our hostess managed to steer the senior of the two to the place of honour on the right of the host, but she could not detach the second wife or persuade her to move to the other side of the table. So, side by side the two wives sat, and our hostess's careful *placement* turned into a game of General Post.'[28] On another occasion, 'when we asked an African colleague to dinner with his wife, he came bringing his 11 year old daughter instead of his wife, and explained that he had brought the child as a treat for having passed her school exam,' a puzzled Grizel recalled. 'I am afraid she must have found a middle-aged dinner party a boring treat, but she appeared to enjoy the food and drank lots of orange squash.'[29]

CHAPTER NINE

Hardships

The finer points of diplomatic etiquette – the *placement* at the dinner table, or the correct length of a morning call – were, contrary to popular folklore, by no means the most pressing problems which might confront the diplomatic hostess. Nor were the solutions necessarily to be found in Marcus Cheke's handbook. Here is Masha Williams describing one of her dinner parties in Baghdad just after the war. In summer temperatures regularly rose as high as 120°F (45°C), and were frequently accompanied by sandstorms which locked them into their own house 'with a perpetual smell and taste of dust'. 'At dinner our guests, sweat pouring down them, glared at each other through the haze, crunching away at gritty food,' Masha recalled. 'The women's hair hung soggy and limp in spite of the hairdresser . . . conversation died and the guests left as soon as they decently could. The dinner party was a disaster. Alan and I, lying sweating on hot sheets, had to laugh.'[1]

The particularly severe conditions – extremes of climate, unhealthy or primitive living conditions, hostile or repressive political regimes – which were to be found in certain parts of the world (all now referred to by the Foreign Office as 'hardship postings') affected every aspect of life. Although Masha's description makes light of the appalling conditions in which she had to work, coping with them required particularly deep reserves of physical and emotional strength.

Extremes of temperature were particularly debilitating. A newly pregnant Masha wrote of that first Baghdad summer, 'We were worn out at 113F, but quite energetic at 110F. I pulled my long hair into a bun on top of my head; I couldn't bear it on my neck. Our thin clothes clung to us as the sweat poured down. We left damp patches on the armchairs. We drooped with exhaustion . . . I got prickly heat; my hands itched horribly, and I had a septic foot. Alan developed boils on his neck.' At night they escaped to the coolest place in the house – the roof, where, like their dinner party food, they often woke up to find themselves covered in layers of gritty dust.

Even women who had been brought up in the tropics suffered in some postings. Peggy Trevelyan, whose father was chief of general staff in India, also found the Baghdad summers oppressive, but was used to adopting local habits and hours in order to survive them as best she could.

There was awfully little that you could do in the summer. The way of life was simply that you got up very early in the morning, when it was cool. And you had breakfast, and I took the children to the Club, to the swimming pool, where we stayed. Came back at lunchtime. Slept for two or three hours because there was nothing you could do between the hours of one and four. And then at five o'clock back to the swimming pool. It was a frightfully boring sort of life.

In the 1950s the Trevelyans at least had the advantage of air conditioning in their bedroom at nights. For diplomatic wives of earlier times there was no such reprieve; they could only take the advice of those who had braved the summer heats before them.

Some words of advice were more useful than others. In his 1883 edition of *Tropical Trials*, Major Leigh Hunt waxed lyrical on the benefits of wearing flannel next to the skin, a practice which the Victorians adhered to with almost religious fervour, even in the most furnace-like conditions. (The magical property of this material lay in its absorption of perspiration, which kept the body's temperature constant. Cotton or linen, on the other hand, merely became damp; when the moisture evaporated and then cooled, a potentially dangerous chill resulted.) Another useful tip was that ladies should always use a hairnet, rather than a nightcap, on retiring to bed. This was on grounds that a hairnet would allow the scalp to breathe. Women who wore their hair in tight rolls and did not loosen them at night, he warned, were liable to perspire and their scalps would suffer such severe attacks of prickly heat that their heads would have to be completely shorn in order to facilitate treatment.

Less alarmist than Major Hunt, Flora Steel, in her 1888 version of *The*

Complete Indian Housekeeper and Cook, was none the less deeply critical of Englishwomen who, fearing the sun, shut themselves away in the dark. She took a brisk but practical line, and advised 'making the sun your *friend*'. She included many sound tips on how to dress: silk, rather than flannel underwear was recommended, with thin serge or nuns' veiling for dresses. She also put forward the revolutionary, but eminently sensible suggestion that in the hottest weather a woman should discard her stays. When, for whatever reason, it was necessary to brave the sun, she recommended that 'a large pith hat should be worn, a real mushroom, that will protect the nape of the neck'. A cork protector, or a quilting of shredded cork (available, of course, from the Army & Navy catalogue) should always cover the spine, and as well as this strange-sounding garment, 'an umbrella covered with white and dipped occasionally in water will make a hot, dangerous walk less dangerous'.

Both Steel and Hunt were united in warning against 'nervousness' and 'want of spirits' when living in hot or tropical conditions; 'nervous hysteria', it was generally agreed, could be brought about by either too much or too little activity. In addition, Flora Steel recommended that 'two or three grains of quinine should be taken morning and evening, and the greatest attention paid to general health'.

Maureen Tweedy learnt to dread not the heat, but the cold. When the embassy grand piano arrived one particularly bitter Korean winter, it was so frozen that the insides had to be thawed out with electric fires. Conditions in Ulan Bator were worse still. 'Everything froze,' Ann Hibbert recalls; 'even the whisky was pretty well frozen by the time it arrived, because it came overland. If you washed a pair of nylons, for instance, and then went out on the balcony they just went *shwwwt,* like that, and froze instantly.' When one of her successors in Mongolia, Jennie Sullivan, was posted there the temperature plunged to −50°C, the severest winter in living memory.

Marie-Noele Kelly experienced some bitter winters in Moscow (where temperatures would reach a mere −30°C). She describes 'The great falls of snow, the massive change brought about in ordinary life and scenery, the biting cold.' And then 'the great January silence which one expects of a stilled countryside, but is eerie in a city of eight million people: a palpable silence in which sounds are so muffled and speech so rare that one hurries on, impelled by a complex of small fears.'[2]

Sheila Whitney remembers a similar sense of oppression during the long, hard Peking winters, when they would often visit the Ming tombs:

> The Sunday occupation of everybody was to go to there and have a picnic. And when it was very, very cold, we would sit in the car – the sun would usually shine through – and I would have three pairs of slacks on, two pairs of tights (one thin, one thick), skiing pants, trousers, three or four sweaters, a hat and an anorak. And when we got out of the car we couldn't sit down to enjoy our picnic, we had to keep walking about otherwise we'd get too cold. And so we took huge bowls of hot soup and things, and just walked about all the time.

Even within the embassy compound, into which the Whitneys later moved, keeping warm was a problem: 'The heating wasn't very good, and it was terribly, terribly cold. I had to sleep in a sleeping bag with about six blankets on top, and even then I'd wake up in the night with every bone in my body aching from the cold.'

But there were many other extreme climatic conditions to be endured. In Japan, as Mary Fraser witnessed in the 1880s, it was the typhoons. In one of her first descriptions she seems almost to revel in the elemental forces at work there, 'Bricks and slates were flying in every direction, trees were uprooted and tossed about like dry leaves, jinrikshas and carriages were blown right over in the streets, and it rained – ramrods!' But then, perhaps recalling the tempest she witnessed on her voyage out to China as a young bride, which ravaged Hong Kong, she becomes more fearful: 'The intense oppression and excitement that I have felt in other typhoons was upon us all; we seemed to be fighting the air, hot, choking, evil air, full of enemies to soul and body . . . the storm reached us, swept over and round and through us in a concentrated fury of attack. Every moment it seemed as if the house must go, and we and it be hurled down to the drowning plain.'[3]

All those who had postings to China dreaded the springtime dust storms which blew in south from the Gobi Desert. Sheila Whitney's flat in the embassy compound was permanently covered with a layer of dust; 'And you could wipe it one minute and five minutes later it was there again. The flats weren't very well built, so all the air came in through all the nooks and crannies round the windows, and through all the brickwork.' But these dust storms were nothing compared to the sandstorms experienced by Miss Tully in North Africa in the 1780s, where tempests might last for ten days at a stretch. The heat was so intense that travellers who had crossed the sands came into town literally dying of thirst. Insects were scorched to death, dropping in huge numbers out of the burning atmosphere. Sand entered every crevice of the houses, and the Tullys were forced to take shelter inside a sealed room; water was thrown on the floor in order to help them breathe. Despite all these precautions several basket-loads of sand had to be swept up several times a day. 'There is no eating or sleeping in this weather,' Miss Tully wrote. People who were unfortunate enough to have to venture out covered their faces with sheets to stop themselves being blinded by the vicious, sand-filled winds which rendered just the simple act of breathing 'so difficult as to occasion death'.

There were those who were quite undeterred by the tougher and more precarious elements of diplomatic life. When Ella Sykes wrote of the many hardships involved in her journey to Kashgar in 1915 that 'Such slight drawbacks matter little to the true traveller who has succumbed to the lure of the Open Road, and to the glamour of the Back of Beyond,' she may well have been exceptional in that she had the heart and soul of an explorer. But many other women, for whom the travelling was not an end in itself, knew just what she meant. 'We were the jungly types on the whole,' admits Pat Gore-Booth. 'We enjoyed these far-flung posts.'

According to Catherine Young, even amongst contemporary wives, the idea of diplomatic service is still very much associated 'with the idea of doing something very different, and a bit adventurous'. When it comes to hardship postings there are still plenty of women who will accept the challenges involved with composure:

All these new places in the ex-Soviet Union, for instance, there's this feeling of pioneering, and of doing something for people who've been under a hard regime for so long. And all right, it's hard, and it's not much fun, and they have pretty lousy accommodation, and the climate is horrid or whatever, but there's always something to uplift. You feel that you're really doing something.

And then the serving concept works a hundred per cent – a hundred and fifty per cent.

Under quite ordinary circumstances a women's private life could be difficult and inconvenienced, but in certain 'pioneering' postings it could be exceptionally tough. Back in 1964, when the Hibberts went to Ulan Bator to set up a British mission, they were the only westerners in a staunchly communist country. Ann soon discovered that her living conditions were to be limited in the extreme. Instead of a home of her own she was to have only a small hotel suite in which to live: 'We had three rooms – a bedroom, a room we used for a dining room, and a sitting room,' she recalls. Her 'kitchen' was a two-ring electric cooker with a tiny oven in the cloakroom next to their 'front door'. The washing-up was done in the handbasin and the slops went down the WC. The Hibberts' routine was to eat lunch in the hotel restaurant, but to prepare their own breakfast and supper, using tins and packets sent out from England. 'The Mongols don't eat bread,' Ann remembers, 'so I had to learn how to make it myself.'

In a recent series of articles in the *BDSA Magazine* some of the current generation of 'Pioneer Spouses' describe their experiences in newly opened embassies, mostly in countries previously within the old Soviet bloc and the former Yugoslavia. When Helen Peart first heard that her husband had been offered the job of opening an embassy in Lithuania she thought it over and agreed to go for one year – 'I felt that one could live anywhere for that period.' To her surprise, when her husband Michael returned that night he 'told me that . . . as it was not known what the living conditions would be, we could go for nine months; if we then felt we could not cope we would be able to walk away without any adverse reaction.' They had exactly nine days in which to pack their bags.

'We travelled with seven suitcases,' Helen remembers, 'with such important items as a toaster; travelling kettle; hairdryer, teabags, packet soups, a tapestry kit (to help me while away the long hours I would be spending in the hotel) and official stationery.' Once in Vilnius they moved into the Draugstye (Friendship) Hotel, 'a large, dismal hotel' which was once used by high-ranking party officials but was subsequently to become the new diplomatic enclave. Their grand-sounding 'suite' consisted of 'a lounge with rather worn and uncomfortable chairs, a bedroom with rock hard single beds pushed together (at least they were beds – other rooms had put-you-up sofas), a bathroom with one plug for both sink and bath and a shower that would only work if one did a balancing act of standing on one foot whilst the other tried to hold up the lever. There was a noisy refrigerator.' Over the next few months the refrigerator was supplemented by a toasted-sandwich maker and a microwave oven. This was just as well because in the hotel dining room 'the meaning of the word "service" was alien to the waiters and waitresses, who would hide when one walked into the restaurant, and when one did get "service" it was not with a smile. They were known in the past to go on strike and leave hotel guests to cater for themselves!' In the end the Pearts took to inviting their guests up to their room for a lunch 'of toasted sandwiches, or corned beef and tomato sandwiches, huddled round our small coffee table'.[4]

The flavour of so many of these accounts – from Belgrade, Zagreb, Sarajevo, Ljubljana (Slovenia), and Skopje (Macedonia), to name but a few – is remarkably similar. Their tone is not only unfailingly cheerful in the face of hardships, but full of relish at the challenge. 'Our delight in being posted to Zagreb [in April 1996] was in sharp contrast to the horror felt by our friends and family,' wrote Philippa Monckton, 'who could not understand why anyone would want to go to "war-torn former Yugoslavia", with two small children and myself being a dia-betic.'[5] Stephanie Hopkinson listed the 'bizarre qualifications' needed by a diplomatic spouse wanting to live a successful and contented life in nearby Sarajevo.

Ability to see/work/don several layers of Damart underwear under a smart outfit/apply make-up in the dark; aptitude for bathing in a cold teacup and keeping one's hair/self/clothes clean and uncrumpled as long as possible (official commitments continue despite non-availability of showering, laundering, and pressing facilities); vivid imagination which converts tinned frank-furters, bread and rice into smoked salmon/steak and chips/a bowl of strawberries and cream/beans on toast or whatever other culinary delights might kindle the tastebuds at the time; candi-dates who thrill at the thought of reading a good book by torch-light or a nice game of candlelit Scrabble will enjoy the leisure opportunities offered by this Post.

When Stephanie left, her verdict was that it had been 'the most challenging, unpredictable and in some ways rewarding 18 months of our married life'.[6]

Of course, sometimes the challenge was simply too much. For Ann Hibbert in Mongolia, the cramped living conditions were merely tiresome; emotionally and psychologically the loneliness of her position was far more difficult to cope with. 'We were completely alone,' she remembers. 'And I had absolutely nothing to do. Living in a hotel we had no housekeeping. We occasionally entertained people but not a lot of them were very keen to come. I missed the children terribly. I had no home. No nothing.'

Even today there are still postings which offer very few rays of light, even for the most adventurous, according to Catherine Young:

It is very difficult at the moment to find someone who accepts going to Lagos, for instance. It is a large embassy, it is interesting politically and commercially, but is absolutely horrible to live in. Security is appalling. You can't shop unless there's an armed guard with you (you get either mugged or slaughtered). You can't drive on certain roads. You can't do this, you can't do that. It's an endless list of can't, can't, can't. The climate is difficult. The facilities are not there. There are absolutely no redeeming features.

A similar sense of hopelessness was experienced by one contemporary family of five, posted to Dacca in Bangladesh when their youngest child was just six months old:

there were no proper medical facilities for hundreds of miles. There was no air-conditioning in the kitchen because the Foreign Office had thought it unnecessary. So every night, with the temperature at over 100°F (38°C), the diplomat's wife stood in the kitchen, dripping with sweat, clad only in her knickers, boiling all the water for the next day in great vats. Every six months, when the cockroaches began to walk over their faces, the mattresses were burned. There was nothing to do and nowhere to go and around them was only abject, ghastly poverty. Her main role outside the family was to act as unpaid, unofficial welfare officer to the junior wives, particularly of the Home Office entry clearance seconds, who had absolutely no experience of being abroad and could not believe what was happening to them.[7]

It is a story with which even that most resilient of diplomatic wives, Isabel Burton, would have sympathized. On one level Isabel Burton seems, psychologically and emotionally, to have been made for the pioneering diplomatic life. 'A dry crust, privations, pain, danger for him I love . . .' she once wrote melodramatically, 'there is something in some women that seems born for the knapsack.' Grand words indeed, but ones which during her short but turbulent diplomatic career, she was to have a great number of difficult and solitary months to contemplate.

Isabel Arundell, born on 20 March 1831 into an aristocratic Catholic family, was not at all a likely candidate to become Richard Burton's wife. Although her looks were much admired by many of her contemporaries, a portrait shows that she was handsome rather than beautiful, with a long, rather heavy face and luxuriant hair. When she first met Richard, in Boulogne, then a popular haunt for impoverished English society, she was a young girl of just twenty, little more than a schoolroom miss. Richard was ten years older and already a celebrity.

Although disapprovingly dubbed 'Ruffian Dick, the White Nigger' during his days in the Indian army, Richard Burton was none the less a traveller and Orientalist of exceptional gifts. He spoke twenty-eight languages (one of them pornography, it was maliciously said) and was at that time the only European to have entered the sacred inner sanctuary at Mecca. He was both a master Sufi and a master of disguise. Obsessed since girlhood with 'gypsies, Bedouin Arabs and everything Eastern and mystic; and especially a wild and lawless life', Isabel found Richard's appearance as dizzyingly romantic as his reputation. He had extremely dark, almost Arab features, the most remarkable of them being 'two large black flashing eyes with long lashes, that pierced one through and through. He had a fierce, proud, melancholy expression; and when he smiled he smiled as though it hurt him . . .' His eyes had a way of looking through the object of his gaze as if they 'saw something behind; the only man I have ever seen, not a Gypsy, with that peculiarity'.

Isabel took one look at Richard and instantly fell so in love that she grew 'red and pale, hot and cold, dizzy and faint'. Alarmed, her parents sent for a doctor, who diagnosed indigestion and prescribed pills. But Isabel knew better. Many years before this meeting in Boulogne, a gypsy princess, Hagar Burton, had cast Isabel's horoscope. 'You will cross the sea, and be in the same town with your Destiny and know it not . . .' the gypsy had written; 'you will bear the name of our tribe, and be right proud of it. You will be as we are, but far greater than we. Your life is all wandering, changes and adventure. One soul in two bodies in life or death, never long apart. Show this to the man you take for your husband: – Hagar Burton.'

In Boulogne Isabel danced a single waltz with Richard, and made up her mind there and then that she was going to marry him. She put aside the sash and gloves which he had touched and, unbeknown to Richard, started to prepare for a life of adventure, for she was attracted as much by the life as by the man. 'If I were a man, I would be Richard Burton', she once wrote in a letter to her mother; 'but being only a woman, I would be Richard Burton's wife . . . I long to rush around the world in an express; I feel as if I shall go mad if I remain at home.'[8] It was to be four years before they met again.

While at home, Isabel was not a woman to waste her time. She engaged a fencing master and learnt to shoot, taking her pistols to pieces and cleaning and oiling them herself. She also learnt to milk cows, to groom and care for horses and to ride astride. She boned up on poultry-keeping, gardening, cooking, washing and fishing. She even learnt how to take the wheels and axles off her pony carriage and put them back on again.

For many years Richard himself had no idea of Isabel's 'long love'. When they met again, and he finally proposed to her, he asked her to think it over first. Isabel was so overwhelmed that for several moments she was literally struck dumb. 'It was just as if the moon had tumbled down and said "You have cried for me for so long I have come . . ."' 'Forgive me,' Richard said, misconstruing her silence, 'I ought not to have asked so much.' But she soon found her voice again. 'I don't *want* to think it over,' she replied, 'I have been thinking it over for five years . . . and I would rather have a crust and a tent with you than be queen of all the world, and so I say now Yes, *Yes*, YES!'[9]

In fact it would be a very long time before Isabel tasted so much as a crumb of the 'wild and lawless life' she longed for. Their engagement still a secret, Richard journeyed to Africa to look for the source of the Nile and they were separated for three long years. When they finally married in January 1861 (nearly ten years after their first encounter in Boulogne), in the face of considerable parental opposition, Richard received his first diplomatic posting. It was to the obscure consular outpost of San Fernando Po, on the west coast of Africa. Even then, the Burtons were forced to remain apart. San Fernando Po, known by the discouraging sobriquet of 'the Foreign Office Grave', was too unhealthy for any white woman, even Isabel. It was not until 1865, when Richard was posted to Santos in Brazil, that Isabel was finally able to join the man who was always 'her Earthly God and King'.

She had cried to share a 'crust and a tent' with Richard and, in Santos, that was just about what she got. The phrase 'a hardship posting', as Santos would be described in today's terminology, does not do full justice to the conditions which prevailed there in the mid-nineteenth century. It was a suffocatingly humid mangrove swamp, infested with mosquitoes and sand-flies. The seas were so rough that they threw up whale bones into the Burtons' garden.

By her own account, Isabel thrived, marvelling at the luxuriance of the vegetation, of the orchids and butterflies and birds, and the extraordinary colours, 'the tints of the opal in fine weather'. But her account, written many years later, revels quite as much in the hardships and horrors of the place as in its beauties. She describes the insects, reptiles and vermin with particular relish: spiders grew 'as big as a toy terrier', and a prick from a single hair caused instantaneous death; if you cut off the tail of a certain large mosquito while it was on you, it would simply carry on sucking, the blood spilling out of it, 'the mosquito being not the least aware of its loss'. Richard, who was apparently quite impervious to the bites of all other insects, was allergic to sand-flies, and liked to have Isabel near him when they were particularly bad. 'It was just like having a "catch 'em alive" for flies, as everything came and bit me,' she explained cheerfully, 'and spared him. The fact is, I had fresh English blood, and it was rather a treat to them.'

In addition to mosquitoes and sand-flies there was the *carapato*, a cross between a tick and a small crab. 'If you ride through a coffee plantation you come out covered with them. I have more than once taken off my riding habit and found my jacket nailed to the skin from the outside,' Isabel wrote gleefully; 'to pull them is to tear your flesh and produce a festering wound.' Instead you had to get into a hot bath, into which two bottles of *cachaxa*, the local alcohol made from fermented sugar-cane, had been poured. 'Cockroaches you don't count,' she went on, 'but you must always look in your sleeves, and dress, and boots, for large horned beetles or spiders or other horrors.' Worst of all, however, were the snakes, which ranged in size from boa constrictors downwards, and which lurked everywhere – in gardens, basements and rafters. 'At night when you walk out you go with a lantern at the end of a stick, for the snake called *jararaquassu* lies curled up at night on the road, looking exactly like a heap of dust and you would certainly put your foot on it; it bites your ankle, and they say that you live about ten minutes.'

And yet for all her bravado, there were moments when even Isabel longed for home. 'I often think a parvenue, or half-bred woman would burst if she had to do what I do,' she wrote in a fit of gloom not long after her arrival in Santos, 'keeping up appearances, lancing boils, coping with insects, with Richard, with everything.' Emotionally she had too much invested in Santos to admit defeat, which makes these rare outbursts all the more poignant. 'I do hate Santos,' she went on. 'The climate is beastly, the people fluffy. The stinks, the vermin, the food, the niggers are all of a piece. There are no walks, if you go one way you sink knee-deep in mangrove swamps; another, you are covered with sandflies.'

But there was far worse in store than mangrove swamps and sand-flies. The Burtons had barely arrived in Santos when Isabel succumbed to her first fever. She outlined the symptoms in detail: 'it consisted of sickness and vomiting, colic, dizziness, faintness, shivering, heat and cold, delirium, thirst, disgust of food.'* The treatment was 'calomel, castor oil, hot baths, blankets, emetics, ice, starvation'.

After the fever came the boils, so many and 'so close together you could not put a pin between them'. For a time these eruptions were so painful that she could neither sit, stand, lie or even kneel, and had to be 'slung up', as she put it, until they healed. A friend gave her a barrel of porter, and 'it was alternately "faint" and "a glass of porter", which revived me for a few minutes, and then more faint and more porter, *ad*

---

* These symptoms are characteristic of any severe febrile illness; she may have had either malaria, dengue or paratyphoid.

infinitum.'[10] She cured herself eventually by drawing a circle of laudanum and caustic alternately around each boil. If one managed to pull through this ordeal, she believed, then one would enjoy better health than ever before (as indeed she did for the next seventeen years).

Although they rarely dwelt upon it, almost all diplomatic women risked illness and disease. We may laugh at Major Leigh Hunt's encomiums on the benefits of flannel, but in the late nineteenth century a 'chill' was no laughing matter.* People could, and did, die from them. There were no inoculations, no serums for snake bite, no jabs against rabies. If Isabel had been bitten by a *jararaquassu*, one of the few pieces of written advice available to her would have been both drastic and use-less: 'If the snake is known to be deadly, amputate the finger or toe at the next joint; or if you cannot do this, run the knife right round the bone, dividing the flesh completely. Let the bitten person suck the wound till you can burn it with anything at hand, carbolic, nitric acid, nitrate of silver, or actual hot iron.'[11]†

Until well into this century, of course, life was more precarious for everyone. A relatively common virus such as influenza was as potentially lethal in London as in Libya,‡ but travelling and living abroad made people more susceptible to illness. It maximized their chances of con-tracting common ailments, and exposed them to many new, and often deadly diseases against which they had no natural immunity or effective medical protection.

In many countries, particularly in Europe, the medical facilities were just as good, if not better, than in England, but women often missed the reassurance of having their own doctors near at hand.§ When

* Many serious illnesses, such as cholera, malaria or yellow fever, could present as a simple 'chill'. Malaria and yellow fever could kill within days; cholera within hours.
† In fact, Isabel is credited with having saved the life of a friend from a rattlesnake bite with rather less drastic means. First, she burnt a hole with matches at the site of the puncture mark. Then she made a ligament with her handkerchief around the wound and forced the man to drink a bottle of whiskey, at the same time keeping him walking about for three hours. The next day her patient, Charles Williams, was in 'perfect health' again. Cf Mary S. Lovell, *A Rage to Live*, p.491.
‡ Most people in Europe died of infectious diseases. In Victorian England most adults died of TB, including a third of all medical students, who succumbed to it *before* the end of their training.
§ They were especially good in France and Germany. Until the First World War, German was the principal international language of medicine.

Harriet Granville heard that she was to go as ambassadress to Paris, one of the few comforts which she had to look forward to was that in France she would have access to English physicians. Psychologically, too, being far away from home was particularly painful during times of sickness.

Deprived of the familiar support of friends and relations, women felt particularly isolated during times of sickness. Disease was everywhere, and young children were especially vulnerable. In Algiers, in the first decade of the nineteenth century, Mrs Blanckley recorded a smallpox epidemic in which 5,000 children died in three months. 'How thankful I ought to be that my children have been vaccinated,' she wrote.[12] Others were not so lucky. Elizabeth McNeill, far away in Persia, witnessed the deaths of three of her four children.

It was not only children who succumbed to the rigours of foreign climates and disease. Adults were vulnerable, too, servants and masters alike. In the 1880s an influenza epidemic overtook the city of Tokyo. According to Mary Fraser, 'Within a week the town was one large hospital.' At times like these the whole domestic pyramid, so carefully and painstakingly constructed, simply collapsed beneath the strain. 'In many houses there was not even a servant who could light the kitchen fire; and one of my friends, too ill herself to go downstairs to do it, kept her family alive with Liebig's extract cooked over a spirit lamp beside her bed. Every engagement was cancelled; people were too ill to ask if even their best friends were still alive.'[13]

Recovery was often a long and painful process. Ann Fanshawe suffered from a fever which weakened her so much that she became 'like an anatomy': 'I never stirred out of my bed in seven months, nor during that time eat flesh, or fish, nor bread, but sack, posset drink, and pancake or eggs, and now and then a turnip or a carrot.'[14]

Richard Burton, too, for all his long experience as a tropical traveller, took many weary months to recover from one Brazilian illness, which took the form of a fever and a debilitating liver complaint.* In the autumn of 1867 he left Santos on one of his solitary expeditions into the interior, canoeing 1,500 miles down the San Francisco river.

---

* Possibly some form of hepatitis (although hepatitis A, the common travellers' hepatitis of today, was often acquired in childhood, which gave lifelong immunity) or even mild yellow fever.

On his return (he had been gone an agonizing four months) Isabel found him on the point of complete collapse, and immediately set about nursing him herself. It almost killed him. Her regime included six cuppings, with thirty-six glasses and twelve leeches, a tartar emetic, ether pills, mustard and orange tea. There was some remedy to be given or rubbed on nearly every half hour.

Isabel's treatments may seem ferocious, but she was desperate – 'We had no doctors up there that I am aware of,' she wrote bleakly. Many diplomatic women in similarly isolated situations had no alternative but to struggle on as best they could, using what little information was available to them. More than twenty years later Flora Steel – whose general advice on hygiene was probably more effective than any of her remedies – betrays a similar ignorance in the face of foreign disease. Her recommendation for treating cholera, for example, was one tablespoon of vinegar and one teaspoon of Worcestershire sauce, or, more drastically, the 'acid treatment', which involved diluted solutions of sulphuric and nitric acid.* 'Even if collapse sets in, and apparent death, hope should not be given up . . . Hand-rubbing, hot bottles, mustard, turpentine, everything should be tried.'

Remedies for even the most common ailments have a touch of desperation about them. For asthma she recommended 'twenty grains of dried datura leaf smoked with ordinary tobacco', while colds and catarrh 'may be almost entirely prevented by small doses of opium'. (Perhaps they worked. Like Isabel, Flora Steel was able to boast that in over twenty years spent in India she had never once been invalided.)

The household medicine cupboard of a typical diplomatic family at this time might have included the following:

1. Powdered ipecacuanah [Made the patient vomit. Still used today in poison and overdose victims. Purgatives were popular Victorian remedies, presumably in the hope that the patient would get rid of toxins, etc.]
2. Purgative powder
3. Sulphate of quinine [Very effective malaria treatment. Still the mainstay of treating malaria.]

* Neither of these would have had any curative effect at all.

4. Chlorodyne [Another name for chloroform and morphine tincture.]

5. Pure carbolic acid [An antiseptic.]

6. Castor Oil

7. Eno's fruit salts

8. One bottle each of M'Kesson and Robbin's compound podophyllin and aloes and myrrh pills ['A rather toxic agent', useful for putting on warts and veruccas. When taken by mouth it was a purgative.]

9. Stick of nitrate of silver [Antibacterial substance, often used for eyes (conjunctivitis), skin infections and ulcers.]

10. Cholera pills

11. Iodine

12. Tabloids of antipyrin

13. ditto phenacetin [antipyrin and phenacetin have analgesic and antipyretic properties.]

14. ditto aspirin

15. Salicylate of soda [For pain relief, but could also be used in skin conditions like eczema and psoriasis.]

16. Boracic acid [A disinfectant.]

17. Cough lozenges

18. Tabloids of grey powder [Tablets of mercury in prepared chalk, used principally as a purgative and antisyphilitic.]

19. Kaye's essence of linseed

20. Lint, cotton, wool, linen

21. Oiled silk

22. Roll of adhesive plaster

23. Bandages

24. Dressing forceps*[15]

In our own century medical advice remained vague. As recently as 1947 Masha Williams found herself nursing her husband Alan through a bout of 'sand-fly fever',† which left him unconscious for days at a

---

* I am very grateful to Dr Matthew Dryden, Consultant in Macrobiology and Communicable Diseases at the Royal Hampshire Hospital, for supplying this information.
† Almost certainly Leishmaniasis – a chronic systemic disease transmitted through the bite of sand-flies.

time. Doctors were hard to come by, and the best Masha could do was to consult a Mrs Chadwick, the wife of the local veterinary surgeon who had lived in Baghdad for thirty years. 'Give him a glass of champagne with a couple of biscuits at mid-morning,' was her stalwart advice.

In the mid 1960s, when her youngest child Kate was just six months old, Jane Ewart-Biggs was horrified at the prospect of going to 'one of the worst climates in the world, a place renowned for its unbearable heat and humidity, where English children who arrive with pink cheeks rapidly take on that yellowish tinge common to the tropics'. In the end, it was the delicate health of her eldest child, Henrietta, who had suffered from periodic bouts of fever in their previous posting in Algiers, which saved the day. They were sent to Brussels instead.

Not all families could hope for such reprieves. The letters written by Miss Tully at the end of the eighteenth century – among the most dramatic accounts ever written about the vicissitudes of diplomatic life – tell an extraordinary tale of resourcefulness and courage in the face of disease.

The surviving biographical details about Miss Tully are fragmentary. It seems likely that she was the sister – or at least a close female relative – of Richard Tully, who was appointed British consul to Tripoli in 1772. Tripoli was the largest of the three Barbary regencies (the other ones were Algiers and Tunis), all of which were subject to the Ottoman Porte. The chief importance of the regency lay in the fact that it was strategically placed on one of the most important trade routes between Africa and Europe. The quickest routes across the Sahara Desert, and across the Mediterranean, converged here, with camel caravans bringing a rich and exotic cargo of black slaves, gold dust, ostrich feathers, ivory, esparto grass and saffron. The importance of Tripoli, which also lay on the western Haj route to Mecca, was reflected in the fact that the local ruler, the bashaw, was the only Barbary sovereign to hold the status of 'three horsetails'. Like Mr Blanckley, the consul in Algiers some forty years later, Richard Tully was there principally to look after British shipping interests, and to secure the release of Britons taken into slavery.

Miss Tully's letters to her unknown correspondent in England cover a period of exactly ten years, from 1783 to 1793, her brother's second tour of duty. Although she lived as one of his family for more than a decade, very few personal details emerge from her letters;* the consul is always, very properly, 'Mr Tully'; his wife 'Mrs Tully'. She makes it clear that she seeks to impart more than mere family chit-chat. 'I purpose simply to relate facts as they occur,' she wrote, 'without the least embellishment, as that, I conceive, would not increase the interest which they may probably inspire.'

What she could not have known when she wrote these lines was that the simple facts which were to be her raw material were not merely the manners and customs of the Moors,† which she might well have had in mind, but the ravages of famine, civil war, and one of the worse cases of the bubonic plague ever to affect the north coast of Africa.

When Miss Tully first arrived in North Africa her first impressions were almost all sensual: the extreme blueness of sea and sky, the blinding whiteness of the town arranged in a semicircle at the harbour's mouth. Although, when viewed at close quarters, Tripoli was in a state of some dilapidation – a result of 'the destructive hand of time' (and the neglect of its ruler, the Bashaw Ali Koromanli) – from a distance it was pleasingly picturesque. The surrounding country was of very pale, almost white, soil. Clusters of cupolas, from the town's numerous baths and mosques, were surrounded by plantations of fig and date trees, where she saw 'camels without number'. There were also numerous beautiful gardens, which gave the whole city 'an aspect truly novel and pleasing'.

Like many diplomatic women, Miss Tully began her life in Tripoli in a position of considerable reflected privilege and power. Following the Ottoman Capitulations of 1761 (see pp. 51–2) as far as the Christian community was concerned, the consuls of the large maritime powers in particular – Britain, France and Holland – were virtual rulers in their own right. As we have seen, the Tully women were on intimate terms with the women in the Bashaw's palace, and not only were there regular visits to the harem; there were also rides and expeditions into the surrounding countryside, visits to the local tombs, camel racing

* The version we have was edited in 1816. There may well have been more family details in the original letters, which are now lost.
† The generic term by which she refers to all North Africans.

on the sands, picnics and feasts in the pleasure gardens of friends.

Having known only the temperate beauties of England, Miss Tully was profoundly impressed. 'It is a wilderness of sweets, beneath thick orange groves, through which the sun's beams but faintly shine,' she wrote, describing the pleasure grounds of the Tullys' particular friend, the Tripolian ambassador Hadgi Abderrahaman.

> White marble channels with rapid clear streams of water cross the garden in many directions; and the air in them is fraught with the scent of oranges, roses, and Arabian jasmine, whose thick shade forms an agreeable contrast with the burning atmosphere surrounding them. In the centre of the largest garden, nearest the house, is a most pleasant golphor* built a considerable distance from the ground. The floors, walls and window seats are lined with Chinese tiles of lively colours: the windows are placed round it, through which honeysuckles, orange flowers and jasmine make their way. The shrubs reflect through them everywhere the most lively green, and fill the whole with the richest perfume.

But in the second year of her residence an altogether more disturbing picture begins to emerge. At first these are scattered details: 'The starved objects we passed this morning in the streets were shocking to behold,' she wrote home. 'A total want of rain occasions this dreadful distress . . . the great must pay for it, but what the poor will suffer must agonise every feeling heart.' Just a few months later the situation had deteriorated still further. There was only enough barley left for two market days; the farmers were reduced to grinding down the bark of date palms to feed their cattle, asses, camels and mules. The Tullys were forced to buy ship's biscuit from the few merchant vessels which passed their way.

By August 1784 Tripoli was 'in so dreadful a state of famine that it is become horrid to walk or ride out, on account of the starved objects that continually die in the street. The Christians have lessened, as much as possible, the consumption of provisions for their table,' in order to give to the poor and starving. 'Every article, even the most

---

* Reception room or pavilion.

trivial, is an enormous price.' But the worst was still to come. News reached them that there was plague in Tunis, only 300 miles away. The Tully women, who had been hoping to evacuate to Malta until the worst of the famine was over, would not now be accepted anywhere in the Mediterranean for fear of infection.

As the famine grew worse, the plague drew slowly nearer. In November Miss Tully wrote hopefully, 'We yet escape the plague, though it is at Tunis,' but by January the following year it was clear that they could not last out long. 'We have hardly a hope of escaping the plague; it increases daily . . .' she wrote in her New Year's letter on 8 January 1785, 'and to add to the misfortune of its reaching us, this kingdom is already in so unhealthy a state from famine that it is thought it will considerably add to its ravages.'

Like a forest fire, the plague spread inexorably. In March they learnt that as many as 700 people were dying daily in Tunis. The danger to the Tullys, as they were painfully aware, was considerably increased because most Muslims refused to take any kind of precautions against it: to do so, they believed, would be to resist the hand of fate, the divine will of Allah. 'As it is contrary to the Mahometan religion to endeavour to avoid contagion, the Moors expose themselves so much to the attacks of the plague, that we have been obliged to defer our visits to the castle, and to Moorish families for some months past,' she wrote in desperation.

The royal women took an unprecedented step. Surrounded by their eunuchs and black slaves, who threatened death to anyone who might try to witness them, they left the castle at night, making a procession through the town to pray at one of the local shrines. But it was no good; on 29 April Miss Tully recorded that 'In the last few weeks several couriers have crossed the deserts from Tunis to this city, disseminating the plague in their way; and consequently the country round us is everywhere infected.' Gradually, her sense of the imminence of the danger begins to infect the normally cool tone of her letters. She describes the symptoms of the disease in horrified detail. The first signs were 'a sort of stupor, which immediately increases to madness, violent swellings and excruciating pains in a few hours terminate in death'.

And then it was upon them. 'Four people who were perfectly well in the morning were taken ill there yesterday afternoon,' she wrote on 27 May; 'they were brought out of the castle last night at ten, and died at midnight. Two of them went raving mad, and they were all afflicted with large swellings on different parts of the body when they died.' By the end of the month the Christian households were desperate. Despite the disapproval of the Bashaw, who feared that once it was known that the country was infected the grain ships would stay away and the country would starve, their preparations for quarantine began.

The success of their quarantine depended upon the absolute strictness with which it was enforced. Most critically, there had to be as little contact with the outside world as possible. For however long it took – and from the beginning it was feared that the quarantine would be a long one – the Tullys would quite literally immure themselves inside the consulate building. Each Christian household hired a set of servants who would remain imprisoned with them until the plague was over: 'Should it be necessary to change servants, or to take in additional ones, it can be done only on condition that they relinquish the cloaths [sic] they have on; go into a bath prepared for them in the *skiffer* or hall of the consular house, and submit to remain in one room a fortnight to ascertain their not having the plague.' The terraces and windows fronting the street were nailed up, and only the 'master of the family' had possession of the keys to all the outside doors. Large jars, each one containing a mixture of camphor, myrrh and aloes, were prepared; the house was fumigated daily with this perfume, and small quantities of gunpowder. All domestic animals, including chickens and ducks, were banished for fear of infection from their fur or feathers.

Even before the quarantine was in force the strictest possible precautions were taken when admitting visitors:

No business is now transacted but with a blaze of straw kept burning between the person admitted into the house and the one he is speaking to.* A friend is admitted only into a matted apartment, where he retires to the farther end of the room to a straw seat, which is not touched after his departure till it is fumi-

---

* Although it was not known then that fleas were the carriers of bubonic plague, these precautions would have been extremely effective.

gated. The keys of all the ways into the house are kept by the master of the family only. If any of the Christian gentlemen are obliged to go out on business during this interval, before the houses are closed, a guard walks before and one behind, to prevent any person approaching too near; and, on returning, the guards are put into quarantine for some days. Without these precautions, it would be impossible to escape this dreadful disorder, the rage of which increases every hour.

'It is impossible to give you a just description of this place at present,' Miss Tully wrote in July, a few weeks after quarantine was imposed; 'the general horror that prevails cannot be described.' The stories which filtered through to them were terrifying. A slave, delirious with sickness, had escaped from the castle and jumped off the battlements, dashing himself to pieces on the rocks beneath. Close friends perished daily. One, Hadgi Mahmute, died in torment 'from the singular instance of the plague having at first seized him in his mouth, producing violent tumours, by which he is now starving: he is at times so raving that many people are required to secure him.'

In terror, the Tullys doubled their precautions. The door onto the street was never opened except, once a day, by Mr Tully himself in order to receive the daily supplies into the consulate. The *skiffer* was divided up into three parts. Mr Tully would go into the first 'hall', from where he would then send one of his servants to unlock and unbolt the door. 'The servant returns, and the person in the street waits till he is desired to enter with the provisions he had been commissioned to buy. He finds ready placed for him a vessel with vinegar and water to receive the meat, and another with water for the vegetables.' Only a very few things could ever be brought into the house without precaution. These included: cold bread, salt in jars, straw ropes, straw baskets, oil poured out of the jar to prevent contagion from the hemp with which it is covered, sugar without paper or box.

When the person has brought in all the articles he has, he leaves them by the account, and the change out of the money given him, and retiring shuts the door. Straw previously placed in the hall is lighted at a considerable distance, by means of a light at the end of a stick, and no person suffered to enter the hall til it is thought sufficiently purified by the fire; after which a servant with a long stick picks up the account and smokes it thoroughly over the straw still burning, and locking the door returns the key to his master, who has been present during the whole of these proceedings, lest any part of them should be neglected, as on the observance of them it may safely be said the life of every individual in the house depends.

No chances, however trivial, could ever be taken with the quarantine procedures. 'To be secure in the midst of this dire contagion, requires a thorough knowledge of its effects,' Miss Tully wrote soberly. Cotton, wool, linen, 'hides with the hair on', hemp and hops were all thought to be potential 'imbibers' of plague particles. Corn, barley, fruit, vegetables and meat, on the other hand, 'are deemed incapable of taking or communicating the infection'. Some strange anomalies existed: 'bread, though perfectly safe after having been baked some hours, is fatally dangerous if handled while it is hot or warm. A peach, or any downy fruit or vegetable, such as unshelled filberts or almonds have been known to communicate the plague. This disorder has been conveyed from friend to friend in a high scented bouquet of flowers; and most perfumes are considered as propagators of this infectious disorder.'

From her prison inside the consulate Miss Tully could hear and see the horrors which went on all around her. 'The cries of the people for the loss of their friends are still as frequent as ever,' she wrote in her next letter, on 1 July; 'not a quarter of an hour passing without the lamentations of some new afflicted mourner.' By now there were so many dead that there was not enough wood to make coffins. Families were reduced to bringing their dead to the door, where 'the first man they can prevail on carries it over his shoulder, or in his arms to the grave' where the bodies – up to 300 a day – were buried at a communal 'mass' at noon each day. Whole families were wiped out. Women demented with grief, veils torn and faces exposed, their hair loose and dishevelled, could be seen wandering the streets. Many people, who had no one left either to bury or to mourn them, staggered to the walls of the European consulates in order to die there, 'whence they were removed with great inconvenience and expense'.

Even for the Tullys, safe in their self-imposed solitary confinement, life was not without problems. Since no one in the house could ever leave it, they were entirely dependent on outsiders employed to bring them their food and other essential supplies. Within the space of seven days a total of eight of these 'providers' were struck down and killed by the plague. However, 'He who was too ill to return with what he had brought, consigned the articles to his next door neighbour, who faithfully finishing his commission, as has always been done, of course succeeded his unfortunate friend in the same employment, if he wished it, or recommended another.' A system which, amazingly, seemed to work.

By August the sickness seemed to have abated a little, but by October it was back again with increased ferocity. It was a pattern which was often repeated. 'In vain the Christians wish to finish their long quarantine, for notwithstanding their houses have been shut six months, they are likely to continue much longer,' Miss Tully wrote wearily in December that year. 'A short time since, few deaths were heard of, but in the last five days they have increased from four a day to fifteen.'

The Tullys were never entirely cut off from the outside world. From the high, flat terrace of their rooftop, aided by Mr Tully's spy-glass, they had a good view across the town and out to sea, and even as far as the neighbouring hills, and Miss Tully was able to witness 'extraordinary scenes'. On one occasion one of the neighbouring households consulted a holy man (possibly a whirling dervish), seeking information on the whereabouts of the 'master of the house'. The *marabut*, as she called him, was dressed strangely, in a blue shirt and trousers, without turban or shoes, and when he arrived he called for a drink 'and immediately broke the vessel he drank out of'. Items of the master's clothing were brought out for him. 'He for a long time, in an act of devotion, turned round with such velocity that his features were not discernible, and continued to do so till he sunk on the ground through fatigue. At other times, he sang and played on the tambourin extremely well, and in the end, according to the duties of his order, washed the feet of those who employed him before he went away.'

Miss Tully continued to write, and receive, letters.

Imprisoned in the midst of increasing pestilence, your kind wishes for a happy new year can effect us but in small degree [she wrote to her English correspondent on 12 January 1786]. The plague seems likely to repeat all the horrors of the last year. Nobody is prepared to meet this second attack, though all were told, at the time the infection seemed to cease here, that a fresh and more severe disease was breeding within the mountains of Guerianno,* which can be seen hence with our glasses, and whence we have now received it.

As the new year progressed, food became alarmingly scarce. Long-awaited ships often failed to bring the expected provisions; supplies were of very bad quality, and cost up to four times the usual price. Wheat was in particularly short supply, and the Tullys were once again reduced to buying up all the biscuit from the few vessels which would venture into the harbour. 'If the plague had not swept off the chief part of the inhabitants, they must have perished by famine,' Miss Tully remarked.

After these first six months the extreme monotony of the Tullys' quarantine was enlivened by the occasional visit, but careful precautions were still taken by all parties: 'Tremendous as it may seem to be in the same room with one who has just passed through a multitude of martyrs to the plague, many of whom were expiring in his sight, yet with proper care danger may be avoided,' Miss Tully wrote. The extreme 'purity' of their techniques – adapted from the ones developed in the Grand Duke Leopold's famous lazarettos† in Leghorn – were as follows:

The drawing room has neither linen, silk, nor carpets; no other furniture than tables and matted chairs: the floor is also matted. Every visitor is his own valet; he is not admitted but in the presence of the master of the house; no servant is permitted to attend him or hand him a chair; and he helps himself to refreshments, which are brought to a corridor, or anti-chamber. This is done to prevent a servant, by inattention, going too near his person; and whatever he has handled, or the chair he has occupied, is not touched for hours after his departure.

* Gharyan, in the Jabal Nefusa.
† Places of quarantine.

The desperation felt by the whole of her family during their long imprisonment is very clear in her comments on one such visit, from the Venetian consul: 'I am happy to think that you must be a stranger to the satisfaction which the sight of a friend now affords us unless you were shut up, as we are, in the midst of pestilence, and in a place where the state of the government and country are equally alarming, and render every one painfully anxious for such accounts as can be depended on, while false ones are continually issuing from chimerical minds.'

Finally, at the end of July 1786, after thirteen long and fearful months, the Tullys came out of their quarantine. It was a moment experienced with relief, rather than rejoicing. The scene which met them was pitiful indeed:

> The city of Tripoli, after the plague, exhibited an appearance awfully striking [she wrote sombrely]. In some of the houses were found the last victims that had perished in them, who having died alone, unpitied and unassisted, lay in a state too bad to be removed from the spot, and were obliged to be buried where they were; while in others, children were wandering about deserted, without a friend belonging to them. The town was almost entirely depopulated, and rarely two people walked together.[16]

(Altogether in the city some 10,000 are known to have died, including half the Jewish population and nine-tenths of the Christian. Outside the town, in the oasis known as Neuschia, a further 25,000 Arabs were buried.)* Thanks to their extraordinary quarantine, all the Tullys survived.

The Tully women must have felt extraordinarily isolated during their seclusion, but they at least had each other. During her seventeen years in Kashgar, Catherine Macartney saw only three other Englishwomen; two of these, a Miss Kemp and a Miss MacDougall, did not appear until 1912, fourteen years after her arrival. The Macartneys received news from India that the two ladies were to come to Kashgar, but 'we

---

* After the plague, in 1790, consular records set the population of Tripoli at 25,000.

had barely got through the Revolution,'* Catherine wrote 'and the country was still disturbed, so my husband, not wanting to have any more women to look after, replied very decidedly: "Do not let them come." But being very plucky and afraid of nothing, they came all the same.' The two women travelled through Ladak, and over the Karakoram range, 'with only native servants, doing a very difficult journey for anyone, and especially for ladies. Only one who has been cut off from the companionship of her own countrywomen as I had been, can understand what it meant to me to have them staying with us for a time.' Although by 1912 she had her children and her household, and she had grown used to her life. It was during the first four years that she experienced 'to the very utmost all that homesickness and loneliness meant'.

Catherine's inability to speak either Turki or Hindustani made her feel particularly cut off and isolated. Worse still, she found that she had almost nothing at all to do. 'All our clothes were new and in good condition, and sometimes I was tempted to cut holes in them that I might be obliged to sew them up,' she wrote years later in her memoir. She did not see much of her husband, who only came home at mealtimes, and it was not long before she began to hate all the people who came to see him, with their ceaseless claims on his time and attention. The Macartneys had very few books and no materials for 'handiwork', and for a time she was in danger of falling into a severe depression: 'nothing seemed worthwhile doing, so utterly slack did I become.'[17]

Although few diplomatic wives have had to suffer the extremes of isolation endured by Catherine Macartney, feelings of loneliness are common to almost all diplomatic women at some time or other. Some women adapt more quickly and easily than others. Mary Fraser once noted these feelings, and their effects, with the philosophical detachment born of her long experience abroad. 'Out here I live my mind life in a curious three time, owing to the enormous distance from home,' she explained in one of her letters home from Japan. 'My Christmas letters had to be written and sent off on November 20th; in a few days they and the quaint collection of gifts that went with them will cause great joy in the little home circle; but I shall have no word of thanks till the end of January or later.' It was not only home

* In January that year China had nominally become a republic under Sun Yat-sen.

life, but also larger events which ceased to have quite the same reality. 'We get in the papers distorted telegrams about events in Europe, but long before the true account of the thing reaches us its very existence has gone out of one's mind; and so, little by little, the vivid interest in home politics dies out, and is replaced by smaller and nearer subjects. But one is not moved or excited about them as one is in Europe.'[18]

Other, more personal events were doubly devastating when they took place far away. Marie-Noele Kelly remembered the dreadful month during her time in Ankara (in other respects her favourite posting) in which both her father and her stepson Richard died (the latter, a young man of twenty-four, in just seven hours from peritonitis) and her terrible grief was intensified by being unable to return to Europe. Ann Hibbert had a similar experience in Singapore in the early 1970s. 'My mother died when we were out there,' she recalls, 'and I couldn't afford the fare to come back for her funeral and so on. One was so terribly cut off.'

However, to have no news at all was much worse. No matter how near or far they were posted, or in what century, most diplomatic women found letters and news from home were intense preoccupations. More important than familiar food and drink, than the climate, or even the roof over their head, the yearning for news from home is the emotional experience which unites each and every woman in this book.

I can remember vividly the intense anticipation in our house in Singapore on 'bag day' (my brothers and I were not great correspondents in those days, but we each had a subscription to an English comic): the feeling of excitement when the post came; the bitter disappointment when it was delayed. There was a sense, even then, that time was measured out by the intervals between each arrival of 'the bag'. In Singapore 'bag day' was once a week, but this was not always the case. 'The routine of the Embassy, such as it is,' wrote Jennie Sullivan from Mongolia, 'is geared to the arrival of the bag each fortnight.' In her case the Queen's messengers not only delivered the longed-for mail from London but were also their only source of fresh food, bringing fruit and vegetables from Hong Kong and Peking.

Nowadays the diplomatic bag is usually delivered by air, but in earlier times the mail took a tortuous mixture of land and sea routes, with varying degrees of reliability. 'From the state of the Elbe, I fear there will be a great retardment in our posts,' wrote Anne Disbrowe in disappointment from St Petersburg in the 1820s. (She was compensated later when, to her joy, two posts came in together; 'so I had a feast for a whole evening and part of the next day, in a second reading of yours and Mama's of 30th and 3rd,' she wrote to her father.)

The correspondence of Harriet Granville, Anne's exact contemporary, is similarly peppered with laments on the shortcomings of the postal system, even though she was only a short hop across the Channel. 'The Poodle and I sat over the fire after dinner yesterday and we are the only people here who sympathise entirely on the subject of the bag. We are agreed that from the moment it was due we cannot feel pleasant in our minds till it arrives.' Her feelings on these occasions were 'a mixture of impatience and nervousness and a great deal of wool-gathering about what it will bring'.[19]

Diana Shipton describes the unique system of runners and riders which linked Kashgar and Shrinagar, in northern India, in the 1940s, complete with shelter and provisions for the men all along the route. They worked in relays, in pairs or in groups of three, and after a journey of twenty-four days, the Shiptons' post arrived with almost miraculous regularity, once a week. 'On Tuesday mornings we woke with that tingle one feels on special days,' Diana recalled. 'Considering the hardships and difficulties of the route – over snow-covered passes, risking avalanches, crossing rivers swollen by melting ice in summer along narrow mountain paths – it was remarkable how promptly and regularly our post was delivered.' Years later she could still vividly remember the effect of those 'magic words', 'the mail has come', and then the solemn ceremony of unpacking it. 'Once the letters had been read and the parcels unpacked a sad flatness descended at the thought of a long week to wait for the next mail. Sometimes the mail bags were empty and then the disappointment and flatness was acute . . . the one post a week meant so much.'[20]

Isabel Burton received letters from home only once a month, as did Mary Sheil in Persia: 'Once a month the post from Europe arrived, and that was a bright and joyful day,' she wrote. 'The 10th of each month mail was "due" and everyone anxiously expecting it, but alas!, we often experienced the truth of the saying "Hope deferred maketh the heart sick" for we were often forgotten in Constantinople.'[21]

In Constantinople itself, half a century earlier, Mary Elgin was unluckier still, once waiting for almost six months for the arrival of a precious letter from her mother. But the record surely goes to Elizabeth McNeill who, in a letter to her sister from Persia, written on 8 April 1828, remarks that her latest home letters are dated 8 June 1827, nearly a whole year previously. The most painful delays of all were not necessarily the longest. It is hard to conceive of the additional anguish which the McNeills must have suffered when the letter informing John that his child Ines (from his first marriage) had died did not reach him until five months after her death.

CHAPTER TEN

Children

The longing for news, the 'famishing hunger for home and one's own people', as Mary Fraser once put it, flowed in both directions. During the writing of this book I was reminiscing with my oldest friend, a diplomat's child like myself, whom I have known since we were at boarding school together aged ten. I was not at all surprised to find that, like me, she has the most vivid memories of the rituals surrounding the arrival of the post: the staircase, the old chest, the anxious craning over the banisters for that glimpse of a familiar envelope or handwriting. 'There was one time when I did not hear from my parents for nearly three months,' she recalls. 'I thought they must be dead.' (An English literature academic, she believes that her chosen field of expertise – eighteenth-century epistolary novels and letters – is no accident.)*

Like that of our mothers, the experience of diplomatic children is enormously varied. 'The myth is that diplomatic life, with all the travelling, new places, new faces, is attractive and exciting for children,' wrote Jane Ewart-Biggs, 'but I believe that nothing could be further from the truth.'[1] Although the necessity of changing houses, schools, friends, food, and even languages every few years, can be problematic for many children, others happily adapt.

My own feelings, while principally positive, are not entirely uncomplicated. I was brought up in Spain (in Madrid and Bilbao) and in Singapore. My memories of both places are vivid, and startlingly happy. In Bilbao, when I was six, we lived in an apartment on a clifftop overlooking the sea. I learnt not only to speak, but to read and write

---

* Many collections of letters have been edited by daughters and granddaughters – Anne Disbrowe's, Elizabeth McNeill's and Mrs Blanckley's, to name but a few.

in Spanish; I came top in catechism (I was the only Protestant pupil in a Catholic convent), and bottom in English. I developed a love for Velázquez and the gorier paintings of Goya. 'My father is a Consel. If any person from England, Scotland, Wales or Irlang is in trouble in any kind of way my Father has to go and loock after them,' I wrote, to my parents' mingled pride and despair, in one of my first school essays. 'My father job is very very inpartant. If ther wer no consels there wode be pepole diing withaut help and all kids of thing. If he doset like eny person he must not just say o I dont like yo I dont want to help you. He must be nice and help hem.'

In Singapore, when I was eight, my brothers and I ran wild in a tropical garden filled with bougainvillaea and frangipane trees. We swam in jellyfish-infested seas and went barefoot for two years. I wrote my first stories, and it was always hot. England was a far-away, drizzle-grey dream, from whence letters and comics turned up occasionally, as emotionally distant as the moon. The utter despair which I experienced two years later, when I was sent to boarding school there, has stayed with me all my life.

Adults are often tempted to believe that because children are not yet physically or emotionally mature they do not experience the 'big' emotions of rage or grief in quite the same way that we do. The pain which I felt on being separated from my family was like a bereavement. For many children at boarding school for the first time it is the nights which are the worst, but for me it was always the mornings. I would wake up in the cold first light to see the stark little chest of drawers at the foot of my bed, with its one regulation photograph frame, and beyond it the melancholy autumn beech leaves, dripping and tapping at the window panes. Then I would hide under the bedclothes, sick to my stomach at the thought of another whole day to get through. After half a term of this complete misery – after which I was supposed to have 'settled in' like everyone else – in some trepidation, I wrote a letter. 'Mummy, Mummy, Mummy, Oh my Mummy...' it began. I don't remember the exact wording of the rest of the letter, but I was sure that the hidden message which lay behind these words, the plea to be taken away, could not be mistaken. It was the only letter to which, although I doubtless had a letter back, I never received a reply. So I stayed at school, and learnt to survive.

Diplomatic life, with its long, enforced separations, was often severely damaging to the natural bonds between children and their parents. (It is extremely striking, on reading a good many of these memoirs, to find that the women often write far more naturally and openly about their pets than they do about their children.) In 1941 Norah Errock's father was posted to Saudi Arabia. The country was considered 'impossible' for small children and so Norah, then aged three, was sent to live with her grandmother in the South of France. She did not see her parents again for two and a half years. Although she does not remember missing them during this time (in fact she had barely any recollection of them at all: when she finally saw her father again, and he took her roller-skating round Lake Geneva, she remembers wondering 'who this strange, very tall person was'), her relationship with them was irretrievably altered; 'it wasn't incredibly close. My father was very strict; in fact they both were. It's difficult looking back. There was always a slight fear: was I doing the right thing? At the same time that I wanted to do my own thing. I'm sure it was the separations as much as anything . . . I certainly would never have thought of confiding in them.'

Those children who were occasionally able to visit their parents abroad found the dichotomy between boarding-school life and home life hard to reconcile. 'I think it is very difficult for children,' says Felicity Wakefield. 'Foreign Office children go back to school and they lead a separate life. At school nobody's interested in what's going on at home. And I think they suffer, and I think they suffer very silently.' Felicity put her youngest son into boarding school at the age of nine.

Foreign Office rules in those days [the 1960s] were that you were allowed one fare a year if you weren't going home on leave that year. So in a three-year posting you'd have your child out twice, and that was a heart-breaking thing to do. It was dreadful. It was dreadful for him. From being a very extrovert little boy he became a rather silent little boy. I think he bears the scars of that now. I do. I mean, it wasn't formative for me, because I was already an adult, but I still suffered. I had this letter from him once. We'd arranged for him to go and spend his Easter holidays with my brother and sister-in-law, and then at the last minute they couldn't have him. But they had friends who ran what they called a children's hotel, a sort of hostel for children whose parents were in the Far East – there were masses of them in those days. So I had this letter from him saying, 'Mummy I'm in a home for unwanted children.' Well, that wasn't very good for the morale, was it?

Suzie Duncan's experience reflects that of many diplomatic children as they grew up:

Yes, I did resent my parents for not being there. I think I resented them until probably quite late, until I was about nineteen, because I was very unhappy at boarding school, and I think I blamed part of that on them, for making me go to boarding school, when I didn't really want to be there. I remember my parents having big fights about it. Well, not fights, but discussions, weighing up the pros and cons of taking us with them, or of one of them even staying in England. So I knew that. And obviously they were doing it for our own good, so that we'd have an education throughout. But I think I did resent the fact that they were so far away, and I think that they missed out on us growing up really because they didn't actually have a clue what I was really doing. Or who my friends were . . . or anything at all.

Forced from an early age to rely on their own resources, children often had no choice but to overcompensate, and to suffer the consequences. 'My parents were not around when I wanted them, but when they got back to London I was 16 and too independent,' is one typical remark.[2] Some were tempted to use these situations, sometimes ruthlessly so, to their own advantage.

At the age of thirteen, my sister turned up at Djakarta airport clad in stiletto heels and with piles of make-up on [recalls one diplomatic child]. It was very much more difficult for my mother to tell her to get rid of them, as the obvious answer was that she had been wearing these sort of things 'for years', and anyway, 'everyone else did'. As there were no other 13-year-old English girls out in Djakarta at the time, it was impossible for my parents to make any comparison. Needless to say, this particular episode set the tone for a recklessly rebellious holiday, with me and my sister contradicting everything we were told, and telling my parents that they didn't know anything about England as they hadn't been there for centuries.[3]

Tensions within the family, caused by the uniquely disruptive rhythms of diplomatic life, have made for some understandably ambivalent feelings towards it. Counsellors at the Family Welfare Department of the Foreign Office had seen increasing numbers of diplomatic children coming to them for help. As a spokesman explains,

> What is noticeable over the last five years is that we are seeing a lot of diplomatic children in their thirties and forties, or even in their twenties or late teens, who have strong feelings about what it meant to them to be a diplomatic child. Mostly they are feelings which are partly positive and partly the opposite. It may cause them to feel strongly about how they should live their lives as adults themselves. They want to talk about what they wished had happened. . . . They wish there had been a group of people like there are now to whom they could have talked. And they wish their parents could have perhaps accepted that there was a negative side to it as well as a positive side.

The boarding school (which was quite happily accepted by many) was not the only negative side of diplomatic life. While numerous children, like myself and my two brothers, have gone on to become incurably restless and nomadic adults, it does not necessarily follow that the offspring of peripatetic parents will share their enthusiasms. Sheila Whitney recalls that her two sons, then aged seven and eight and a half, took a distinctly dim view of China when they came out for their first holiday there in 1967. It had an inauspicious start. Owing to bad weather the flight to Peking took four days. They spent one night in Copenhagen, which was not too bad, but were also forced to overnight in Omsk and Irkutsk, where the hotels were terrible.

> You know, the rats were THAT big, and by the time they'd finished the story the rats were as big as THIS, and horrible. So they didn't enjoy the flight at all.
> When they did arrive the peasants, who had come in from all the far corners of China, were curious about them. They hadn't

ever seen a foreigner before, or blue eyes and blond hair, because of course they are all very dark. And they kept touching the boys, and so they *hated* that. And so the first thing we did was to go and buy them a black hat, you know those Chinese hats that have a flap at the front and back, and so they pulled them right down here, you know, right down, and hid behind these hats.

When the next holidays came around, the boys categorically refused to go back. 'We had a letter from their prep master,' Sheila recalls, 'saying, the boys don't want to come out. But we insisted that they did. I won't say that they enjoyed it thoroughly, but it was much better than it had been.'

Norah Errock did not enjoy living in Saudi Arabia when she joined her parents there at the age of seventeen. 'There was virtually nothing there,' she recalls. 'We took one trunk each, and that was about it. You read the same books over and over again. I can remember Sinclair Lewis and Hudson, who wrote terribly sickly stories about life in South America.' The heat and humidity were appalling – 'you did tend to just sit and drip' – and so were the insects. 'I can remember the lovely size of our balcony, and looking out at the sea, but being eaten up by mosquitoes. It sounds wonderful, sitting out on the balcony, sipping whatever it was, gin and lime, but being eaten alive. That was the abiding remembrance: of wanting to enjoy something, but there would always be something to stop it.'

One of Norah's chief problems was how to fill her day. 'Somebody taught me Arabic, and that I thoroughly enjoyed, but that only took about an hour. I think I did the stores, and giving out things to the cook. Then in the afternoons we used to go out and play golf. There was a nine-hole golf course which was entirely desert. The greens were made up of oiled sand. Then in the evenings it was sitting on the balcony. It was a very quiet life.'

Worse still was the absence of anyone of her own age. 'I was extremely lonely. I used to do a lot of writing letters, but even that tails off after a while because what I was writing about was of very little interest to them. There was a war on: by then they were in the services, or working on farms. That was the hardest thing, because you got completely out of the habit of making friends.' Coming back to England was 'a complete culture shock. . . . I thought again that everyone would be fascinated to hear what I'd been doing, and of course no one was in the least bit interested.' '"Where are you from?"' echoes another diplomatic daughter. 'When I was growing up I never did know how to answer that question.'

Whatever ambivalence we may feel about our childhoods, for almost everyone there have been times, some of them sublime, which compensate for the bleaker moments. 'Did I Win Or Lose?' is the title of one lyrical description of a diplomatic childhood published in 1996 in the *BDSA Magazine*. Despite the boarding schools, the separations and the lack of continuity, postings abroad, it claims, give a powerful focus to our most cherished childhood memories. 'I was born in post-war Vienna and christened, just weeks later, in Schönbrunn Palace, then the Catholic chaplaincy. Food was limited, and my staple baby food was brains,' wrote Denise Holt. When she was two, her family moved to Moscow.

I remember little, but we were there when Stalin died, and for the Queen's Coronation. I still have the silver cigarette box given to my father for helping to organise the grand Ball by which the Embassy marked the latter – but I recall best the horror at spilling chocolate ice-cream down the front of my new, beautifully smocked, party frock at the Ambassador's children's party. The country dacha where we spent weekends had fairies at the bottom of the garden: only years later did I discover they were dragonflies.

In Japan Denise learnt to speak fluent Japanese (forgotten on the cruise home); she still has her first kimono. In post-war Beirut 'it was scary but exciting to go to school lying flat on the floor of my father's VW, and to hear shells whistling overhead while we were on the beach, marking the 6 pm curfew.' Holland was 'bicycles, trams, Saint Nicholas, chocolate letters spelling out your name, skating on the canals and learning to make my own way about a foreign city at the age of eleven'. Even when Denise went to boarding school there were still holidays in Persia,

camping in the Elburz mountains, swimming in the Caspian Sea, or – most thrilling – seeing the Blue Mosque and other pearls of Isfahan ... My father's last post was Sofia: for me, grown up parties, learning to ski from the Embassy dacha and discovering the Black Sea Coast before Western tourists had heard of it. The sickly smell of attar of roses, empty cobbled streets, a lovely balcony draped in wisteria, celebrating Easter at a wonderful midnight Russian Orthodox celebration. Did I win or lose from my childhood? What do you think?[4]

These memories of childhood Arcadia, experienced by many diplomatic children when the family was together, are often echoed by their mothers. When asked why they favoured a particular posting, many of the women I spoke to answered, 'Because I had all the children with me.' Mothers who were forced to leave their children often found the separation quite traumatic. 'Nothing,' wrote Sir Geoffrey Jackson poignantly in his book *Concorde Diplomacy*, 'will ever convey the stoical anguish of the exiled mother, watching that twice-yearly charter-flight hoist itself from some tropical runway, bearing back to school – or, surely, to the nightmare of some unimaginable aeronautical catastrophe – the small, subdued, slightly sweating tweed-jacketed figure she loves best of its kind in the world.'[5] '"You must be quite used to this,"' a visiting politician's wife once said to my mother as she returned to the house after one such farewell. 'But one never was.'

Sending one's children away was quite difficult enough for women brought up in a culture where boarding school was the norm. For foreign-born wives, with no such expectations or cultural conditioning, it was far harder to accept. According to Paraguayan-born Veronica Atkinson,

When we were posted to China I felt very claustrophobic because my children were all at boarding school. I couldn't ring them. I didn't have a sister or a family close by who could go and see my kids. And I was thinking, 'Heavens above, I should have them with me.' I had to get used to the idea that boarding school was the thing for a diplomatic family, but at the time I felt very upset because of the distances.

Norah Errock, too, speculates on the pain which her mother must have felt when she sent her three-year-old daughter away. 'My mother was Romanian,' she explains. 'It must have been a terrible introduction to English life, to leave her children. I think she would probably have liked to have stayed behind with us, but my father certainly would not have agreed. He felt very much that the wife's place was with the husband. And I think she was influenced by my grandmother's feelings, which would have been exactly the same.'

Although conditions for diplomatic families have improved considerably, progress has been painfully slow. In 1970, under pressure from an increasingly tough-minded DSWA, the chief of administration admitted in a speech at the Annual General Meeting: 'It is the unalienable right of people to have children. The nation sends us abroad, and it is an inalienable right to unite parents and children every holiday.' Today, as a result of this long campaign, the Foreign Office now pays for three return fares per child, per year, and for two tickets for children over eighteen who are still in full-time education.

Until the 1970s, however, this was very far from being the case. The historian Ruth Dudley Edwards sums up the situation: 'Men with little understanding of what constitutes a normal family life, have made the rules for the Diplomatic Service, and men, whose only criteria were financial, determined the allowances.'[6] But although the conditions may have been created by 'the service', most wives still colluded with it. The tone of Lady Kirkpatrick's 1960 'Serving Abroad' speech to the newly formed Foreign Service Wives Association was typical of the attitude which prevailed. 'Of course we are miserable at being separated,' was her advice, 'but it can't be helped.' When Marie-Noele Kelly was posted to Argentina during the war, she left her eldest son Bernard at school at Downside. 'I knew I should not see him for a year or two,' she wrote matter-of-factly.

In public, the stiff upper lip prevailed; in private, leaving one's children was 'pain and grief every time'. 'I think one of the bad things in our generation was the fact that the children were only allowed out for the summer holidays,' says Ann Hibbert. 'The office only paid for one flight a year, and I think that was extremely hard.' When she was posted to Mongolia in 1964 Ann had to put her youngest son, then aged seven, into boarding school: 'I couldn't explain where we were going. We were completely out of touch. Letters would take three weeks to get there and three weeks to get back. I was always rather upset by receiving a letter from him saying, "I've lost one of my bedroom slippers, what shall I do?"'

The choice which women faced was an unenviable one. A handful decided to opt out of the system and stay at home with their children, but most did not. Very few diplomatic wives can allow themselves to be as clear-sighted about it as Lady Gore-Booth. Although she minded 'desperately' when the time came to send her eight-year-old daughter to boarding school, she had no doubts about it: 'I had made the decision early on, and I don't think that everyone does it this way, that my husband came first, and that we'd make the best arrangements we possibly could for the children.' It was not merely a question of an English education; like many diplomatic parents, the Gore-Booths felt that their children needed 'a sheet anchor', and that the best 'sheet anchor' was boarding school back in England. However, Lady Gore-Booth admits, 'They must have suffered terribly because they were shipped off to their grandparents, which was a terrific generation gap, in the holidays. What they have told us since is that they didn't miss us so much when they were seven as when they were seventeen, and all their emotional problems – this was the '60's – were crowding in on them and they did miss their parents tremendously. It was very sad.'

The stronger a woman's sense of her role within the diplomatic partnership, the more clear-sighted she tended to be over such choices. In her memoir *Pay, Pack and Follow* Jane Ewart-Biggs is brutally honest over the conflicting claims of husband and children. 'My worries about the children's health and welfare had in some ways isolated me from Christopher's preoccupations,' she wrote of her time in Algiers. 'He, in turn, felt excluded by my concentration on the children.' And yet those choices never got any easier. Each time her son Robin went back to England, where he was at school with my two brothers, 'it was like suffering a physical and mental amputation'.

How often did women regret the choices they made? When Anne Disbrowe travelled to St Petersburg in 1825 to join her husband, she had made a difficult decision in good faith. Considering the sea journey to be too dangerous for children, she had left her two small daughters with her parents at Walton Hall. Her elder daughter, Charlotte (who would later edit her mother's letters, some of which were written to her as a little girl, publishing them privately in 1878), was three. Her younger child, Albinia, known to the family as Sissey, was a baby who could 'neither speak nor walk alone' when Anne left her.

'Did you not pity me at leaving my precious babies?' she wrote to a friend shortly after her arrival in Russia. 'It was, and is, still a most painful separation, but I have the comfort of knowing that they are in better care than my own, and that they are as well and happy as possible. I have their pictures, and by dint of scolding myself into good behaviour, I really bear my lot extremely well,' she added bravely.

A few weeks later, spotting two little girls out of her window, 'just the size of my two darlings', she becomes even more wistful: 'If I could see them also, so well wrapt up, trotting along the quay, apparently not minding the cold. Heigh ho!' But as the months continue a note of impatience can be detected. 'I am getting more and more longing to see our little treasures . . . when I see any passages about our being at Walton together I never dare trust myself to thinking "how it will be"; but I skip over the lines at quick as possible. I hardly ever dare talk about my pets, Walton, you . . . or England.'

The winter months brought no hope of reprieve. The tumultuous events of the latter part of 1825 and the beginning of 1826 – the death of Alexander I in December, the Decembrist Uprising, the abdication of Constantine and the plans for the coronation of the new Tsar, his brother Nicholas – all conspired against the speedy return to England for which Anne had been hoping. The following spring she wrote home in a sombre mood. She had been away from England for nearly a year, and the comfort she had derived from thinking of her children as safe and happy at Walton Hall was wearing thin. 'I must not call them babies any more. I could cry to think of it, no longer playthings, but growing up, educating, mannering young ladies, and I have lost a whole year of them, just the most interesting of their youth – what a pity!'

Then, just when the coronation plans were finally underway, the Empress Elizabeth (wife of the recently deceased Alexander) also died. The court in St Petersburg – and with it the entire diplomatic corps – was thrown into another long and gloomy round of official mourning. The coronation and all its fêtes were suspended. 'In short,' Anne wrote, 'the greatest confusion and uncertainty prevails.'

In the light of these disastrous developments, the Disbrowes seriously reconsidered their decision not to bring their children out to Russia with them. Anne, torn between her longing to see them and her fears for their safety, agonized. In the end, after much soul-searching, her misgivings over the perils of both the voyage and the Russian climate won the day. 'I think that the separation will cause me the smallest degree of unhappiness of the two alternatives,' she wrote; 'and then I know they are so well off with you all and I alone am the sufferer, and this consideration must console me.'

But she was very far from being consoled. To her great private disquiet, the question of how long Mr Disbrowe would be required to stay in St Petersburg remained as uncertain as ever. Lady Strangford, the wife of the British ambassador, had died (Anne was with her when 'the fit came which carried her off'); no replacement ambassador had been appointed, and at this stage it was not at all clear whether or not they were expected to travel to Moscow, along with the rest of the court and the diplomatic corps, for the new Tsar's coronation. 'We are in total darkness as to our future,' she wrote. Outwardly Anne's life continued much as before, but the strain was beginning to show. In desperation she began to cut out dress patterns for the two little girls, 'just so as to have something to do around them'.

By June that year she was frantic.

These last two days seem to have lengthened the separation from my darling pets, at least as many months. The day before yesterday completed the long, long year that has elapsed since I was blessed with a sight of those two precious rosy faces peeping under the green bonnets and driving off in such glee. It makes my heart ache to think of it, and yet I can think of little else. If I could only look forward to some certain period of our return, but this suspense, this total ignorance of when this happy event is likely to take place makes me doubly sad. . . . Send me a curl from each of the dear pates. God bless them.

Finally, after months of uncertainty, and at very short notice, the Disbrowes received notice that they were to go to Moscow after all. The Duke of Devonshire (Harriet Granville's brother) had been appointed ambassador extraordinary* for the occasion. He brought with him a

---

* A temporary ambassador, who would not be permanently resident in Russia, but who was appointed specifically to represent the British monarch, George IV, at the coronation.

large retinue of twenty-three servants and nineteen horses, but no wife. It would fall to Anne, as the principal English lady, to do the honours for him. Temporarily, she was entranced. 'Do you not rather envy me going to Moscow! To Moscow!' she wrote. 'Who thought some thirty years ago that it would ever be my lot to write a letter in Moscow? Well, but so it is.'

And yet, in amongst the relentless round of balls and fêtes in Moscow, all of which are described with a lucid and witty pen, lurks the continual ache of her children's absence. 'It is now a whole week since I last heard of those two precious darlings that occupy so much of my thoughts. I am almost *au bout de ma Nature*, and do not know what I shall do if this cruel separation lasts much longer: no prospect of a new ambassador either, and consequently no present hope of relief.' Despite her very real anguish, there is never any suggestion that she should return to England alone.

It was not until March 1828, nearly three years after Anne had left England, that she was finally reunited with her children. 'Until I am actually in the carriage I cannot quite give credence that I really and truly shall again see my darlings and you all,' she wrote. A strange sense of unreality permeates the description of her departure. 'To think that they are learning anything beyond talking and walking seems so very queer to me, I cannot make up my mind to it at all, and for the first few days I am sure I shall not be quite certain that they really are my children.'[7]

Anne Disbrowe paid a high price in leaving her children behind in England, but her fears for their health and safety were well-founded. Mary Fraser tells of a pitiful scene which took place at a diplomatic reception just before their arrival in Vienna in 1880. The Empress, who spoke perfect English, had two stock questions which she would put 'without fear or favour' to every woman who was presented to her: 'Do you ride?' and 'Have you any children?' 'The wife of an English Secretary, instead of replying when it was put to her, burst into uncontrollable weeping,' Mary wrote. 'She had lost her two little ones the year before.'[8]

It was an all-too-familiar story. The kind of medical treatment available for children at that time was still very rudimentary and often outlandish. In *The Complete Indian Housekeeper and Cook*, Flora Steel devoted a whole chapter to 'Hints on the Management of Young Children'. Recommendations for 'Paget's Germ-Free Feeding Bottle and Milk Food' (available from the ubiquitous Army & Navy Stores),* were detailed in amongst recipes for 'powder of rhuburb' (sic) for diarrhoea, and Brand's Essence of Beef for keeping up a child's strength after a bout of bronchitis. As always, Steel's advice was sensible, practical and wholesome, her rule of thumb being 'plenty of milk, plenty of air, plenty of flannel'. There was, however, the odd lapse. A section headed 'Advice on Teething' contained the following hint: if the tooth was visible through the gums, 'take the child's head between your knees, its body being held firmly by another person, and with a small sharp lancet or penknife, and a steady hand, cut the gum through to the tooth. This affords great relief. . . .'[9]

Maintaining a child's physical health was not the only problem. Parents often worried about the cultural implications of bringing up small children abroad.

The mother will have to be ever watchful to counteract the more or less evil influence of native servants [wrote Major Leigh Hunt in *Tropical Trials*]. Take care to keep your children *of all ages* with you as much as possible, for, if left to the society of native servants, not only will they most assuredly contract native habits in the way of eating, gesticulating with the hands when talking etc. Habits that once acquired are so difficult, often impossible, to break off – but, rapidly picking up the language, their little minds will soon become contaminated with ideas and expressions that would utterly horrify a mother did she herself understand the language of the country.

In Persia, Mary Sheil observed how the nurses she employed to look after her children would tear their hair and scratch their bosom 'when in a passion' – behaviour which, to her distress, her daughter Frances learnt to imitate exactly.

It was, however, through observing these same nursemaids that Mary gradually came to a much deeper understanding of the Persians – of

---

* In Peking, at that same period, Mary Fraser noted that the rival Allenbury's Feeder was in vogue amongst legation mothers.

which the Major would have heartily disapproved. Once, during the terrible summer heat, she left her children alone with their two Persian servants at their mountain summer camp, while she and Colonel Sheil went to take the waters at Ask, in the mountain province of Mazenderan (she believed that she was the first European woman to visit there). 'In no country could they have been treated with more kindness, attention and respect,' she wrote, with a mother's relief, on her return. 'English agents are often brought into contact with bad classes, and they hastily assume the whole nation to be equally vicious.' Besides, there were far more serious threats to her children's well-being. In Persia so many children died young, she noted; only three out of every ten children were likely to survive into their third year.[10]

Childbirth itself was enormously dangerous, as much for the mother as for the baby. Its perils were often greatly exacerbated by the conditions abroad. Like many diplomatic women, Mary Elgin missed the comforting presence of her own mother during her first confinement in Turkey: 'I was very, very ill,' she wrote, 'but indeed, poor Poll always suffers more than other people in every illness.'[11] Recovery was often both painful and slow.

I am now able to give you some account of myself with my own hand [wrote Mrs Vigor after the birth of her first child in St Petersburg in 1733], though really I look so pale and thin that if you were to see me I fancy you would not know your old friend ... for though it is three months since I was brought to bed, I have not been out of my room yet, but as my spirits are good I hope my strength will soon come; though, between you and me, as this is the first I should be horribly frightened if I was to find myself in the same condition again.[12]

The following year she had recovered sufficiently to attend 'an entertainment' given by the Empress to celebrate the taking of Dantzick,* but was still too weak to dance.

Others were more robust. 'I wish you joy of your niece, for I was brought to bed of a daughter five weeks ago,' Lady Mary Wortley Montagu wrote to her sister from Constantinople in March 1718. 'I

* Danzig or Gdańsk, on the Baltic Sea.

don't mention this as one of my diverting adventures, though I must own that it is not half so mortifying here as in England, there being as much difference as there is between a little cold in the head, which sometimes happens here, and the consumptive coughs so common in London.' The Turkish attitude to childbirth interested her greatly, and she recorded her observations in detail. To her delight, there was no equivalent to the English tradition of confinement for women who were giving birth – in her view an additional 'curse' which her sex were obliged to endure. 'Nobody keeps to their house a month for lying in,' she wrote, 'and I am not so fond of any of our customs to retain them when they are not necessary.' Mary was able to return all her visits after just three weeks.

Another aspect of Turkish life she found less easy to understand. It was considered a greater social shame to be married and have no children than it was, in Europe, to be 'fruitful' before marriage. Turkish women, Lady Mary observed, went to enormous lengths to 'make proofs of their youth', synonymous in Turkish eyes with fertility, often killing themselves with the various 'quackeries' which they employed to this effect:

> Without any exaggeration, all the women of my acquaintance that have been married ten years have twelve or thirteen children, and the old ones boast of having had five-and-twenty or thirty a piece, and are respected according to the number they have produced. When they are with child 'tis their common expression to say they hope God will be so merciful to them to send them two this time, and when I have asked them sometimes how they expected to provide for such a flock as they desire, they answer that the plague will certainly kill half of them, which, indeed, generally happens without much concern to the parents, who are satisfied with the vanity of having brought forth so plentifully.

Her friend the French ambassadress had indeed taken this custom to heart: 'She has not been here much above a year and has lain in once and is big again.'[13]

Diplomatic women of the eighteenth and early nineteenth centuries are generally far more open on the delicate subject of childbirth than their successors. Mary Sheil, writing in the mid nineteenth century, does not allude directly either to her pregnancies or to the births of her children. Much of what we learn about her family life is by inference alone: only by carefully calculating the dates, for example, do we realize that she was already pregnant when she made her uncomfortable three-and-a-half-month journey to Tehran.

Ann Fanshawe, on the other hand, whose memoir was transcribed in 1676, is almost disconcertingly breezy on the subject. Her extraordinary tales of adventure – of pirates, shipwrecks and high diplomacy – are freely interspersed with information of a far more personal nature: 'In the latter end of this summer I miscarried, when I was near half-gone with child, of three sons, in two hours one after another,' is one typically sanguine observation. 'And my daughter Mary died in Hertfordshire in August.'

The matter-of-factness of her tone is easily misconstrued. It was not that women were indifferent to the loss of their children; it was simply too common an occurrence to merit much comment. Throughout her married life Ann Fanshawe was almost continually pregnant, an exhausting but not unusual state of affairs for a woman of that era. Between 1644, the year of their marriage, and 1666, when her husband died, Ann gave birth to a total of six sons and eight daughters, miscarrying of a further six children (nine if you count the triplets). This means that over a period of twenty-two years, she was pregnant for a total of more than twelve of them. If all the children she conceived had lived, she would have presided over a massive brood of twenty-three children.* As it was, of the fourteen who were 'born and christened', only five lived to see their majority.

Occasionally Ann left her very youngest child behind when she was off travelling on her diplomatic missions with Richard; one of her daughters, Betty, remained 'at nurse' in England while she was away in Portugal. On the whole, however, the family took their chances together. On the detailed inventory of the 'Household and Belongings', which the Fanshawes took to Spain in 1664, appears a Mrs Kestian, governess, and a Mrs Ursula Fawcett, 'servant to young gentlewomen'. But even on Richard's earlier, and far riskier diplomatic missions during the Civil War, Ann took her family with her – a

---

* It would have been a complicated family. Of the boys, three were called Richard and two were called Henry, and of the girls there were two Anns and three Elizabeths.

considerable risk. On Richard's very first mission to Spain, Sir Edward Hyde, one of two resident British ambassadors in Madrid at that time, recorded their arrival. 'Dick Fanshawe has arrived at Malaga with his wife, children, and a family of twelve persons,' he wrote in a letter of 4 April 1650, adding soberly, 'What shift he will be able to make to live I cannot imagine. I myself do not know how to get either bread or money.'[14] Inevitably perhaps, given that she had already endured 'the sword and the plague' in Galway, and a threatened attack by Turkish pirates on the high seas, Ann almost immediately proceeded to give birth again, although her new daughter lived only a few days.

Ann was passionately attached to those children who did survive. The death from smallpox of her nine-year-old daughter Ann – known as 'Nan' – filled her with grief. She was 'the dear companion of our travels and sorrows'. But her sons were particularly important to her. The death of her eldest son Richard in October 1658, also from smallpox, left her shattered in both mind and body. As she recalls the event in her memoir, which was written down nearly twenty years later, the despair in her voice is still terrible to read. 'Both my eldest daughters had the small pox at the same time, and though I neglected them, and day and night tended my dear son, yet it pleased God they recovered, and he died, the grief of which made me miscarry, and caused a sickness of three weeks.' He was eleven and a half years old.

Few descriptions can equal the howl of anguish which came from the pen of Mary Elgin after the death of her son in 1805. On their return to England from Constantinople in February 1803, despite the rumours of a renewal of hostilities between England and France, the Elgins had unwisely decided to travel back overland (sending their two children home separately by the safer sea route). In May, after the Treaty of Amiens had finally collapsed, Napoleon took hostage every English traveller in France. Despite their diplomatic status, the Elgins were detained. William, Mary Elgin's youngest child, was born in captivity in France following year. He died on 18 April 1805, just a month after his first birthday. Mary was inconsolable:

Pray for me, my dearest Mother, take me in your arms; your prayers will be heard tho' mine were not listened to. I have lost my William, my angel William – my soul doated on him, I was wrapt up in my child. From the moment of his birth, to the fatal night it pleased God to call him, I have devoted myself to him. I am resigned to the Will of the Almighty, but my happiness is destroyed forever . . . *My William, my adored William is gone . . . gone . . . and left me here.*

Bless your Miserable Child
What a birthday is this.[15]

In an uncertain world, the decision as to whether or not to keep her children with her abroad was perhaps the most important one which a woman could take during her diplomatic career. Ann Fanshawe chose to take her family with her on her travels. Anne Disbrowe decided against it. Both, in their own ways, suffered the consequences, but the choice was rarely a simple one. As the story of Elizabeth McNeill shows, even when a painful decision had been reached, the complexities of diplomatic life often made it very hard to execute.

Elizabeth, or Eliza Wilson was the ninth child of John Wilson, a wealthy merchant and manufacturer of gauze in Paisley, near Glasgow in Scotland. After his death, his wife moved to Edinburgh with her family, where they maintained a secure and respected position in society. It was there, in 1822, that Elizabeth met John McNeill, a tall and strikingly handsome widower of twenty-seven. They were married on New Year's Day 1823. Just six months after their wedding Elizabeth, already four months pregnant, set out with her husband to make the exhausting three-month journey to Persia, where she was to spend more than ten years of her life. They arrived safely in Tabriz, in northern Persia (in present-day Azerbaijan), where all Europeans were obliged to reside, on 8 October. Two months later their first child, Margaret, was born.

John McNeill, a doctor by training, was not a conventional diplomat but an employee of the British East India Company. Diplomatic links with countries on the borders of British India were frequently maintained directly by the East India Company itself (and later, after the 1849 Mutiny, by the government of India) rather than by London. The main diplomatic mission in Tehran, founded in 1798 and administered alternately by the Foreign Office in London and the Indian government, was preceded by a 'Political Residency', set up in 1763 under the company's control in Bushire, on the Persian Gulf. Early trading relations, which date from the beginning of the seventeenth century, were later supported by increasingly political ties. Persia's strategically vital position on one of the main overland routes to India made it an important ally. Under the 1814 Treaty of Tehran, Persia had engaged to obstruct any power seeking to pass through the country for the purpose of invading India. Originally a response to the threat from Napoleon, this vital alliance with Persia became, as the century progressed, a powerful buffer against the growing strength and expansionist tendencies of Russia. The 'Eastern Question' was to become John McNeill's great area of expertise.

In 1823 most of this was still before him, but John McNeill had already proved himself to be an extremely able young man. The year before his marriage, under the company's aegis, he had already served as assistant medical officer on one diplomatic mission to Persia, accompanying the British chargé, Mr Willock, from Bombay to Tehran. Now, just two years later, he was promoted to assistant chargé, and in this capacity, on 18 February 1824, he set out once again to accompany Mr Willock to Tehran. Margaret was too young to undertake such a long journey in freezing temperatures, so Elizabeth stayed behind with her in Tabriz. It was to become a familiar pattern. Although the marriage was a love match, and when John was at home they led 'a very quiet and happy home life', from the beginning it was an extremely solitary existence for Elizabeth. As the capital of Azerbaijan, Persia's richest province, Tabriz was an important centre (the Crown Prince, Abbas Mirza, had his court here), but the Shah, and the centre of power, remained in Tehran. In a single year John once calculated that he had travelled between 1,500 and 2,000 miles, much of it between Tabriz and Tehran. On this first trip alone he was away for nearly four months.

A practical and extremely devout Scotswoman (both the McNeills were Episcopalians), Elizabeth made the best of it and helped her husband in many ways. Most of her days, however, were spent looking after her family: her eldest daughter, the delicate Margaret, soon had a sibling, Hester Mary.

It was a lonely time. Although Tabriz was a regular staging post for those travelling to and from India,* for long stretches during her

* The main route was by sea from Bombay up the Persian Gulf, and then overland, north through Persia and Russia.

ten-year residence in Persia Elizabeth saw no other European woman but her children's nurse, Mrs Robinson. For a short period Madame Mazarowitch, the wife of the Russian envoy, accompanied by her little boy, came out to join her husband. Elizabeth was delighted at the addition to the tiny European community then resident in Tabriz. 'I hailed the arrival of anything rational as a boon for heaven,' she wrote, pronouncing Madame Mazarowitch to be 'lady-like, sensible, and pleasant'. On the whole, though, Elizabeth, like her successor Mary Sheil, was extremely isolated, both emotionally and physically. However, being blessed with a gentle and hopeful disposition, and happy in her domestic rounds, she did not complain. 'I can truly say that I have never seen her express the slightest discontent at the numerous inconveniences to which she has occasionally been subjected,' wrote her husband fondly.

Elizabeth's situation was greatly improved in 1827, when the new British envoy, Colonel Macdonald, who had at last arrived from India, received permission to move his entire suite to Tehran. The new British mission house was built 'in European style, with a broad flight of steps leading up to a Doric portico between two projecting wings'; the view was of the snowy mountains of Elburz which, seen through the cypresses of the garden, had 'a most beautiful effect'. Not only could she spend more time with John; she and her children would at last be able to take some part in Persian life.

Elizabeth's pride in her children can be appreciated in her detailed description of her visit to the royal harem. John McNeill had cured the Shah's favourite wife and one of her children, and in gratitude they issued Elizabeth with an invitation to the harem. Unusually, Elizabeth did not go alone, but took both her little girls and their nurse with her. The four set off in some style, she wrote to her sister, Jane Wilson:

Myself on a led horse, dressed in white satin with broad lace flounces, my blue stones etc; Mag in a bobbinette dress over pale blue satin, with Jessie Beatson's beautiful cap newly done up; Hester Mary in virgin white, and Robertson in a brown poplin gown she got from our beloved mother. My outward garb was a great wide cloak of crimson silk lined with pale blue, and a large *calash* of the same. You are aware that the point of a lady's finger even dare not be seen in Persia. I had four running footmen of my own before me, and three of Mr Willock's behind me.

Like the other diplomatic women who were granted this rare privilege, once inside the royal harem Elizabeth was almost overcome by the opulence of the scene which greeted her:

Nothing could exceed the splendour, the magnificence, the dazzling richness and brilliance of the scene. The slave girls were blazing in diamonds and rubies, brocade and spangles. Their dresses, originally of the richest stuffs, were so closely embroidered with pearls and precious stones that little else could be seen. Their hair hung loose, and their heads were ornamented in various ways with jewels . . . The Queen sat on a crimson velvet cloth which was richly embroidered with pearls, and reclined against a large square cushion of the same material, with this difference only, that the pearls were here so close together as to leave almost no portion of the velvet visible. Her own dress was most magnificent. The precious stones alone cost, independent of setting, about £150,000.

This already overwhelming display was augmented, if that were possible, not only by the walls of the harem – three sides of which were covered entirely with mirrors – but by the entire contents of the Shah's treasury:

On the niche above her head was placed the Crown of the Shah (an exquisite thing), and on each side of it a Persian black lamb's skin cap, ornamented with sprays of the largest diamonds. Beside her lay the famous armlets of the Shah, in one of which is the diamond called 'the Sea of Light'.* In the various other niches

* Exactly 100 years later Vita Sackville-West, never easily impressed, was flabbergasted by the sight of the Shah's jewels: '. . . suddenly, and as with a physical start, my eyes and thoughts came together, as gears engaging; I stared, I gasped; the small room vanished; I was Sinbad in the Valley of Gems, Aladdin in the Cave. The linen bags vomited emeralds and pearls; the green baize vanished, the table became a sea of precious stones. The leather cases opened, displaying jewelled scimitars, daggers encrusted with rubies, buckles carved from a single emerald; ropes of enormous pearls. Then from the inner room came the file of servants again, carrying uniforms sewn

were candlesticks, dressing materials, basins, and caskets, all of the purest gold and precious stones.

After the usual courtesies had been observed – the sprinkling of her hands with rose water, the scented coffee offered in tiny gold- and emerald-encrusted cups – Elizabeth's children were introduced. Margaret, 'terrified out of her wits by the glare of the diamonds', could not be persuaded anywhere near the Queen's throne, and was carried off in disgrace. The baby Hester Mary, on the other hand, 'received a royal embrace, and was pronounced a beauty'. When the visit was over they were all presented with gifts – for Elizabeth, 'a large ornament of diamonds, rubies, emeralds, and pearls'; 'ornaments of jewels' were fastened on each of the children's caps. Hester, who had found special favour, was also given 'a pair of beautiful little pearl bracelets' fastened onto her fat wrist by the Queen herself. Even Robertson received 'a handsome black shawl (cashmere) of which you may be sure she is not a little proud'. They returned to 'the English palace, on the steps of which we found Mr Willock, Mr Shee, and Papa, all dying with impatience to hear the account of the secret place'.

Elizabeth's delight at being able to show off her children to the Persian queen is all the more poignant because it was to be so short-lived. The timid Margaret, always a delicate child, had been almost constantly ill with 'painful, weary attacks', and died soon after on 22 September 1826, just a little short of her third birthday. 'Elizabeth has shown her usual strength of mind,' John wrote to her sister 'and amidst all her grief has behaved with composure. Her desire to prevent the affliction of her own mind from injuring the infant she was nursing gave force to her natural resolution.'

But this was only the beginning of the McNeills' misfortunes. Not long after her sister, Hester, hitherto as 'fat as a little pig', also began to decline, a victim of the Persian 'climate'. At enormous personal cost, the McNeills decided to send her back to live with Elizabeth's

---

with diamonds; a cap with a tall aigrette, secured by a diamond larger than the Koh-i-Nur; two crowns like great hieratic tiaras, barbaric diadems, composed of pearls of the finest orient ... We plunged our hands up to the wrist in the heaps of uncut emeralds, and let the pearls run through our fingers' (*Passenger to Teheran*, p. 103). The Persians were delighted at the effect of the Shah's treasures upon foreigners. 'The ministers laughed at our amazement and incredulity,' Vita noted.

sister in Edinburgh. The three-month journey, which Elizabeth undertook alone with Hester, very nearly killed her. Mother and child often passed whole days and nights at a stretch in their carriage, and when they did find a miserable lodging for the night they were often kept awake by fleas and other insects. At Ekaterinagorod they were forced to observe a fifteen-day quarantine in a filthy hovel. Hester fell ill with a fever, and Elizabeth contracted such a severe bout of dysentery that she was afraid she might die.

When she finally returned to Persia, having left Hester in Edinburgh, Elizabeth had been away a year, a full six months of which had been spent travelling, 'much of it in very wild country, without adequate protection, and with almost no comforts but those afforded by the help of a few friends along the way'.

Back in Tehran the McNeills' fortunes seemed to take a turn for the better. They received news that John had received a promotion, and had been appointed political resident in Bushire in the Persian Gulf. To her joy, Elizabeth was expecting another baby. Despite her pregnancy, now in an advanced stage, on 22 December, in the depths of winter, the McNeills set off for the gulf. In order to avoid crossing the high mountains north of Bushire, they took a circuitous route – first west, through the Iraqi deserts, then south down the Tigris to Baghdad, and from there to the gulf. 'The accommodation in Persia is not particularly luxurious,' Elizabeth wrote, 'but in Arabia, it is fifty times worse. We slept every night in the stables of caravansaries, as black as pitch, liker the dens of robbers than the sleeping-places of Christians. Sometimes we were nearly suffocated with smoke, none of the places having either windows or chimneys.'

On the Tigris they were shot at by Arabs, 'who kept firing random shots until at last the ships' company were obliged to fire the boat's big gun', but there was worse to come. The plague was raging in Baghdad and at Bussorah, and at the same time the weather grew worse. 'Snows have not, in the memory of man, ever been so deep as this year,' wrote Elizabeth, then just weeks away from her confinement. The only shelter was offered by caravanserais, now filled with hundreds of dead bodies, victims of the plague. They had no choice but to press on through the snow, which in places lay six feet deep. 'On two occasions we came to places the day after travellers had perished,' Elizabeth wrote to her sister, and we saw flocks of sheep lying frozen to death. My *tukt* [litter] without exaggeration fell from 12–20 times daily. I had often to walk from five to seven miles knee-deep in snow or mud. John never got leave to sit on his horse half an hour at a time, and had he not been with me with his powerful arm and steady mind the tukt would oftentimes have been abandoned to its fate.

In February, two months into this appalling journey, when they were just a day's journey from Bussorah, John received dispatches informing him that his appointment had been cancelled. The new governor of Bombay, Lord Clare, had taken the unprecedented step of altering the appointments made by his predecessor. John was to stay in Tehran as first assistant and medical officer to the new envoy, Captain Campbell.

The McNeills were in a quandary: where should they go now? Should they press on or turn back? Elizabeth's situation was critical. News that the plague had now reached Bushire, where a thirty-day quarantine had been imposed, decided them. They managed to reach Hamadan, in Persia, where, against all the odds, Elizabeth's child Eliza was safely born on 30 March 1832.*

When the McNeills finally arrived back in Tehran, five months after they had left it, they tried to take up the thread of their lives, but things were never quite the same again. Even the extraordinarily stoic and resourceful Elizabeth seemed despondent:

My spirit is occasionally weary and worn out with various discomforts, to which, for us, there seems no end . . . I feel such an additional loathing to everything connected with the country that, were John sure of being made *Ellchee* [Envoy] at the end of five years, I feel that I could scarcely rejoice in it, or, in fact, any aggrandizement that is to keep us longer from our home, our child, our brethren, and the rational uses of existence. I struggle all I can against these feelings, but I find it all in vain; sleeping or waking, they are ever present in my thoughts.

* It was the right decision. The plague in Bushire became so severe that the residency had to be abandoned. All the Europeans took refuge on Corgo, a sandy island three or four miles long and only half a mile wide, where they lived in tents for four months. In Bushire 2,000 bodies lay dead and unburied in the streets.

In January 1834 another daughter, Margaret Ferooza, was born, but the following month Eliza died, and in April a letter came informing Elizabeth that there had been a scarlet fever epidemic in Edinburgh. Both her sister Jane and her daughter, little Hester, were dead. Having seen so many of her other children die, and having sent Hester to a place where she, at least, would be safe, what can Elizabeth have felt on reading this letter? The fact that letters took many months to reach Persia meant that Hester had been dead for some time while her mother remained in ignorance, a thought which must have tortured her all her life.

In May Elizabeth and the four-month-old Margaret Ferooza left to make the weary journey back to England. John McNeill, left alone in Persia, was also close to despair. 'Elizabeth set out with our poor babe for England,' he recorded. 'It is right that an attempt should be made to save it at whatever sacrifice to ourselves, but it is neither stouter in frame nor more healthy in appearance than its brother* and sisters. How, then, can we expect to see it survive when they have all been taken away.' A letter to Elizabeth, written shortly after this, clearly shows his depressed state of mind.

When I reflect on the many chances against our meeting again, and how much these must be increased by prolonging our separation, I sometimes think I do wrong in remaining here to struggle on – for what? For the chance, the distant chance, of one day (if I live) being able to spend a hundred or two more per annum in England than I can do now. I have found the house most desolate today, so much so that it quite overcame me. My solitary dinner stuck in my throat.

In fact, John McNeill did live to be *ellchee* to Persia. Just two years later, in 1836, he resigned from the East India Company, and was appointed 'Minister Plenipotentiary and Envoy Extraordinary from the Court of St James to the Shah of Persia'. You will be relieved to know that Elizabeth and Margaret Ferooza both reached Edinburgh safely. By the time John finally retired, in 1842, he had risen to become the

* It is not clear when this child was born. Possibly he was the baby, even younger than Hester, whom Elizabeth was nursing when Margaret died.

acknowledged expert on the Eastern Question; he was lionized by London society, and honoured with the Civil Grand Cross of the Bath. With Elizabeth and his 'Pettie' as his side, he went on to enjoy a respected and prosperous retirement as 'the handsomest and proudest man in Edinburgh'.[16]

CHAPTER ELEVEN

Dangers

In 1971 the following message appeared in the DSWA's *Spring Magazine*, under the title: 'A Message from Lady Douglas-Home, Lady Greenhill,* the Chairman and the Committee':

> We are all worried about the kidnap threat and very conscious of the strain that the danger and restriction of movement places on whole families in certain countries. All of us were delighted by the happy outcome of the Cross case,† and we are very proud of them both. We are proud, too, of the way in which Mrs Geoffrey Jackson is facing her present ordeal. The administration is doing all it can to help.

At that time Evelyn Jackson (now Lady Jackson – Googoo to her friends), whose husband had been kidnapped in January that year by a Uruguayan terrorist group, still had a further six months of her ordeal to endure. The Jacksons had been posted to Montevideo in 1970. The high incidence of kidnappings throughout Latin America at that time, and a general sense of unease and foreboding which had affected Geoffrey since their arrival, had persuaded him that he might well be a victim. According to Evelyn, this meant that the Jacksons had ample time to plan their strategy:

> Geoffrey said, 'Now when it happens, I want you to get into the first plane back to London. You go to Mr Heath, Sir Alec Douglas-Home (who was Foreign Secretary) and Denis Greenhill

---

* Wives of the Foreign Secretary and the head of the Foreign Office respectively.
† Jasper Cross had been kidnapped in Canada.

(who was the head of the Foreign Office), and you tell them what I want: no exchange of prisoners, no negotiations, no ransom to be paid. And he also added – and this was very strong – and no publicity. I'm going to see it through.

For all her husband's premonitions, the day he was taken was very much like any other.

I'd hurt my back, and I was in the bath [Evelyn remembers], so I said to Geoffrey, 'Don't go without getting me out,' because Reuben, our butler, was a wonderful man, but he wasn't a lady killer, and I didn't want him to have a slippery woman to get out of the bath. So Geoffrey got me out of the bath and he said, 'I've got an appointment, so I'm off.' And he gave me a big kiss and he went. About half an hour later the butler came in and he said, '*Embajadora*, do you know where the ambassador was going?' So I looked at him and I said, 'Reuben, he was going to his office.' And he said, '*Embajadora*, he's not there.' So I said, 'Let's turn on the radio,' and so we put the radio on and it said, '*El Embajador de Gran Bretaña* etc etc etc.'

Geoffrey Jackson had been kidnapped by Tupamaro terrorists.*
Evelyn was already packing her bags for London when the minister of foreign affairs, a friend of the Jacksons, came round with his head of protocol.

He said, 'Googoo, Geoffrey has been kidnapped – what do you want me to do for you?' So I said, 'Get me on the first plane out, and you can tell the press that are at the door that I'm not talking to anybody. That Geoffrey wants: no exchange of prisoners, no ransom, and no negotiations.' And, of course, I knew then that I'd killed him. Because I was confirming what we had decided.

---

* The Marimiento de Liberación Nacional took 'Tupamaro' from Tupac-Awaru, last scion of the Incas. Brought up in eighteenth-century Peru as a Spanish hidalgo, he later led a movement for indigenous rights and was executed in 1784. His name became a synonym for 'troublemaker'. It was taken up by a small group of Uruguayan guerrillas dedicated to the overthrow of the current order of society.

But what else could I do? That was what Geoffrey wanted, and I was his wife, and that was my duty.

Back in London Evelyn took the only course available to her: she settled down to wait. It was only much later, when her husband was finally released, that she was able to piece together some of the details of what had happened.

He was underground for nine months, in a cage. A cage made from chicken wire. On a very hard slab of concrete. With a mattress which wasn't a mattress: just foam, which was in bits. He lived in his underpants. It was very hot down there. He never saw a face – they always wore those black masks – and he never knew where he was. They were trigger happy. They'd sit there and he'd hear them fooling around with their rifles. And he didn't say anything, ever, but he would draw them. And he would draw a Tupamaro woman with a mask on, pushing a baby in its little bassinette. The baby was in a mask, too.

At the time, back in London, Evelyn knew nothing of this. 'I drove John Ling [at the Foreign Office's South American Department] mad I'd ring him up every morning and say "Have you got any news?", and he'd say "No, I haven't." So I'd keep him on the phone and we'd discuss things.' Although for most of the time she was able to keep an open mind, she was still haunted by the possible consequences of following Geoffrey's instructions. 'I thought, Well, I've killed him. What have they to wait for? But they didn't. I think they admired his bravery.'

Until Geoffrey Jackson's release, nine months later, Evelyn received no communication at all from the kidnappers. She had no idea whether he was alive or dead. Despite the DSWA's message of support, she found herself very isolated in her anxiety for her husband: 'I think the wives could have kept in touch, one of them, every other day, a different one, just to say, "Are you still alive? Is there anything we can do for you?" But no. No joy.'*

* The one exception was Angela Greenhill, wife of the head of the Foreign Office, who was 'very kind and very decent'.

Dramatic though Evelyn Jackson's experience may have been, in diplomatic life it is by no means unique. At various times, in various trouble spots around the world, wives have been evacuated, bombed, shot at, besieged; their husbands injured, kidnapped and even killed. Once again the BDSA magazines provide both a catalogue and an interesting barometer of how women regarded these experiences. Most wives involved in dangerous or traumatic situations assumed a peculiarly English form of stoicism – 'Cake and Shrapnel for Tea' was one recent, typically humorous offering from a wife in Beirut. In 1972 an article by Mrs Pat Vincent, wife of the ambassador to Nicaragua, whose aeroplane had recently been hijacked on a flight from San Salvador to Managua, appeared, sandwiched in between 'Living in Geneva' and 'Letter from Swaziland'. 'Without over-dramatising the situation, being a victim of a "secustro" or hijack,' she wrote, 'is not exactly amusing.'[1]

In times of real crisis the emotional and psychological costs are far greater than these carefully constructed masks might suggest. 'You get involved,' Catherine Young explains. 'Maybe not everybody, but I think the majority of us get involved.' During Catherine's posting in Syria in the 1980s the British embassy was trying to secure the release of British hostages in the Middle East, most of whom came out via Syria.

That was a big tension while we were there: hostages. And I remember the worst time probably for Rob was when two Brits* had been taken by the Libyans: they knew that they were beginning to get them out and just at that time there was that American strike in Tripoli, and within two hours the two chaps had been killed. Revenge. And you know, the hours, the nights. There was constantly someone on duty in the Embassy to make sure that someone would always be there if there was a call. An enormous amount of effort at all levels put in and . . . It took us a long time to get over that one. You do live it, absolutely, absolutely.

Even when they are not direct targets, diplomats and their families are still extremely vulnerable in any potentially volatile political situation. Sometimes, just being there is enough. And besides, as Googoo Jackson puts it, 'We're always in the middle of a revolution. They just

* Leigh Douglas and Philip Padfield. They were executed on 17 April 1986.

wait for us to arrive, and then they get cracking . . . such is life in the Foreign Office.'

Jennifer Duncan, posted to Mozambique during the seventies when the revolution started, recalls how

> For several months it wasn't safe to go out, so I used to sit at home listening out for the shooting. My husband is partially deaf, so when it started I used to ring him up to tell him what direction I thought the fighting was coming from. Once I rang him and said, 'The shooting's started again; I think it's coming from downtown.' Stanley, who was lying flat on the floor under his desk at the time said rather tersely, 'Yes, I know. And for God's sake get off the phone, all the other lines are down and this is the only one we've got left.' The rebels had just taken the radio station across the road from his office.

Diplomatic families have occasionally had reason to regret their prominent status. In Tripoli in 1791, during a revolt spearheaded by the Bashaw's son, Sidi Useph, not only the Tullys but many others, including the French and Venetian consuls and their families, took refuge in the British consulate. According to Miss Tully, 'As soon as Sidy Useph arrived within sight of the town, the Greeks, Maltese, Moors and Jews brought all their property to the English house.' The building, a large and secure house which had once been the residence of the Bey (the Bashaw's eldest son), was reinforced by armed soldiers stationed on the rooftops, and even a canon from one of the Venetian ships. 'Every room was filled with beds, and the galleries were used for dining rooms. The lower part of the building contained the Jewesses and the Moorish women, with all their jewels and treasures. There was likewise a great quantity of jewels in the house belonging to the Bashaw, which was in the possession of some of the Consuls, to be returned to him at a future time.'

Although she was at home on leave, visiting her two sons, Sheila Whitney remembers only too well the events in China of August 1967. The rapidly escalating frenzy of the Cultural Revolution (1966–76) was by now being directed not only at 'counter-revolutionary' Chinese, but also at foreigners. The Indonesian embassy had been sacked and burned, and the Soviet embassy invaded. In Hong Kong, in an effort to stop the mass demonstrations there, the authorities had closed down communist newspapers, and were prosecuting some of their journalists for inciting and participating in violence. When the British embassy in Peking received, and rejected, an ultimatum from the Chinese, serious trouble was bound to follow. On the night of 22 August the British mission in Peking was burnt to the ground by Mao's Red Guards. Sheila's husband Ray, along with the other few remaining British diplomats, was seriously assaulted as he tried to escape.

> There were twenty-three of them, including one wife because she looked after the library. And they all went into one of the back rooms [the embassy's secure area] because they could hear the mob yelling for them. And then they suddenly felt fire, and they realized that the whole building was alight and they had to get out of the back door. I think there were five women. And they each took three or four men round one woman and tried to protect her against the mob, but they did ghastly things to them all the same.

> Punches and blows rained down on them; the women had their hair wrenched from their heads and most of their clothing was ripped off. 'Ray was pulled away from the door and bashed around, and he was clinging to the railings so that they couldn't drag him off, and his hands were hit. And he really thought he was going to be bludgeoned to death. He really thought that was it. He said he thought he'd never see us again.'

Back in England, appalled and helpless, Sheila and her two sons watched the news on television.

> The boys were very, very upset about it because they knew of the hostility that they had encountered – it was a feeling in the air, not anything that you could really touch. You just felt the atmosphere. They were so worried about it that they didn't work for a whole year at school, they just couldn't settle down. I visited them every weekend, you know just to say, 'Well, at least I'm here.' And we went to the chapel and I tried to reassure them as much as I could. But they were just terrified of what might happen to Ray in Peking.

In the 1970s any kind of official support for these casualties of diplomatic life was almost unknown: most, like Evelyn Jackson, were obliged to sit it out on their own. Neither the BDSA (then still the DSWA, and in 1971 only ten years old), nor the Medical and Welfare Department of the Foreign Office (which, according to Ruth Dudley Edwards, in those days was still perceived as 'a particularly cross school matron') – bodies which might have provided some kind of support – were willing or able to help. Evelyn's suggestions for a roster of wives to keep in touch with women in a similar position to hers fell on deaf ears. Many years after his release Sir Geoffrey Jackson was still bitter on the subject. 'When first [my wife] pointed out this special loneliness of a wife desperately awaiting news of a husband missing or endangered overseas, the immensely "senior wife" present interjected, "But wives at home aren't expected to be social." '[2]

Today, however, a much more sophisticated safety net of advice and counselling is on offer.

If there was a violent scenario now we would insist on seeing everybody [explains one of the Foreign Office welfare counsellors], I think we have learnt that over the years. As a department we don't like to insist; we feel that we should give people a choice as to whether they want to come and see us. But I think now we probably *would* insist. And we would do it fairly quickly. For example, if a bomb went off in some post overseas I think we would try to get there within a week . . . three days perhaps. And we would be very clear as to how we could be of most use to people.

In 1976, when Jane Ewart-Biggs's husband Christopher, then the British ambassador to Ireland, was killed by a bomb, these services were in a still distant future. Instead, members of the embassy (where my father was then counsellor, the number two in the office, automatically becoming chargé d'affaires after the ambassador's death) drew together to support Jane and her family as best they could during the long, dark weeks immediately following the assassination. My mother recorded the events in a long letter, written on that occasion as a diary, which she later sent to my grandmother,

Wednesday, 21st July, 1976

Sheila McMullen [wife of the military attaché] rang me about 10 to say had I heard anything as their policeman had heard on his walky talky that there had been an explosion up at Glencairn [the residence]. I pooh-poohed this slightly, thinking it must have been a gasmain blowing or something. Spoke to John Goulden [in the office] who sounded disturbed and said they were in the process of finding out what had happened – something I guessed obviously had. 10 minutes later J [my father, John] rang me to say that in fact there had been an explosion under the Ambassador's car and the first report was that Brian O'Driscoll [ex butler and for two weeks the chauffeur] had been killed and Christopher the footman seriously injured. Also others. The children and I are devastated. Matthew and Katie rush to their rooms sobbing their hearts out.* Andrew stands mutely beside me as I too burst into tears. J tells me to stand by the phone as of course I must go up to Glencairn and see the children: Henrietta 15, Robin 12, and Katie 8. Their mother left for England last night before I came to take all the children, theirs and mine, to the cinema. Christopher EB was entertaining Brian Cubbon and his secretary Judith Cooke from the Northern Ireland Office to dinner, J and John Golden etc. there too. This was a routine visit and nothing of any significance.

J tells me not to go up until I'm told as it is all confusion up there and details garbled. We listen to the 10.30 RTE news. A programme just before is interrupted to tell us that a land mine exploded under the British Ambassador's car, and that he and one other person had been killed. Brian O'Driscoll and Brian Cubbon are in hospital very seriously injured. I pace the house distraught not knowing *what* to do. I feel I must get up to Glencairn. At last the phone rings – J again to confirm that in fact Christopher EB has been killed and the secretary, but that the two Brians are alive, but their condition critical. Will I go up to Glencairn and take over – and tell the children.

Children calm by this time and I fly off leaving K. beside the telephone to take messages which are already flooding in. I drive up there to find of course the road leading up to Glencairn

* I was then fifteen; my brother Matthew twelve, and Andrew ten.

blocked by army trucks by the score, batteries of police cars, the inevitable photographers and of course gawpers who block my way and madden me. I eventually get to the front of the house by the back way, also blocked by soldiers with guns at the ready, helicopters are hovering overhead. I arrive to find the staff in a bad way and all wanting me to hear their version of when they heard the bang. No children in sight. I ask Christopher [the footman], dear Christopher, looking ashen, to find them for me. They are in the garden, Katie the little one still upstairs. Christopher sweetly insists on giving me a snort of whisky to give me some extra courage. I find Henrietta and Robin playing with a newly acquired spaniel, and I ask them to come for a little walk with me round the garden. They are obviously quite unaware of what has happened (the explosions as you know occurred outside the gates around a bend, along which incidentally I must have passed at least six times the day before. The explosive having been packed beforehand in an underground culvert, ready to be set off electronically at the right moment.)

I break it to them as gently as it is possible to break such impossible news – and my words came out so crudely it seemed. I feel entirely inadequate and for a few moments they are inconsolable. We stay in the garden and walk and walk, but they are now mute, and there are no more words to say. They ask no questions, thank goodness, as to details. I know so little as yet myself. We return to the house having decided that we won't tell Katie but that Jane would tell her on her return. I promised them Mummy would be back that night. I only hope to God this is possible.

Phone call from the F.O. in London. Jane who was driving down to London from Liverpool had been intercepted by the police. However she had already heard the news on her car radio. Can you imagine? She spoke to me from Michael Palliser's office. (He is Permanent Under-Secretary.) She wanted to talk to the children. I persuaded her not to as this couldn't help. However her message to them was that she was on her way back NOW and would be with them as soon as possible. I tell her this is the only thing that matters to them and she is satisfied, Thank God. The Private Sec. tells me an RAF plane is flying her home as soon as it can be prepared and that a Senior FO man would be with her.

Sheila McMullen arrives to give me moral support. She, and I and the children have some lunch, but no-one has any appetite. I have told my Katie to hold the fort and get the lunch. She says the phone hasn't stopped ringing. After lunch I take the children back to our house. Mine are a bit shy, no-one knows what to say. However they behave beautifully and I'm proud of them. The boys play billiards etc and Katie copes with an utterly silent Henrietta. We hear that the plane is due in at 4.30. We must be there when she arrives so the EB children and I leave for Glencairn. Little Katie asks innumerable questions as to why there are so many soldiers, policemen, armoured cars, helicopters, cars, people etc, everywhere. I go and play tennis with Robin while we wait, Henrietta has gone to ground. Jane arrives flanked by Richard Sykes* and J; I don't know who looks more ashen. Jane goes out into the garden with the children, and they stay out there for half an hour and then slowly trail back in.

I rush back home, ring Kath [a family friend] who says of course she'll have the children for as long as I want (she has already rung twice to offer help). I pack a few things for myself as I am obviously going to stay the night at Glencairn.

Dinner consists of J and I, Richard Sykes, Jane and her children, a ghastly meal with her breaking down from time to time. She wants to go in to the hospital to see Brian O'Driscoll and Brian Cubbon but as they are on the danger list still this obviously is not possible. (Mrs Cubbon has arrived on the same aircraft to be with her husband and is living at the hospital.) I suspect she also wants to see Christopher. Brian Cubbon had suspected spinal injuries and head injuries and cuts, and Brian O'Driscoll is reported to be in better shape though with bad bruising, facial cuts, a practically severed arm and possible internal lung injuries. J eventually goes off saying he will look in on Kath and the children. The EB children all go off to sleep with Jane, and I sleep in little Katie's bed. Richard Sykes is in the Yellow Room.

END OF FIRST DAY

* The Under-Secretary of State from London. Just three years later, in 1979, Richard Sykes was himself assassinated, also by the IRA, when he was serving as ambassador to The Hague.

Thursday, 22nd July, 1976

I spent a wretched night hardly sleeping at all. I couldn't get out of my head the thoughts that the car had apparently gone about 60ft in the air (weighs 2 tons this specially made Daimler) and caused a large crater right in the middle of the road. It was obviously a well-planned operation with split second timing that it hit the first of a convoy of four cars. I eventually got up with the light at 5 am, wandered down to the big kitchen and made myself some tea, taking it out, and walking round the garden in lovely early morning light. All seems so peaceful. It's all hard to believe. I dozed off for an hour and Bridie [the housekeeper] wakes me at 8 o'clock with more tea. I have a good bath and come down alone to breakfast. See the awful headlines . . . The wives come up as I suggest, only they don't come one at a time, but in pairs. First Joan Townsend and Audrey – everybody stands and sits around drinking. Then Marion Harris and Vi Harris.

After lunch I went to Kath's where we all sat in the kitchen and discussed the horror. I took the children back up to Glencairn to play with EBs. We all stay to dinner. J and Jane go off to see the two Brians and she comes back considerably shaken as we knew she would. She also went and saw Christopher. We had warned the hospital first so that some facial surgery could be done beforehand. They said they needed at least one hour's notice for this to be done. Garret Fitzgerald [the Irish Foreign Minister] was there seeing the two Brians and actually went with her into the mortuary – I gather he was a marvellous support. He comes back with them and Joan joins us a little later. I take the children back to Kath, but return to spend another night here.

Friday, 23rd July

Fiona Camber, Christopher's departing secretary, is supposed to be coming up to take the secretarial side in hand coping with the mail, constant telephone etc. etc. However she is ill and Carole Crook [an embassy wife] arrives which I'm glad about as she will do well. We start a few files and get a proper diary going. I'm constantly on the phone myself. The system here works badly and one spends hours moving backwards and forwards to the pantry where the old switchboard lives. I have a long talk to Denis

Greenhill in London whom she has asked to do the address at the St Margaret Memorial Service next Friday – today week . . .

3pm The Prime Minister and Mrs Cosgrave here to see Jane. Don't stay very long. Mrs Cosgrave asks after my family . . . No news from the two Brians. We discover later that Brian O'Driscoll nearly went this afternoon while under anaesthetic for stitching 16 stitches round his lip. There had been more damage than they realised to his lungs and he nearly stopped breathing. No change in Brian Cubbon who is still in intensive care . . .

We all sleep at home in our own beds and this is good. We now have a 24 hours guard round the house and J has two Special Branch men always with him. I wish however that they were not in uniform as this only tells everyone where we are. On the Saturday they get put into plain clothes.

Saturday, 24th July, 1976
[Day of Christopher Ewart-Biggs's cremation in England] Drive out with J and escort to Glencairn, 9 o'clock, to collect Jane. We drive out in convoy with outriders to get us through red lights, traffic etc. to Baldonnel Airport [the military one]. I hate this as they [the police] love the excitement of commanding the traffic and causing traffic jams etc. to get us there at great speed. We drive in at the gates at Baldonnel where two guards of honour salute Jane as we drive through to where a waiting RAF Andover is on the tarmac – the coffins, thanks goodness, having been already taken on board.

Fitzgeralds and John Burke there to meet us, plus the press of course. Eric Townsend and Bob Harris had been doing all the donkey work of organising coffins etc. Poor Bob also had the horrific job of identifying the bodies at St Vincent's Hospital . . . They board the aircraft and we all stand and see it taxi to the end of the runway. Had long chat with Joan Fitzgerald about what we shall wear next Wednesday etc. They have been enormously concerned and involved with us over this tragedy and obviously felt very deeply. The coffins are being taken to Northolt and a cremation service at Golders Green. The Gouldens hold the fort at Glencairn and have lunch up there with their children, too. I

arrive after lunch and take Henrietta and Robin and collect my
children. First we went shopping mainly to buy Robin's birthday
present. He is 13 on Monday. Then we go off for a sailing
expedition. It was rather disastrous as it turned out. Everyone was
tired and it was rather cold. First Matthew, Kate and Henrietta
went out. They were nearly rammed by the ferry and they had
awful trouble sailing back. Secondly, Matthew, Robin and Andrew
went, this was slightly better. However I don't think anyone
enjoyed it much. All flags were flying at half mast - including the
one at the office.

Sunday, 25th July, 1976
All stagger up latish and tired. J talks to surgeons re Brians.
They both have up days and down days. Brian Cubbon has been
through a down patch. Still both in intensive care ... J takes
Matthew to the Pembroke Cricket Club where he has been welcomed with open arms and asked to play in a match. Everywhere
we go people are full of courtesy and commiseration and want
to apologise to us for what has happened.

6pm We gallop up to Glencairn where the Fitzgeralds are due
and we discuss his memorial address over cups of tea. The Dean
of St Patrick's Rev. Griffin and Rev. Bradley arrive to discuss the
order of service for Wednesday, ie should we have the National
Anthem and/or Irish National Anthem, which incidentally is a
battle song not a hymn. The clerics decide against and want The
Londonderry Air played as we walk out. Down here it is of course
known as 'Danny Boy' not Londonderry Air. You *never* call it the
Londonderry Air here. Jane impresses on them that it mustn't
be a sad service, the hymns must be rousing and the prayers short
– Christopher was an agnostic. The theme was to be one of hope
rather than sadness.

Dinner is late and after the children go off to play hide and
seek in the garden which they do with the guards, hiding in their
boxes etc. I gather they join in the fun but ask that the children
do not do it again as a policeman's reaction to being suddenly
jumped on from behind is liable to be violent! ... At 1.30 pm
we say we *must* take the children home. They have to be dragged
away from their hide and seek.

Monday, 26th July, 1976

Up early to pack up Robin's birthday presents . . . Matthew had cycled up early that morning on his bicycle. It is such a help that they get on so very well together.* My Kate too is beginning to get through to poor mute Henrietta who hardly utters. Matthew is going to sleep out in the tent that Robin has in Glencairn's gardens. This pleases both of them . . .

Carole Crook blows her top as Jane has decided the library can no longer be used as an office. This has meant moving all the files etc. onto the floor of the little ante-room.

Early night. Take sleeping pill but are awakened after midnight by Fergus Pyle [editor of the *Irish Times*] to query whether we are really leaving out Irish National Anthem (Is this Wise?). I reckon he is quite right and it should be in.

Tuesday, 27th July, 1976

Ruth Reed from the Commercial Dept. up at Glencairn to help prepare the flowers in hall and sitting rooms ready for television programme and wake tomorrow after the Service. I take A and K up to the Glen. Jane is lying on her bed having a facial and I go off with Henrietta and my Katie to *Ib Jorganseb* boutique in Molesworth Street to buy Henrietta something suitable for tomorrow. Thank goodness we find eventually a creamish pleated skirt and blouse to go with her dark green velvet jacket which looks sweet with her red hair. Jane, thank God, approves. I then send the girls off and look for something suitable for myself – a very nice mushroom woollen skirt and jacket and cream blouse, very super – very expensive!

Robin and Matthew look tired after their night in the tent. I don't think much sleeping got done . . . Riding for the children cancelled as EB children had to be dressed up and ready for television appearance. We find a score of cars, television lights blazing in the drawing room. They go over the thing twice and a row ensues I think between ITN and the BBC over timing embargo, plenty of gin gets consumed all round.

Carole Crook has hysterics over the secretarial work which is

* Matthew and Robin were in the same form at the Dragon School in Oxford.

overwhelming her. She is in need of more help and I ring up two more wives to get their help here tomorrow. I go at about 6 pm as Jane, Dick [Jane's brother] and children all coming for dinner.

Wednesday, 28th July, 1976

The Memorial Service is today, so we each take half a pill to stop us churning over all night. We get the GPO to call us at 7.30. J sits down to a boiled egg in his morning coat (and top hat borrowed from Frank McMullen) leaves 8.15 for Baldonnel to collect Hattersley, his P.S., Westbrook and du Boulay (both Protocol and F.O.). Children and I leave 8.45 as it turned out far too early. I'm terrified of not finding a parking space and I've decided I want to drive myself rather than get someone from the office to collect us. Our policeman suggests we park in the forecourt of Kevin Street Police Station which is just round the corner from St Patrick's . . . Children look quite respectable though I haven't had time to get the boys' Dragon School hair cut. We arrive far too early and walk around and around the grounds of St Patrick's, nagging them not to kick the stones or go on the swings and slides.

We wait until 9.40 before slowly walking in. Meet Bob Harris and Marion with Lauren Cubbon and we all walk in together. Bob luckily is there to show us where to go, though there is a mass of ushers all falling over themselves. The front of the church where we are to be in the South Aisle is flooded with brilliant television light, so cruel for Jane, but the whole service is being televised. Sheila and Frank are there, F in his splendid dress uniform of the Gunners. The children sit beside them and I sit in front to wait for the others. Most of the embassy staff have already arrived and are sitting in their seats behind us. J, Hattersley, etc. arrive. Hattersley is beside me and makes polite noises. He mutters that memorial services should not be televised and I agree. Ministers and dipsos arrive and sit in their allotted seats. Then Jane and Dick and the children arrive and sit in front of us. The service is beautiful, not too moving and the music and choir very good, a lovely Bach anthem. The President reads the 'Though I speak with tongues of angels' chapter with a slightly hammy style, and Garret reads the Donne far too quickly for anyone to grasp properly. However, his address was splendid and said with great conviction and feeling. No breaking down and Jane behaves with great calm. After, Jane and family, then the President, then Hattersley and I and J and Co. all walk down the aisle and gather in a little Lady Chapel at the back for the President to speak to Jane ... We all come out and drive back to Glencairn with enormous feelings of relief that all had gone well.

Both the Brians, Brian Cubbon and Brian O'Driscoll, survived the bombing. Jane Ewart-Biggs was made a life peeress in 1981 as Baroness Ewart-Biggs of Ellis Green, and went on to lead a highly successful political career of her own as Labour spokesman on home affairs, overseas development and consumer affairs in the House of Lords. She died in 1992.

Although Christopher Ewart-Biggs's assassination by the IRA was an extreme and tragic case, it is a measure of the very real risks involved in diplomatic life that there are few families who have not been involved in some serious incident. In the case of my own family, this involvement was at one remove: although we had driven over that IRA bomb at least four times the day before, we were never direct targets. Other families, such as the Ewart-Biggs or the Atkinsons, caught up in the Romanian revolution following the downfall of the Ceauşescu regime, were not so lucky.

It was the middle of December, and Veronica Atkinson's three children – Carina, Paul and Nicholas – had just arrived for the Christmas holidays. On 21 December 1989 the President appeared on his balcony to make a speech, and for the first time as he was talking there was 'a rumbling in the crowd'. It was a spontaneous expression of discontent. 'Somebody shouted, and he got perplexed,' Veronica remembers.

This was something that he had never heard before. Somebody daring to do that. And it was then that the whole thing erupted. It was not orchestrated. It was just like a hurricane taking place. Unexpected. And then he escaped in a helicopter ... and this was the Revolution, you see.* And what followed was of course a

* The government's plans to exile a dissident Protestant pastor, Laszlo Tokes, to a remote village had provoked an anti-Ceauşescu protest movement in the city of Timisoara. On 17 December, four days before the rally to which Veronica refers, hundreds of demonstrators had been killed in the state's subsequent crackdown.

sort of unbelievable happiness. They were all shouting and screaming and in the streets people were shouting '*libertate*'. And the housewives would go and kiss the soldiers. And suddenly there was a group of people who said, 'O.K., let's do something. This is the end.'*

At first, however, there were few signs that a revolution, the 'Christmas Revolution', as it later became known, was happening at all. Instead it was, in the words of Veronica's son Paul,†

like a party on the streets . . . there is so much festivity and jubilation – probably what it was like at the end of WWII. Everyone is wild, excited and joyous, not one person seems to be otherwise. Everyone exchanges 'V' signs and huge smiles. Everyone cheers as we and other foreigners drive past. On one occasion a group starts clapping and shouting 'We love you English!' We leave the car at the Embassy and take to the streets by foot. Huge piles of what were formerly books eulogising the megalomaniac dictator and his supposedly 'learned' wife litter the streets. I myself take great pleasure in keeping the fires going when there are parts of books as yet untouched by the flames in some places. Graffiti is scrawled on shop windows and walls: '*A cazut dictatorul*' '*A cazut savanta*' (the dictator has fallen, the learned one has fallen) are amongst many slogans to be seen . . . It is marvellous to witness this mass celebration and to feel part of it (even if in a very insignificant way), an amazing outburst of emotion and happiness. I feel happy for these poor people who have suffered for so long.

The first sign of something more than a euphoric street carnival came that evening when heavily armed troops, with tanks and armoured personnel carriers, moved in to protect the television station, about 200 yards away from the British residence. Veronica received a phone call from her husband Michael, the British ambassa-

---

* In fact, it was the army chief of staff, General Stefan Gusa, who called on his soldiers to defend the uprising.
† I am very grateful to Paul Atkinson for allowing me to use his account of the Romanian revolution.

dor, to say that about 2,000 Securitate, Ceauşescu's elite secret police, still loyal to their President, were about to take over the station.

Later that night the fighting started. Although it had been agreed that, as a precaution, the family should not sleep in any of the rooms facing the street, the Atkinsons could not resist peering out of the windows from time to time.

The sight is astonishing [Paul wrote], and bears a striking resemblance to a scene out of one of the *Star Wars* films – tracer bullets are whizzing like lazer beams in all directions at roof level, and it causes no surprise when a loud thud whacks the roof. Mum joins me and we crouch down and view the spectacle for a short time . . . No movement can be seen in the wooded area opposite which surrounds the TV station and so I drag Mum away.

After that Veronica describes the rapidly deteriorating situation.

My eldest son Nick was shaving in the bathroom and he was just passing across the threshold to his bedroom when a bullet broke the glass of his window. I don't know whether his curtain was open and some soldiers had seen him and then aimed at him. But the fact is that had he stayed in that room he would have been killed. It was then that he shouted and said, 'They are shooting at us; let's go down to the basement.' And as we were going down the staircase they were shooting at the glass – probably from the house next door – which was of course splashing all over the place and we had to go covering ourselves. And the shooting followed us even to the kitchen door.

Hiding with her three children in the basement that night, Veronica describes how 'You get conditioned to hearing gunfire, and you think, OK, I am immune, the house is immune, it is nothing to do with us. We are safe . . . perhaps it could be safer not to be too close to the windows, but this will finish soon. But, in fact, it didn't.' Sheltering in the basement with them were their two maids. 'One of the girls was absolutely hysterical,' Veronica remembers. 'I could just sense that she knew something. She was too nervous to hide it. My older son Nicholas, who was used to dealing with large crowds of youngsters, because at that time he was working with ACIS, the American Cultural Institute, really knew how to calm this woman, and say to her, "Look, look; don't panic, don't shout, they are going to come otherwise."' Little by little, the truth dawned on them. The gunfire was not merely happening around them;

> They were actually aiming *at* us. Why? We didn't *know* why. Only when the shots went inside the house did we realise that there were Securitate people somewhere in the house with us. And the maid, obviously she was part of the Securitate network and she wanted to tell them, 'Look, they are here.' Because she didn't owe us any loyalty, and at that stage she was just in panic. And then we started thinking, 'Are they going to kidnap us? Are they going to kill us?' And the minutes were ages. The seconds were just years. And you were thinking 'When is this going to finish? A big bomb is going to finish with us.'

As they had suspected, the fighting was indeed aimed straight at the residence. Although Veronica was unaware of it at the time, half a dozen of Ceauşescu's Securitate had broken into the house and had taken up positions in one of the attic rooms overhead. 'Our dogs also were in the attic,' she explains, 'but in another room, and at one stage we thought that they had shot the dogs. They opened the door and heard the dogs barking at them. We heard a few shots, and it was only then that we actually realized that we had people in the house.'
As the night wore on the fighting grew worse.

> With such an intensive shooting the building was shaking. It was a very strong, large building and yet we could feel how it was responding to the vibration of all these shots, from all these different kinds of weapons. There comes a moment when you begin to think, we must pray. That is the only thing which will give us some peace and it did, it did. We actually made a little circle and held hands and prayed Our Lord's Prayer. And you know it was almost like magic. You could feel 'OK, we are going to be safe, we are going to be safe'.

But their ordeal was not over.

We knew the shooting had to finish because it was so intense. It was lasting an hour, two hours. We were terrified, of course. I had been thinking, they are going to come and *raptar* [rape] my daughter. And so I said to the others, if they come we are going to throw tins of coke and 7Up, because those were the only weapons that we had. We had bottles there – we had been sitting on the crates – and these were our only defence. Then came this silence, you see, and there was a lull in the fighting. And suddenly we heard 'Hello, hello'. But the 'hello' sounded European, and not Romanian. And so Nicholas went to the back door and a German diplomat came in, and he said, 'Look, we have seen what has been happening to your house. Come with us now, there is a lull. Come as you are.' Luckily we had our coats along a corridor close to the stairs, and we just picked up our coats and went out. And as we went out, because there was snow, there was a lot of silence suddenly. No wind, nothing.

Two days later, when the Atkinsons were finally able to return to their house, they found that it had been almost completely burnt to the ground. Although they had lost nearly everything, it was some time before Veronica could take in anything other than the fact that they had survived. 'At that stage I just couldn't have cared less whether the house was burning or not burning, or whether I had lost anything, because I was glad to be alive.' After almost forty-eight hours without sleep, she had become 'automatized'. In their home, now a burnt-out shell, 'There was an atmosphere of death. I went to the room of the children and it was so destroyed that the suitcases that they had started packing were completely submerged in the rubble. Pictures were on the ground. Lamps were on the ground. You know how it is.' Even though there was total silence, a sixth sense told her that there were still people hiding there.

Two days later, on Christmas Day (the very day on which Ceauşescu was tried and then executed), Veronica and her children were evacuated to Bulgaria. The day after that, exhausted, and with little more than the clothes they stood up in, they flew back to England.

When you have been in a situation like this the trauma only starts afterwards. When we arrived here, the children and I, it seemed eerie to see all these people because we didn't have anything with us. We had to start from a toothbrush, you know. So of course the next day we went shopping, and all we could see were these people satiated with presents, because it was the 26th or 27th December. It was unreal to see normal life taking place. And you know, they didn't have a clue that we had been in the situation we had been in, living in this very poor country. For us it was a surreal experience.

The experience of danger affects people in many different ways; they are often surprised by their reactions. 'Some of those unwanted experiences are in retrospect the most golden,' Felicity Wakefield explains; 'although you don't realize it yourself at the time. It is those ones which really make you what you are.'

After living in Cyprus in 1955, during the EOKA guerrilla campaign against the British,* being evacuated from Egypt during the Suez Crisis in 1956, and caught up in riots in Benghazi in 1967 (where the mobs tried to burn their house down), Felicity has lived in more of her share of the world's trouble spots. 'People used to say, "What's going to happen there?" when we were posted somewhere, because we had a reputation for things happening to us.'

In 1975 Peter Wakefield was posted as ambassador to Beirut. 'It had started in April, the troubles with armed elements,' Felicity remembers.

When we arrived, in May, there was a curfew and nobody on the streets. You never knew who was who or what they were up to. It changed all the time in Beirut. So our first summer there started out as quite alarming. My second son, who was at art school, came out for his holidays, and we were sitting out on this balcony at the front of our house, where we used to sit every evening and have a drink. And I said to him, 'Isn't it funny that bird that they have here. I've never heard it anywhere else. It makes a sort of *sing . . . sing* noise.' And he said to me, 'Mummy, that's no bird, that's *bullets*.' And so I said, 'Well, do you think we ought to

---

* EOKA (Ethniki Organosis Kipriakou Agonos), the National Organization of Cypriot Struggle, was formed by Greek Cypriots wanting union with Greece, who were trying to drive out the British occupying forces. (Cyprus had become a British crown colony in 1925.)

be sitting here because I don't!' And he said, 'No, perhaps we shouldn't.' And so we went indoors.

It was not until the beginning of September, however, when her children had returned to England, that the fighting started in earnest. Despite the dangers, Felicity was determined that her place was by her husband's side:

I felt that very strongly. That Suez experience* was very deep in me. When the Foreign Office wanted to evacuate everybody I said, 'Now wait a moment. I don't think that's right. You don't employ the wives. You can't order us to go. You can say to us, it would be sensible if you went, and make it easy for us to go. You can help us. But you can't tell us you've got to go if it's against our better judgement.'

So Peter put it to them: he suggested that anyone who didn't have children, who wanted to stay, and took the job of a secretary or whatever they were good at, should be able to – thereby making it less necessary to keep on the single secretaries in the embassy. Single people were much more vulnerable under those conditions. So we ended up having a group of married people running the embassy. I worked as Peter's PA. That surprised the Lebanese. They couldn't understand why I should be answering the telephone in the office. To make it easier for them I'd say, 'Yes, I'll tell the ambassadress.'

Under these conditions, the Wakefields prepared to sit it out together.

We had nothing. No security of any kind except our wits. And when the fighting was raging about 100 to 200 yards away from our house, Peter and I decided that we had better go and sleep in an embassy flat the other side of town. We stayed there for about two weeks, but our neighbours in Zaris, where the residence was, were appalled. They said, 'The ambassador's leaving. He

---

* After the women had been evacuated, all the men were imprisoned by the Egyptians inside the embassy buildings: for several weeks she was unable to find out what had happened to her husband.

knows. Something terrible is going to happen here.' They always thought we *knew* what was going on, and they were all very demoralized by our going away, so we decided to go back. We were surrounded by blocks of flats and we used to watch people on the balconies, firing. I don't think they were what were always euphemistically known as *les éléments armées* – the Lebanese one met at parties used to call them 'the Elizabeth Ardens' – but it was extremely dangerous. We had a cellar, but it was full of cockroaches and I wouldn't sleep there. It was horrible. But we did sleep in a downstairs bedroom, when things started whizzing about us too much. You could hear glass breaking in the neighbouring houses and that kind of thing.

And then the Foreign Office hired a private security company to protect us. We had these ex-SAS soldiers sleeping in the house. We used to have about four of them at a time, sometimes more. And two of them went with us everywhere.

The guards were a comfort, but as Felicity points out,

if someone lobs a mortar bomb at you a security guard isn't much use. At that stage they were not taking western hostages. On the whole the foreigners, as long as one was sensible and not known as being a friend of any particular faction, we didn't feel that we were targeted.

We were given bullet-proof vests which we were supposed to wear when we went out. I didn't wear it round the house, but if I went into the garden I had a vest. And President Ford sent me a helmet. I still have it; they painted it with a daisy. I never wore it, it was an extremely uncomfortable thing. It would have been sensible, but I would have felt a twit really.

And in fact a mortar bomb did land on the residence one afternoon. Five minutes before we got there. We'd been to lunch with a neighbour and drove up, and this thing had just gone off. It would have killed us if we had happened to be walking in at that moment.

The day after the mortar had exploded, I stayed in the house together with a member of the embassy staff to mend the telephones. And we were going back to the office together in my car, and just as we came towards the chancery building a bomb landed in the road and our car went from being in the right hand lane to being in the lane on the other side of the road. It was just blown across. And when we got to the chancery everyone was in the cellar.

The Wakefield children, back at school in England, went through agonies: 'It was very frightening for them. Our youngest son was still at boarding school. He was at Ampleforth and the monks said that his work was suffering. I think he was very anxious. You know, he heard things on the radio. I don't know what one ought to do as a parent. The children kept saying, "You ought to come home. You shouldn't be there." I think they thought we should both come home.'
And yet Felicity found that she could not.

It was frightening, but you get used to the fear and you don't want to leave. This is a very interesting aspect of danger, which you don't understand until you have experienced it. When the danger is removed, your adrenalin stops, and you have withdrawal symptoms. And you have to go back. You have to go back to the danger. You feel that it is important that you are there. I think a lot of the Lebanese had this. I certainly did. When you are living like that – 'what's going to happen now?' – and that is removed, you feel that life is boring. I think that's what a lot of soldiers go through in war. They say they've enjoyed the war, they've enjoyed the danger. The danger part is like a drug. I did not realize it to start with, but I eventually did. I began to realize, this is stupid. And then somebody in the Foreign Office said, 'You're hooked on danger'; and I was.

CHAPTER TWELVE

Rebel Wives

'I think it is fair to say that perhaps too much is asked of diplomatic wives,' Jane Ewart-Biggs once reflected. It was not enough that they should be shot at and bombed; that they should have their children taken from them, or wasted away by tropical disease, their husbands kidnapped and even killed. Even in the face of wars, revolutions and myriad other calamities, there were always certain standards to be maintained: 'They are always expected to be there; to look nice, to say the right thing; to have no definite views of their own; to remember everyone's names; not to complain; and so on. Sometimes they rebel.'[1]

For a strong-minded few, rebellion was a simple matter: they simply declined to take part in diplomatic life at all. 'I am not a good person for you to be married to,' Vita Sackville-West wrote to her husband, Harold Nicolson. 'You love foreign politics; and I love literature, and peace, and a secluded life.'[2] When Harold was posted to Persia, despite the compensations of 'a beautiful country and a proud and romantic people', Vita refused to be part of it. 'She would visit him there, but she would not be lodged in a Legation compound as his *légitime,*' explained her son Nigel, 'and be made to sit at dinner-parties in her correct order of precedence with a white card beside her plate proclaiming her "The Hon. Mrs Harold Nicolson", when she could be V. Sackville-West at Long Barn, with her writing, her garden and Virginia.'*[3]

Although she found it painful to be parted from Harold, her independence was more important. The role of the 'correct and adoring young wife of the brilliant young diplomat' – with which she toyed briefly, as a newly-wed – was one which she would later regard with

* The novelist Virginia Woolf, her lover.

little short of revulsion. 'That was the only period in my life when I achieved anything like popularity,' she wrote. 'I was no longer plain, I took adequate trouble to make myself agreeable. Harold was loved by everyone who met him – we were, in fact, a nice young couple to ask out to dinner. Oh God, the horror of it! I was so happy that I forgot even to suffer from *Wanderlust*.'[4]

Life in the legation compound in Tehran, where she visited Harold twice, only confirmed her suspicions. 'God, the people here!' she complained to Virginia Woolf on her second visit, in a letter of 9 February 1927. 'They're still talking about the same things as when I left, only now they have got me as a new victim, *"Alors, chère amie, vous avez fait bon voyage?" "Etes-vous contente, chère madame, de vous retrouver à Teheran?"* And I behave so pretty, and answer it all as though it were the most important thing in the world.'

In a rare concession to conformity Vita had decided to buy a hat for the Shah's coronation which, as an albeit temporary member of the British legation, she had been invited to attend. But in Vita's hands even such a simple task became an assertion of independence. Her travelling companion, Dorothy Wellesley, described the shopping expedition in Cairo: 'She was furious at having to get a hat. Ronnie [Balfour] and I stood outside; a whole hour passed. At last she emerged, wearing some sort of black hat into which she had stuck one of the largest emeralds I ever saw. The effect was miraculous. Someone said: "She looks like the Empress Zenobia."'[5]

Diplomatic life, in Vita's eyes, was a collection of people thrown together 'through a purely fortuitous circumstance, with nothing in common except the place we happen to find ourselves in'. The Persians, with their 'limp, oriental methods' and their 'grubby old cashmere dressing gowns', fared no better beneath her grand but narrow gaze. But it was Vita who was the odd one out. ('I like this in the aristocracy . . . ,' Virginia Woolf once wrote to her sister Vanessa, 'I like the complete arrogance and unreality of their minds.')[6] The limitations of conversation in Tehran continued to be a source of special grievance. 'Foreign diplomats do not talk about copulation with the same ease, candour and readiness as our friends in England,' Vita wrote to Virginia. 'Correctness is the order of the day, so we never get any further.'[7]

For Vita, with her artistic instincts and her unconventional but aristocratic upbringing, this kind of overt rebellion was a great deal easier than it was for most diplomatic women. There was enormous pressure to conform, but the traditional closeness of the diplomatic partnership – happily and willingly embraced by so many women – did not work for everyone. Those who were naturally of a more independent, liberal, or – perish the thought – bohemian cast of mind found the sometimes stifling conventions of diplomatic life very hard to bear.

When Felicity Wakefield was posted to Egypt in 1956, Cairo was still 'a very colonial place'. Social life revolved around the club.

> One went to the Gazira Club. I didn't like that kind of life. I am an artist and I've always been interested in fringe ways of doing things. I didn't want to sit in the Gazira Club and play bridge or mahjong, or whatever it was. That's not me at all. In the club there was a sign up saying NO DOGS OR NANNIES BEYOND THIS POINT. Things were like that. It wasn't peculiar, but it was the order of it that really upset me. I thought it was so insulting to my nanny.

On a later posting to Benghazi she had even greater cause to complain: 'I did not want to be a consul-general's wife very much. I wanted to be having a giddy time in London,' she confesses. The British army was still stationed in the Libyan desert after the war and, to her horror, she found that they expected her to behave 'like a matron'.

> They expected me to go and inspect. You know, the sort of thing that here, the royal family go and do, or the mayor's wife, or the vicar's wife. They like to have visits. And I once said: 'I wish you'd stop asking me to visit your kitchens and ask me to visit your guns.' They never asked me to do anything again after that. I'd made a joke of it. I wasn't meaning to be bolshy. I was always going to do it, and I was going to do it as well as I could. I just thought it was funny that they should want me to visit in this very pompous sort of way, when I wasn't that sort of person at all. I was very relieved when they all went.

Even fully paid-up subscribers to the partnership ideal sometimes balked at the work. In Paris in the 1820s Harriet Granville complained bitterly – as many an ambassadress both before and after her – about the ceaseless demands on her time and energies. 'It is frivolous, eternally frivolous,' she lamented. As the consul's wife in Baghdad over 100 years later, Masha Williams heartily agreed with her. It was impossible to refuse invitations without giving serious offence, she noted bitterly. 'The whole Colony knew where and when we were invited. It was unreasonable to go out so often, but it was expected of us – it was our job.' Masha found the artificiality of her position very hard to bear.

We Embassy wives were all acting a part, as though we were on the stage. I would have enjoyed discussing Alan's illness, our housing problems, the manners of the Office, but disloyalty apart, this would not become the Personage they expected me to be. It was this nightly performance that was exhausting. And the formality. The presence of the Consul and his wife made every function formal. It was as much a strain as being the bride's mother every evening.[8]

More junior wives were affected too. Their lesser status within the hierarchy meant that they had little control over the increasingly onerous demands that were made of them. One former diplomatic wife (now divorced), who married into the Foreign Office in 1951, was told 'in no uncertain terms' that it was her duty to help her husband (then a third secretary) and serve her country. They were to be no excuses, not even a difficult first pregnancy, for not attending diplomatic functions when en poste. When she nearly had a miscarriage on her sea voyage back to Rangoon after her mid-term leave, the ship's doctor took pity on her and wrote a letter to the ambassador's wife to say that she must be more careful. 'This was such a good thing because she felt that there should be no let-up and was at a dinner party herself when her last baby began to arrive!'

Her husband was similarly demanding. After the birth of her second son, in Vienna, he insisted that she attend a ball just two weeks after the birth. 'I had to be stitched into my dress!' she remembers. 'Questions were asked why I wasn't at cocktail parties at 6 in the evening. How things have changed!'

Out and out insurrection, however, was not something that came naturally to the Foreign Office wife. Peggy Trevelyan, for one, finds it amazing that wives accepted the more ridiculous conventions: 'Looking back on it now, I can't imagine why we didn't rebel.' But, on the whole, they did not. The culture, however intransigent it was felt to be, was still a largely self-perpetuating one. 'We had one wife in the embassy who refused to do anything beyond the odd evening party,' confesses the would-be rebel who was once reluctantly stitched into her ballgown, 'and we were all full of scorn for her.'

As they reached more senior levels, women who as junior wives had themselves been lectured and bullied by their ambassadress, often felt, with some justification perhaps, that it was now 'their turn', which perhaps explains the legendary *folie de grandeur* associated with many ambassadresses and heads of mission wives.

By far the greatest single deterrent to rebellion was the perception that a wife's willingness to toe the line contributed vitally to the success of her husband's career. And husbands, naturally, were not shy of using it to make their wives conform.

Although she had no legal or contractual obligations to the service, a wife's 'performance' was none the less subjected to an annual review by the head of mission.* Peggy Trevelyan remembers those days only too well. On her first posting to Baghdad, she had many bitter confrontations with her ambassadress.

> At one point she said that I was ruining my husband's career and that I would be reported back to London. This was simply because she had been away and I had been to visit the Regent's wife, and I didn't tell her, immediately, the moment she came home. Having been talked to rather severely by her I came out in an absolute rage and said to my husband that I was never going to stick my neck out again. I felt very rebellious, but it didn't last. And he said, 'Don't take it to heart. Everybody knows what she's like and it's not going to be a black mark against you or me or anybody else.'

Not everyone was so understanding. The perception that a wife's 'performance' contributed vitally to the success of her husband's career meant that the reverse was also true. As that most trenchant arbiter

---

* Heads of mission did not mince their words, either. My father remembers one damningly laconic comment, 'It would have been better if he had never married her.'

of diplomatic duty, Marie-Noele Kelly had written, 'Just as the right sort can make all the difference to her husband's local position and influence, so one who is inefficient, disagreeable, disloyal, or even merely stupid, can be, locally, a millstone around his neck.' And there have been many millstones: women whose husbands, even when their wives did embrace the duties of diplomatic life, were left wishing heartily that they had not.

One such unfortunate was Walter Townley. Although from a social point of view his wife, Lady Susan, was unquestionably 'the right sort', her thick skin, her reckless indiscretion and her highly developed sense of her own importance made her a disastrous diplomatic wife.

Lady Susan came from an aristocratic background. One of the nine children of the seventh Earl of Albemarle, she had an eccentric upbringing at Quidenham, in Norfolk, with her siblings (by her own admission, 'certainly the naughtiest children I have met in fact or fiction').* In 1896 she married Walter Townley, then a young second secretary at the British legation in Lisbon.

The Townleys moved on, first to Berlin, then to Rome, Peking and Constantinople, from where, in 1905, Walter was posted as counsellor to Washington, 'the Mecca of all diplomatists who cannot be appointed to London'. At first all went well, and the Townleys were favourably received. The 'Yellow Press' – as the society journals were known – painted Walter's past career in 'glowing colours', while Lady Susan was deemed to be 'a bright, brainy, winsome and accomplished little lady . . . one of the most valuable acquisitions which the Diplomatic Corps had had in years!' If they had left it at that perhaps disaster would have been averted, but Lady Susan took exception to the 'impertinent' attention to which her dress, her appearance and even her conversation were subjected.

Day and night, journalists on the look-out for sensational paragraphs for their papers pursued her.

---

* Lady Susan's father, Lord Bury, had the same highly developed sense of humour as his daughter. One of their neighbours in Norfolk, who hated Lord Bury but was naturally unable to insult him to his face, hit upon the happy expedient of buying an ugly yellow dog which he christened Berry. 'Whenever my father came along, this man would yell insults at his dog. "Down Berry, or I'll give you such a thrashing." "Get out of my sight you d—d beast, Berry!" My father delighted in the joke, and I think he took particular pleasure in walking past Mr Witman's house and to giving him a chance to air his feelings.'

It was remarked that I wore my jewels 'in a manner made famous by the infamous Leonor Telles' (who was she?) [wrote Lady Susan witheringly], also that 'on State occasions' I wore 'a diagonal sash of blue and white' (it happened to be green, red and white, the grand cordon of Sheffakat) 'upon which gleamed a resplendent decoration, i.e., the Order of the Garter, the Victoria Cross, or some such bric-à-brac.' Could anything surpass this!

They got her family connections 'mixed', referring to her father as the seventh earl of Aberdeen. 'They found out their mistake in time, however, and got on the right track at last when they discovered in Lady Susan "the real daughter of a *bona fide* Earl who goes to parties duly tagged and labelled as such." No only was I "the daughter of the late belted Earl of Albermarle", but incidentally I was also "the sister of the present holder of the belt".' Lady Susan, in no mood for jokes, found the whole thing 'pushing and vulgar to the last degree'.

When a particularly persistent reporter from 'a horrible little society newspaper' telephoned her very late one night, asking what form her entertainments in America would take, she was determined to have her revenge. On the spur of the moment she answered that she would, of course, be continuing her series of 'Octaves'; 'What are they?' queried the puzzled reporter.

'Surely,' I said, 'you can't be so behind the times in this country as never to have heard of "Lady Susan's Octaves". Why, they are known and discussed all over Europe!' 'Indeed! This is most interesting. Please tell me about them,' begged the excited pressman, scenting a sensational paragraph for his paper.

So I told him about them! 'Oh, my Octaves,' I said airily, 'are merely little dinners of eight given every eight days to eight selected guests. Eight viands are served and eight wines drunk, whilst the eight chief topics of the moment are discussed. I am surprised you have not heard of them over here.'

Lady Susan's entirely imaginary 'Octaves' were duly reported. When it was discovered that she had been 'merely chaffing', the Yellow Press were extremely unamused. The Townleys' press honeymoon was over. Lady Susan had found their methods 'pushing and vulgar'; now, the compliment was returned. 'From that day they never spared me, and I became the constant butt for their gibes and comments.'

Although her every word and action continued to be reported, the winsome and accomplished 'little lady' was now lampooned in the press as a monster of English snobbery and conceit. It was not only her practical joke at the society press's expense which was the cause. 'Lady Susan allows her wit to flow unrestrained – American institutions generally stimulate her conversational attractiveness,' claimed one report. 'A dinner-party was astounded recently by a remark of hers that the greatest circus in America was the White House.' 'She disdains also to play second fiddle to the wives of Senators or any mere Commoner, and Washington hostesses are in despair,' read another. Lady Susan was also credited with having said of two well-known senators that 'their toothpicks alone would keep them out of the homes of even the middle classes of England'. Her pretensions as a would-be leader of fashion fared no better. A cartoon in one paper caricatured her as 'an overdressed puppet, dragging along two marionettes at the end of a string'. The title read: 'Lady Susan leads the fashion'.

Rarely has the official *raison d'être* of the diplomatic wife – to nurture and cultivate friendly relations with the host nation – been so successfully sabotaged. There is no record of what the hapless Walter thought of his wife's antics, not least her blatant anti-Americanism, but for him the worst was yet to come. A rumour – 'cruel and perfectly baseless', according to Lady Susan – was put about that she did not get on with Lady Durand, the wife of the ambassador, Sir Mortimer. 'She [Lady S. T.] declined to walk into dinner after Lady Durand,' sneered one report, 'who is the daughter of a Church of England curate.' Worse still, she was said to be plotting to have Sir Mortimer recalled from his post.

'Such bad taste', as Lady Susan chose to describe this truly disastrous state of affairs, would not have mattered so much if the story had not been taken up by *The Times* back in England. Their Washington correspondent filed a damaging report: '*The Springfield Republican*, one of the most trustworthy and influential newspapers in this country, says that Lady Susan Townley must share with the President the doubtful honour of having caused the retirement of Sir Mortimer Durand.' By now even the long-suffering Walter had had enough; he obtained leave to go home and consult with the Foreign Office with a view to taking up the matter officially. A leading lawyer had assured the Townleys that they could get record damages if they chose to bring libel suits against some of the papers concerned. 'But the Foreign Office advised my husband to do nothing,' Lady Susan concluded regretfully, 'and this advice he was obliged in his official position to accept!'

Although the Townleys' diplomatic career continued until after the First World War, in 1919, thanks to the monumental 'indiscretions' of his wife, Walter was advised by the Foreign Office that he would not be receiving further promotion. He handed in his notice and, possibly with some relief, retired to the country to breed large black pigs. 'More remunerative,' as Lady Susan concluded, 'and less exacting than Diplomacy.'[9]

Lady Susan's vulgarity and tactless flamboyance were completely at odds with the traditional diplomatic qualities of discipline and reserve. And yet, for all its apparent conservatism, diplomatic life has a strange way of attracting, and even embracing, the unconventional and the eccentric.

Unlike Lady Susan Townley, Isabel Burton was in many ways the paradigm of an intelligent, efficient and loyal wife, but few couples were so spectacularly ill-suited to diplomacy as she and her husband Richard. His sense of the social refinements required by his new-found profession was extremely rudimentary: when a London hostess asked him to bring her back a souvenir of his travels he took a human scalp out of his pocket, and tossed it languidly across the dinner table at her. 'He *would* defend cannibalism, too,' Isabel sighed.

Fortunately, in Santos, which was very nearly as obscure as San Fernando Po and not much healthier, the social duties required of the new consul and his wife were few. None the less there was a sizeable British community – mainly railway employees (a line between Santos and São Paulo, some eighty miles into the interior, was being constructed). Richard, who never paid the slightest attention to them otherwise, had a rhyme which he was fond of quoting to Isabel:

They eat and drink and scheme and plod,
They go to church on Sunday,
And many are afraid of God
And more of Mrs Grundy.*

* See footnote, page 76.

Between them, Richard and Isabel spent a lifetime offending the 'Grundys' of the various countries they were posted to.

After the heat and loneliness of Santos, Richard's next posting, as consul in Damascus, was, for Isabel, 'the earthly fulfilment of paradise'. It was to be her first taste of the mystic east, the dream of her childhood: 'I am to live among Bedouin Arab chiefs: I shall smell the desert air; I shall have tents, horses, weapons, and be free.' They were not the usual sentiments of a British consul's wife.

Isabel's devotion to Richard was total. On paper, at least, she continued to be a paragon of wifely duty.

> I interested myself in all his pursuits, and I was a most fortunate woman in that he allowed me to be his companion, his secretary, and his aide-de-camp. I looked after our house, servants, stables, and animals. I did a little gardening. I helped my husband, read and wrote, studied Arabic, received and returned visits, saw and learnt Damascus through, till I knew it like my own pocket . . . Our lives were wild, romantic and solemn.

But not everyone saw things in quite the same light. The 'Emperor and Empress of Damascus', as they were not altogether kindly known, were a bossy couple. Their increasingly unorthodox ways extended even into their marriage. Isabel's devotion to Richard was, naturally, not like that of any ordinary wife. She submitted herself to his will with such fervour that he was able to mesmerize her, even at a distance: 'he used said simply to say, "sleep", and I did,' she wrote. Another of Richard's peculiarities was that he never told her to do anything directly, but used to leave her notes in odd places – in a book she was reading, or a drawer which she opened frequently. She soon grew adept at detecting his 'go seek' expression, and knew, also by his expression, when she had succeeded. In this way they developed a kind of private language, 'and could speak before outsiders in this way, without speaking a word out loud'.

Isabel claimed that she and Richard always made a point of being 'thoroughly English and European' at the consulate; 'but when *not* obligatory, we used to live a great deal *with* the natives, and *as* the natives, for the purpose of experience,' she explained. Amongst the

European society of Syria, however, such behaviour was viewed with a certain *froideur*. Not only did Isabel frequent Turkish baths and spend days on end in harems, but she had taken to smoking the *narghileh*, or water pipe. Her fondness for wearing man's dress when she went travelling with Richard, especially, was considered not just eccentric, but thoroughly reprehensible.

But on her frequent journeys through the desert with Richard Isabel found it far easier to adopt this costume than to struggle with Victorian corsets and crinolines. Despite her pink-and-white English complexion and what had become a magnificent bosom, on these occasions she always claimed to have been accepted as Richard's son; the Syrian man's robes were all drapery 'and did not in the least show the figure'. Although Richard was a hard task master – he kept his wife in the saddle for up to fifteen hours a day, until she was sobbing with fatigue – Isabel had never been so happy in her life. This was how she had always longed to live. In the desert 'there is no-one to check your spirits,' she wrote, intoxicated, 'the breath of the desert is liberty.'[10] The Grundys of diplomacy were certainly not going to stop her now.

Long after she was forced to leave her beloved Damascus,* Isabel retained many of her Syrian habits, continuing, with magnificent disregard for convention, to puff on her *narghileh* and rim her eyes sootily with kohl. But despite this unorthodoxy an element of the Catholic schoolgirl always remained: in later years she apparently took to wearing a luxuriant golden wig.

Eccentric and wayward though she may have been, Isabel brilliantly exploited the possibilities of her marriage into diplomatic life in order to fulfil her own ambitions. While her methods may have been the object of both censure and ridicule, her status as Richard's wife was beyond question. The same could not be said for everyone. Despite the social conventions of the day, there were plenty of diplomats who, unofficially at least, conducted more exotic relationships. Englishmen, 'so formal at home, liked to lead a disorderly life when abroad', observed Chateaubriand, who became French Foreign Secretary in

---

* In August 1871 Richard was recalled in disgrace by the Foreign Office for exceeding his authority. He had expelled a British missionary and his wife, and also a group of Jewish money-lenders who had been living under British protection.

1822, in his memoirs.[11] And diplomats, naturally, could be just as susceptible to such a life as anyone.

In 1858 Sir Henry Bulmer, the ambassador to Constantinople, bought the tiny island of Yassida, where he built a neo-Gothic house for his mistress, a mysterious siren known as the Princess of Samos. Likewise Lionel Sackville, Vita Sackville-West's grandfather, met the Spanish gypsy dancer Pepita, 'The Star of Andalucia', when he was a young attaché at the British legation in Stuttgart. Although he could never marry her (even if he had wished to, she was already married), he installed Pepita in her own establishment in Arcachon, in southern France, and went on to father seven illegitimate children. Even the Duke of Wellington, who was appointed ambassador to Paris after the Napoleonic Wars, left his wife behind in England and became infatuated with the beautiful singer Grassini. He used to make her lie on a sofa raised up on a dais, it was said, so that she could be more easily admired by his guests. But all these women existed on the unspoken fringes of diplomatic life. As *demi-mondaines* none of them was officially accepted, either as consort or as hostess; none had been, nor was ever likely to be, presented at court. They were therefore barred from 'society'.

Remarkably, however, there was a handful of such women who did manage to gain acceptance in diplomatic circles. One of these was Pepita's own daughter (and Vita Sackville-West's mother) Victoria, who despite her illegitimacy went on to become a leader of Washington society. Another equally extraordinary woman who was able to pull off this apparently impossible feat was Emma Hamilton.

Emy Lyon – as Lord Nelson's 'beloved Emma' started out in life – was born in 1765 into rural squalor in north Wales. In her early teens she escaped to London, where she found employment as a nurserymaid. From there her exact progress is obscure, but it seems likely that she soon fell into the hands of a local procuress, Mrs Kelly. The late eighteenth century was the great age of courtesans, women who serviced the rich and titled – often, like Kitty Fisher and Perdita Robinson, the Prince of Wales's mistress, combining the stage and prostitution. By the time she was sixteen Emy Lyon was well established in this career, living for several years under the 'protection' of the aristocrat Charles Greville. When Greville had no further use for her, he passed her on to his uncle, the British envoy to the Kingdom of the Two Sicilies, Sir William Hamilton.*

Sir William Hamilton was thirty-five years older than Emy, or Emma Hart, as she now styled herself. For thirty-six years the 'Envoy Extraordinary' to the court at Naples, Sir William was one of the most cultured and civilized minds of the eighteenth century. He was a passionate collector of antiquities (his Etruscan vases became a world-famous collection), and when his nephew first wrote to him proposing that he take Emma on, he seems to have regarded her as little more than another beautiful museum piece. 'The prospect of possessing so delightful an object under my roof soon causes me some pleasant sensations,' he wrote back, 'but they are accompanied with some anxious thoughts as to the prudent management of this business.'[12]

But Sir William had reckoned without Emma. She arrived in Naples on 26 April 1786, her twenty-first birthday. At that time the capital of the Kingdom of the Two Sicilies was the third largest in Europe, the most beautiful and exciting metropolis in the Mediterranean. Emma was made for it. As a young girl she had been very pretty, but by now she had matured into a truly exquisite beauty. She was described by the German poet Goethe, who saw her there the following year during his tour of Italy: she had a beautiful face, a perfect figure, and long dark hair which fell almost to her knees. Sir William 'does nothing all day but look at me and sigh', Emma wrote to Greville.

Sir William was not the only one. Before long the whole of Naples, it seemed, was at her feet. Crowds of *lazzaroni*, the most impoverished but voluble inhabitants, followed her when she went out. In drawing rooms her singing 'left some dying, some crying, some in despair'. Artists flocked from all over the region, beseeching her 'to lend them her shining countenance for an hour'.[13] Not even the clergy were immune to Emma's charms. 'The [Neapolitans] have all got it in their heads I am like the virgin [Mary],' she wrote to Greville, 'and they do come to beg favours of me. Last night their was two preists came to our house & Sir William made me put the shawl over my head & look

* What sounds today like a piece of cold-blooded exploitation was, by the standards of the late eighteenth century, an act of unusual consideration. There was nothing to stop Greville, like her previous 'protector', simply abandoning Emma to a far less certain fate on the streets of London.

up & the preist burst in to tears & kist my feet & said God had sent me a purpose.' Even by hot-blooded Neapolitan standards, Emma was a sensation.

In February of the following year Sir William wrote to Greville expressing his satisfaction with her progress: 'Our dear Em goes on now quite as I cou'd wish, improves daily, and is universally beloved.' Emma, who always had the highest possible opinion of herself (and perhaps, too, an understandable desire to show Greville what he had given up), penned an even more fulsome description of her success. 'I walk in the Villa Reale every night, I have generally two princes, two or 3 nobles, the English minister & and the King, with a crowd beyond ous,' she wrote to Greville, rubbing it in. 'The Queen likes me much & desired Prince Draydrixton [Dietrichstein] to walk with me near her, that she might get a sight of me, for the Prince when he is not with ous, he is with the Queen & he does nothing but entertains her with my beauty.'

In fact, whatever her other successes, Emma was deceived when it came to the Queen's opinion of her. Although she and Sir William lived in separate apartments and, according to Sir William, 'give no scandal', it was widely known in Naples that the court did not approve. While the Neapolitan *cavalieri* were more than happy to be charmed by Emma's beauty, no one was in any doubt about her origins. Queen Maria Carolina, the wife of King Ferdinand I (and the sister of Marie Antoinette), was heard more than once expressing her displeasure 'that a man, honoured with an important mission, an English Minister, should live publically with a prostitute taken from the very streets of London'.[14]

By the summer of 1787, despite royal disapproval, Emma was Sir William's acknowledged consort. Amazingly, she had even begun to preside over his 'deplomatic diners'. 'We sett down thirty to dine, me at the head of the table, mistress of the feast,' Emma wrote, gloating to Greville. She described her appearance in detail: 'drest all in virgin wite & my hair all in ringlets reaching all most to my heals. I assure you it is so long that I realy lookd and moved an angel. Sir Wm said so.' That night she went to the opera, where to her delight Sir William had a box near the King and Queen. Her dinner guests, the commander and officers from a visiting Dutch ship, attended her in her box 'and behaved to me as tho I was a Queen. . .'[15]

But, even in the hedonistic and permissive climate of southern Italy, there were limits. Although Sir William went nowhere without Emma, with whom he was increasingly besotted, he took great care not to let her appear in places where her presence would cause offence. Emma was quite astute enough to realize this. 'He as no diners, but what I can be of the party,' she wrote, 'no body comes with out they are civil to me; we have allways good company.' But the good company at Sir William's residence, the Palazzo Sessa, remained almost exclusively male. Emma was not received at court, and none of the aristocratic ladies of Naples, or the wives of Sir William's diplomatic colleagues, would have dreamt of visiting her, even in the august setting of Sir William's elegant palazzo.

All this changed, however, when Emma's 'Attitudes', as they were known – a series of improvised *tableaux vivants* in which she posed in a flowing sequence of scenes from antiquity – became increasingly famous amongst travellers to Naples. In March 1787 Goethe witnessed one of her very first performances. Sir William had a Greek costume made for her and, dressed in this simple garment, Emma

lets down her hair and, with a few shawls, gives so much variety to her poses, gestures, expressions etc that the spectator can hardly believe his eyes. He sees what thousands of artists would have liked to express realised before him in the movements and surprising transformations – standing, kneeling, sitting, reclining, serious, sad, playful, ecstatic, contrite, alluring, threatening, anxious, one pose follows another without a break. She knows how to arrange the folds of her veil to match each mood, and has a hundred ways of turning it into a head-dress. . .

In an age quite unused to moving imagery the display caused a sensation. 'This much is certain,' Goethe concluded: 'as a performance it's like nothing you ever saw before in your life.'[16]

As the fame of Emma's 'Attitudes' grew, they gradually became one of the sights to be seen in Naples, along with the wonders of antiquity or Vesuvius itself. Two years later, in 1789, she was regularly entertaining visitors to the embassy, not only with her 'Attitudes', but with singing and dancing with a tambourine. Her voluptuous rendition of the tarantella was much admired.

As she had already shown, with the ready transference of her affections from Greville to Sir William, Emma had a pragmatic head on her shoulders as well as a beautiful face. Now she grew ambitious, too. She was determined to become respectable.

With Sir William's help, Emma worked hard: she entertained his guests, took music lessons three times a day, dancing lessons with the Queen's dancing master three times a week, and learnt drawing, French and Italian. At the King's birthday party in June that year Sir William finally took the plunge and Emma attended her first official diplomatic dinner, to which only English guests were invited. Later that same year the Duchess of Argyll, who was travelling in Italy for her health, not only seemed to take to Emma herself, but agreed to present her to her two daughters. An unchallenged rumour circulated that Emma and Sir William were secretly married. Slowly, Emma's position in society was changing.

In January 1791 Sir William gave a great ball at the Palazzo Sessa. Emma had now been a part of his establishment for five years, and her position was assured. Although Queen Maria Carolina still refused to receive her at court, even the most aristocratic ladies of Naples no longer scrupled to visit the British residence while Emma presided. The 400 guests who were invited included 'all the foreign ministers and their wives, and all the first ladies of fashion, foreyners and neapolitans'. From then on the British embassy became a focus for social life in Naples. 'Every night our house is open for small partys of fifty or sixty men and women,' Emma wrote. 'She is much visited here by ladies of the highest rank and many of the *corps diplomatique*,' confirmed one English visitor to Italy, Heneage Legge.[17]

Of course, not everyone approved. Mrs Legge was outraged when Sir William suggested that Emma should act as her companion whilst she was in Naples. According to Sir Gilbert Elliot, the viceroy of Corsica, Emma still had a vulgar country accent and the easy manners of a barmaid. She was undeniably beautiful, but when left to her own devices she exhibited a deplorable taste in clothes. Her 'Attitudes' were almost universally admired by her contemporaries (although for one witness, the Comtesse de Boigne, they were 'one of those things where there is only a step between the sublime and the ridiculous'), but the same could not be said for her singing. Emma claimed, as Emma would, that her singing always reduced her audiences to grateful tears of emotion. Lady Palmerston, however, one of the many hundreds of English visitors who visited Naples at that time, was of a rather different opinion. 'I like [her] too well not to wish she had never learned to sing,' she wrote in a letter home. 'Her voice is powerful but perfectly without harmony and I am sure she has no ear.' None the less, she conceded, Emma was 'a very extraordinary character'.

The rumours of a secret marriage, put about by Emma, continued. Although Sir William was still very fond of her, and had found her behaviour as his mistress exemplary, as a diplomat he was well aware of the implications of such a marriage; 'whilst I am in a public character, I do not look upon myself at liberty to act as I please,' he wrote to his friend Sir Joseph Banks, 'and such a step I think would be imprudent and might be attended with disagreeable circumstances.' Despite Emma's new respectability, many of her fellow Britons would find it hard to stomach her elevated status: 'But as I have experience that of all Women in the World, the English are the most difficult to deal with abroad, I fear eternal tracasseries, were she to be placed above them here, & which must be the case, as a Minister's Wife, in every Country, takes place of every rank of Nobility.'

In the summer of 1791 Sir William and Emma went on home leave, living openly together at his establishment in London. Emma was the most talked about woman in town. Although she was now accepted in some circles, no one was surprised when Queen Charlotte refused to receive her at court. Nonetheless, rumours that a secret marriage had taken place in Naples continued to circulate. Under pressure from Emma, Sir William's remaining scruples were fading. In August he received the unspoken consent of the King, and on 6 September 1791, finally, they were married.

Back in Naples, Emma's triumph was complete. As Lady Hamilton, she was now received at court, and the last remaining sticklers were forced to accept her. Even her spelling had improved. 'We have many English at Naples,' she wrote to her friend, the painter Romney; 'Ladys Malmsbery, Malden, Plymouth, Carnegie, Wright etc. They are very kind and attentive to me; they all make it a point to be remarkably civil to me.' Even Queen Maria Carolina now made it her business to befriend Emma. In the fight against the French Republicans, who had already beheaded her brother-in-law, Louis XVI, the British were the kingdom's most powerful ally. On 12 July 1793 the Anglo-Neapolitan

Treaty of Alliance was signed. As the wife of the British envoy, Emma was now a personage to be carefully cultivated.*

Among the most vivid and powerful women in diplomatic history there have been some wonderful oddballs, but very few have actually rebelled against the system. Those who found the life less than perfect generally kept quiet about it, or resorted to subterfuge (Countess Granville's sly strategies for outwitting *les élégantes* in Paris come to mind). Some, like Vita Sackville-West, refused to be part of the traditional camp-follower life, but their actions had no wider implications; they showed little interest in trying to change things for anyone else. And even the most outrageous – Isabel Burton, for example – happily operated from within the system (or, as in the case of Emma Hamilton, devoted years of her life trying to get into the system in the first place).

'I can't imagine why we didn't rebel,' Peggy Trevelyan ventured, but the fact was that until the 1970s hardly anyone else could imagine it either. By then, however, times began to change. Back in Britain the first Women's Liberation demonstration was held in London in March 1971; the following year saw the first issue of the radical feminist magazine *Spare Rib*. And on 1 January 1976, under a new Labour government, the Equal Pay Act came into force. For diplomatic women, the vast majority of whom were living abroad, it was through the rather less trenchant DSWA that the *zeitgeist* found its voice.

The DSWA newsletters – which, in the early 1960s, voiced so many of the cultural assumptions governing domestic diplomatic life – now became an unexpected mouthpiece of change. While they could hardly be called either radical or feminist, a new and refreshing steeliness none the less began to creep into their pages. The contentious question of working wives, for instance, was raised and debated. Although there had never been any written rules on the subject, until now it had always been assumed that diplomatic wives did not, indeed should not, work. An article by Margaret Ibbot entitled 'The Role of the Foreign Service Wife: a Personal View' appeared in the *Spring Newsletter*

---

* It was not until some years later, after the Battle of the Nile in 1798, that Nelson met and fell in love with Emma Hamilton, by then a powerful and flamboyant figure. What she had gained in respectability, Emma had also gained in girth. The following year another British envoy's wife, Lady Elgin, en route to Constantinople, noted that 'She is indeed a Whapper!'

of 1976. She was not talking about the technical questions of work permits and diplomatic immunity (in some countries, if the wife obtained a permit to work she was automatically forced to give up her immunity from civil actions. Contrary to what is usually believed, her political immunity was never affected. In every case, a wife was obliged to secure the permission of the head of mission first.) Instead, her bitterness was directed at those who applied pressure 'designed at the very least to make me feel apologetic that I should wish to have a job of my own. Other wives particularly have made it clear where they think all diplomatic wives' duties lie – with the post in particular and with the FCO in general, and that personal interests, professional or otherwise, must come last.' Many women who had had careers before their marriages agreed with her. 'The knowledge that all one's learning and training is draining away and that left to oneself one could contribute little to the world,' she wrote, 'is a bitter and destructive experience.'

More radically, some of the younger women were beginning to question the very role and *raison d'être* of the diplomatic wife. Margaret Ibbot's article challenged previous assumptions to the very core: 'she should not, indeed does not, break [her husband] by refusing to be an unpaid curate. Even less does she make or break the Diplomatic Service. The fear that she might is sustained by a few officers and more frequently by dutiful, but I think misguided wives, anxious to justify and magnify the importance of their role.' More rebelliously still, she pointed out: 'however much a wife chooses to help her husband, she is not, as a simple matter of fact, an employee. She has not been trained, she is not paid, and perhaps more important, she has no real authority herself, nor is she subject to authority from the office or other wives ... The blunt truth is that wives owe the post and the office nothing at all.'[18] Of course, not everyone agreed. But the first serious calls for change had been sounded, and their repercussions have been felt right up to the present day.

CHAPTER THIRTEEN

Contemporary Wives

It is not unusual for Chris Gardiner, one of the very newest breed of diplomatic spouse, to serve Ferrero Rocher chocolates at his dinner parties in Kyiv. It's a good joke, he acknowledges, if a little worn. Chris is a retired school teacher and education officer, and is one of the increasing numbers of male 'trailing spouses' who accompany their diplomat wives on postings. He admits to being surprised by the extent to which he was forced to change his assumptions about the Foreign Office after his marriage in 1994. 'They're all Colonel Blimps, aren't they?' he says. 'I don't think people know what the hell diplomats really do. They think everyone is over fifty and an old Cambridge-type duffer, when in fact people actually come from all sorts of backgrounds.'

Much the same could be said of diplomatic spouses (of whom, in 1998, 13 per cent were male). A man of many parts, Chris is quite content with the domestic role which his wife's job has conferred on him. 'My job is to do the shopping and the preparation. You know, I wear the pinny.' He meets with many different reactions to his new position, 'scaring the Ukrainian men to death' – they could not believe that he was prepared to swap roles with his wife. The assumptions about the way he lives, however, are remarkably similar: 'People think you live with cut glass chandeliers and flunkies with white gloves, when in fact we live in what looks like a council block which might grace the Elephant and Castle, in conditions which can be fairly tough at times.'

On the Ivory Coast, Alex Sutherland was at first regarded with suspicion by the inhabitants. As the husband of Britain's first married woman ambassador, Veronica Sutherland, he came to the task with a certain notoriety. Although he had his own job, as the UK's executive director at the African Development Bank, *Monsieur l' Ambassadrice*, as he became known locally, soon found himself rustling up lunches and dinners single-handedly, with the same panache as any more traditional diplomatic wife. And if the Ivorians had any lingering doubts, they were confirmed when Alex turned up to a Queen's Birthday Party wearing his kilt with some élan. 'Veronica was always treated as the most important woman in the room, while I was always regarded as the least important man,' he recalls. 'I usually got to sit next to the mistresses and unmarried daughters, and became very adept at discussing the relative merits of shopping expeditions to Paris and Geneva. It's Geneva they prefer, by the way.'

The old myths about Foreign Office life, it seems, are unusually resistant to change. Change, nonetheless, has occurred. On the eve of the twenty-first century, diplomatic 'wives' – which include growing numbers of men, foreign-born spouses and unmarried partners – bring with them an increasing variety of outlooks. A particularly refreshing article in a 1997 *BDSA Magazine* was contributed by one sartorially challenged wife, who admitted that 'dressing up' to embassy life had been a terrifying ordeal. A professional dress consultant gave her some useful tips, including a price guide. As a farmer's daughter, for whom dress had been more or less irrelevant as long as it was practical, she related the prices she was given to her own rather more down-to-earth shopping list:

Belt	£35	(10 laying hens)
Shoes	£75	(50m chicken wire)
Handbag	£80	(2 fat lambs)
Jacket	£185	(3 breeding ewes)
Blouse	£80	(2 × 12' metal 7-barred gates)
Trousers	£105	(500m barbed wire *and* 50 wooden fencing posts)
Sweater	£85	(huge metal water trough)
Skirt	£85	(2 tons good straw)
Dress	£180	(2 tons really good hay)
Suit	£275	(½ milking cow)
Coat	£265	(other ½ milking cow)
Scarves		
large	£50	(4 vet's call-out fees)
small	£25	(12 stable buckets)
metre		
square	£100	(½ ton cow cake)[1]

Diplomatic spouses have come a long way since the days, not all that long ago, when Lady Kirkpatrick would blithely instruct them on the importance of absolute dedication to 'the service'. It was not only in the senior positions that this ethos of absolute loyalty was imbibed. In a 'Woman's Hour' broadcast of April 1968 Mrs Enid Venables, wife of a 'junior member of the diplomatic corps', could be heard dutifully toeing the party line. 'Do you think, in fact, that diplomats' wives should go with them, or do you think that they are a bit of a luxury?' enquired the interviewer. 'No, certainly not,' replied Mrs Venables. 'I think that diplomats' wives can, should and must fulfil a very definite function and diplomatic life is very much a question of team work,' her clipped English tones tinkled out across the ether. 'They must do this. The wife must do her share, entertaining for her husband and she can be very, very helpful making contacts for him and, for instance, joining local organizations and charities. She meets the wives, through them their husbands, and in this way contacts are made. This is all extremely helpful to the husband.'

This rich and fulfilling sense of partnership which Enid Venables felt with her husband was one shared by countless other diplomatic wives before and after her. Also implicit in her comments, however, is another unspoken assumption, the very one which Lady Kirkpatrick had so forcefully spelt out in her speech. Following marriage to a diplomat, certain obligations and duties were imposed on wives not only by their husbands, but in some indefinable way by the service itself. Their husbands' job became, *de facto*, their job too. Although she did not feel like going out every night, Enid Venables explained to her interviewer, she knew that it was her duty to do so. 'You don't do it from choice. It's just part of the job. You must do it, and if you feel like staying at home with a good book, well this isn't always possible.'

Despite the fact that a diplomatic wife had no legal or contractual obligation to the Foreign Office, in practice the service could, and did, exert enormous control over 'its wives' in all sorts of ways. During the 1970s one subject of hot debate was the right of diplomatic wives to take salaried employment while they were abroad. While in the past permission was often refused for technical reasons – loss of diplomatic immunity, for example – there was another unspoken agenda at work. As the anthropologist Hilary Callan noted astutely in her 1975 essay

'The Premiss of Dedication', those who spoke out in favour of allowing wives to work argued 'to a man' that a wife's usefulness to the mission 'was likely to be enhanced by her having a job – provided, everyone agrees, that she does not neglect her official duties'. It is not hard to see, she added, that the threat of a competing set of responsibilities generated 'ambivalent feelings' amongst the authorities, which would seek to assert their control.[2]

There was a certain opaqueness in the Foreign Office rulings on the subject. 'A lot of people are under the illusion that you were forbidden from working, but it was never written down,' explains Annabel Black, who, like Hilary Callan, is both a diplomatic spouse and an anthropologist. In fact, the only written ruling on the subject, stipulating that a wife should seek permission from the head of mission before taking on employment, was enshrined in the *officer*'s terms of employment, and was thus never legally binding on his wife.

The ideal relationship between spouses and the service has been debated for over twenty years now – ever since Margaret Ibbot, and other independent-minded women, began to question some of these assumptions. On the face of it, progress has been slow; many of their questions are still largely unresolved. 'We are called DS [Diplomatic Service] or FO [Foreign Office] spouses,' stated Catherine Young in her chairman's address to the BDSA 1996 conference. 'Does that really mean that we are married to the Foreign Office? Many will answer with a heart-rending "yes"!'

At the turn of the twenty-first century embassy culture is still able to exert great pressure. Diplomatic life is not, and never has been, merely a collection of people (principally men) doing a job. It's a shared way of life, often sustained under extreme and sometimes very dangerous conditions, in which wives and families are very closely involved. Whereas so many other great institutions, such as the Church, or politics, or the trade union movement, have lost much of their power to motivate people on a communal level, the diplomatic service still defines people's sense of themselves.

And as a group, diplomatic spouses remain strikingly self-aware. This collective feeling is one which has, if anything, grown rather than diminished over the last forty years. The literature published by the BDSA contains some of the most compelling evidence of this, as wives (and now husbands too) continually debate and analyse the delicate, and sometimes seemingly impossible balance between their own needs and those of 'the role'. Even the most disenchanted have found ingenious ways of expressing themselves, not only through magazine articles and opinion pieces, but through questionnaires and even academic papers. The ground-breaking 1978 report, *Some Reflections on the Role of the Diplomatic Wife*, commissioned from Dr Eric Miller at the Tavistock Institute of Human Relations in London, brought, for the first time, the cool analytical skills of a sociologist to bear on the problem.

The debate reveals a wide range of opinions and temperaments, but also a certain steely clear-sightedness which is definitely paying off. Diplomatic wives may not be rebellious in any conventional sense of the word, but there is no doubt that a quiet revolution is taking place. For all its lingering flavour of the coffee morning and the charity bazaar, the BDSA, which speaks for more than 4,000 diplomatic spouses, has become a rather 'stroppy little group', to coin one member's refreshingly undiplomatic phrase. 'I would scare some of them off if I said, "We're running a small union here,"' comments Chris Gardiner, who recently took over the BDSA branch in Kyiv, 'but that's exactly what we're doing, because we're acting collectively.'

This unofficial union has had a long list of successes in taking on the Foreign Office administration and forcing them to adopt more 'Family Friendly Policies'. The right of wives to work, which as recently as 1975 was still described by one Foreign Office official as 'contentious', has now been firmly established; efforts are made to help them by, for instance, employing them where possible at the mission itself. There were extra fares for children at boarding school, a family welfare officer was appointed in 1978, and a counselling service introduced in 1989. The conditions for spouses and families abroad have improved in many ways: there is now a salaried community liaison officer at some posts, and spouses who pass Foreign Office language exams receive payment. Those who help with official entertaining at home can now claim the labour costs of cooking and waitressing as part of their entertainment allowance. Extra funding has been secured for heads of mission wives, who in some missions can now apply for the position of residence 'housekeeper' (at local rates). The Secretary of State has now agreed that spouses who are unable to work abroad should receive compensation for lost pension rights. (The money, in an increasingly budget-conscious age, has yet to be found, but the principle has been established.)

And yet, for all the changes that have been made, the 'collective morality' within individual missions abroad remains remarkably strong. While the Dragon Empress ambassadresses of old, brow-beating 'their' wives into making meat balls for the Queen's Birthday Party, are now no more than a cherished folk-memory, almost all contemporary spouses feel that they are still required to conform to type. 'People feel under pressure still, they really do,' explains Annabel Black. Her own experience of diplomatic life, in Brussels in the early 1990s, began relatively late in her life, but is typical of many modern women, even those with careers and expectations of their own. 'I was a fully grown woman. I had been independent for years, supporting myself and working, and living a totally different life. And academic life is very different from diplomatic life to say the least.'

In her view, what makes diplomatic life unique (and different from the experience of many other people 'married' to their spouses' professions – the Church or the army, for example) is the highly representational aspect of embassy life.

What is very specific is the fact of being on show, and I think that affects people. Very soon after I came to Brussels I really did notice myself changing. At first it was all rather good fun, going to all these parties and meeting all these new people, and feeling very much an outsider. And observing it really, in a sort of quasi-anthropological way. Then one day someone I knew sent round a copy of Marcus Cheke's handbook as a joke, because it was so funny. But then I found myself looking at it, you know, really in earnest when I had to go out to some 'do'. I'd look to see what time I should arrive, and how I should introduce people, and so on. I was monitoring my own behaviour in ways that I had never done before. For instance, you are very aware at diplomatic parties that you mustn't step out of line or get tiddly, as opposed to academic parties where people do go over the edge quite a lot. And wanting to be well turned out and to put on a good face. And feeling the obligation to entertain. Even though they say that you don't have to do that in Brussels, I felt myself pulled into it.

It is not only women who feel this. Male spouses, too, if they do decide to accompany their wives overseas, admit to feeling the pull.

From what I hear the service has always expected their higher level diplomats to have a spouse who is very much part of the team [explains Chris Gardiner]. I think it's different if your role is not representational. But if the post is representational then the spouse has a very real role in producing a household that is fit for visitors to that outpost in Britain, wherever you are. Your household is on show, you've got dinner parties to give, you appear at the elbow of the diplomat at diplomatic functions. You don't have to, you don't need to take part, but in many ways there's enormous pressure on you to do just that. Part of our job in Kyiv is to host dinner parties, for Ukrainian MPs or whatever, and *of course* there is an expectation that I will take part. I'm not going to sit there dumb. I'm part of the package as far as the service is concerned. An unpaid part of the package. I'm quite convinced that that is what the Foreign Office ideally would like. They don't want a load of unaccompanied diplomats. Particularly the higher-up you go. There is a huge household to run. A computer program to run, now, managing the accounts. Managing the staff. You're running a small hotel. A small hotel which is Britain.

Even the very youngest and most junior diplomatic spouses, for whom the representational role has always been far less onerous, still feel a considerable degree of pressure. 'It's very difficult to prevent yourself being drawn in to a certain extent, because the embassy is your immediate social structure,' says thirty-one-year-old Susie Tucker, a doctor of music and wife of a former second secretary to Prague and Slovakia. 'Until you do put down roots overseas those are the people you have to rely on. You are one of the "wives of the embassy".'

Not all diplomatic spouses are happy with this status quo. The same vigorous collective persona which has made them so successful and effective as a pressure group, is, paradoxically, one of the greatest sources of conflict and unhappiness within the service. 'I don't think that being "a wife" confers on me any obligation whatsoever to take on the role that is still expected,' Susie goes on. 'But a lot of husbands do expect it. I'm just lucky in that mine does not.' Even today, amongst the youngest and most independent wives, there is a very real fear that it is all too easy to become subsumed by embassy life. By setting up her own company, a desk-top publishing service, Susie hopes that she will not only create a valuable buffer against too many demands on her time, but also a sense of purpose and identity of her own. Not everyone, however, has either the opportunity or the resources to construct these safety nets.

The older wives have spoken out with bitterness about their lost years, and younger wives such as Susie have taken note: 'The older I get the more determined I am not to do things against my will, and not to be carried along by it. You only live once, and when I get to retirement age I'm not going to think, "God, I wish I'd given a few more dinner parties." What I'm going to think is, "God, I wish I'd done something more with my life."'

'God, I wish I'd done something more with my life' is a cry with which counsellors from the Medical and Welfare Department at the Foreign Office are extremely familiar. While many women are happy with the life, and willing to give it their all in ways which have changed little in the last forty years or so, others are increasingly reluctant to play the game. Many young, ambitious, career-minded spouses choose not to follow their partners abroad at all.

However, there are those who feel they had no choice. For them, the changes of the last twenty years have come too late. The full and unquestioning identification with their husbands' jobs may no longer be enough, but in the past it provided a vital psychological prop. 'Women around fifty feel they have given up a lot in terms of a career of their own,' explains one Foreign Office counsellor. 'And then when they get to fifty they wonder where they are.'

It is not only jobs which are sacrificed. In diplomatic life a continuing sense of loss can permeate almost every aspect of life. 'You settle down for three or four years, you go off again, you settle again, you move again. Your children in general go away, when other parents in the UK are not experiencing that. You lose job opportunities; you lose friends; you lose identity, I think.'

Foreign-born spouses find the loss of their own culture particularly hard to bear. Korean-born Eui-Jong Han Karmy speaks eloquently –

not only for herself, but for many others in her situation – about her fear of isolation, both within the embassy community itself during postings abroad, and also during 'home' postings in the UK. 'Foreign born spouses need to be posted back to their country to maintain their relationship with their family,' she explains. 'I have been waiting for a posting to Korea for the last twenty years. I hoped the children would be able to hear my language spoken around them. They are now nineteen and seventeen!' The cultural prejudice of her own family presented another almost unsurmountable obstacle. 'I went back to Korea after seven years of marriage. I had not heard or spoken my language all this time. My family had forgotten all about me and met my children, then aged five and three, for the first time. I felt bewildered, guilty and strange. The airfare had been too expensive even to think about it until then.'[3]

Loss of identity, in whatever form it is experienced, is exacerbated by what counsellors call 'the camp-follower thing'. The role of the diplomatic spouse remains fundamentally a supporting one.

They can't always be themselves because they are also representing their country, or their husband is, so the feeling perhaps is that if they express views which are a little bit odd or way out it may reflect badly on the husband. You have a pseudo-smile, a pseudo-persona who does all this, and although some people find that easy, other people don't. After twenty years or so maybe you get a bit sick of it, and you'd prefer to do your own thing.

The loss of identity experienced by many spouses is 'about having to put on a false self, and perhaps becoming increasingly uncomfortable with it'.

Although the collective identity of diplomatic spouses remains remarkably strong, its foundation has shifted dramatically. Uncomplaining, self-abnegating loyalty to 'the service' may now largely be a thing of the past, but amongst many diplomatic couples the idea of a husband and wife as a team or partnership has remained remarkably strong.

Now, as in the past, there is no job in the world in which wives (and now husbands, too) are so deeply involved in their spouses' work. 'I think my loyalty is not to the Foreign Office at all,' explains Chris

Gardiner succinctly. 'My loyalty is to my wife.' Even the most vehemently independent would agree with him. 'I will help Seamus when I can,' says Susie Tucker. 'But I'll do it because of him, because I know it is part of his job. It's not pure duty.' Nowadays, however, such loyalties work both ways. 'Seamus knew that what he did would make it much harder for me to follow any career myself than if we lived in London,' Susie says. 'When we got married he said, "If you ever want me to leave the office and do something else, I will. Tell me, and I'll do it." Because of that I'd probably never ask him, but it means I don't feel any kind of resentment towards him.'

Diplomatic spouses are divided on the question of whether or not their role will continue into the twenty-first century. In a recent survey carried out by the BDSA, although 53 per cent thought the role would still be important, a substantial 41 per cent thought it would not. Morale, across the board, is said to be low, and the position of spouses is still in a state of flux. For all the uncertainties, the continuing debate is also their greatest hope for the future. Some, such as Annabel Black, think that it is one which will never be resolved. More optimistically, one senior wife said recently: 'It is a case of the role is dead, long live the role.'

Ultimately, the contemporary spouses who are happiest with their lot are those who combine a flexible approach to life with a love of adventure, qualities which diplomatic wives have shared ever since Lady Winchilsea took to the seas in 1661. In a sense their story has now come round in a full circle. In the future, I suspect, their lives will mirror far more closely those of their earlier sisters like Mrs Blanckley, sewing shirts for shipwrecked sailors on the coast of Algiers, whose time and energies were freely given.

Many, of course, will choose to pursue their own path. However, the fact that it is all but impossible to follow a conventional career or profession whilst trailing a diplomat around the world is not an insurmountable stumbling block to everyone.

I've got friends who definitely say they would never do it, and would hate to do it, and say it's just not them. They just want to have a stable career here, and that's what their life is about [explains one young diplomatic wife]. But I'm quite happy that my life could be about all kinds of things.

It astonishes me now, even though I'm not very far into the thing, that I have had friends who have done just that. They've stayed in the same career, in the same house, in the same part of London, since we all left university. They've both got glittering professional careers and two lovely kids. They're both carrying on down the same path. And I just think: How can they do it? Don't they want to make radical changes? Don't they feel that they've got stuck in a rut? And the answer is, no they don't. But I would. And one of the things about it is the feeling that you are going to get a kick, every four years or so, and told, 'Right. OK. You've done that. Now move on, try something else.' And I think it's quite exciting really. Don't you?

NOTES

Prologue

1. Raphaela Lewis, *Notes from Everyday Life in Ottoman Turkey*, B. T. Batsford, London, 1971.
2. *A Narrative of the Success of the Voyage of his Excellency the Lord Heneage Finch, from Smyrna to Constantinople; his arrival there, the manner of his entrance into Pera, and of his audience with the Grand Vizier and Grand Seignior.*
3. Ibid.

Introduction

1. Jane Ewart-Biggs, *Pay, Pack and Follow*, Weidenfeld & Nicolson, London, 1984.
2. Lady Mary Leonora Sheil, *Glimpses of Life and Manners in Persia*, John Murray, London, 1856.
3. Letter of 22 December 1802, in Nisbet Hamilton Grant (ed.), *The Letters of Mary Nisbet of Direlton, Countess of Elgin*, John Murray, London, 1926.
4. Garett Mattingly, *Renaissance Diplomacy*, Jonathan Cape, London, 1955.
5. Marie-Noele Kelly, *From Dawn till Dusk*, Hutchinson, London, 1960. See also Phyllis S. Lachs, *The Diplomatic Corps under Charles II and James II*, Rutgers University Press, New Jersey, 1965; *The F.C.O.: Policy, People and Places, 1782–1995*, Library and Records Department, Foreign and Commonwealth Office, April 1991.

Chapter One: Getting There

1. Miss Ella Sykes and Brigadier-General Sir Percy Sykes, KCIE CB CMG, *Through Deserts and Oases of Central Asia*, Macmillan, London, 1920.
2. Ibid.
3. Major S. Leigh Hunt, *Tropical Trials; A Handbook for Women in the Tropics*, W. H. Allen & Co., London, 1883.
4. Mrs Hugh Fraser, *A Diplomatist's Wife in Many Lands*, 2 vols., Hutchinson & Co., London, 1911; vol. I.

5. Diana Shipton, *The Antique Land*, Hodder & Stoughton, London, 1950.
6. Mary King Waddington, *Letters of a Diplomat's Wife, 1883–1900*, Smith, Elder & Co., London, 1903.
7. Mrs Elizabeth Broughton, *Six Years Residence in Algiers*, Saunders & Otley, London, 1839.
8. Lesley Blanch, *The Wilder Shores of Love*, John Murray, London, 1954.
9. Isabel Burton, *The Life of Captain Sir Richard F. Burton*, Chapman & Hall, London, 1896.
10. Historical Manuscripts Commission, *Manuscripts of the Marquess of Down-shire*, vols. I–VI, Her Majesty's Stationery Office, 1988.
11. Flora Annie Steel and Grace Gardiner, *The Complete Indian Housekeeper and Cook*, William Heineman, London, 1911.
12. Angela Caccia, *Beyond Lake Titicaca*, Hodder & Stoughton, London, 1969.
13. Vita Sackville-West, *Passenger to Teheran*, Hogarth Press, London, 1926.
14. Letter to Virginia Woolf, 9 March 1926, in Louise de Salvo and Mitchell A. Leaska (eds.), *The Letters of Vita Sackville-West to Virginia Woolf*, Hutchinson, London, 1984.
15. Fraser, op. cit.
16. Lady Mary Wortley Montagu, *The Turkish Embassy Letters*, introduced by Anita Desai, Virago Press, London, 1994.
17. Lady Macartney, *An English Lady in Chinese Turkistan*, Ernest Beern, London, 1931.
18. Lady Susan Townley, *The Indiscretions of Lady Susan*, Thornton Butterworth Ltd, London, 1922.
19. Maureen Tweedy, *A Label Round My Neck*, Terence Dalton Ltd, Suffolk, 1976.
20. Steel and Gardiner, op. cit.
21. Sheil, *Glimpses of Life and Manners in Persia*.

Chapter Two: The Posting

1. Sheil, *Glimpses of Life and Manners in Persia*.
2. Letter to Virginia Woolf, 15 March 1926, in de Salvo and Leaska, *Letters*.
3. Ewart-Biggs, *Pay, Pack and Follow*.
4. Wortley Montagu, *Turkish Embassy Letters*.
5. Caccia, *Beyond Lake Titicaca*.
6. Masha Williams, *The Consul's Memsahib*, The Book Guild Ltd, Sussex, 1985.
7. Tweedy, *Label Round My Neck*.
8. Ibid.
9. Miss Tully, *Letters Written During a 10 Years Residence at the Court of Tripoli, 1783–1793*, Arthur Barker Ltd, London, 1957.
10. Grant (ed.), *Letters of Mary Nisbet of Direlton, Countess of Elgin*.

11. Ann Fanshawe, *Memoirs of Ann, Lady Fanshawe*, John Lane, The Bodley Head, London, 1907.
12. Tweedy, op. cit.
13. Shipton, *The Antique Land.*
14. Macartney, *An English Lady.*
15. Mary Fraser, *A Diplomatist's Wife in Japan: Letters from Home to Home*, Hutchinson, London, 1899.
16. Broughton, *Six Years Residence in Algiers.*

Chapter Three: Partners

1. Broughton, *Six Years Residence in Algiers.*
2. Andrew Henderson, *The Life of John, Earl of Stair*, London, 1749.
3. *Letters from a Lady who resided some years in Russia to her friend in England*, London, 1775.
4. Quoted in Beryl Smedley, *Partners in Diplomacy*, The Harley Press, West Sussex, 1990.
5. Macartney, *An English Lady.*
6. Anne Disbrowe, *The Original Letters from Russia*, The Ladies Printing Press, London, 1878.
7. Florence MacAlistair (ed.), *Memoir of Sir John McNeill, GCB, and of his second wife, Elizabeth Wilson*, John Murray, London, 1910.
8. D. B. Horn, *The British Diplomatic Service 1689–1789*, Clarendon Press, Oxford, 1961.
9. Fanshawe, *Memoirs.*
10. Kelly, *From Dawn till Dusk.*
11. Marcus Cheke, His Majesty's Vice-Marshal of the Diplomatic Corps, *Guidance on foreign usages and ceremony, and other matters, for a Member of His Majesty's Foreign Service on his first appointment to a Post Abroad*, FCO, January 1949.
12. 'Serving Abroad', in *FSWA Newsletter*, 1960.
13. Quoted in 'Women in Diplomacy, The FCO, 1782–1994', *History Notes*, No. 6, Historical Branch of the Foreign and Commonwealth Office, May 1994.
14. Williams, *The Consul's Memsahib.*
15. Kelly, op. cit.
16. Quoted in the *DSWA Newsletter*, Spring 1976.
17. Ewart-Biggs, *Pay, Pack and Follow.*

Chapter Four: Private Life

1. *Letters from a Lady* ...
2. Steel and Gardiner, *The Complete Indian Housekeeper*.
3. Macartney, *An English Lady*.
4. Sheil, *Glimpses of Life and Manners in Persia*.
5. Kelly, *From Dawn till Dusk*.
6. Sykes, *Through Deserts and Oases*.
7. Burton, *The Life of Captain Sir Richard F. Burton*.
8. Kelly, op. cit.
9. Sheil, op. cit.
10. Rosemary Watts, *A Military Memsahib*, Owl Press, Salisbury, 1994.
11. Burton, op. cit.
12. Kelly, op. cit.
13. Iona Wright, *Black Sea Bride*, Square One, Upton upon Severn, 1997.
14. Ibid.
15. Grant (ed.), *The Letters of Mary Nisbet*.
16. MacAlistair, *Memoir of Sir John McNeill*.
17. Macartney, op. cit.
18. Wright, op. cit.
19. Wortley Montagu, *Turkish Embassy Letters*.
20. Shipton, *The Antique Land*.
21. Wright, op. cit.
22. Leigh Hunt, *Tropical Trials*.
23. Sykes, op. cit.
24. Shipton, op. cit.
25. Fraser, *A Diplomatist's Wife in Japan*.

Chapter Five: Embassy Life

1. Cheke, *Guidance on foreign usages* ...
2. Kelly, *From Dawn till Dusk*.
3. F. Leveson Gower (ed.), *Letters of Harriet, Countess Granville*, vol. I, Longmans, Green & Co., London, 1894.
4. Letter to Virginia Woolf, 15 March 1926, in de Salvo and Leaska, *Letters*.
5. Wright, *Black Sea Bride*.
6. Steel and Gardiner, *The Complete Indian Housekeeper and Cook*.
7. Sheil, *Glimpses of Life and Manners in Persia*.
8. Quoted by Iona Wright in 'The Lar Valley', *DSWA Magazine*, Spring 1968.
9. Ibid.
10. Fraser, *A Diplomatist's Wife in Many Lands*, Vol. I.
11. Paul Gore-Booth, *With Great Truth and Respect*, Constable, London, 1974.
12. Lady Henderson, *DSWA Magazine*, Spring 1976.

13. Cheke, op. cit.
14. Waddington, *Letters of a Diplomat's Wife.*
15. Williams, *The Consul's Memsahib.*
16. Tweedy, *Label Round My Neck.*
17. Ibid.

Chapter Six: Ambassadresses

1. Waddington, *Letters of a Diplomat's Wife.*
2. Ruth Dudley Edwards, *True Brits: Inside the Foreign Office,* BBC Books, London, 1994.
3. Leveson Gower, *Letters of Harriet, Countess Granville,* Vol. I.
4. Quoted in Betty Askwith, *Piety and Wit: A Biography of Harriet, Countess Granville* (London: Collins, 1982).
5. Ibid.
6. Cynthia Gladwyn, *The Paris Embassy,* Collins, London, 1976.
7. Leveson Gower, op. cit.
8. Katie Hickman, 'The Dutiful and the Damned', *Sunday Telegraph,* 9 October 1994.
9. *DSWA Magazine,* Spring 1976.
10. Kelly, *From Dawn till Dusk.*
11. Fraser, *A Diplomatist's Wife in Many Lands,* Vol. I.
12. Leveson Gower, op. cit.
13. Williams, *The Consul's Memsahib.*
14. Philip Ziegler, *Diana Cooper,* Hamish Hamilton, London, 1981.
15. Quoted in ibid.
16. Quoted in ibid.
17. Quoted in ibid.
18. BDSA magazine, Autumn 1998.

Chapter Seven: Public Life

1. Leveson Gower, *Letters of Harriet, Countess Granville,* Vol. I.
2. Fanshawe, *Memoirs of Ann, Lady Fanshawe.*
3. Wortley Montagu, *Turkish Embassy Letters,* 14 September 1716.
4. Disbrowe, *The Original Letters from Russia.*
5. Grant (ed.), *The Letters of Mary Nisbet.*
6. *Letters from a Lady* . . .
7. Wortley Montagu, op. cit.
8. Sheil, *Glimpses of Life and Manners in Persia.*
9. Broughton, *Six Years Residence in Algiers.*
10. Lady Anne Macdonell, *Reminiscences of Diplomatic Life,* R. & R. Clark Ltd, Edinburgh, 1913.

11. Grant, op. cit.
12. Ibid.
13. Wortley Montagu, op. cit.
14. Lady Susan Townley, *My Chinese Notebook*, Methuen & Co., London, 1904.
15. Fanshawe, op. cit.
16. Fraser, *A Diplomatist's Wife in Many Lands*, Vol. I.
17. Waddington, *Letters of a Diplomat's Wife*.
18. Disbrowe, op. cit.
19. Leveson Gower, op. cit.
20. *Letters from a Lady* . . .
21. Sackville-West, *Passenger to Teheran*.

Chapter Eight: Social Life

1. Burton, *The Life of Captain Sir Richard F. Burton*.
2. Cf. Horn, *The British Diplomatic Service 1689–1789*.
3. Townley, *The Indiscretions of Lady Susan*.
4. Fraser, *A Diplomatist's Wife in Many Lands*.
5. Macartney, *An English Lady in Chinese Turkistan*.
6. Shipton, *The Antique Land*.
7. Tully, *Letters*.
8. Sheil, *Glimpses of Life and Manners in Persia*.
9. Macartney, op. cit.
10. Fraser, *A Diplomatist's Wife in Japan*.
11. *DSWA Magazine*, Spring 1972.
12. Tully, op. cit.
13. Kelly, *From Dawn till Dusk*.
14. Sykes, *Through Deserts and Oases*.
15. *BDSA Magazine*, Spring 1976.
16. 'What Can the British Cook?', *BDSA Magazine*, Spring 1976.
17. Sykes, op. cit.
18. 'The Back of Beyond – Ulan Bator', *BDSA Magazine*.
19. 'My Kisses for Bing', *BDSA Magazine*, Autumn 1997 (first published in *Punch*).
20. Kelly, op. cit.
21. Vita Sackville-West, *Pepita*, The Hogarth Press, London, 1937.
22. Victoria Sackville, *The Book of Happy Reminiscences for My Old Age*, 1922; quoted in above.
23. Susan Mary Alsop, *Lady Sackville: A Biography*, Weidenfeld & Nicolson, London, 1978.
24. Quoted in ibid.
25. 'Representing Your Country Abroad', *BDSA Magazine*, Spring 1976.

26. Stanley Tomlinson, *Handbook on Diplomatic Life Abroad*, Foreign and Commonwealth Office, July 1974.
27. Williams, *The Consul's Memsahib*.
28. 'Etiquette South of the Sahara', *BDSA Magazine*, December 1966.
29. Other sources: Lady Troubridge, *The Book of Etiquette*, The Kingswood Press, London, 1958; Horn, op. cit.

Chapter Nine: Hardships

1. Williams, *The Consul's Memsahib*.
2. Kelly, *From Dawn till Dusk*.
3. Fraser, *A Diplomatist's Wife in Japan*.
4. Helen Peart, 'A Decent Place', *BDSA Magazine*, Spring 1996 (in the series Pioneer Spouses).
5. 'New Countries – New Posts', *BDSA Magazine*, Autumn 1996.
6. Ibid.
7. Dudley Edwards, *True Brits*.
8. Quoted in Lesley Blanch, *The Wilder Shores of Love*, John Murray, London, 1945.
9. Ibid.
10. Burton, *The Life of Captain Sir Richard F. Burton*.
11. Steel and Gardiner, *The Complete Indian Housekeeper and Cook*.
12. Broughton, *Six Years Residence in Algiers*.
13. Fraser, op. cit.
14. Fanshawe, *Memoirs*.
15. Steel and Gardiner, op. cit.
16. Tully, *Letters*.
17. Macartney, *An English Lady in Chinese Turkistan*.
18. Fraser, op. cit.
19. Leveson Gower, *Letters of Harriet, Countess Granville*, Vol. I.
20. Shipton, *The Antique Land*.
21. Sheil, *Glimpses of Life and Manners in Persia*.

Chapter Ten: Children

1. Ewart-Biggs, *Pay, Pack and Follow*.
2. Davina Palmer, 'Diplomatic Childhood?', *BDSA Magazine*, Autumn 1971.
3. Ibid.
4. Denise Holt, 'Did I Win or Lose?', *BDSA Magazine*, Spring 1996.
5. Sir Geoffrey Jackson, *Concorde Diplomacy*, Hamish Hamilton, London, 1981.
6. Dudley Edwards, *True Brits*.
7. Disbrowe, *The Original Letters from Russia*.

8. Fraser, *A Diplomatist's Wife in Many Lands*.
9. Steel and Gardiner, *The Complete Indian Housekeeper and Cook*.
10. Sheil, *Glimpses of Life and Manners in Persia*.
11. Grant, *The Letters of Mary Nisbet*.
12. *Letters from a Lady* ...
13. Wortley Montagu, *Turkish Embassy Letters*.
14. Quoted in Fanshawe, *Memoirs*.
15. Grant, op. cit.
16. MacAlistair, *Memoir of Sir John McNeill*.

Chapter Eleven: Dangers
1. *BDSA Magazine*, Autumn 1972.
2. Quoted in Dudley Edwards, *True Brits*.

Chapter Twelve: Rebel Wives
1. Ewart-Biggs, *Pay, Pack and Follow*.
2. Quoted in Nigel Nicolson, *Portrait of a Marriage*, Weidenfeld & Nicolson, London, 1973.
3. Ibid.
4. Quoted in ibid.
5. Dorothy Wellesley, *Far Have I Travelled*, James Barrie, London, 1952.
6. Letter of 22 May 1927, in Nigel Nicolson and Joanne Trautman (eds.), *Letters of Virginia Woolf*, 6 vols., The Hogarth Press, London, 1975–80; vol. 3.
7. Letter to Virginia Woolf, 19 February 1927, de Salvo and Leaska, *Letters*.
8. Williams, *The Consul's Memsahib*.
9. Townley, *Indiscretions of Lady Susan*.
10. Burton, *The Life of Captain Sir Richard F. Burton*.
11. Chateaubriand, *Mémoires d'Outretombe*, quoted in Cynthia Gladwyn, *The Paris Embassy*, Collins, London, 1976.
12. Flora Fraser, *Beloved Emma: The Life of Emma, Lady Hamilton*, Weidenfeld & Nicolson, London, 1986.
13. Ibid.
14. Ibid.
15. Roger Hudson (ed.), *Nelson and Emma*, Folio Society, London, 1994.
16. Johann Wolfgang von Goethe, *Italian Journey, 1786–1788*, trans. W. H. Auden and Elizabeth Mayer, Collins, London, 1962.
17. Quoted in Fraser, *Beloved Emma*.
18. *DSWA Newsletter*, Spring 1976.

Chapter Thirteen: Contemporary Wives

1. Georgina Armour, 'Dressing Up', *BDSA Magazine*, Autumn 1997.
2. Hilary Callan, 'The Premiss of Dedication', in Shirley Ardener (ed.), *Perceiving Women*, Malaby Press, London, 1975.
3. Eui-Jong Han Karmy, 'From a Different Perspective: FCO Life as a Foreign-Born Spouse', *BDSA Magazine*, Spring 1998.

BIBLIOGRAPHY

Books and Book-Length Sources

Alsop, Susan Mary, *Lady Sackville: A Biography* (London: Weidenfeld & Nicolson, 1978).

Askwith, Betty, *Piety and Wit: A Biography of Harriet, Countess Granville* (London: Collins, 1982).

Blanch, Lesley, *The Wilder Shores of Love* (London: John Murray, 1954).

Broughton, Mrs Elizabeth, *Six Years Residence in Algiers* (London: Saunders & Otley, 1839).

Burton, Isabel, *The Life of Captain Sir Richard F. Burton, by his wife, Isabel Burton* (London: Chapman & Hall, 1896).

Caccia, Angela, *Beyond Lake Titicaca* (London: Hodder & Stoughton, 1969).

Hilary, Callan, *The Premises of Dedication*, see *Perceiving Women*, edited by Shirley Ardener (London: Malaby Press, 1975).

Chance, James Frederick, List of Diplomatic Representatives and Agents, 1689–1762 (London, 1913).

——List of Diplomatic Representatives, 1789–1852 (London, 1934).

Cheke, Marcus, His Majesty's Vice-Marshal of the Diplomatic Corps, *Guidance on foreign usages and ceremony, and other matters, for a Member of His Majesty's Foreign Service on his first appointment to a Post Abroad* (Foreign and Commonwealth Office, January, 1949).

Clark, Ruth, *Sir William Trumbull in Paris, 1685–1686* (Cambridge: Cambridge University Press, 1938).

Disbrowe, Anne *The Original Letters from Russia*, (London: The Ladies Printing Press, 1878).

Dudley Edwards, Ruth, *True Brits: Inside the Foreign Office* (London: BBC Books, 1994).

Elgin, Mary, *The Letters of Mary Nisbet of Direlton*, ed. Nisbet Hamilton Grant (London: John Murray, 1926).

Ewart-Biggs, Jane, *Pay, Pack and Follow* (London: Weidenfeld & Nicolson, 1984).

Fanshawe, Lady Ann, *Memoirs of Ann Fanshawe* (London: John Lane The Bodley Head, 1907).

Foote, Mrs, *Recollections of Central America and the West Coast of Africa* (London: T. Cantley Newby, 1869).

Fraser, Flora, *Beloved Emma: The Life of Emma, Lady Hamilton* (London: Weidenfeld & Nicolson, 1986).

Fraser, Mrs Hugh, *A Diplomat's Wife in Many Lands*, Vols 1 & II (London: Hutchinson & Co., 1911).

Fraser, Mrs Hugh, *A Diplomat's Wife in Japan* (Tokyo: John Weatherhill, 1982).

Gladwyn, Cynthia, *The Paris Embassy*, (London: Collins, 1976).

Gore-Booth, Paul, *With Great Truth and Respect* (London: Constable, 1974).

Henderson Andrew, *The Life of John, Earl of Stair* (London, 1749).

Horn, D.B., *The British Diplomatic Service 1689–1789*, (Oxford: Clarendon Press, 1961).

Hudson, Roger (ed.), *Nelson and Emma* (London: The Folio Society, 1994).

Jackson, Geoffrey, *Concorde Diplomacy* (London: Hamish Hamilton, 1981).

Jones, Raymond A., *The British Diplomatic Service 1815–1914* (Gerrards Cross: Colin Smythe, 1983).

Kelly, Marie-Noele, *From Dawn 'till Dusk* (London: Hutchinson, 1960).

Lachs, Phyllis S., *The Diplomatic Corps under Charles II and James II* (New Jersey: Rutgers University Press, 1965).

Leigh Hunt, Major S., *Tropical Trials; A Handbook for Women in the Tropics* (London: W.H. Allen & Co., 1883).

Leveson Gower, F. (ed.), *Letters of Harriet, Countess Granville* Vol. 1 (London: Longmans, Green & Co., 1894).

Lewis, Raphaela, *Notes from Everyday Life in Ottoman Turkey* (London: B.T. Batsford Ltd., 1971).

Lovell, Mary S., *A Rage to Live: A Biography of Richard and Isabel Burton* (London: Little, Brown and Company, 1998).

MacAlistair, Florence, *Memoir of Sir John McNeill, G.C.B. and of his second wife Elizabeth Wilson, by their Grand-daughter Florence MacAlistair* (London: John Murray, 1910).

Macartney, Lady, *An English Lady in Chinese Turkestan* (London: Ernest Benn, 1931).

Macdonell, Lady Anne, *Reminiscences of Diplomatic Life* (Edinburgh: R & R Clark Ltd., 1913).

Mattingly, Garett, *Renaissance Diplomacy* (London: Jonathan Cape, 1955).

A Narrative of the Success of the Voyage of his Excellency the Lord Heneage Finch, from Smyrna to Constantinople; his arrival there, the manner of his entrance into Pera, and of his audience with the Grand Vizier and Grand Seignior.

Pepys, Samuel, *The Diary of Samuel Pepys*, Vols 1 and 2 (London: Everyman, 1906).

Robinson, Jane, *Wayward Women – A Guide to Women Travellers* (Oxford: OUP, 1990).

Sackville, Victoria, *The Book of Happy Reminiscences For My Old Age*, 1922.

Sackville-West, Vita, *Pepita* (London: The Hogarth Press, 1937).

Sackville-West, Vita, *The Letters of Vita Sackville-West to Virginia Woolf*, ed. Louise de Salvo and Mitchell A. Leaska (London: Hutchinson, 1984).

Sackville-West, Vita, *Passenger to Tehran*, (London: Hogarth Press, 1926).

Sheil, Lady Mary Leonora, *Glimpses of Life and Manners in Persia* (London: John Murray, 1856).

Shipton, Diana, *The Antique Land* (London: Hodder & Stoughton, 1950).

Smedley, Beryl, *Partners in Diplomacy* (West Sussex: The Harley Press, 1990).

Steel, Flora Annie & Grace Gardiner, *The Complete Indian Housekeeper and Cook* (London: William Heineman, 1911).

Sykes, Miss Ella and Brigadier-General Sir Percy Sykes, KCIE CB CMG, *Through Deserts and Oases of Central Asia* (Macmillan, 1920).

Tomlinson, Stanley, *Handbook on Diplomatic Life Abroad* (Foreign and Commonwealth Office, July 1974).

Townley, Lady Susan, *The Indiscretions of Lady Susan* (London: Thornton Butterworth Ltd., 1922).

Townley, Lady Susan, *My Chinese Notebook* (London: Methuen & Co., 1904).

Troubridge, Lady, *The Book of Etiquette* (London: The Kingswood Press, 1958).

Tully, Miss, *Letters Written During a 10 Years Residence at the Court of Tripoli, 1783–1793* (London: Arthur Barker Limited, 1957).

Tweedy, Maureen, *A Label Round My Neck* (Suffolk: Terence Dalton Ltd., 1976).

Ure, John (ed.), *Diplomatic Bag – An Anthology of Diplomatic Incidents and Anecdotes from the Renaissance to the Gulf War* (London: John Murray, 1994).

Vigor, Mrs., *Letters from a Lady who resided some years in Russia to her friend in England* (London: 1775).

Waddington, Mary King, *Letters of a Diplomat's Wife, 1883–1900* (London: Smith, Elder & Co., 1903).

Watts, Rosemary, *A Military Memsahib*, (Salisbury: Owl Press, 1994).

Williams, Masha, *The Consul's Memsahib* (Sussex: The Book Guild Ltd, 1985).

Wortley Montagu, Lady Mary *The Turkish Embassy Letters*, Introduced by Anita Desai (London: Virago Press, 1994).

Wright, Iona, *Black Sea Bride* (Upton upon Severn: Square One, 1997).

Ziegler, Philip, *Diana Cooper* (London: Hamish Hamilton, 1981).

Papers and Periodicals

'The Dutiful and the Damned', Katie Hickman, *The Sunday Telegraph*, 9 October, 1994.

DSWA and BDSA Magazines, 1960–1998.

'The English Embassy at Constantinople 1600–1762', by A.C. Wood, *The English Historical Review*, Vol 40., London, 1925.

'The Supervising of the Barbary Consulates during the Years 1756–1836', by Hilda Lee, *Institute of Historical Research Bulletin*, Vol 23–24, London, May 1950.

Manuscripts of the Marquess of Downshire, Vols I–VI, Historical Manuscripts Commission, Her Majesty's Stationery Office, London, 1988.

Private Papers of British Diplomats 1782–1900, The Royal Commission on Historical Manuscripts, Her Majesty's Stationery Office, London, 1985.

The F.C.O. Policy, People and Places, 1782–1995, Library and Records Department, Foreign and Commonwealth Office, April 1991.

Women in Diplomacy, The F.C.O., 1782–1994, History Notes, No. 6, Historical Branch of the Foreign and Commonwealth Office, May, 1994.

Black, Annabel, 'The Changing Culture of Diplomatic Spouses: Some Fieldnotes from Brussels', *Diplomacy and Statecraft*, Vol 6, March, 1995.

INDEX